3

Strengthening Health System Governance

Better policies, stronger performance

The European Observatory on Health Systems and Policies supports and promotes evidence-based health policymaking through comprehensive and rigorous analysis of health systems in Europe. It brings together a wide range of policymakers, academics and practitioners to analyse trends in health reform, drawing on experience from across Europe to illuminate policy issues.

The European Observatory on Health Systems and Policies is a partnership between the World Health Organization Regional Office for Europe, the Governments of Austria, Belgium, Finland, Ireland, Norway, Slovenia, Sweden, the United Kingdom, and the Veneto Region of Italy, the European Commission, the World Bank, UNCAM (French National Union of Health Insurance Funds), the London School of Economics and Political Science, and the London School of Hygiene & Tropical Medicine. The Observatory has a secretariat in Brussels and it has hubs in London (at LSE and LSHTM) and at the Technical University of Berlin.

European
Observatory
on Health Systems and Policies
a partnership hosted by WHO

Strengthening Health System Governance

Better policies, stronger performance

Edited by

Scott L. Greer, Matthias Wismar and Josep Figueras

Mc
Graw
Hill
Education Open University Press

PROMOTIONAL COPY - NOT FOR RESALE

Open University Press
McGraw-Hill Education
McGraw-Hill House
Shoppenhangers Road
Maidenhead
Berkshire
England
SL6 2QL

email: enquiries@openup.co.uk
world wide web: www.openup.co.uk

and Two Penn Plaza, New York, NY 10121-2289, USA

First published 2016

A catalogue record of this book is available from the British Library

ISBN-13: 978-0-335-26134-5
ISBN-10: 0-335-26134-5
eISBN: 978-0-335-26135-2

Library of Congress Cataloging-in-Publication Data
CIP data applied for

Typeset by Aptara, Inc.

Printed and bound by CPI Group (UK) Ltd, Croydon, CR0 4YY

European Observatory on Health Systems and Policies Series

The European Observatory on Health Systems and Policies is a unique project that builds on the commitment of all its partners to improving health systems:

- World Health Organization Regional Office for Europe
- Government of Austria
- Government of Belgium
- Government of Finland
- Government of Ireland
- Government of Norway
- Government of Slovenia
- Government of Sweden
- Government of the United Kingdom
- Veneto Region of Italy
- European Commission
- World Bank
- UNCAM
- London School of Economics and Political Science
- London School of Hygiene & Tropical Medicine

The Series

The volumes in this series focus on key issues for health policy-making in Europe. Each study explores the conceptual background, outcomes and lessons learned about the development of more equitable, more efficient and more effective health systems in Europe. With this focus, the series seeks to contribute to the evolution of a more evidence-based approach to policy formulation in the health sector.

These studies will be important to all those involved in formulating or evaluating national health policies and, in particular, will be of use to health policy-makers and advisers, who are under increasing pressure to rationalize the structure and funding of their health system.

Academics and students in the field of health policy will also find this series valuable in seeking to understand better the complex choices that confront the health systems of Europe.

The Observatory supports and promotes evidence-based health policy-making through comprehensive and rigorous analysis of the dynamics of health care systems in Europe.

Series Editors

Josep Figueras is the Director of the European Observatory on Health Systems and Policies, and Head of the European Centre for Health Policy, World Health Organization Regional Office for Europe.

Martin McKee is Director of Research Policy and Head of the London Hub of the European Observatory on Health Systems and Policies. He is Professor of European Public Health at the London School of Hygiene & Tropical Medicine as well as a co-director of the School's European Centre on Health of Societies in Transition.

Elias Mossialos is the Co-director of the European Observatory on Health Systems and Policies. He is Brian Abel-Smith Professor in Health Policy, Department of Social Policy, London School of Economics and Political Science and Director of LSE Health.

Richard B. Saltman is Associate Head of Research Policy and Head of the Atlanta Hub of the European Observatory on Health Systems and Policies. He is Professor of Health Policy and Management at the Rollins School of Public Health, Emory University in Atlanta, Georgia.

Reinhard Busse is Associate Head of Research Policy and Head of the Berlin Hub of the European Observatory on Health Systems and Policies. He is Professor of Health Care Management at the Berlin University of Technology.

Contents

List of contributors

Naomi Chambers, Professor of health management, University of Manchester, United Kingdom

Jonathan Cylus, Research Fellow, European Observatory on Health Systems and Policies, LSE Health, London School of Economics and Political Science, United Kingdom

Josep Figueras, Director, European Observatory on Health Systems and Policies and Head, WHO European Centre for Health Policy, Belgium

Scott L. Greer, Associate Professor, Health Policy and Management, School of Public Health, University of Michigan, USA and Senior Expert Advisor on Health Governance, European Observatory on Health Systems and Policies

Patrick Jeurissen, Chief, Strategy Group Ministry of Health & Chief Program Fiscal Sustainability at Radboud University Medical Centre, the Netherlands

Maria Joachim, PhD Research Scholar, Health Services Organization and Policy, School of Public Health, University of Michigan, USA

Panos Kanavos, Associate Professor in International Health Policy, Department of Social Policy and Deputy Director, LSE Health, London School of Economics and Political Science, United Kingdom

Yiannis Kyratsis, Assistant Professor, Health Management & Leadership, City University London, United Kingdom

Eva Lieberherr, Environmental Policy Analyst, Natural Resource Policy Group, Swiss Federal Institute of Technology Zurich (ETHZ) & Environmental Social Sciences Department, Swiss Federal Institute of Aquatic Science and Technology (Eawag), Switzerland

Denise F. Lillvis, PhD Research Scholar, Health Services Organization and Policy, School of Public Health, University of Michigan, USA

Hans Maarse, Professor Health Policy Analysis, Maastricht University, the Netherlands

Russell Mannion, Professor of Health Systems, Health Services Management Centre, University of Birmingham, United Kingdom

Charlotte McKee, Exeter University, United Kingdom

José R. Repullo, Professor, Health Planning and Economics, National School of Public Health, Instituto de Salud Carlos III, Spain

William D. Savedoff, Senior Fellow, Center for Global Development, USA

Peter C. Smith, Emeritus Professor of Health Policy, Imperial College Business School, United Kingdom

Ewout van Ginneken, Senior Researcher, Health Care Management, Technical University Berlin, Germany

Nikolay Vasev, Visiting Researcher at European Observatory, PhD Student, Department of Political Science, University of Copenhagen, Denmark

Iestyn Williams, Senior Lecturer, Health Services Management Centre, University of Birmingham, United Kingdom

Matthias Wismar, Senior Health Policy Analyst, European Observatory on Health Systems and Policies, Belgium

Olivier Wouters, Research Associate, LSE Health, London School of Economics and Political Science, United Kingdom

Foreword

Health is a political choice, and both good health governance and good governance for health require governments to continuously make important and sometimes difficult choices, choices that may have consequences on access to health services, the quality of health care and on financial hardship for those using the services. These choices are often made difficult by structural challenges in the processes. For example, how can we improve access to health care for vulnerable groups when essential user data is not available? We have structural challenges in developing informed and evidence-based policy, one example being reliable and thorough information from stakeholders. When seeking advice and input on policy issues, it is often the best-informed and invariably the best-resourced actor who participates and not necessarily those with the greatest health needs. An additional challenge is that the political choices taken are not always fully implemented: patient centredness is not always prioritized; services may be misaligned with patients' needs and expectations; and accountability may be absent. It may even be the absence of the rule of law which affects the implementation of our political choices. Informal payments and corruption are still manifest and remain a barrier to efficient and equitable health systems in some countries. Likewise, analytical blunders and policy failures are not unknown: what appeared well on paper was not implementable in practice.

In these times of global challenges to health and health systems, we need to look further at how to implement the political choices for health and well-being, and support countries in their goals to strengthen access, quality of services and financial protection. The economic and financial crisis has given us many lessons learned on the gaps between evidence, political choice and practice. A number of countries have tried to use the crisis as an opportunity to strengthen efficiency through health policy reform; however, all too often, austerity policies and cost-containment prioritization have impacted on past achievements.

One way to improve our political choices for health, especially in hard times, is to strengthen health system governance, as this study elaborates. Governance is defined as how societies make and implement collective decisions. This timely book argues that transparency, accountability, participation, integrity and policy capacity are the building blocks of governance. It presents a detailed framework for analysis and reform, which is called TAPIC – Transparency, Accountability, Participation, Integrity and Capacity. This framework is tested and illustrated by eight concrete case studies, including a set of diverse and current health system reform topics.

Health 2020, the health policy framework for the WHO European Region, stresses the importance of governance for improving both health and well-being, as well as strengthening people-centred health systems. Health 2020 acknowledges that the implementation of governance for health requires new leadership roles for both Ministries of Health and the health sector, including reaching out to and strengthening cooperation with other sectors and new partners. The framework presented in this study could contribute to the development of a practical analytical governance tool, not just for health systems but in the implementation of the whole-of-government and whole-of-society approaches to health and well-being. I therefore warmly welcome this timely contribution to our common quest to improve both health governance and governance for health in the European Region.

Monika Kosinska
Programme Manager
Governance for Health
WHO Regional Office for Europe
July 2015

Acknowledgements

With this book, we are hoping to contribute to improved health system governance in Europe. Our aim is to contribute to the development of a common tool that helps to identify, analyse and address health system governance problems in countries. To this end, we have developed in this volume a practical conceptual framework on which this tool could be based. We have tested this framework by means of case studies and literature reviews. This would not have been possible without the input of a large variety of individuals.

We would like to mention the invaluable input of our academic colleagues who helped us at an early stage in developing the conceptual framework of this book, although we may have taken decisions slightly different from their comments. We are, in particular, grateful to Merilee Grindle, José Repullo, Richard Saltman and Peter C. Smith.

We received important input from our colleagues from the WHO Regional Office for Europe. Juan Tello helped us at the inception of the book project and Erica Barbazza provided an instructive scoping review of governance concepts. Later in the process Agis Tsouros discussed with us conceptual questions and commented on early drafts of the manuscript. We are particularly grateful to Monika Kosinska who helped us at the end of the project to thrash out some key observations and practical conclusions.

The quality of the volume depends a lot on critical minds helping us to identify inconsistencies and weaknesses. We would like to thank Antonio Duran (Técnicas de Salud), Holly Jarman (University of Michigan) and all the chapter authors for detailed and helpful comments on the first chapters, including the draft conceptual framework. We are particularly grateful to our external reviewers, Albert Weale (University College London) and Kai Mosebach (University of Applied Sciences, Ludwigshafen on the Rhine), who provided rigorous comments and gave us directions.

We tested earlier versions of the conceptual framework and the draft chapters with a variety of audiences. Among the large number of talks we delivered on the subject, we would like to mention the presentations and discussions with conference participants at the European Health Management Association's (EHMA) 2013 and 2014 annual conferences in Milan and Birmingham, the European Health Forum Gastein (EHFG) in 2013, the European Union Public Health Association's 2014 meeting in Brussels, and audiences at Maastricht University in 2014 and 2015. We would like to thank participants for their very helpful and at times challenging comments.

Part I

TAPIC: a framework for analysing and improving health system governance

chapter one

Introduction: strengthening governance amidst changing governance

Scott L. Greer, Matthias Wismar and Josep Figueras

The world is cluttered with good health policies gone wrong. They are adopted but badly executed, or produce unintended effects, or fall prey to corruption and ineptitude. Sometimes the trouble is political, and sometimes it is financial, but sometimes it is in the way things are done – in governance.

The reason we need to understand and improve governance is that it is through governance that societies and health systems manage conflict, make collective decisions and exert authority (Fox 2010). For governance, it is a great challenge to weave a web of actors, such as social insurance funds, professions, agencies, governments at different levels, NGOs, and even private companies, who are capable of formulating and accepting a direction, aligning their efforts, and then carrying out their duties. Governance problems include corruption, misaligned incentives, regulatory capture, unintended effects of badly thought-through policies, nepotism, incompetence, lack of trust and difficulties with long-term planning.

In this book, we proceed in a diagnostic manner, starting with the premise that the reason to care about health systems governance is that it can lead to policy failures. Adoption of a problematic policy or non-implementation of an otherwise feasible and well-supported policy can often be traced back to governance problems. To summarize our argument, which will be presented in more detail in Chapter 2, governance is the structure of decision-making and policy implementation in a system. It is characterized by its pattern and routinization rather than dependence on charisma or leadership, and it is 'sticky'. Decisions about governance shape and constrain future decisions about substance.

Governance, our review concludes, has five key attributes: (1) accountability; (2) transparency; (3) participation of affected interests; (4) integrity; and (5) policy capacity. Governance problems can be traced to one or more of these attributes, which can mean too much, too little, or the wrong kind of them. Case studies illuminate key health policies in light of the five aspects of governance, showing the difficulty and value of improving governance for health.

The first part of this chapter presents the most widely cited reasons why the governance of health systems is so frequently discussed: it is simply not clear that we understand how governance in health systems really works. Increasing complexity and increasing awareness of complexity mean that simple models of health systems and politics seem untenable.[1] The result has been an efflorescence of theories about understanding the locus and nature of governance in modern health systems and societies.

The second part of the chapter presents an equally vibrant debate: the search for good governance. Many good health policy ideas have foundered on poor governance; simple and complex policies alike have failed in systems for reasons that are not to do with money, or political will, but stem from troubles in governance. Repeated disappointment with policy formulation and implementation drives repeated waves of interest in the practical improvement of governance. Together, those two sections of the chapter set the stage for this book. They show the importance and practical relevance of efforts to understand and strengthen governance in health systems. The third and final part of the chapter briefly presents our approach, worked out in more detail in Chapter 2, and the plan of the volume.

Our framework is developed for governance in general. Kickbusch and Gleicher (2011) focus on the broad, 'horizontal', relationships across sectors that constitute and can solve many of the 'wicked' intersectoral problems related to population health and equity. The case studies in this work are narrower in focus, taking as their topic the 'vertical' governance of health and public health systems. Just as Health 2020's priorities (WHO Regional Office for Europe 2012) will be unattainable without a strong whole-of-society focus and horizontal policy work (Hunter 2012; Brown et al. 2014), the priorities will be unattainable if health systems are not up to playing their necessary role, and making their necessary changes due to weaknesses in their specific governance arrangements. Chapter 5 discusses ways to extend the analysis beyond health systems governance to governance for health.

Why care about governance?

Governance is the systematic, patterned way in which decisions are made and implemented (discussed in more depth in Chapter 2). Governance shapes the capacity of the health system to cope with everyday challenges as well as new policies and problems. It works in the absence of especially good leaders, and is a defence against especially bad leaders. Politics might be seen as the art of the possible, and the greatest politicians the ones who can perceive new possibilities. Governance is the complex of institutions and rules that determine what is possible.

The governance of a health system therefore shapes its ability to respond to the various well-documented challenges that health systems face today: demographic changes including ageing, migration and changing gender roles; epidemiological changes such as the growth of chronic and non-communicable diseases, as well as the ever-present threat of infectious disease outbreaks; economic changes such as the rise of part-time and service sector jobs, and changes in the growth and prosperity of the different countries; political changes such as the need to comply with EU law; medical changes such as the seemingly endless new technologies, many of them very expensive, and the limits on human resources; and social changes, including changes in patients' and professionals' view of their roles. It shapes the ability of systems to produce equitable, sustainable, quality health care (Ottersen et al. 2014) and survive crisis (Boin et al. 2005: 64). These governance challenges shade over into resilience in the face of crisis.

There are also problems of bad governance. Health governance problems and the vulnerability of health care systems to informal payments and corruption are problems for health care and health outcomes (Gaal et al. 2006; Vian 2008; Radin 2009). Recent European Union studies of corruption found that the health care sector was the most likely to have corruption problems (European Commission 2014: 6) and that improved governance of areas such as pharmaceutical policy was crucial to improving health system performance (European Commission 2013).

In addition to these reasons, many European health systems are facing often unprecedented financial pressure. A number of Eurozone states, in particular, are facing cuts to health expenditure rarely seen before in their country's history. Health systems have faced cost containment pressures for decades, but in many countries the adoption of austerity policies since 2008 has posed challenges beyond previous experiences. Austerity puts tremendous pressure on systems, not just to deliver health care with fewer resources, and perhaps respond to increased need, but also to maintain their basic integrity when more people are competing for fewer resources (Karanikolos et al. 2013; McDaid et al. 2015). Even when we consider the waste in many systems, it is an enormous governance challenge to survive austerity (Olafsdottir et al. 2013), let alone reform systems during this period (e.g., Meneu and Ortún 2011), as Repullo discusses in Chapter 11. Improving their governance means cutting away waste and fat, but waste and fat can reflect governance problems that make them, in many cases, harder to cut away than bone and muscle (Greer 2014).

More broadly, the quality of governance affects the ability of the health system to be sustainable, universal and of high quality, and can generally affect the ability of a whole society to pursue social goods. Governance problems, especially corruption, go together with inequality. Governance problems impede effective public policy that might remedy the inequality. That is the trap: bad governance is best addressed by making people less dependent, but policies that reduce inequality and dependence are vulnerable to bad governance (Uslaner 2008; Rothstein 2011; Svallfors 2013). It should be no wonder that there is a correlation between the quality of government, which includes governance, and happiness (Charron et al. 2013). In other words, governance and a good society go together – in vicious or virtuous cycles.

Discussing governance shifts the focus from individual policies and individual people to the structure of the system within which they work, be it the ministry, the health system managers, the professionals, the regulators or the market participants. It is too simple to wait for a great leader, and leaders can often disappoint. It is also too simple to assume a functioning market will arise and deliver a desired outcome. Markets alone are highly unlikely to produce optimal policy outcomes in health (Hammer 2003). Only with appropriate governance do market mechanisms produce egalitarian, sustainable and high quality health systems. Designing governance is always an activity undertaken for some reason, and in health systems the reason should be health.

Why do we need a framework?

Why, then, do we need a framework to analyse and alter health systems governance? This section presents four frequently cited reasons (see also Savedoff 2012; Kickbusch and Gleicher 2014). The first kind of justification is the demand for frameworks that allow us to understand and improve health systems' governance in Europe as part of a broader effort to measure and strengthen health systems. The second is that we have deficient or dated conceptual models. The third kind of justification for a framework for governance is that the political, institutional and social context of health policy is changing. Academic and practical literature on governance and its changes is voluminous and contradictory, but it is possible to characterize the broad outlines of what we mean when we discuss the challenges of understanding and strengthening governance. The fourth and final kind of justification for a governance framework follows from the previous two: coordination is more of a challenge due to the increasing complexity of health services and the increasing complexity of their political environment. It is the challenge of coordination, or alignment, as it is sometimes known.

Health system performance and consistency in recommendation and action

In Europe, there is an increasing need to speak with one voice when talking about health system governance. This need grows out of an increased interest in the theory and practice of health system performance assessment at both national and international level and the reform plans emanating from this. Most governments are striving to improve the performance of their health systems. They have developed large numbers of indicators and complex data collection methodologies monitoring medical outcomes, patient experiences, efficiencies, quality of services and timely access to health care. Often, international comparison is used to benchmark the performance of the domestic health system (Papanicolas and Smith 2013). At the European level, the European Semester, as part of the EU fiscal governance, brings together surveillance, assessment, benchmarking and recommendations. Country-specific recommendations are issued for many policy fields, including health systems. These recommendations particularly stress the need to improve the performance of health systems (Greer et al. 2014). Developing expertise in health systems performance assessment is one of the stated responsibilities in the mission letter sent by the President of the European Commission to the incoming Commissioner for Health & Food Safety.[2] And there is already an Expert Group on Health Systems Performance Assessment working at the EU level.[3] The Member States of the WHO European Region stipulated in the Tallinn Charter of 2008 that health systems need to demonstrate good performance.[4] This was supported by numerous supporting studies and preceded by the WHO in 2000 which focused on health systems and health system performance assessment (WHO 2000; Murray and Evans 2003). With its quality indicators project, the OECD has also contributed substantially to this agenda.

Once identified, poor health system performance should result in a debate about causes. There might be financial reasons, linked to revenue collection, pooling and purchasing. Luckily, there are widely used robust frameworks that can provide guidance for policy-makers and scientists alike (Mossialos et al. 2002; Thomson et al. 2009; WHO 2010, 2012). Poor performance linked to the delivery process can equally build on well-researched conceptual frameworks (Kringos et al. 2010). For governance, however, there is no such framework or at least no clarity about the different frameworks.

The lack of good governance frameworks impedes learning from each other in the countries of Europe. Without a common analytical framework, good research remains incomparable. Single studies that seem to make sense in their context cannot be checked against other studies regarding the plausibility of results and conclusions since they differ too much in conceptual terms. This missed opportunity for learning from each other is a waste of resources and a failure to make the most out of the diversity of European institutional settings, which, in principle, provide an ideal test bed for comparative governance analysis.

The lack of common governance frameworks leads ultimately to inconsistencies in advice. Countries are often seeking input and advice from international agencies and global consultancies. But without a common governance framework, this input will amount to a cacophony, which confuses the client rather than clarifying the issue. Moreover, this cacophony might be sourced from consultants, which has the effect of undermining their technical credibility.

In summary, it is hoped that based on this research, international agencies will take the opportunity to develop simple tools for governance analysis that can be shared across and between agencies and organizations.

Models and borders

A second reason to ask for a clear governance framework is that the older models which guided our thinking are being questioned. Models are staples of thinking about health systems: social health insurance (Bismarck) and national health service (Beveridge) systems, for example (Esping-Andersen 1990; Freeman 2000). Even if there were always exceptions – social insurance taxes in the United Kingdom, *Länder* funding for hospitals in Germany, a small NHS for miners in France and a big NHS for veterans in the United States (Oliver 2007; Longman 2010) – the models were comforting. We thought we knew where power lay, what the trade-offs were and how the basic system worked.

But now there are more and more systems that seem not to conform. The Estonian health finance model is perched on the dividing line with a single social health insurance fund financed by payroll taxes; its separation from government, the presence of business representatives on the supervisory board, and its payroll tax base sound like social insurance, but concentrating health expenditure in a single nationwide agency tightly linked to the government sounds more like the approach found in traditional national health systems such as in the United Kingdom. The Dutch system of private but tightly regulated health insurers, discussed by Ewout van Ginneken in Chapter 6, is another example of a system that seems to defy old typologies; is it social health insurance if people are mandated and sometimes subsidized to buy tightly regulated policies from competitive private insurers? And what is the value of forcing such systems into older templates?

Part of the reason the models seem to be broken is that the component parts have taken very different shapes. Basic organizational borders have lost coherence that they once appeared to have. On one hand, social insurance systems are frequently becoming more tightly regulated and driven by the state, while, on the other hand, many NHS systems are experimenting with new forms of private-sector provision. Attempts to coordinate and integrate care interfere with the traditional roles of doctors and payers such as health ministries or social insurance funds. Information technology opens up the possibility of new forms of care, health and coordination – as well as seemingly endless expenditure, managerial troubles and disappointment. Attempts to improve public health, such as communicable disease control and surveillance, or connections between public health, preparedness and security (Lakoff and Collier 2008), disrupt old organizational borders, while a focus on population health almost automatically brings the conceptually disruptive challenges of inserting Health into All Policies (Leppo et al. 2013). If it is not clear what the borders of 'health' should be (Fox 2003; Hart 2006; Kickbusch 2007) or what the division of labour within the sector might be, then it is no wonder that it seems hard to make clear suggestions about what is happening or who is in charge. And if the world has changed, then it is incumbent on policy-makers and researchers to understand the changes and adapt the models, as well as policy tools and initiatives, to the world – rather than the other way around.

Locus

A third reason to seek a governance framework is that the broader political system might be changing, and with it the locus of authority. First, territorial politics are changing. There has been a widespread trend towards decentralization of health policy authority to regional elected governments in Europe since the 1960s (Saltman and Bankauskaite 2006; Hooghe et al. 2010; Adolph et al. 2012; Costa i Font and Greer 2012), with potential benefits in terms of democracy, responsiveness and policy as well as costs in terms of intricate coordination problems, cost- and blame-shifting, complex or lacking accountability, and the expense of running multiple government departments.

The trend towards decentralization to elected regional governments in many countries has occurred at the same time as increasing integration at the European and, possibly, global levels. European Union health policy, a vestigial issue at best in 1995, is now a consequential set of issues ranging from the regulation of patient mobility to pharmaceuticals market access to the regulation of blood products (Greer 2009; Mossialos et al. 2010; Greer and Kurzer 2013; Greer et al.

2014). Since the financial crisis, a troika of the European Commission, the International Monetary Fund and European Central Banks have been specifying health policy measures for Eurozone countries in financial distress, including some very precise and expensive policy priorities such as e-Prescribing (Fahy 2012). The troika's work brought all the complexity and potential disappointment that come with the use of conditional lending as a policy tool (Greer 2014). It is also upending much of what we thought was established knowledge about the politics and roles of the European Commission, the European Council and the European Central Bank as well as the IMF (for the expanded role of the EU in health and fiscal policy, see Greer et al. 2014).

Above even the EU level, a complex and poorly understood web of global trade and legal institutions such as the World Trade Organization, Bilateral Investment Treaties, regional free trade agreements and investor–state dispute resolution systems operate, further shaping and constraining health policy options (McGrady 2011; Jarman 2014). A variety of new actors such as the Global Fund and the Gates Foundation have joined established organizations such as the WHO, the Rockefeller Foundation and the World Bank, spawning a whole academic field of 'global health governance' studies (Buse et al. 2009; Parker and Sommer 2010). They are making and trying to implement decisions in patterned ways, which makes them part of health governance, but they are not traditional governments at all. Their interaction with older systems of governance can change the meaning and importance of both (Yeates 2002).

Complexity and coordination

The fourth reason for a new approach to governance, particularly one focused on health rather than individual organizations, is the complexity of interconnectivity and the challenge of making policy in a complex environment. If it is hard to find the borders between models, and between countries, and it is hard to find the locus of authority, then it should be no surprise that complexity is growing, and growing more visible (Kettl 2000). Where different governments share power, they ought to coordinate, but might genuinely disagree on policies. Such are the issues created by multi-level democracy, and it produces webs of more or less effective agreements, networks and plans that in turn create new complexity. Complexity is not just confined to relations between elected governments or international arenas. Health systems have long been governed by complex networks of more or less public organizations: social insurance funds, professional organizations, territorial boards with responsibility within larger health systems. Their power is frequently changing, and often being reduced at the hands of both pro-market and regulatory initiatives – professional associations, for example, are losing influence over payment systems and quality control in many states. The power and autonomy of a social insurance fund, or medical college, or hospital board – or a regulator – are often changing in ways that are not well mapped.

Adding a significant European level to health policy produces new challenges – how is a local health manager supposed to interpret claims made by a patient under some new directive (Greer and Jarman 2012; Greer and Martín de

Almagro Iniesta 2013)? Reinvigorating, or even just reorganizing, international health governance adds more actors, arenas and opportunities, and increases the number of imponderables for even for the most highly regarded experts: e.g., how do investor–state dispute mechanisms constrain public health regulation (Jarman 2014)? Even when the state claims greater authority, by, for example, replacing negotiated medical payment systems with tariffs, it merely creates new demands for data, staffing, and probably agencies to do the work, and thereby new demands for coordination (Tuohy 2003). At the same time, population health programmes and inter-sectoral governance put the complexity of health policy in direct contact with the complexity of other policy areas (McQueen et al. 2012).

Even without policy-makers blurring models of financing and delivery, and even without constitutional change and globalization adding levels of intergovernmental complexity and politics, there is increasing complexity emerging from the intertwining of clinical developments, communications, demographics, increasing income inequality, and health services policy. The profile of populations in many of the world's countries includes an ever-increasing proportion of people with multiple chronic ailments who live for decades and require a very different set of health services from the ones established in the mid-twentieth century. Attentiveness to mental health issues, likewise, changes the demands on health systems and societies. Staffing requirements are different (and larger), integration between inpatient, outpatient and community care is demanding and hard, professional boundaries are challenged, and the very persistence of chronic conditions and medication regimes for them creates new potential safety hazards. It does not help that many countries organize social care locally and health care regionally or centrally, adding intergovernmental to interorganizational and interprofessional coordination problems. As policy-makers, professionals and patients struggle to integrate health and social services, they are creating new problems and systems that can be hard to characterize, evaluate, manage or govern.

Finally, governments and bureaucracies public or private tend to be good at routine tasks, but have trouble responding to crises or making major changes, which means that coordination and change are both difficult (Kettl 2008). Governments are often tempted to respond to a crisis with a reorganization. The problem is that reorganizing without addressing governance failures will often just create a different kind of rigid or dysfunctional system (Kettl 2000).

How do existing theories discuss systems governance?

The sheer volume of literature on good governance, governance strengthening, smart governance or any other kind of adjectival combination with the word 'governance' means that there is a text for every taste, from the most obscure to the most practical. What is often missing is a combination of simplicity and practicality for the right level. For example, there are many arguments put forward about what boards should do (e.g., the Higgs and Cadbury Codes in the United Kingdom, which set out clear visions of what boards should be and do), but it is frequently hard to see what exactly boards do in reality, and fundamental conceptual questions about what boards are for, or what their accountability really might be, remain unanswered (Chambers 2012 and Chapter 13 of this book).

While governance is a term widely used in health policy, political science and public administration, the concept of 'good' governance first arose in studies of corporate governance in the United States and United Kingdom. To this day, much of the literature on good governance comes from those early sources, and focuses on how to design organizations that will have appropriate internal controls, strategic development, and shareholder or stakeholder representation in decisions. It often just means 'good management' in the hands of such writers (Woods 1999). In policy debates, governance is invoked by all manner of advocates and analysts (Frederickson 2005; Batniji et al. 2014). If almost everybody is in favour of good governance, then arguments are about what it means rather than whether it is desirable. It can mean many things. It can mean the behaviour of individual organizations (e.g., the composition and performance of the supervisory board), it can mean the manner in which decisions are made in society, and it can mean the organization and relationships within the health sector.

The aspirations of those who would improve governance are legion, and frequently somewhat confusing. Good governance is well articulated, if not always philosophically coherent or implemented, at the level of individual organizations, and to be found in codes of conduct for good hiring, board behaviour or professional ethics (Mehta 2007). It is less well articulated, and much more hotly debated, when we turn to the interactions among different organizations. Orchestrating good governance in a whole health system is a key task, and is equally challenging to establish, measure and implement.

This section reviews the approaches to health systems governance. We concentrate on ones that focus at the system level and try to characterize the challenges and responses facing health systems. We start with attempts to measure governance, and then identify two major theoretical approaches, both of which have had and continue to have an influence on real public policies: the rationalist and the network-based.

Measurement

Measuring and counting give a tangibility to statements – what's measured is what's managed – and it is therefore no surprise that there are various efforts to measure and compare governments (Diamond and Morlino 2005; Norris 2010; Larmour 2012: 71; Fukuyama 2013; Stanig and Kayser 2013) with important applications in health (Mackenbach and McKee 2013; Batniji et al. 2014). They are discussed in more detail by Savedoff and Smith in Chapter 4. Comparative data and rankings permit what is called 'naming and shaming' in the United Kingdom, highlighting the failings of countries relative to each other and attempting to clarify their strong and weak points (Bevan 2010; Elliott 2013). They are essentially benchmarking exercises, testing existing governance in different countries against an ideal kind of liberal democratic state.

To pick just a few: the World Bank has a large series of Worldwide Governance Indicators[5] that evaluate countries on such values as rule of law and regulatory quality, as well as its annual Doing Business survey. The OECD has a similar series designed for its high-income countries. The Bertelsmann Foundation provides Sustainable Governance Indicators.[6] Transparency International runs surveys of corruption.[7] Gothenburg University collects a wide variety of public sector, government and academic indicators in its large Quality of Government (QOG) databases (Rothstein 2011; Charron et al. 2013).[8] A collaboration between Gothenburg and Notre Dame Universities is assembling a still more comprehensive data set on governments (Coppedge et al. 2012).[9] The Hertie School of Governance also has an ambitious Governance Report (Hertie School of Governance 2013). The United Nations Development Program (UNDP) has a set of more specific capacity indicators (UNDP 2010).

On one hand, there is some consensus among their indicators about what good governance means: rule of law, good regulation, fiscal probity and sustainability. On the other hand, the indices incorporate many value judgements – intentionally, as with the World Bank's focus on the market, enabling public administration – and unintentionally, as when the 'good enough' data available adds a bias to findings. At their best, they incorporate parts of the complexity of interorganizational relationships, but they are frequently limited to evaluating the public sector (which is the object of most of the reform efforts, and frequently seen as an obstacle to good governance in the rest of the society). They run all the methodological risks of large-scale efforts to reduce complex systems to quantitative indicators. Presumably time and competition will show which indices are most useful in this still-new field of inquiry. Finally, such indicators of good governance are only as good as the data informing them and the theories that give them shape. They are necessarily theoretically and normatively driven. That directs our attention to the theories underlying such measurements.

Theories of governance

There are two broad approaches to governance that scholars and policymakers tend to adopt: the rationalist approach that notably led to New Public Management and its reliance on contracting, outsourcing and markets; and the later theory of network governance that sought to compensate for some of the failings of rationalist models by emphasizing networks, cooperation and partnership (following Bevir 2013: 129–48). These theories are our focus, addressing the interactions between organizations – the shifting boundaries, unclear authority and spiralling complexity of coordination that drive so much interest in governance.

The focus on systems matters because health systems are more than the sum of individual organizations. Organizations can have good boards and internal audit and still, collectively, produce a dysfunctional health system. There is nothing about the average management presentation on 'good governance' that will align different organizations and agendas to produce a coherent result. We can see this in the 2013 Francis Report on poor care in Stafford Hospital in England: dozens of different organizations could and perhaps should have done something about dangerous conditions in a particular hospital, but none did. Rather than blame the governance of the *system* in which many different actors failed to hold the hospital accountable, the report focuses on the internal governance of the hospital. Nobody should characterize the English NHS as if it were a group of atomistic, independent organizations whose operations are their own business, but when it came time to analyse a failing of governance, that is how the inquiry went about it.[10]

Both sets of theories have been extensively studied in theory and practice. But it is worth noting that they are essentially deductive, starting with first principles borrowed from economics in the first place (notably transaction cost economics and Chicago School economics, two very different traditions), and sociology and public administration, in the second. One focuses on incentives facing putatively rational agents; the other, on the complexity of networks, the ingenuity of people and the pliability of their incentives, goals and strategies.

New Public Management and principal–agent models

New Public Management (NPM) was an international movement promoting privatization, contracting and regulation in an effort to introduce market-like disciplines and greater accountability to public services such as health (Hood 1991; Osborne and Gaebler 1992; Frederickson 1996; Klein 1998). In health systems, this meant a variety of widely disseminated reforms including purchaser–provider splits, greater managerial autonomy for providers, greater private sector participation in provision, more use of independent regulators and agencies for specialist functions, and outsourcing ancillary functions such as catering and estate management. It often made accountability more complex and often ineffective, while increasing coordination problems and costs (Dunleavy et al. 2006; Eymeri-Douzans and Pierre 2011). Underlying much NPM is a basic set of theories of how health and other systems work. It is essentially individualistic, rationalist and focused on the use of market and contract rather than hierarchy or network.

One of the lasting legacies of NPM and the use of micro-economic analysis is the use of principal–agent models. Economists typically render accountability using this model (Bevir 2013: 139–45; for an excellent critique, see Borowiak 2011: 53–77). In principal–agent models, one actor (e.g., doctors) works for another (e.g., the state) and analysis focuses on making the relationship work better in the face of misaligned incentives and imperfect information (Bevir 2013: 139–40). They are essentially simplifying models rather than descriptions and do have great force in illuminating decisions of policy-makers when trying to assert control over others (McNollgast 1990; Huber and Shipan 2002; Przeworski 2003).

The problem, of course, is when simplifying heuristics are taken for description (Page 2012a, 2012b). Frequently the relationship is more fiduciary than about agency. Most organizations in modern society in no reasonable sense 'work for' anybody else: they have resource dependencies, and are shaped by law and money, but their interactions are hardly comparable to those of property owners and plumbers. Governments' accountability has long been contested. Most governments claim to work for their people, but that claim tells us nothing about the presence and functionality of mechanisms to make sure that they are actually accountable to those people. Only abstractly does the medical profession 'work for' the payers who finance health care in the health care system; nobody can dispense with the doctors that they have, which means that medical reform is about interorganizational negotiations and pressures, and accountabilities between doctors, professional organizations, payers and governments rather than only writing contracts (Marmor and Klein 2012). Instead, the way to think about these problems is to view organizations in the round – in their interconnections, resource dependencies and accountability relationships.

    The other problem with principal–agent models is that most organizations are enmeshed in a web of relationships, each of which imposes different requirements, often for good reasons, but which are not easy to reduce to principal–agent relationships. Can we regard a hospital's management as the agent of a health ministry if it is also answerable to regulators of all sorts (safety, quality, environmental, building standards, etc.), a broader range of politicians than the models suggest (in government, out of government, local, regional and national), influential community members (local activists, the press), and purchasers such as insurance funds, staff, professionals, professional networks, possibly shareholders and other regulators if private, accrediting agencies and others (Marmor 2001; Healy and McKee 2002)? To return to the Stafford example, the assumptions of a principal–agent model might clarify a prescriptive piece of advice about who should have been accountable to whom. But could it explain what happened, other than to note a failure? Such a complex environment, including diverse lines of accountability, is a fact of life and a challenge for policy and management. It is also complex enough that modelling it in a principal–agent relationship would be to oversimplify it.

Network governance approaches

Network governance is another broad way to consider these problems. This model followed rationalist models in the 'parade of the paradigms' that characterizes public management (Pollitt 2013). Network theorists start with the complexity that principal–agent modelling handles so badly, and puts trust in expert networks, or coordinated groups of leaders, to manage their joint responsibilities and align their different capabilities and organizations. It is an approach that grows out of the broader field of public administration, which has been struggling for decades with the importance of networks and the weakness of older conceptual models of public action (Rhodes 1996; Frederickson 1999; Peters 2013). Some of the interest in network and other new models of governance has come as a response to the policies adopted under NPM. For example, it turned out that purchaser–provider division produced coordination difficulties where cooperation would work better, and that problems such as territorially concentrated pockets of poor health would respond better to partnership working than to market incentives.

    There are two major empirical problems with analysing governance solely in terms of networks and partnerships. One is that networks and partnerships are everywhere and nowhere. Finding networks is not that hard: people tend to talk to each other. What is harder to define, find and arrange is networks that govern:

that do actually align organizations and forces for collective ends. What can look like networked governance from one angle can be an amorphous, frustrating landscape of meetings, bickering and missed opportunities from another.

The second is that network governance does not simply replace hierarchy and law. The most effective cases of experimentalist, new, networked governance are where the participants agree on the problem, do not agree on the answer, and face a problematic 'default penalty' if they do not organize themselves adequately (Sabel and Zeitlin 2007, 2010). In communicable disease control, for example, there are strong incentives to collaborate (the disease is the problem and uncontrolled spread is a bad outcome, and so the authorities have the incentive to puzzle out solutions together). That might explain why what appears to be a very badly organized sector generally functions well in Europe. Outside such situations, it frequently seems that networks work best in the 'shadow of hierarchy' – where there is ultimately some powerful player, possibly less informed or responsible, that can step in when experts fail (Héritier and Lehmkuhl 2008; Héritier and Rhodes 2011). For example, if professional associations do not successfully discipline their members, the legal system and the state can step in. This is an incentive for the professional associations to do their jobs well. If social health insurance funds do not contain costs effectively, their failure is an invitation to the state to intervene.

Some ambitious efforts of the 1990s to put forth 'governance' as a uniquely network-based alternative to traditional 'government' and markets (e.g., Peters and Pierre 1998; Stoker 1998; Frederickson 1999) foundered on these two problems (Lynn Jr. 2011; Peters 2013). On one hand, networks are not always apparent or do not exert the right kind of governing authority; and on the other, they often work best when there is some kind of authority in the background to give them legal force or oblige them to do their jobs well. The inescapability of networks and the many virtues of networks do not mean that they can be the whole basis for health system governance.

Summary

There are two broadly influential ways to approach systems-level governance, reviewed in this section. One, with its affinities in economics and roots in the popular NPM of the 1980s and 1990s, focuses on contracts, competition, incentives and principal–agent models. A second, with its affinities in sociology and public administration focuses on the power and effectiveness of networks in what its advocates call, variously, experimentalist, new, and network governance. Both contribute a great deal to clarifying puzzles of governance, and have influenced policies as diverse as privatization, contracting, patient choice, agency creation, intersectoral policy, and the whole of government joined-up approaches. Examining them has contributed to our framework by highlighting the effectiveness of networks, the complexity of accountability and the related difficulty of using simple frameworks, and the difficulty of drawing clear distinctions between different kinds of governance. The next section presents our more inductive framework, drawn from a literature review rather than this kind of deductive framework.

Health systems governance: plan of the book

In this book, we follow an inductive, diagnostic approach that stands in contrast to these theories. It is inductive because it is built on an extensive literature review, including practical and practitioner literature, and it is diagnostic, because it is built on regarding governance problems as one category of problems that can cause a health policy failure. It is in contrast to the more deductive, academic theories above, which risk providing overly simple answers (as experiments in NPM have frequently demonstrated). It is also in contrast to many discussions of good governance, presented in Chapter 2, which can appear to be arbitrary and utopian in their long lists of desirable aspects of governance (Grindle 2004). The aim is to provide policy-makers with a practical synthesis of the governance literature that directs their attention to potential and real faults in governance, in health care systems and more broadly in governance for health.

Part I TAPIC: a framework for analysing and improving health system governance

We start with the premise, more fully explained in Chapter 2, that the core reason to care about governance is that it affects which policies are chosen and how well they work. A certain quality of governance is a necessary condition to avoid policy failure. Making and implementing authoritative collective decisions are hard. Based on a review of health policy and public administration literatures, the chapter identifies and defines five mutually exclusive attributes of governance that influence the kind and consequences of decisions a system makes: what we call the TAPIC framework:

Transparency
Accountability
Participation
Integrity
Capacity

None of these attributes are an unqualified good thing; as with all good things, they can be excessive or used wrongly (participation, for example, can be a costly impediment to action or a creator of bias if done to excess or with the wrong mechanisms). For each attribute, there is a series of different associated policy and administrative tools: transparency is enhanced by freedom of information legislation, integrity is enhanced by clear job and organizational role definitions, capacity is enhanced by hiring skilled policy staff, and accountability is promoted by clear mandates and reporting, while some tools such as strong conflict of interest policies promote several attributes (e.g., transparency, integrity and accountability). They should be properties of systems as well as individual organizations; it should be possible to see clear accountability for each organization as well as the map of accountability relationships, and capacity should be a property of each organization as well as a system.

Chapter 3 goes into these attributes and techniques in more depth, focusing on ways to identify which ones are lacking and which kinds of techniques might be adopted by those who identify a problem in one of these aspects of the health systems. There is an extensive literature in health policy and public administration about governance, and the chapter draws on it to present common techniques used to strengthen various aspects of governance.

Chapter 4 gives conventional international answers to the question of how to improve governance, reviewing the 'good governance' literature with a special focus on efforts such as that of the World Bank and the OECD to define good governance and measure it. It then addresses a key issue: how to measure good governance, and what it means to do so, in terms of directing attention to different issues, data sources and countries, and what it means for policy-makers who would improve governance in their own organization or system.

Chapter 5 then draws the model of health governance, as tested and elaborated in the Part II case studies, into the broader realm of governance *for health*. The TAPIC framework's components were drawn from studies of governance, in health, for health and in general, and accordingly should contribute to policies for health beyond health systems.

Part II Sectoral case studies on health system governance

Part II, then, introduces case studies of different policy areas. The case studies were selected to be policy areas that pose challenges for governance – areas where well-thought-out and economically rational policies can go wrong in the hands of weakly governed systems. Governance is fundamentally about organizing and exercising power, and that can be very difficult. We chose hard cases in which the high stakes, discretion, complexity and interplay of contradictory incentives make it hard to manage the systems.

Our first four policy areas are about situations where key health system organizations – purchasers and regulators – must be well governed if they are to deliver good outcomes for the system:

- regulation of private insurance;
- public–private finance of health care services and facilities;
- establishment of an impartial and effective health technology (HTA) assessment agency;
- pharmaceutical pricing and regulation.

These first four case studies have a key component in common: they involve very complicated feats of alignment among multiple actors, not all of whom have the collective interest at heart and can lead to disaster if the public authorities' regulatory efforts fail.

To successfully regulate an insurance market so that it produces equitable outcomes; to successfully authorize and buy pharmaceuticals without excessive expense or even risk to patient safety; and to successfully decide whether to make or buy a care facility, then write and monitor a robust contract – these are all tests for the key organizations governing a health system. They involve designing and manipulating the incentives facing large for-profit companies; they involve high levels of information and monitoring; they risk all manner of dysfunction among regulators and buyers, from bribes to legislative interference to 'revolving doors' to underpaid ineptitude; contracts are usually shielded from public scrutiny; the stakes are high enough and nonlinear enough[11] to mean everybody has an incentive to invest in legal and perhaps illegal influence and actions; and they have a high level of technical complexity and opacity that makes it challenging to have individual organizations, let alone the whole system, be transparent, accountable, participatory, capable and have integrity. They are, in short, key tests of governance in the system, and in the key organizations where authority resides. Systems that fall short might want to eschew them if possible (every system needs medicines, but not every system can risk a failed big Private Finance Initiative, PFI), or urgently strengthen their governance.

The last four chapters focus on more intractable systemic problems: three areas where governance is less 'dangerous' but still capable of vastly influencing the coherence, alignment and outputs of health systems:

- intergovernmental relations (case study areas: blood and communicable diseases);
- austerity;
- primary care reform;
- hospital governance.

In these four cases, small differences can have big effects on the health system and its objectives as well as the broader political system. Intergovernmental relations is an area that interferes with the simplicity of democratic ideals, since it means that multiple governments, some with different electoral bases, others sharing an electorate, can argue about policies and each other's powers. How can intergovernmental relations be well governed? The incentives facing elected politicians are not always in favour of alignment and coordination. It would often be negligent for a regional politician who opposes the state's policy not to think of ways to prevent it. Austerity, meanwhile, is a highly controversial situation to be working in but also a policy imperative for many health policymakers. Even if evidence on the benefits of curtailed health budgets is debated, it has been implemented in many countries and presents a challenge to governance. Doing austerity 'well', preserving the most essential services and investments and perhaps even gaining the benefits of reform depend substantially on governance. Primary care is changing everywhere, as new organizational and payment forms attempt to change its organization and role in many countries. As Kyratsis discusses in Chapter 12, governance can lead to very different results. It highlights the difficulty of establishing accountable, transparent and participatory mechanisms, and the challenges facing governments as they try to make policy. Finally, hospitals are difficult to manage, difficult to reform, expensive and politically important, which makes their reform a challenge for governance that Chambers, Joachim and Mannion address in Chapter 13.

Each case study chapter is written to a template. It first introduces the issue, with the EU or one or more European countries as its case studies. It then identifies the key aspects of governance, and places to look for problems, in terms of our five diagnostic attributes: are the levels of transparency, accountability, participation, integrity or policy capacity adequate to the task at hand? If not, what are the effects on the performance of the system? Are those effects – the acknowledged problems in the case study areas and systems – due to governance problems, or to other difficulties (such as misconceived policy or lack of resources?). And what policies are being discussed, or might be discussed, to address governance deficiencies?

Conclusion

The governance of a health system directs the energies of the people within by shaping the markets, bureaucracies, professions and organizations in which they work. It can direct them to different ends using different means, and is always being reinvented, bit by bit, every day. It shapes politics and markets, which are both ubiquitous in human life. It goes beyond leadership and a focus on getting good people,[12] assuming instead that the governance of their actions matters.

It is customary to bemoan politics in health, as in so many other aspects of life. Politicians are rarely popular creatures, in part, because their task in life is to defuse, manage, mobilize, and ignore conflict. Wherever there are clashing interests, there will be some politics. The most important clashing interests, such as those who want more or less health care expenditure, those who want more or less chemical regulation, those who want higher or lower taxes, and so forth, tend to be in the sights of the formal political system, where they are yoked to political ambition and opposition, so that even if an opposition party has little substantive interest in a topic, it can still have incentive to raise the topic and challenge the government (Hood 2010: 992).

Governance structures political competition. Sometimes governance systems limit the scope of formal political competition, for example, by creating independent agencies separate from the health ministry, or limiting the political affiliations of civil servants, or otherwise creating systems beyond politics, guided by tripwires so that everybody will identify a political influence on their behaviour. For example, it is easier to identify political pressure on an independent agency governed by an appointed board, as Williams discusses in Chapter 8, than on a part of the ministry which is staffed by people whose job is to serve the minister. Sometimes it biases the political system towards one outcome or another; for example, accounting conventions often make public health expenditure or health care innovations look like an expense with no guaranteed future benefit (a particular problem for efforts to promote Health in All Policies). Regulatory impact analysis and proportionality tests can bias policy-making towards business interests at the expense of health (Smith et al. 2010; Jarman 2014); health impact assessment is in part an effort to reciprocate by biasing policy-making towards health (Greer and Lillvis 2014). In short, governance systems limit and channel public and political conflict, and ideally lead it to produce the advantages of informed, thoughtful, consensual policy.

Governance also shapes markets, and without appropriate governance, health markets can malfunction badly. The place of markets in health systems is controversial, with strong arguments for almost any imaginable use of market mechanisms. The mere fact that there are arguments about how much market a given system should have – whether the EU should have cross-border pharmacy markets, whether competition between private and NHS providers in England is a good idea, whether free choice of social insurance fund is equitable – tells us something important. Markets in health are inevitably the creatures of their governance. From basic levels, such as patents and property rights that underpin and shape markets, to the detailed policies involved in the introduction and regulation of market mechanisms, the quality of governance and its biases shape the entrants, business and effects of markets in health (Carpenter 2010, 2012; Carpenter and Moss 2013).[13]

Ideally, in health governance, systems should bias the health system, including its competition and economic incentives, and broader political systems towards universal, quality, sustainable health care and good public health. Just how they might do that – and how the rules of governance can channel the universality and creativity of politicians – has been the subject of argument and thought since the dawn of theory, and the subject of scientific inquiry since the birth of the social sciences. Working politicians and policy-makers have developed a wide range of governance systems that deliberately over-represent some interests, make some policies harder to change than others, constrain some people more than others, and otherwise shape decision-making to produce their desired ends (Greer and Lillvis 2014). Political scientists and scholars of health policy and public administration study those techniques, and the ways policy-makers in different contexts can tilt the debate in favour of health. We draw upon those social scientists, and their findings, in the subsequent chapters.

Notes

1 Perhaps the two best collections on the topic of governance old and new, and why it matters, are Peters and Savoie (2000) and, on the broader topic of government quality, Charron, Lapuente and Rothstein (2013). See also the compendium of academic research in Levi-Faur (2012).
2 See: http://ec.europa.eu/commission/sites/cwt/files/commissioner_mission_letters/andriukaitis_en.pdf (accessed 2 April 2015).
3 See: http://ec.europa.eu/health/systems_performance_assessment/policy/expert_group/index_en.htm (accessed 2 April 2015).
4 See: http://www.euro.who.int/__data/assets/pdf_file/0008/88613/E91438.pdf (accessed 2 April 2015).
5 See: http://info.worldbank.org/governance/wgi/index.asp.
6 See: http://www.sgi-network.org/index.php?page=faq.
7 See: http://www.transparency.org/research/cpi/overview.
8 See: http://www.qog.pol.gu.se/.
9 See: https://v-dem.net/.
10 See: http://www.midstaffspublicinquiry.com/report. The inquiry sat from 2010 and reported in 2013.
11 Nonlinearity here means that the rewards for winning vastly exceed the rewards for coming in second, as is particularly notable with large capital investment contracts (Warner 2007).
12 A focus on the right cadres is a feature of some regimes that do well despite looking weak on governance indicators as we discuss them. See Rothstein (2015) and Huang (2013) for relevant discussions.

13 For an introduction to the extensive literature underpinning this paragraph, see Swedberg (2009).

References

Adolph, Christopher, Greer, Scott L. and Massard da Fonseca, Elize (2012) Allocation of authority in European health policy, *Social Science & Medicine*, 75: 1595–603.

Batniji, Rajaie et al. (2014.) Governance and health in the Arab World, *Lancet*, 383: 343–55.

Bevan, Gwyn (2010) Performance measurement of 'knights' and 'knaves': differences in approaches and impacts in British countries after devolution, *Journal of Comparative Policy Analysis*, 12: 33–56.

Bevir, Mark (2013) *A Theory of Governance*. Berkeley, CA: University of California Press.

Boin, Arjen, 't Hart, Paul, Stern, Eric and Sundelius, Bengt (2005) *The Politics of Crisis Management: Public Leadership Under Pressure*. Cambridge: Cambridge University Press.

Borowiak, Craig T. (2011) *Accountability and Democracy: The Pitfalls and Promise of Popular Control*. Oxford: Oxford University Press.

Brown, Chris, Harrison, Dominic, Burns, Harry and Zigho, Eric (2014) *Governance for Health Equity: Taking forward the equity values and goals of Health 2020 in the European Region*. Copenhagen: WHO Regional Office for Europe.

Buse, Kent, Hein, Wolfgang and Drager, Nick (eds) (2009). *Making Sense of Global Health Governance: A Policy Perspective*. Basingstoke: Palgrave Macmillan.

Carpenter, Daniel (2010) Confidence games: how does regulation constitute markets? in Edward J. Balleisen and David A. Moss (eds) *Government and Markets*. Cambridge: Cambridge University Press, pp. 164–90.

Carpenter, Daniel (2012) Is health politics different? *Annual Review of Political Science*, 15.

Carpenter, Daniel and Moss, David (eds) (2013) *Preventing Regulatory Capture: Special Interest Influence and How to Limit It*. Cambridge: Cambridge University Press.

Chambers, Naomi (2012) Healthcare board governance, *Journal of Health Organization and Management*, 26: 6–14.

Charron, Nicholas, Lapuente, Victor and Rothstein, Bo (2013) *Quality of Government and Corruption from a European Perspective: A Comparative Study of Good Government in EU Regions*. Cheltenham: Edward Elgar.

Coppedge, Michael, Gerring, John and Lindberg, Staffan (2012) *V-Dem: Varieties of Democracy Project Description*. South Bend, IN: University of Notre Dame Kellogg Institute.

Costa i Font, Joan, and Greer, Scott S. L. (eds) (2012) *Federalism and Decentralization in European Health and Social Care*. Basingstoke: Palgrave Macmillan.

Diamond, Larry and Morlino, Leonardo (eds) (2005) *Assessing the Quality of Democracy*. Baltimore, MD: Johns Hopkins University Press.

Dunleavy, Patrick, Margetts, Helen, Bastow, Simon and Tinkler, Jane (2006) New Public Management is dead: long live digital-era governance, *Journal of Public Administration Research and Theory*, 16: 467–94.

Elliott, Heather A. K. (2013) European Union information infrastructure and policy, in Scott L. Greer and Paulette Kurzer (eds) *European Union Public Health Policies*. London: Routledge, pp. 36–50.

Esping-Andersen, Gosta (1990) *The Three Worlds of Welfare Capitalism*. Princeton, NJ: Princeton University Press.

European Commission (2013) *Study on Corruption in the Healthcare Sector* (HOME/2011/ISEC/PR/047-A2). Brussels: European Commission. Available at: http://ec.europa.eu/dgs/home-affairs/what-is-new/news/news/docs/20131219_study_on_corruption_in_the_healthcare_sector_en.pdf.

European Commission (2014) *EU Anti-Corruption Report* (COM(2014)38). Brussels: European Commission. Available at: http://ec.europa.eu/dgs/home-affairs/e-library/documents/policies/organized-crime-and-human-trafficking/corruption/docs/acr_2014_en.pdf.

Eymeri-Douzans, Jean-Michel and Pierre, Jon (eds) (2011) *Administrative Reforms and Democratic Governance*. London: Routledge.

Fahy, Nick (2012) Who is shaping the future of European health systems? *BMJ*, 344: e1712.

Fox, Daniel M. (2003) Population and the law: the changing scope of health policy, *Journal of Law, Medicine and Ethics*, 31: 607–14.

Fox, Daniel M. (2010) The governance of standard-setting to improve health, *Preventing Chronic Disease*, 7: A123.

Frederickson, H. George (1996) Comparing the reinventing government movement with the New Public Administration, *Public Administration Review*: 263–70.

Frederickson, H. George (1999) The repositioning of American public administration, *PS: Political Science and Politics*, 32: 701–11.

Frederickson, H. George (2005) 'Whatever happened to public administration? Governance, governance everywhere, in Ewan Ferlie, Lawrence E. Lynn Jr. and Christopher Pollitt (eds) *Oxford Handbook of Public Management*. Oxford: Oxford University Press, pp. 282–304.

Freeman, Richard (2000) *The Politics of Health in Europe*. Manchester: Manchester University Press.

Fukuyama, Francis (2013) What is governance? *Governance*, 26(3): 347–68.

Gaal, Peter, Belli, Paolo P. C., McKee, Martin and Szócska, Miklós (2006) Informal payments for health care: definitions, distinctions, and dilemmas, *Journal of Health Politics, Policy and Law*, 31: 251–93.

Greer, Scott L. (2009) *The Politics of European Union Health Policies*. Maidenhead: Open University Press.

Greer, Scott L. (2014) Structural adjustment comes to Europe: lessons for the Eurozone from the conditionality debates, *Global Social Policy*, 14: 51–71.

Greer, Scott L., Fahy, Nick, Elliott, Heather, Wismar, Matthias, Jarman, Holly and Palm, Willy (2014) *Everything You Always Wanted to Know about European Union Health Policy but Were Afraid to Ask*. Copenhagen: WHO Regional Office for Europe on behalf of the European Observatory on Health Systems and Policies.

Greer, Scott L. and Jarman, Holly (2012) Managing risks in EU health services policy: spot markets, legal certainty and bureaucratic resistance, *Journal of European Social Policy*, 22: 259–72.

Greer, Scott L. and Kurzer, Paulette (eds) (2013) *European Union Public Health Policies: Regional and Global Perspectives*. London: Routledge.

Greer, Scott L. and Lillvis, Denise (2014) Beyond leadership: political strategies for coordination in health policies, *Health Policy*, 116(1): 12–17.

Greer, Scott L. and Martín de Almagro Iniesta, Maria (2013) How bureaucracies listen to courts: bureaucratized calculations and European law, *Law & Social Inquiry*, 39(2): 361–86.

Grindle, Merilee S. (2004) Good enough governance: poverty reduction and reform in developing countries, *Governance*, 17: 525–48.

Hammer, Peter J. (ed.) (2003) *Uncertain Times: Kenneth Arrow and the Changing Economics of Health Care*. Durham, NC: Duke University Press.

Hart, Julian Tudor (2006) *The Political Economy of Health Care: A Clinical Perspective*. Bristol: Policy Press.

Healy, Judith and McKee, Martin (2002) The role and function of hospitals, in Martin McKee and Judith Healy (eds) *Hospitals in a Changing Europe*. Milton Keynes: Open University Press/European Observatory on Health Care Systems, pp. 59–80.

Héritier, Adrienne and Lehmkuhl, Dirk (2008) The shadow of hierarchy and new modes of governance, *Journal of Public Policy*, 28: 1–17.

Héritier, Adrienne and Rhodes, Martin (2011) Conclusion: new modes of governance: emergence, execution, evolution and evaluation, in Adrienne Héritier and Martin Rhodes (eds) *New Modes of Governance in Europe: Governing in the Shadow of Hierarchy*. Basingstoke: Palgrave Macmillan, pp. 163–74.

Hertie School of Governance (2013) *The Governance Report 2013*. Oxford: Oxford University Press.

Hood, Christopher (1991) A public management for all seasons? *Public Administration*, 69: 3–19.

Hood, Christopher (2010) Accountability and transparency: Siamese twins, matching parts, awkward couple? *West European Politics*, 33: 989–1009.

Hooghe, Liesbet, Marks, Gary and Schakel, Arjan (2010) *The Rise of Regional Authority: A Comparative Study of 42 Democracies*. London: Routledge.

Huang, Yanzhong (2013) *Governing Health in Contemporary China*. London: Routledge.

Huber, John D. and Shipan, Charles C. R. (2002) *Deliberate Discretion?: The Institutional Foundations of Bureaucratic Autonomy*. Cambridge: Cambridge University Press.

Hunter, David J. (2012) Tackling the health divide in Europe: the role of the World Health Organization, *Journal of Health Politics, Policy and Law*, 37(3): 867–78.

Jarman, Holly (2014) *The Politics of Trade and Tobacco Control*. Basingstoke: Palgrave Macmillan.

Karanikolos, Marina et al. (2013) Financial crisis, austerity, and health in Europe, *The Lancet*, 381: 1323–31.

Kettl, Donald F. (2000) The transformation of governance: globalization, devolution, and the role of government, *Public Administration Review*, 60: 488–97.

Kettl, Donald F. (2008) *The Next Government of the United States: Why Our Institutions Fail Us and How to Fix Them*. New York: W. W. Norton & Company.

Kickbusch, I. (2007) Health governance: the health society, in David McQueen, Ilona Kickbusch, Louise Potvin, Juergen Pelikan, Laura Balbo and Thomas Abel (eds) *Health and Modernity*. Frankfurt: Springer, pp. 144–61.

Kickbusch, I. and Gleicher, D. (2011) *Governance for Health in the 21st Century: A Study Conducted for the WHO Regional Office for Europe*. Copenhagen: WHO Regional Office for Europe.

Kickbusch, I. and Gleicher, D. (2014) *Smart Governance for Health and Well-Being: The Evidence*. Copenhagen: WHO Regional Office for Europe.

Klein, Rudolf (1998) Self-inventing institutions: institutional design and the UK welfare state, in Robert E. Goodin (ed.) *The Theory of Institutional Design*. Cambridge: Cambridge University Press, pp. 240–55.

Kringos, Dionne S., Wienke Boerma, G. W., Hutchinson, Allen, van der Zeel, Jouke and Groenewegen, Peter P. (2010) The breadth of primary care: a systematic literature review of its core dimensions, *BMC Health Services Research*, 10: 65.

Lakoff, Andrew and Collier, Stephen S. J. (2008) *Biosecurity Interventions: Global Health and Security in Question*. New York: Columbia University Press.

Larmour, Peter (2012) Interpreting corruption: culture and politics in the Pacific Islands, in Peter Larmour, *Interpreting Corruption: Culture and Politics in the Pacific Islands*. Honolulu: University of Hawai'i Press.

Leppo, Kimmo, Ollila, Eeva, Pena, Sebastián, Wismar, Matthias and Cook, Sarah (2013) Health in all policies: seizing opportunities, implementing policies, *Julkaisuja* (STM), 2013: 9.

Levi-Faur, David (eds) (2012) *The Oxford Handbook of Governance*. Oxford: Oxford University Press.

Longman, P. (2010) *Best Care Anywhere: Why VA Health Care Is Better Than Yours*. San Francisco: Berrett-Koehler.

Lynn Jr., Lawrence J. (2011) The persistence of hierarchy, in Mark Bevir (ed.) *The Sage Handbook of Governance*. Thousand Oaks, CA: Sage, pp. 218–36.

Mackenbach, Johan P. and McKee, Martin (2013) A comparative analysis of health policy performance in 43 European countries, *European Journal of Public Health*, 23: 195–201.

Marmor, Theodore R. (2001) *Fads in Medical Care Policy and Politics: The Rhetoric and Reality of Managerialism*. London: The Nuffield Trust (Rock Carling Fellowship Lecture 2001).

Marmor, Theodore R. and Klein, Rudolf (2012) *Politics, Health, and Health Care: Selected Essays*. New Haven, CT: Yale University Press.

McDaid, David, Sassi, Franco and Merkur, Sherry (eds) (2015) *Promoting Health, Preventing Disease: The Economic Case*. Maidenhead: Open University Press.

McGrady, Benn (2011) *Trade and Public Health: The WTO, Tobacco, Alcohol, and Diet*. Cambridge: Cambridge University Press.

McNollgast (1990) Positive and normative models of procedural rights: an integrative approach to administrative procedures, *Journal of Law, Economics and Organization*, 6: 307–32.

McQueen, David, Wismar, Matthias, Lin, Vivian, Jones, Catherine, St-Pierre, Louise and Davies, Maggie (2012) *Inter-sectoral Governance for Health in All Policies: Structures, Actions and Experiences*. Copenhagen: WHO Regional Office for Europe on behalf of the European Observatory on Health Systems and Policies.

Mehta, Michael D. (2007) Good governance, in Mark Bevir (ed.) *Encyclopedia of Governance*, Thousand Oaks, CA: Sage, pp. 360–4.

Meneu, Ricard and Ortún, Vicente (2011) Transparencia y buen gobierno en sanidad. también para salir de la crisis, *Gaceta Sanitaria*, 25: 333–8.

Mossialos, Elias, Dixon, Anna, Figueras, Josep and Kutzin, Jose (eds) (2002) *Funding Health Care: Options for Europe*. Maidenhead: Open University Press.

Mossialos, E., Permanand, G., Baeten, R. and Hervey, T. K. (eds) (2010) *Health Systems Governance in Europe: The Role of European Union Law and Policy*. Cambridge: Cambridge University Press.

Murray, Christopher J. L. and Evans, David B. (eds) (2003) *Health Systems Performance Assessment: Debates, Methods and Empiricism*. Geneva: WHO.

Norris, Pippa (2010) Measuring governance, in Mark Bevir (ed.) *The Sage Handbook of Governance*. Thousand Oaks, CA: Sage, pp. 179–99.

Olafsdottir, Anna Elisabet, Allotey, Pascale and Reidpath, Daniel D. (2013) A health system in economic crisis: a case study from Iceland, *Scandinavian Journal of Public Health*, 41: 198–205.

Oliver, Adam (2007) The Veterans Health Administration: an American success story? *Milbank Quarterly*, 85: 5–35.

Osborne, David and Gaebler, Ted (1992) *Reinventing Government: How the Entrepreneurial Spirit Is Transforming the Public Sector*. Reading, MA: Addison-Wesley.

Ottersen, Ole Petter et al. (2014) The political origins of health inequity: prospects for change, *Lancet*, 383: 630–67.

Page, Edward (2012a) Bureaucracy: disregarding public administration, in Jack Hayward and James Connelly (eds) *The Withering of the Welfare State: Regression*. Basingstoke: Palgrave Macmillan, pp. 101–19.

Page, Edward (2012b) *Policy Without Politicians: Bureaucratic Influence in Comparative Perspective*. Oxford: Oxford University Press.

Papanicolas, Irene and Smith, Peter C. (eds) (2013) *Health System Performance Comparison: An Agenda for Policy, Information and Research*. Maidenhead: Open University Press.

Parker, Richard and Sommer, Marni (eds) (2010) *Routledge Handbook of Global Public Health*. London: Routledge.

Peters, B. Guy (2013) Toward policy coordination: alternatives to hierarchy, *Policy & Politics*, 41: 569–84.

Peters, B. Guy and Pierre, John (1998) Governance without government? Rethinking public administration, *Journal of Public Administration Research and Theory*, 8: 223–43.

Peters, B. Guy and Savoie, Donald D. J. (2000) *Governance in the Twenty-first Century: Revitalizing the Public Service*. Montreal: McGill-Queen's University Press.

Pollitt, Christopher (2013) 40 years of public management reform in UK Central Government: promises, promises, *Policy & Politics*, 41.

Przeworski, Adam (2003) *States and Markets: A Primer in Political Economy*. Cambridge: Cambridge University Press.

Radin, Dagmar (2009) Too ill to find the cure? Corruption, institutions, and health care sector performance in the new democracies of Central and Eastern Europe and Former Soviet Union, *East European Politics & Societies*, 23: 105–25.

Rhodes, Roderick Arthur William (1996) The new governance: governing without government, *Political Studies*, 44: 652–67.

Rothstein, Bo (2011) *The Quality of Government: Corruption, Social Trust and Inequality in International Perspective*. Chicago: University of Chicago Press.

Rothstein, Bo (2014) The Chinese paradox of high growth and low quality of government: the cadre organization meets Max Weber, *Governance*, early online view.

Sabel, Charles F. and Zeitlin, Jonathan (2007) Learning from difference: the new architecture of experimentalist governance in the European Union, *European Law Journal*, 14: 271–327.

Sabel, Charles F. and Zeitlin, Jonathan (eds) (2010) *Experimentalist Governance in the European Union: Towards a New Architecture*. Oxford: Oxford University Press.

Saltman, Richard B. and Bankauskaite, Vaida (2006) Conceptualizing decentralization in European health systems: a functional perspective, *Health Economics, Policy and Law*, 1: 127–47.

Savedoff, William D. (2012) *Global Government, Mixed Coalitions, and the Future of International Cooperation*. Washington, DC: Center for Global Development.

Smith, Katherine E., Fooks, Gary, Collin, Jeff, Weishaar, Heide and Gilmore, Anna A. B. (2010) Is the increasing policy use of impact assessment in Europe likely to undermine efforts to achieve healthy public policy? *Journal of Epidemiology and Community Health*, 64: 478–87.

Stanig, Piero and Kayser, Mark (2013) Governance indicators: some proposals, in Helmut K. Anheier (ed.) *Governance Challenges and Innovations*. Cambridge: Cambridge University Press, pp. 189–220.

Stoker, Gerry (1998) Governance as theory: five propositions, *International Social Science Journal*, 50: 17–28.

Svallfors, Stefan (2013) Government quality, egalitarianism, and attitudes to taxes and social spending: a European comparison, *European Political Science Review*, 5: 363–80.

Swedberg, Richard (2009) *Principles of Economic Sociology*. Princeton, NJ: Princeton University Press.

Thomson, Sarah, Foubister, Thomas and Mossialos, Elias (2009) *Financing Health Care in the European Union*. Copenhagen: WHO Regional Office for Europe on behalf of the European Observatory on Health Systems and Policies.

Tuohy, Carolyn Hughes (2003) Agency, contract and governance: shifting shapes of accountability in the health care arena, *Journal of Health Politics, Policy and Law*, 28: 195–215.

UNDP (2010) *Measuring Capacity*. New York: UNDP Capacity Development Group. Available at: http://www.undp.org/content/undp/en/home/librarypage/capacity-building/undp-paper-on-measuring-capacity.

Uslaner, Eric M. (2008) *Corruption, Inequality, and the Rule of Law*. Cambridge: Cambridge University Press.

Vian, Taryn (2008) Review of corruption in the health sector: theory, methods and interventions, *Health Policy Plan*, 23: 83–94.

Warner, Carolyn M. (2007) *The Best System Money Can Buy: Corruption in the European Union*. Ithaca, NY: Cornell University Press.

WHO (2000) *The World Health Report 2000: Health Systems: Improving Performance*. Geneva: World Health Organization.

WHO (2010) *The World Health Report 2010: Health Systems Financing: The Path to Universal Coverage*. Geneva: World Health Organization.

WHO Regional Office for Europe (2012) *Health 2020: A European Policy Framework Supporting Actions Across Government and Society for Health and Well-being*. Copenhagen: WHO Regional Office for Europe.

Woods, N. (1999) Good governance in international organizations, *Global Governance*, 5: 39–61.

Yeates, N. (2002) Social politics and policy in an era of globalization: critical reflections, *Social Policy and Administration*, 33(4): 372–93.

chapter two

Governance: a framework

Scott L. Greer, Matthias Wismar, Josep Figueras and Charlotte McKee

This chapter presents our approach to governance in the following steps: it first defines governance, then identifies the situations in which governance deserves attention from those who want to improve health systems, then discusses the five attributes of governance that we identify, and concludes by discussing the trade-offs involved in speaking about or trying to improve governance.

What is governance?

Our approach starts with a common reason to care about the structure and strengthening of governance: policy failure. Health policy, like development policy and many other areas of endeavour, is subject to a repeated pattern in which specific policy ideas are proposed, and then fail due to bad design, implementation, corruption, ineptitude or unforeseen consequences. Privatization of state-owned hospitals enables corrupt appropriation of assets if the agency making the sale lacks integrity and transparency. Extension of universal health care can be undermined by 'informal payments' or doctors going private if organizations are not clear about policing bad behaviour and accountability to public authorities does not work. Pharmaceutical policy can be made needlessly expensive and even dangerous if opacity, lack of regulatory agency accountability, and poor information or policy design allow conflict of interests, mistaken market authorizations or inflated payments. Top-down reforms of all sorts, such as reorganizations of hospital systems or payment systems, can fail if the people who must implement them were excluded from policy formulation and feel no ownership of the policy. Reliance on regulated markets, such as insurance, can create problems if the regulators do not feel accountable and need not justify their actions. Any reform can be defeated by rigid bureaucracies that might prevent corruption but clearly prevent action. In short, even the best ideas, with adequate funding and political support, can fail to produce the right effects due to the problems of weak governance.

In the aftermath of such disappointments, scholars and international organizations will often turn to the shape and strength of governance for diagnoses.[1]

Why did the policy fail in implementation, or produce unintended effects? Their answer is frequently one word: governance. Something was wrong with the governance – the institutions, laws or frequently the politics of a given system.

But what is governance? Very long and normative lists get made, most of which appear rather arbitrary when compared (see Table 2.1) and are insensitive to context (Bevir et al. 2003; Andrews 2013), as was notably the case with the widely exported New Public Management (Hood 1991; Dunleavy et al. 2006) or many applications of transaction cost economics (for which, see Williamson 1981, 1996).

For us, the definition of governance is 'the process and institutions through which decisions are made and authority in a country is exercised', in the World Bank's words.[2] The definition yokes together decision-making processes and structures that give those decisions force. It covers the patterned, structured aspects of decision-making, from legislative procedure and judicial review to appointment procedures and professional regulation. Much of the art of the politician is in evading such constraints while creating new constraints on his or her successors. Much of the art of the good health policy-maker lies in restructuring governance so that properties such as accountability and participation skew health systems toward the objectives of quality, sustainable, universal health systems (Greer and Lillvis 2014).

Governance is, in Travis' terms, about 'how things are done', in contrast to the more common health policy focus on 'what should be done' (Travis et al. 2003: 290).[3] It means that coordination (in a sense, the ultimate human activity) is easier and possible (Peters 2013), which also means that it can contain, respond to and resolve conflict (Peters and Savoie 2000). Our review of the literature found many syntheses and frameworks for understanding governance (some notable reviews with application to health are found in Travis et al. 2003; Savedoff and Gottret 2008; Saltman et al. 2011a; Barbazza and Tello 2012). The problem with most of them is that they are lists of desirable attributes and look arbitrary or utopian. As Table 2.1, which is the reprinted table from Barbazza and Tello (2014), suggests, it can be hard to explain why political stability, quality or accountability appear in some definitions of good governance and not in others. As Grindle (2004, 2007) elaborates, making long lists of desirable attributes and calling them all 'good governance' can hinder both thought and action: thought because it is not clear what is really necessary, and action because few or no societies can realistically achieve all of the things associated with good governance at once.

Our approach to governance is minimalist. The point of improving governance is to improve policy performance, meaning better formulated and implemented policies. While better governance is always desirable, the key issue is that governance must be 'good enough' (Grindle 2004): good enough to permit a country to advance, and good enough to manage the policies it must implement. For example, regulating private insurance or pharmaceuticals requires contending with wealthy industries that can both suborn and intellectually defeat regulators in the less well-governed systems. It might be that depending on private insurance for collective health outcomes is a luxury for countries with very good governance. Pharmaceuticals are inescapable, and pharmaceutical governance is a target for those who would undermine governance

Table 2.1 Common dimensions of governance across literature reviewed

Dimensions of governance	UNDP (1997)	World Bank (1999)	WHO (2000)*	Travis et al. (2002)*	Islam (2007)	WHO (2007)	WHO/EURO (2008)*	Siddiqi et al. (2009)	Lewis & Pettersson (2009)	Mikkelsen-Lopez et al. (2011)	Baez-Camargo & Jacobs (2011)	Kickbush & Gleicher (2012)	Council of Europe (2012)	Smith et al. (2012)	Wendt (2012)	Kaplan et al. (2013)
Control of corruption		▓								▓	▓					
Democracy													▓			
Human rights								▓				▓	▓			
Ethics and integrity		▓										▓				▓
Conflict prevention								▓								
Public good													▓			
Rule of law	▓	▓						▓								
Accountability	▓				▓	▓	▓		▓	▓			▓		▓	▓
Partnerships									▓				▓	▓		
Formulating policy/strategic direction	▓			▓			▓		▓						▓	▓
Generating information/intelligence				▓			▓					▓		▓		
Organizational adequacy/system design									▓						▓	▓
Participation and consensus	▓	▓														
Regulation								▓								▓
Transparency	▓	▓											▓			
Effectiveness	▓			▓			▓						▓		▓	▓
Efficiency				▓			▓	▓	▓				▓			
Equity	▓												▓			
Quality													▓			
Responsiveness	▓				▓			▓					▓			▓
Sustainability													▓			
Financial and social risk protection							▓									
Improved health																

Note: A shaded box is used to identify the explicit reference to a given element in the work of the corresponding author(s). The three groupings applied (fundamental values; sub-functions; outcomes) are the authors' own and therefore may not be explicitly used to characterize dimensions in the respective works.

*Refer to health stewardship.

Source: Barbazza and Tello (2014).

in pursuit of personal or corporate profit. Special attention should therefore be paid to strong governance in pharmaceutical policies, and overly complex innovations should be avoided. Weak governance makes it unlikely that any given policy initiative will be adopted and implemented well, and very good governance is a prerequisite for particularly complex and political issues such as regulating private insurance to public ends.

The result should be useful as a diagnostic tool (Brown et al. 2014: 1): when things are going wrong, which aspects of governance need to be strengthened? If a policy were to be adopted, what might be the governance threats to its success? What aspects of policy-making and implementation affect its likely success and could be changed to improve the quality, accessibility and financial sustainability of health systems? What things are going well, such that it might be wise to leave them alone or reinforce them?

Is it a governance problem?

Our diagnostic approach treats governance insofar as it is a source of policy problems. So, the first step in understanding or avoiding policy failure is a simple one: is it a governance problem? There are obvious rival hypotheses for explaining policy failure, retrospectively or prospectively. Failure to recognize when a problem is not predominantly about governance is common, and leads to reorganizations and governance changes that can distract from addressing the real problems or even make them worse. The clearest alternative sources of problems are:

- *Lack of financial resources.* Many policies require funds that are not always provided.
- *Lack of political will.* This is an omnibus term that lacks precision and combines issues as different as party manifestos, the personal preferences of ministers and referendum campaigns. Its value lies in highlighting the importance of political support, and the importance of both parties and individual politicians.
- *Lack of legality.* Many policies can be challenged in courts, including under EU law and international (trade or investment) law.
- *Fundamental flaws in the policy idea.* Some policies can be chosen and implemented well, and still backfire or produce serious problems. In principle, better governance makes it more likely that policies are chosen wisely and well, but this cannot be guaranteed. Some policies are adopted for reasons other than the collective good.
- *Governability.* Some things cannot be resolved or even managed (Jessop 2007).
- *Disagreement.* Finally, it is a mirage to think that better governance will eliminate disagreement and politics. Not everybody can win, regardless of the openness and transparency of the political process. Consequently, it has to be accepted that while better governance can smooth and manage disagreement, it cannot and should not eliminate politics.

Distinguishing among these different reasons for policy failure is an empirical matter. Among them, a governance failure is most likely when a policy with no salient problems (e.g., a legal and good idea with a plausible evidence base), adopted with adequate financing and political support, fails to produce the desired effects. Governance should also affect the likelihood that a good policy is adopted, by making sure that there are good evidence and appropriate interests involved in the conversation (so, for example, in signatories of the Framework Convention on Tobacco Control, it would not be good governance for tobacco interests to participate in the policy-making process, and it is a governance failure when they do influence policy) (Jarman 2014).

Elements of governance: the TAPIC framework

If there is a problem of governance, then our diagnostic approach's next step is to ask, what kind of problem might it be? Of all the different ways to make decisions and exercise authority, which ones are most likely to lead to policy that is implemented and has its intended effects?

At this point we adopted an inductive, rather than deductive, approach (as discussed in Chapter 1, there are many deductive, theoretical approaches to governance, few of which draw on the thought that international organizations and practitioners have put into governance). This involved reviewing a variety of studies that catalogue different attributes imputed to good governance in health and public administration more generally (Travis et al. 2003; Bevir 2007; Savedoff and Gottret 2008; Siddiqi et al. 2009; Labonté 2010; Kirigia and Kirigia 2011; Kickbusch and Gleicher 2011, 2014; Saltman et al. 2011a; Barbazza and Tello 2012; Thomas et al. 2013; Brown et al. 2014) as well as broader literature on public administration and governance (see Chapter 3) (Peters and Savoie 2000; Bevir 2012; Levi-Faur 2012).[4] The Appendix to this chapter presents many of the sources. From this, a list was produced of about 60 attributes of governance, which frequently referred to the same phenomena with slightly different definitions (see samples in the Appendix to this chapter). We reduced them to broad categories which do not overlap, which vary independently, and which make it more likely that decision-making and the exercise of authority mean effective collective action for collective objectives in health. Each category has its own literature, ranging from codes of conduct to consultants' PowerPoints to philosophical and scholarly meditations, but in each case it is possible to give a coherent definition. The result was five categories: transparency, accountability, participation, integrity and capacity. We refer to it as the TAPIC framework.

It is important to stress that these are components of governance rather than ingredients of good governance. Governance problems can be usefully found and understood in these terms – even if the answer is that there is too much of a given attribute or that it has been poorly implemented. They are all words with positive connotations. It is hard to be explicitly opposed to something like integrity, accountability, participation or transparency. But policies made or justified in the name of accountability, or participation, or transparency can be costly and unproductive, and in some forms can compete with other desirable values such as efficacy and flexibility. The framework orients towards important components of governance, but does not mean that more of each component is simply better.

Transparency

Transparency means that institutions inform the public and other actors of both upcoming decisions and decisions that have been made, and of the process by and grounds on which decisions are being made (based on Woods 1999: 44). It has a powerful heritage in Western thought about good government: Max Weber wrote: 'Every bureaucracy seeks to increase the superiority of the professionally informed by keeping their knowledge and intentions secret' (1958: 233), and Jeremy Bentham wrote:

> The enemies of publicity may be collected into three classes: the malefactor, who seeks to escape the notice of the judge; the tyrant, who seeks to stifle public opinion, whilst he fears to hear its voice; the timid or indolent man, who complains of the general incapacity in order to screen his own.

and James Madison wrote: 'Knowledge will forever govern ignorance; and a people who mean to be their own governors must arm themselves with the power which knowledge gives.'[5]

Often conflated with accountability, transparency is different. There can in principle be transparency without accountability, simply because an organization chooses to keep the world informed. There can also be accountability without transparency, as can happen with commercially confidential transactions.

Transparency mechanisms include:

- watchdog committees;
- inspectorates;
- regular reporting;
- Freedom of Information legislation (FoI);
- performance managing/reporting/assessment;
- clear and useful public information: such as open meetings, clarity about key personnel, and information presented in clear and usable formats: for example, datasets should be in usable formats rather than PDFs.

The common theme of transparency mechanisms is that they make it possible to understand an institution, identify possible malfeasance or incompetence, and adapt plans to its behaviour. In principle, it can also be an anti-corruption measure, and has worked as such (Vian et al. 2010).

At its worst, transparency means minimal dissemination: e.g., a website and annual report. Actions that are billed as promoting transparency can be quite the opposite. Every consumer knows the phenomenon of 'transparent' fine print that enables a company to charge extra fees, deliver worse service or ignore complaints. Every researcher is familiar with the phenomenon of a government agency that withdraws access to raw data and replaces it with 'user-friendly' but much less useful graphics-filled reports and apps, in the name of greater public access. Given that public perceptions of transparency do not always correlate with actual transparency (de Fine Licht 2014), transparency for health services often should mean that data and decisions are available to experts who can challenge a decision and the decision-making process as well as simple explanations of decisions and their grounds for the public.

Too much transparency can simply drive politics and decision-making underground. Badly implemented FOI can drive government work into the shadows by leading policy-makers to conduct their business in private and without notes, which snarls intra-governmental communications. Before simply adopting transparency measures, policy-makers should consider their costs and whether they will disproportionately benefit the best-resourced lobbyists; for example, mechanisms that promote or depend on litigation are expensive and most likely to be used by industry or other monied interests.

At its best, transparency produces information that is available, useful and accurate so that it can be used by those who would rely on, plan with or seek to influence the organization. The result is trust. If patients, citizens investors and other organizations know how, when and why decisions are made, then they will be able to plan accordingly and work out how to contribute their views and knowledge, or challenge the policy-makers (Greer and Lillvis 2014). It is worth noting that many highly effective systems do not depend on average citizens using data. It is enough, in many cases, that NGOs, experts and affected interests are able to understand government data and sound the alarm.

The key limitation on transparency, though, is that it can backfire in systems where civil society is weak and interest representation is biased. Greater transparency can give well-resourced lobbies more time to prepare campaigns and start to influence policy. Given that good public health policy often injures the interests of well-resourced lobbies, transparency about process can be actively harmful to good policy (Best 2005). Clarity about decisions and their grounds means what it says. It does not mean that policy-makers should extensively telegraph their thinking so that well-resourced lobbies can intervene. This is especially important in political systems with less-balanced interest group representation.

Accountability

Accountability involves explanation and sanction (Weale 2011: 64). A much-defined concept, it can be stated at greater length as a relationship between an actor (such as an agency) and a forum (such as a legislature) in which the actor must inform the others of decisions, must explain decisions, can be mandated and can be sanctioned (Tuohy 2003; Brinkerhoff 2004; Castiglione 2007; Weisband and Ebrahim 2007; Urbinati and Warren 2008: 396; Bovens 2010; Bovens et al. 2010; Bevir 2013: 141–7). These attributes are distinct but linked. Informing and explaining – giving an account of one's actions – are the core of accountability in one sense. Equally, though, there must be consequences if the action and explanation are inadequate – notably, if there is a mandate that has been violated (e.g., an obligation to ensure patient safety, or financial probity or effective planning).

Accountability mechanisms, reviewed in Chapter 3, include:

- contracts;
- other financial mechanisms, such as pay for performance;
- laws that specify objectives, reporting and mechanisms;
- competitive bidding;
- organizational separation;
- conflict of interest policies;
- regulation;

- delegated regulation;
- standards;
- codes of conduct;
- choice mechanisms that create 'horizontal accountability' by letting users 'vote with their feet' and thereby attempt to create accountability to users at the margin who might leave rather than accountability to public authorities or a diffuse public (Le Grand 2007; Schillemans 2008; Meijer and Schillemans 2009).

Not all of these mechanisms work equally well in different circumstances, and they obviously all work quite differently. It can be easier to pass a law than write and enforce a complex public–private partnership (PPP) contract, or to regulate big and opaque companies such as insurers or medical devices firms (as discussed in Chapters 6–9).

Accountability has a number of virtues that make it popular, perhaps foundational, in discussions of good governance. Without it, all kinds of incompetence, shirking, bloat and malversation are possible. It is often pursued in unproductive ways, with public sector managers rigorously held to account for meals or travel expenses, which is easy but resource-intensive, and less accountable for their major decisions (Behn 2001; Warren 2006; Flinders and Moon 2011). It can be introduced relatively easily, in large part because it is very hard to argue against it in public (Landwehr and Böhm 2011: 684).

Good accountability enables administrative discretion. Klitgaard wrote that monopoly of a power plus discretion minus accountability equals corruption. Since accountability is hard, many policy-makers have opted for limiting discretion in public services, or undermining the monopoly. The problem with limiting discretion is that it can increase rigidity and bureaucracy and even opportunities for petty corruption far more than it reduces corruption (Klitgaard 1988; Warner 2007).[6]

It is better to focus on good accountability relationships so that discretion can be expanded, morale raised, and the skills of workers used to their fullest. Rather than a backward-looking model in which agents are punished for failure to comply, clear accountability can even create a better relationship in which the expertise and experiences of the agents help the principals understand better what they want. A combination of clarity about objectives and opportunity for experimentation, including feedback that allows the goals to be modified as everybody learns about the problem, is optimal. Such a relationship permits flexibility, learning and more engaged workers, and therefore effectiveness, without notably encouraging corruption or waste (Sabel 2001).

The first big problem of accountability is: accountability to whom? This is essential to understanding the functioning, organization or power relationships of any part of a system. Social insurance funds are generally not accountable to the finance ministry in the way that health departments are, courts are not accountable to the government in the way regulatory agencies can be, and governments' accountability to their legislatures and the press also varies. Getting the direction of accountability relationships right for the purposes of health is important.

The second big problem of accountability is that there can be a lot of it, such that it is hard to understand, and can interfere with efficiency. Most organizations in health systems, or our complex societies in general, are embedded in webs of accountability rather than simple delegative or fiduciary relationships (Tuohy 2003). They can be sanctioned by, and do explain themselves to, many actors. Consequently, finding and defining accountability relationships empirically are not as simple as it might seem and quick judgements might be misleading. This means that identifying accountability relationships should be prior to trying to make policy for a given sector. For policy, it frequently means that reducing the number of accountability relationships can make an organization more effective. A simpler accountability relationship (for example, to a single ministry) can be more effective than a thicket of confusing relationships (Greer et al. 2014a).

The third problem is that accountability can go wrong – delegated regulators can be captured, codes of conduct ignored, contracts litigated endlessly. This means that accountability mechanisms are crucial. Accountability means less if those accountable do not actually account for their actions, or if they are held accountable only for inconsequential things because that is easy for bureaucracies to do, or if they remove so much discretion that agents cannot perform their tasks effectively.

The fourth problem is that accountability is often invoked as justification for policies and theories that are hostile to the public sector and justify very tight controls over bureaucracy. Part of the problem is that the assumption of bureaucratic laziness, shirking and empire building is the 'founding myth' of a very large practical and scholarly literature whose empirical base is remarkably thin (Page 2012: vii). Punitive accountability measures can be both unnecessary and damaging – unnecessary if an organization already has accountability and service in its culture, and damaging if they waste time and energy, lower morale or introduce distrust. The assumption that managers are intent on undermining their own mission can be very damaging if turned directly into accountability policy without sufficient thought (Behn 2001).

Participation

Participation means that affected parties have access to decision-making and power so that they acquire a meaningful stake in the work of the institution (based on Woods 1999: 44; see also Tritter and McCallum 2006; Banyan 2007; Weale 2007; Urbinati and Warren 2008; Tritter et al. 2010; Stewart 2013). The need for participation does not only grow from democratic theory, though participation is the core virtue of democracy. Rather, the need for participation comes from the problems that come when decisions are made and authority exercised without the participation of affected populations. Participation mechanisms include:

- stakeholder forums;
- consultations;
- elections;

- appointed representatives;
- legal remedies;
- choice mechanisms;
- advisory committees, ad hoc or otherwise;
- partnerships;
- surveys;
- joint budgets, joint workforce, etc. (when the problem is the participation of different parts of government in a particular policy area); and
- more radically democratic innovations, such as participatory budgeting (Seekings 2013) and citizens' juries (Bevir 2013: 187–206).

Archon Fung (2006) argues that effectively structured participation improves three things. First, participation can be a route to legitimacy and ownership; while it will not always reconcile differences (not everybody can be happy), the participation of key implementers is usually necessary to avoid sabotage or just poor implementation. This argument fits with broader normative and social scientific understandings of legitimacy. Second, participation can produce information that means policies are more just. Lobbyists can bring industry concerns, but if participation is structured well, it can also bring in other citizen and NGO perspectives. Third, according to Fung, participation also improves the effectiveness of policy, notably by providing information. Consulting affected parties can produce very useful information (about, for example, the functioning of little-understood public services that a government is thinking about reforming, or about practical difficulties that might arise from a proposed policy). Even regimes that are unquestionably authoritarian have developed participation mechanisms to gain the benefits (Dominguez 2011: 574). Klitgaard and collaborators (2000), specifically, suggest that it is a powerful tool against corruption.

As with these other components of governance, it can seem like participation is self-evidently good and more of it is better, but there are costs to participatory mechanisms, they can fail, and their contribution is better for some things than for others. A key problem with participation is that its justification is often unclear; what do we want from a given kind of participation (Greer et al. 2014c)? Simply creating participation mechanisms can create problems for no obvious gain, and many of the best decisions are made in private. It is better to think about pay-offs from participation, such as different perspectives, information or assistance. The definition of participation as engagement of legitimate affected parties in pursuit of specific benefits creates an exclusion criterion; for example, tobacco companies should be excluded from discussions of tobacco control. Too many access points in general will lower the costs of access for lobbyists, producing complex and biased legislation. Fewer, more public, better-defined and justified forms of access for affected populations therefore produce better and more representative policy (Ehrlich 2011).

Participation can mean opening up governmental deliberations that were already open to lobbyists, so that NGOs can at least be informed about events and make their views clear (Jarman 2011). In such a case, a participation policy is about trying to redress imbalances between those with and those without resources in the interests of justice, ownership, and information. Much more locally, participation can also mean finding out what local communities think, so that policy-makers can avoid trouble or provide services better. Naturally, these require very different mechanisms.

Then, it must be stressed that participation highlights conflict. Sometimes it is impossible to have a consensus or universal ownership: there are winners and losers, but at least there is some overall procedural legitimacy (Scharpf 2009) if there was participation, and information might have been incorporated. This means that while participation is good, too much of it can skew or prevent decisions. Increasing opportunities to block decisions – veto points – is generally correlated with less generous health systems that are reformed less effectively through changing times (Immergut 1992). Ultimately, somebody needs to make a decision.

Sometimes it is hard to find representatives of affected interests who can provide useful information, legitimacy or ownership. It is notoriously hard to find patient representatives at the policy level because patients are so diverse and fragmented as a group, and the result is often advocates whose representativeness and therefore ability to add legitimacy, information or ownership are questionable. Sometimes people do not want to participate. Just as not all patients want to exercise choice, not all patients wish to be engaged in the management of their health systems (Greer et al. 2014b; Greer et al. 2014c).

And, finally, participation is hard. It requires understanding of policies, interests, structures and different conceptual languages as well as, in some cases, different languages entirely. This means that good representation is expensive and takes time to develop, which in turn means that representation can be biased towards well-resourced interests if it is not carefully designed and supported.

All of this points to the need to be careful with the extension of participation mechanisms, recognizing their cost and potential contribution to gridlock, bias and polarization as well as their benefits, and justify them in terms of practical benefits for the justice, legitimacy and effectiveness of health policies. Finally, despite all the criticism, accountability to a minister, to a legislature and ultimately to voters is a powerful form of accountability that often does what is needed. Few forms of participation have so long and effective a track record as electoral democracy, and it is not a good idea to compare really existing democratic governance, with its flaws, to various theoretical democratic ideals that have not had to be implemented in reality.

A useful starting criterion for participation is that it should bring one or more of Fung's advantages, without creating bias and complexity through too many opportunities suited to well-resourced lobbyists, while also respecting expertise. For example, in developing disease treatment, participation can bring specific benefits but can also create needless costs. Aronowitz (2012) concludes from the cautionary tale of Lyme disease vaccines that '[Inclusion] should not be valorized in itself but for what it brings: fairness, accurate research sampling, different perspectives.' Rather than trying to include on principle, the benefits of participation should be considered carefully and with an eye to the distributional implications of different forms of participation (Ottersen et al. 2014). In other words, specifying that participation means affected interests, and is neither indefinite nor determinative, gives us an exclusion criterion: participation is for a purpose.

Integrity: the Weberian virtues

Integrity has many synonyms and related terms: predictability, anti-corruption, ethics, rule of law, clear allocation of defined roles and responsibility, formal rules, stability. It means that the processes of representation, decision-making and enforcement should be clearly specified. All members should be able to understand and predict the processes by which an institution will take decisions and apply them; individuals should have a clear allocation of roles and responsibilities (based on Woods 1999: 46; see also Larmour 2012: 56; Sabet 2012). These are the basics of well-functioning, long-lasting, trustworthy organizations, as social scientists since at least Max Weber have argued: clear allocation of roles/responsibilities, and a clear process relating them (Weber 1978).

Integrity mechanisms include:

- solid and well-rewarded internal career trajectories that allow high-level officials to be rewarded for service rather than seeking profit or positions outside government;
- internal audit (to ensure that money moves appropriately);
- personnel policies (hiring, job descriptions, procedures to weed out flawed people);
- legislative mandate;
- budget;
- procedures (e.g., document management, board behaviour, minuting meetings);
- audit;
- clear organizational roles and purposes.

In a sense, integrity is good management. That should not obscure its virtues, or the helpful and harmful roles accountability can play. Integrity is good for state-building (Silberman 1993) and democratic stability (Cornell and Lapuente 2014).

Just as accountability can be turned into form-filling, integrity can also simply mean bureaucracy. Worse, bureauracies can encode problematic political preferences.[7] They can seem to have costs in effectiveness, efficiency and speed (though frequently the problem is just the size of the bureaucracy). This might be why, as Grindle (2012) notes, we have the paradox of developing countries seeking to adopt exactly the kind of rigid integrity reforms (e.g., civil service laws) that rich countries are explicitly trying to undermine (e.g., with political appointees). The detail involved in much integrity policy makes it hard to generalize, but frequently the solution is to match integrity in the form of day-to-day controls and clear budgeting with clear and effective accountability, so that the potentially endless bureaucracy of integrity measures must be balanced against the demand that the people actually do their jobs and allow others to do the same. It is also important to focus on some of the less-constraining forms of integrity policy, such as clear organizational missions and understanding of roles, since those might produce benefits while reducing the apparent need for the more time-consuming and morale-damaging forms of integrity such as the (surprisingly common) intense scrutiny of minor expenses claims. Finally, it is possible to overstate the benefits of organizational clarity – no health system's organization chart is clear and it need not be, as Chapter 10 on intergovernmental relations shows – but it is hard to overstate the benefits to an organization of a clear sense of mission that will allow its staff to focus on key goals. At times, it is worth starting a new organization simply to achieve that.

Policy capacity

Policy capacity refers to the ability to develop policy that is aligned with resources in pursuit of goals (Forest et al. 2015). Edward Page refers to the home of policy capacity as the 'policy bureaucracy' – just as some bureaucratic organizations build cars or deliver mail, there is a small bureaucracy near the top of any government that turns raw material such as ideas and political will into coherent policy (Page and Jenkins 2005; Page 2007). It is to be evaluated for its 'power-serving' capacity: the ability to do the staff work and analysis to turn a political idea into a thought-out proposal, or explain why it is risky (Page 2010, 2012). It is not usually the origin of political ideas (Kingdon 2003; Page 2006). Rather, it is the part of government that transforms ideas into workable, well-designed policies. If it succeeds, it can allow governments to formulate innovative and effective policies for health in the face of resistance (Fox 2010: 10–13). If it fails, it can abet a wide range of policy failures (e.g., King and Crewe 2013: 257, 313, 329, 382).

Mechanisms to improve policy capacity include:

- intelligence on performance, so that the central policy-makers can identify problems and gauge the effects of what they are doing;
- intelligence on process (e.g., understanding of legal and budgetary issues and the system that is being changed);
- research/analysis capacity (e.g., trained staff with skills such as research and the ability to identify and work with useful outsiders);
- staff training, to improve their technical policy capacity (e.g., if a doctor is hired in a health ministry, provide opportunities to complement medical education with policy education);
- hiring procedures, to improve the quality of the policy bureaucracy;
- procedures to incorporate specialist advice into policy formulation and recommendations;
- good buy/make decisions (i.e. develop sufficient in-house capacity to manage contractors such as consultancy firms and know when it is more efficient to do the work and when it is more efficient to contract in the work) (Coase 1937).

Policy capacity does not just come from hiring intelligent young people. It requires experience of and integration with the broader organization, and broader government. Neither does it just require data, big or otherwise. Data are not the same thing as knowledge, and data projects can absorb resources and attention that might be better invested in understanding the system.

Policy capacity refers to the specific technical resources at the disposal of a top policy-maker – a fairly small number of skilled people with academic training and experience of government in most cases. They are the ones who are, or are not, good enough at details to develop regulatory frameworks without loopholes or incentive structures that produce the right effects. They are the ones who vet ideas for their legality, budgetary coherence and other problems that can arise from rushed or badly staffed policy-making.

Policy capacity is rarely a bad thing. Its costs are mostly opportunity costs (or are borne by those who benefit from incompetence among decision-makers). The risks are frequently that it will be cut, to save costs, or that it will become distanced from decision-making. Health ministries are not generally the most powerful parts of government, or even necessarily health systems, and it is easy to underplay the benefits of investing in their policy capacity (Greer 2010). On one hand, it is always easy to justify a position in something more important than the policy or evaluation section of a health ministry. The benefits of hiring an extra doctor can always seem to outweigh the benefits of an extra analyst, even if the analyst might inform changes that make the existing doctors much more efficient and effective. On the other hand, it is easy to create units of disconnected smart people, who will be prime targets for later cuts. Ministers frequently have good reasons to be unhappy with the preferences and skills of the policy capacity they inherit, and letting them choose some key advisors is nearly universal for that reason. It is also easy to rely on consultants, whose outside ideas and speed are frequently counterbalanced by their cost, lack of creativity and lack of local expertise. At a minimum, pairing consultants with one's own policy capacity can make the consultants' work better value.

Too little, too much or the wrong kind?

Accountability, transparency, participation, integrity and capacity are all words with very positive connotations, but they frequently interfere with some other good things: speed, efficiency, effectiveness, flexibility, creativity, empowerment and innovation. Many theories of governance are about constraining and regularizing power, which can conflict with its effective use. They almost seem to assume the organization, or system, and then focus on its maintenance and constraint. Even if, in the long term, constrained and effective power is more effective, legitimate and stable, it can always be argued that in an individual case what is required is action.

In principle, as the studies cited here and elsewhere show, all five aspects of the framework can improve the effectiveness, creativity, efficiency and flexibility of a health system. In practice, they can also have excessive costs. Transparency, for example, can be put in the service of making politics mechanistic and elitist (Best 2005) or can widen the gap between what happens on paper and what really happens (Hull 2012). Accountability can focus on little rather than big things and turn into a demotivating waste of resources (Behn 2001). That is why they should be regarded as aspects of organization rather than normative goals – more is not always better.

The final step in a diagnostic or prospective analysis of health systems governance, then, is to think about whether the problem is too little, too much, or the wrong kind of an attribute:

- Too little can mean that the absence of enough policies promoting an attribute produces the effects discussed. Using participation for an example, top-down policies made with little participation risk being illegitimate, unjust, ineffective, or needlessly expensive and coercive. They might be better formulated if there had been a process increasing ownership among implementers and information available to decision-makers (including information about local preferences and politics that would not appear in conventional policy-making evidence). A lot of damage has been done by policy-makers who focus on what is measured rather than by what is managed, and who might not pay enough attention to the distortions in measurement. It is also possible to erode existing capacities. For example, repeated reorganization can erode integrity, by reducing the clarity of roles and missions, reducing individuals' loyalty to and understanding of their role, diminishing policy capacity by reassigning people and tasks, and even turning reorganization and its facilitation into people's core skill (Pollitt 2007).
- Too much can mean that an excess of one attribute is interfering with policy and its implementation, as with, for example, overly detailed internal controls that force documentation for trivial expenses in the name of integrity, or transparency requirements that mean nobody writes anything down. Accountability can frequently have costs if it means that an organization has too many conflicting accountabilities (given that any organization worth discussing already has many); this is, for example, the problem of too many different inspectorates visiting the same hospital. It can also mean that a regulator or professional organization lacks the insulation necessary to do a job well. That is often the case in innovative organizations (research governance justified by ethical concerns can stifle innovation in this way without necessarily improving the ethical quality of the research enterprise) (Bosk 2007; Schrag 2010). Successful innovation and bureaucratic effectiveness come from having the right amount, so that an organization is embedded in its environment but still autonomous enough to take action (Evans 1995). Transparency, finally, can become a problem if it is taken to mean more than clarifying decisions and their grounds. Extensive transparency about the decision-making process (as against who made the decision) can allow well-resourced interests to intervene. This is particularly a problem when there is an imbalance in interest group resources and access. In general, every structural governance solution works better when there is more political competition, because it creates more challengers who can use governance to force improvements.
- The wrong kind, finally, means that the mechanism is ill-judged: too costly, too rigid, too easily used to block action, or too easily manipulated by particular

interests. Participation, for example, risks both entrenching specific unrepresentative interests and slowing decision-making if structured badly. It is unclear, for example, how much industry and public participation there really should be in health technology assessment or communicable disease control. Likewise, special elections for specialist governments responsible for a given function, such as health, can have low and heavily biased turnout compared to general elections (Greer et al. 2012; Greer et al. 2014c) and can even be manipulated by politicians to reward incumbency and distort the electorate (Hajnal and Trounstine 2005; Berry 2009; Anzia 2013). It might seem intuitive that special elections to special governmental bodies will improve participation, but it is risky – a costly affirmation of the status quo at best, and able to be manipulated by special interests at worst. Perhaps the best demonstration is with regulation. There is an unwarranted assumption that regulators will always be 'captured' by the interests that they regulate, despite a large volume of research showing that well-designed regulatory agencies can avoid capture and serve the intended, public, interest (Carpenter and Moss 2013). Likewise, the problem of too many inspectorates in England's Stafford Hospital case coincided with the wrong kind of accountability (see Chapter 1: the Francis Report ended up focusing on individual managers rather than the many people to whom they were supposed to account for their actions).

Conclusions: 'governance is about conflict resolution'

Governance problems are not the only kind of problems health policies and systems face: inadequate finances, poor street-level technical resources, political decisions, political conflict and overstretched resources can all damage the ability of a society to take collective decisions and exercise power to a collective end. But governance is a recurrent problem, identified when policies and systems do not work, falling prey to ineptitude, conflict of interests, bureaucratic rigidity or poorly thought-out policies. Understanding governance weaknesses, and being able to identify them, is important to making good policy and implementing it.

A governance problem is likely to be at work when an adequately financed proposal with political support produces unexpected or no effects due to flawed or poor implementation, or when a system produces dysfunctional results with its resources. It is particularly likely to be at work when the problems are failed implementation, misalignment, or unexpected results due to gaming of the system or lack of coordinated activity. Good governance should improve the quality of decisions, but it is not the sum of the political system, and politics can produce compromises and ideologies that are not always constructive. That is the right of a government, for at least in principle its citizens can punish it for bad performance.

Governance, likewise, is part of the development and implementation of policy, but has its limits. Solving macroeconomic problems with public sector reform in the manner that the EU is pursuing with Greece, has at best a checkered history of success. Likewise, making good governance a precondition for resources has not always been a success; starving a health system of resources is as likely to create zero-sum competition and gaming of rules as it is to promote virtue. So, not all problems are problems of governance, but weak governance can interfere with efforts to solve problems.

The components of governance that we distilled from a large body of literature are accountability, transparency, participation, organizational integrity and policy capacity. They can vary independently. Accountability without transparency, for example, is common, such as when regulatory agencies do not have to report back in detail on their decisions and procedures. Likewise, organizational integrity can operate without participation or transparency, as with any high-handed bureaucracy that is admired for its efficiency and disliked for its arrogance. A participatory, transparent and accountable organization, common in small organizations, can often have weak internal organization and integrity; its other virtues keep it from becoming corrupt.

The five attributes are broadly mutually reinforcing, and if they slow down decisions, they might make them better and better implemented. Accountability works better if transparency is present, since transparency strengthens control mechanisms. Transparency works well with participation, since it produces more informed and trusting participation and connects decisions with new information. Integrity works well with participation since it makes it clear who is making the decisions and what behaviour is proper or improper. Organizational capacity is hard to achieve without organizational integrity since policy skills are limited in weak, nepotistic or corrupt bureaucracies, and it can be hard to recruit and use good staff without coherent jobs and career structures. Even if only one aspect of governance improves, it is linked to other aspects that might be open to improvement as a result; exploiting linkages between small victories to create improvements, as Albert Hirschman (1981) discussed, is crucial to change in the real world.

Going beyond the use of governance as a diagnostic, if not forensic, tool, there is a more forward-looking question: is there a specific aspect of governance in a given system that makes policy failure likely, and is it advisable to try to change the feature of governance, or to change the policy so that it is less vulnerable? Some ideas, such as the use of private insurance in regulated markets (Chapter 6), or major PFIs (Chapter 7), might turn out to demand such good governance that even well-governed systems would be advised to avoid them (see also the superb King and Crewe 2013, on PFI problems). Avoiding policies that demand unrealistically effective governance arrangements is a good policy idea in itself; a second best would be to try to remedy relevant governance deficiencies before implementing policies that make big demands on governance.

We should end on a note of humility. Governance is the structure of decision-making and coordination across a system or society, and the complexity of societies interacts with the many things that different people think they are doing within those societies. It does not mean that everybody agrees – participation does not mean that everybody is happy, capacity does not mean that everybody is hired, and transparency does not mean that everything is understood. What it means is that the system is capable of withstanding the many conflicts over every kind of procedure and priority that are a normal part of life, and still producing and implementing coherent policies for health. In fact, a focus on governance improvement can distract us from both better priorities and the things that are working well despite apparent unorthodoxy (Leys et al. 2002; Brinkerhoff and Goldsmith 2005; Grindle 2012), can be mere signals to earn external approval (Andrews 2013), or can turn into a charter for an 'anti-politics' that damages good governance, democracy, and the policies themselves (Ferguson 1990; Larmour 2012). It is better to focus on identifying the aspects of governance that will bias politics, markets and practice towards health and resilience rather than something else.

This framework identified five aspects of governance, the patterned aspects of decision-making, that in many studies have appeared important in explaining the ability of health systems to provide accessible, quality, sustainable health. There is no necessary advantage to simply adding mechanisms in these areas. A system can have too much of them, or too little of them, or the wrong kind of them, and that will explain policy failures not otherwise explicable in terms of finances, law or the basic policy idea. No governance is neutral; it always has structural winners and losers, and health systems governance should be designed for health. Governance will never wipe out politics or markets, but it can pattern decisions, and politics, in ways that support health.

Notes

1 Perhaps the most visible case was the shift made by the international financial institutions (the World Bank, the IMF) from structural adjustment (a list of policy proposals with little interest in implementation) to governance-strengthening in the 1990s, after it became clear that each aspect of structural adjustment policy could be subverted (Greer 2014). It is not clear, of course, that any amount of good governance could have survived structural adjustment or that structural adjustment would have had the desired effects in a country with any given kind of governance.

2 'What is Governance?' Available at: http://go.worldbank.org/G2CHLXX0Q0. See also the WHO definition: 'a wide range of steering and rule-making related functions carried out by governments/decisions makers as they seek to achieve national health policy objectives that are conducive to universal health coverage. Available at: http://www.who.int/healthsystems/topics/stewardship/en/ and (Peters and Pierre 2004).

3 In the 1990s, some academics attempted to define governance in contrast to government, as if governance had replaced government (Peters and Pierre 1998; Stoker 1998). This artificial and unhelpful distinction is effectively rebutted by Lynn Jr. (2011) and Bevir (2010).

4 Travers et al. (2003) focus on stewardship rather than governance, and Thomas et al. (2013) on resilience, but many of the actions of a good steward are those which contribute to and form part of responsible governance, which improves health system resilience.

5 The Bentham quote is from Jeremy Bentham, *The Works of Jeremy Bentham*, vol. 2 *(Judicial Procedure, Anarchical Fallacies, Works on Taxation)* (1843), available at http://oll.libertyfund.org/titles/1921. The Madison quote is from his letter to T. W. Berry, 4 August 1822, available at http://press-pubs.uchicago.edu/founders/documents/v1ch18s35.html.

6 See also the important corrective discussion at: http://globalanticorruptionblog.com/2014/05/27/klitgaards-misleading-corruption-formula.

7 Weber himself, for example, underplayed the anti-democratic bias of the Imperial German bureaucracy (Wehler and Traynor 1985).

Appendix Examples of concepts in the relevant literature

Category	Wording
Accountability – *a relationship between an actor (such as an agency) and a forum (such as a legislature) in which the actor must inform the other of decisions, must explain decisions, and can be sanctioned*	• *Travis et al., 2002*: subnational health authorities accountable to central government who 'ensure that they collectively provide effective stewardship' • 'formulation of a strategic policy framework' – including institutions for monitoring performance • 'ensuring (formal) tools for implementation: powers, incentives, and sanctions' • 'ensuring accountability and answerability to the population' • 'set and enforce rules, incentives, and sanctions for other actors' • *Woods, 1999*: 'accountability' • *UNDP, 1997:* 'accountability' • *Barbazza et al., 2012*: 'accountability'– differentiates between vertical and horizontal accountability • 'co-ordination' • *Kaufmann et al., 2010*: 'Voice and Accountability', including free press, etc. • *European Commission, 2004*: 'rule of law and administration of justice' • 'democratization' • 'transparency and accountability' • *Sir Alan Langlands, 2004*: 'good governance means engaging stakeholders and making accountability real' • *Brinkerhoff et al., 2008*: 'institutional checks and balances' • 'clear and enforceable accountability' • *Siddiqi et al., 2009*: 'accountability' • *Omaswa and Boufford 2010*: 'standard setting/regulation (monitoring and oversight): public and private sectors' • *Council of Europe, 2012:* 'accountability' • 'integrity' • *Saltman et al., 2011b:* 'accountability arrangements' • *Newman, 2001*: 'recognizing the blurring of boundaries and responsibilities for tackling social and economic issues' • 'a move away from hierarchy and competition as alternative models for delivering services, towards networks and partnership traversing the public, private and voluntary sectors' • *European Commission, 2001*: 'accountability' • *CIPFA, 1994*: 'accountability/holding individuals responsible for their actions by a clear allocation of responsibilities and defined roles' • *WHO, 2007*: 'accountability' • (ensuring all health system actors are held publicly accountable. Transparency is required to achieve real accountability') • *WHO 2012*: Health 2020, 'accountability' • *Sustainable Governance Indicators, 2011*: 'executive accountability'

(Continued)

Appendix Examples of concepts in the relevant literature (*continued*)

Category	Wording

Transparency – *institutions inform the public and other actors of decisions coming and decisions taken, and of the process by and grounds on which decisions are taken*	• *Woods, 1999*: the practical means for ensuring accountability
	• *Sir Alan Langlands, 2004*: 'good governance means promoting values for the whole organization and demonstrating the values of good governance through behavior'
	• *Brinkerhoff et al., 2008*: 'transparency in policymaking, resource allocation and performance'
	• *Siddiqi et al., 2009*: 'transparency'
	• *Omaswa and Boufford 2010*: 'collecting and disseminating information'
	• *Council of Europe, 2012*: 'transparency'
	• *European Commission, 2001*: 'openness'
	• *European Commission, 2004*: 'transparency and accountability'
	  • ('Transparency and accountability exist when the P/P incorporates mechanisms for keeping the stakeholders fully involved, at regular intervals, in the decision-making process, and fully informed of the implementation and results. This implies that stakeholders are answerable to those whom they represent on the fulfillment of their obligations, and that they undertake to inform and consult their constituencies at regular intervals. This will require clearly delineated tasks and responsibilities, effective flows of information and mechanisms ensuring that decisions and sanctions are enforced.')
	• *CIPFA, 1994*: 'openness/disclosure of information'
	• *Kickbusch and Gleichert, 2012*: 'governing by collaboration' ('smart governance for health should bring about better, deeper engagement with various social actors, facilitated by greater transparency and should be held accountable by social values')
	  • 'transparency'– 'a necessary element for building trust in collaborative governance systems'
	• *WHO, 2012*, Health 2020: 'transparency'
	• *Sustainable Governance Indicators, 2011*: 'freely accessible information'

Participation – *affected parties have access to decision-making and power so that they acquire a meaningful stake in the work of the institution*	• *Woods, 1999*: participation and ownership
	• *Barbazza and Tello, 2012*: 'participation and consensus'
	• 'participation'
	• *UNDP, 1997*: 'legitimacy and voice'
	  • 'Fairness'
	• *WHO, 2000*: 'collecting and using information'
	• *PAHO, 2002*: 'social participation in health'
	  • 'evaluation and promotion of equitable access to necessary health services'
	• *European Commission, 2004*: 'civil society'
	  • 'decentralization'
	  • 'participation and ownership'
	  • 'equity'

Category	Wording

	• *Brinkerhoff et al., 2008*: 'responsiveness to public health needs and beneficiaries'/citizens' preferences while managing divergences between them'
	  • 'the legitimate exercise of beneficiaries'/citizens' voice'
	• *Siddiqi et al., 2009*: 'participation and consensus orientation'
	• *Omaswa and Boufford 2010*: 'international liaison'
	• *Council of Europe, 2012*: 'participation'
	• *Newman, 2001*: 'the emergence of "negotiated self-governance" within communities, cities and regions, based on new practices of coordinating activities through networks and partnerships'
	  • 'opening up decision-making to greater participation by the public'
	  • 'a broadening of focus by government that goes beyond institutional concerns to encompass the involvement of civil society in the process of governance'
	  • 'recognizing and incorporating policy networks into the process of governing'
	• *European Commission, 2001*: 'participation'
	• *Scharpf, 1997*: 'input-orientated legitimacy'
	• *WHO, 2007*: 'collaboration and coalition building'
	• *Kickbusch and Gleichert, 2012*: 'governing by engaging citizens'
	  • 'governing through independent agencies and expert bodies'
	• *WHO, 2012* Health 2020: 'the right to participate in decision-making'
	  • 'governments are also committed to establishing structures and processes that enable increased involvement of a wider range of stakeholders'
	• *Grindle, 2004*: 'the representations of interests'
	• *Sustainable governance indicators, 2011*: 'guaranteed opportunities for democratic participation and observation'
	  • 'Citizens' participatory competence'

Integrity – *the processes of representation, decision-making, and enforcement should be clearly specified. All members should be able to understand and predict the processes by which an institution will take decisions and apply them; individuals should have a clear allocation of roles and responsibilities*	• *Travis et al.*: 'a country's government, through its health ministry, remains the "steward of stewards" for the health system'
	  • 'Formulation of a strategic policy framework' – 'clear definition of roles'
	  • 'Ensuring stewards' powers are commensurate with responsibilities' – titles/theoretical power matches actual power of governance, and inequalities between regions are decreased by giving equal power/funds to each region, or centralizing power to allocate funds
	• *Woods, 1999*: 'Procedural Fairness' – rules and standards be created and enforced in an impartial and predictable way'
	• *Kaufmann et al., 2010*: 'Political stability and absence of violence/terrorism'

(Continued)

Appendix Examples of concepts in the relevant literature (*continued*)

Category	Wording

	• *European Commission, 2004*: 'human rights'
	• 'anti-corruption'
	• *Sir Alan Langlands, 2004*: 'good governance means performing effectively in clearly defined functions and roles'
	  • 'good governance means taking informed, transparent decisions and managing risk'
	• *Brinkerhoff et al., 2008*: 'responsible leadership to address public health priorities'
	  • 'efficient and effective service provision arrangements, regulatory frameworks and management systems'
	• *Siddiqi et al., 2009*: 'rule of law'
	• 'ethics'
	• *Omaswa and Boufford., 2010*: 'direct (or contract) management'
	• *Council of Europe, 2012*: 'organizational arrangements'
	• *Barbazza and Tello, 2012*: 'regulation and persuasion'
	• *Saltman et al., 2011b*: 'institutional arrangements'
	• *Newman, 2001*: 'a shifting of the role of government to a focus on providing leadership, building partnerships, steering and coordinating, and providing system-wide integration and regulation'
	  • 'replacing traditional models of command and control with "governing at a distance"'
	• *European Commission, 2001*: 'coherence'
	• *CIPFA, 1994*: 'integrity/straightforward dealing and completeness'
	• *Kjaer, 2010*: 'network management'
	• *WHO, 2007*: 'regulation'
	  • 'policy guidance' ('Formulating sector strategies and also specific technical policies; defining goals, directions and spending priorities across services; identifying the roles of public, private and voluntary actors and the role of civil society.')
	• *Grindle, 2007*: 'structural/institutional stability'

Policy capacity – *refers to the ability to develop policy that is aligned with resources in pursuit of societal goals. It is the process that political ideas undergo in order to become workable, well-designed policies*	• *Travis et al., 2002*: 'generation of intelligence' 'identifying and interpreting essential knowledge for making decisions from a range of formal and informal sources'
	  • 'creating a fit between policy objectives and organizational structure'
	  • 'Generation of intelligence' – use of opinion polls to inform decisions
	  • 'building and sustaining partnerships'
	• *Barbazza and Tello, 2012*: 'organizational adequacy'
	• 'collaboration'
	• *Kaufmann et al., 2010*: 'government effectiveness'
	  • 'Regulatory Quality' ('capturing perceptions of the ability of the government to formulate and implement sound policies and regulations that permit and promote private sector development')

Category	Wording
	• *WHO, 2000*: 'defining the vision and direction of health policy'

• *WHO, 2000*: 'defining the vision and direction of health policy'
  • 'influencing global research and production to meet health goals'
  • 'providing an evidence base to guide countries' efforts to improve the performance of their health systems'
• 'exerting influence through regulation and advocacy'
• *UNDP, 1997*: 'direction'
• *PAHO, 2002*: 'monitoring, evaluation and analysis of the health situation of the population'
  • 'public health surveillance, research and control of risks'
  • 'development of policies and institutional capacity for planning and management in public health'
  • 'strengthening the institutional capacity for regulation and enforcement in public health'
  • 'human resource development and training in public health'
  • 'ensuring the quality of personal and population-based health services'
  • 'research, development and implementation of innovative health solutions'
• *European Commission, 2004*: 'public administration'
  • 'Organizational adequacy' ('Organizational adequacy deals with the suitability and capacity of the organization/s in question to implement the activities they are mandated to undertake. Such organizations will be in a position to command the legitimate resources necessary for the effective implementation of the activities. The organization's capacity to critically participate in the formulation and implementation of the activities is an important element to contribute to sustainability.')
• *Sir Alan Langlands, 2004*: 'good governance means developing the capacity and capability of the governing body to be effective'
  • 'good governance means focusing on the organization's purpose and on outcomes for citizens and service users'
• *Brinkerhoff et al., 2008*: 'evidence-based policymaking'
• *Siddiqi et al., 2009*: 'strategic vision'
  • 'effectiveness and efficiency'
  • 'responsiveness'
  • 'intelligence and information'
• *Lagomarsino et al., 2009*: 'collect information'
  • 'set priorities'
  • 'build capacity'
• *Omaswa and Boufford 2010*: 'policy making'
  • 'collecting and disseminating information'
  • 'technical assistance/capacity building'
  • 'support for research and training'
• *Saltman et al., 2011b*: 'decision-making capacity'
• *Newman, 2001*: 'developing more reflexive and responsive policy tools'

(Continued)

Appendix Examples of concepts in the relevant literature (*continued*)

Category	Wording
	<ul><li>'innovation in democratic practice as a response to problems relating to the complexity and fragmentation of authority, and the challenges this presents to traditional democratic models'</li><li>*European Commission, 2001*: 'effectiveness'</li><li>*WHO, 2007*: 'system design'</li><li>'intelligence and oversight' ('Ensuring generation, analysis and use of intelligence on trends and differentials in inputs, service access, coverage, safety; on responsiveness, financial protection and health outcomes, especially for vulnerable groups; on the effects of policies and reforms; on the political environment and opportunities for action; and on policy options')</li><li>*Kickbusch and Gleichert, 2012*: 'governing by mixing regulation and persuasion' ('smart governance for health concerns how governments respond strategically to health challenges: the choices they make about which mixture of instruments to use, which partners, at which levels of government and society to engage and when')</li><li>'governing through adaptive policies, resilient structures and foresight'</li><li>*WHO 2012*, Health 2020: 'setting targets'</li><li>'smart governance will anticipate change, [and] foster innovation'</li><li>'developing adaptive policies, resilient structures and foresight'</li><li>*Grindle, 2007*: 'organizational capacity'</li><li>*Grindle, 2004*: 'efficient use of resources'</li><li>'effective delivery of services'</li><li>*Sustainable Governance Indicators, 2011*: 'Executive capacity'</li></ul>

References

Andrews, Matt (2013) *The Limits of Institutional Reform in Development*. Cambridge: Cambridge University Press.

Anzia, Sarah F. (2013) *Timing and Turnout: How Off-cycle Elections Favor Organized Groups*. Chicago: University of Chicago Press.

Aronowitz, Robert A. (2012) The rise and fall of the Lyme disease vaccines: a cautionary tale for risk interventions in American medicine and public health, *Milbank Quarterly*, 90: 250–77.

Baez-Camargo, Claudia, and Eelco, Jacobs (2011) *A Framework to Assess Governance of Health Systems in Low Income Countries*. Basel: Basel Institute on Governance.

Banyan, Margaret E. (2007) Participation, in Mark Bevir (ed.) *Encyclopedia of Governance*. Thousand Oaks, CA: Sage, pp. 660–4.

Barbazza, Enrica and Tello, Juan (2012) *A Scoping Review on Governance for Health and Well-Being in the Context of 21st Century Government and Society*. Copenhagen: WHO Regional Office for Europe.

Barbazza, Erica and Tello Juan E. (2014) A review of health governance: definitions, dimensions and tools to govern, *Health Policy* 116(1): 1–11.

Behn, Robert D. (2001) *Rethinking Democratic Accountability.* Washington, DC. Brookings Institute.

Berry, Christopher R. (2009) *Imperfect Union: Representation and Taxation in Multilevel Governments.* Cambridge: Cambridge University Press.

Best, Jacqueline (2005) *The Limits of Transparency: Ambiguity and the History of International Finance.* Ithaca, NY: Cornell University Press.

Bevir, Mark (ed.) (2007) *Encyclopedia of Governance.* Thousand Oaks, CA: Sage.

Bevir, Mark (2010) *Democratic Governance.* Princeton, NJ: Princeton University Press.

Bevir, Mark (2012) *Governance: A Very Short Introduction.* Oxford: Oxford University Press.

Bevir, Mark (2013) *A Theory of Governance.* Berkeley, CA: University of California Press.

Bevir, Mark, Rhodes, Rod R. A. and Weller, Patrick (2003) Traditions of governance: interpreting the changing role of the public sector, *Public Administration,* 81: 1–17.

Bosk, Charles L. (2007) The new bureaucracies of virtue or when form fails to follow function, *PoLAR: Political and Legal Anthropology Review,* 30: 192–209.

Bovens, Mark (2010) Two concepts of accountability: accountability as a virtue and as a mechanism, *West European Politics,* 33: 946–67.

Bovens, Mark, Curtin, Deirdre and 't Hart, Paul (2010) Studying the real world of EU accountability: framework and design, in Mark Bovens, Deirdre Curtin and Paul 't Hart (eds) *The Real World of EU Accountability: What Deficit?* Oxford: Oxford University Press, pp. 31–62.

Brinkerhoff, Derick W. (2004) Accountability and health systems: toward conceptual clarity and policy relevance, *Health Policy and Planning,* 19: 371–9.

Brinkerhoff, D. W. and Bossert, T. (2008) *Health Governance: Concepts, Experiences, and Programming Options.* Washington, DC: United States Agency for International Development. Available at: http://www.healthsystems2020.org/files/1914_file_Governance_Policy_Brief_FIN_2.pdf.

Brinkerhoff, Derick W. and Goldsmith, Arthur A. A. (2005) Institutional dualism and international development: a revisionist interpretation of good governance, *Administration & Society,* 37: 199–224.

Brown, Chris, Harrison, Dominic, Burns, Harry and Zigho, Eric (2013) *Governance for Health Equity Taking forward the equity values and goals of Health 2020 in the European Region.* Copenhagen: WHO Regional Office for Europe.

Carpenter, Dan and Moss, David (eds) (2013) *Preventing Regulatory Capture: Special Interest Influence and How to Limit It.* Cambridge: Cambridge University Press.

Castiglione, Dario (2007) Accountability, in Mark Bevir (ed.) *Encyclopedia of Governance.* Thousand Oaks, CA: Sage, pp. 2–8.

CIPFA (1994) *Corporate Governance in the Public Services.* London: Chartered Institute of Public Finance and Accountancy.

Coase, Ronald H. (1937) The nature of the firm, *Economica,* 4: 386–405.

Cornell, Agnes and Lapuente, Victor (2014) Meritocratic administration and democratic stability, *Democratization,* 21(6): 1286–304.

Council of Europe (2000) *Recommendation No. R (2000) 5 of the Committee of Ministers to Member States on the Development of Structures for Citizen and Patient Participation in the Decision-Making Process Affecting Health Care.* Strasbourg: Council of Europe.

Council of Europe (2012) *Recommendation CM/Rec(2012)8 of the Committee of Ministers to Member States on the Implementation of Good Governance Principles in Health Systems.* 1149th meeting of the Ministers' Deputies: Council of Europe. Available at: https://wcd.coe.int/ViewDoc.jsp?id=1976095&Site=CM&BackColorInternet=C3C3C3&BackColorIntranet=EDB021&BackColorLogged=F5D383.

de Fine Licht, Jenny (2014) Transparency actually: how transparency affects public perceptions of political decision-making, *European Political Science Review,* 6: 309–30.

Dominguez, Jorge (2011) The perfect dictatorship? South Korea versus Argentina, Brazil, Chile and Mexico, in Byung-Kook Kim and Ezra F. Vogel (eds) *The Park Chung Hee*

Era: The Transformation of South Korea. Cambridge, MA: Harvard University Press, pp. 573–602.

Dunleavy, Patrick, Margetts, Helen, Bastow, Simon and Tinkler, Jane (2006) New public management is dead: long live digital-era governance, *Journal of Public Administration Research and Theory,* 16: 467–94.

European Commission (2001) European Governance. White Paper. Brussels, European Commission. Available at: http://eur-lex.europa.eu/LexUriServ/LexUriServ. do?uri=CELEX:52001DC0428:EN:NOT.

European Commission (2004) *Handbook on Promoting Good Governance in EC Development and Co-Operation.* Brussels: European Commission. Available at: http:// ec.europa.eu/europeaid/what/governance/documents/handbook_2004.pdf.

Evans, Peter (1995) *Embedded Autonomy: States and Industrial Transformation.* Princeton, NJ: Princeton University Press.

Ferguson, James (1990) *The Anti-Politics Machine: Development, Depoliticization, and Bureaucratic Power in Lesotho.* Cambridge: Cambridge University Press.

Flinders, M. and Moon, D. S. (2011) The problem of letting go: the 'Big Society', accountable governance and 'the curse of the decentralizing minister', *Local Economy,* 26: 652–62.

Forest, P.-G., Denis, J.-L., Brown, L. and Helms, D. (2015) Health reform requires policy capacity, *International Journal of Health Policy and Management,* 4(5): 265–6.

Fox, Daniel M. (2010) *The Convergence of Science and Governance: Research, Health Policy, and American States.* Berkeley, CA: University of California Press.

Fung, Archon (2006) Varieties of participation in complex governance, *Public Administration Review,* 66: 66–75.

Greer, Scott L. (2010) Editorial introduction: health departments in health policy, *Social Policy & Administration,* 44: 113–19.

Greer, Scott L. (2014) Structural adjustment comes to Europe: lessons for the Eurozone from the conditionality debates, *Global Social Policy,* 14: 51–71.

Greer, Scott L. and Lillvis, Denise (2014) Beyond leadership: political strategies for coordination in health policies, *Health Policy,* 116(1): 12–17.

Greer, Scott L., Wilson, Iain, Stewart, Ellen E. A. and Donnelly, Peter P. D. (2012) *Health Board Elections and Alternative Pilots: Final Report of the Statutory Evaluation.* Edinburgh: Scottish Government.

Greer, Scott L., Jarman, Holly and Azorsky, Andrew (2014a) *A Reorganisation You Can See from Space: The Architecture of Power in the New NHS.* London: Centre for Health and the Public Interest.

Greer, Scott L., Stewart, Ellen E. A., Wilson, Iain and Donnelly, Peter P. D. (2014b) Victory for volunteerism? Scottish Health Board Elections and participation in the welfare state. *Social Science & Medicine,* 106: 221–8.

Greer, Scott L., Wilson, Iain, Stewart, Ellen E. A. and Donnelly, Peter P. D. (2014c) Democratizing public services? Representation and elections in the Scottish NHS. *Public Administration.*

Grindle, Merilee S. (2004) Good enough governance: poverty reduction and reform in developing countries, *Governance* 17: 525–48.

Grindle, Merilee S. (2007) Good enough governance revisited, *Development Policy Review,* 25: 533–74.

Grindle, Merilee S. (2012) *Jobs for the Boys: Patronage and the State in Comparative Perspective.* Cambridge, MA: Harvard University Press.

Hajnal, Z. and Trounstine, J. (2005) Where turnout matters: the consequences of uneven turnout in city politics, *Journal of Politics,* 67: 515–35.

Hirschman, Albert O. (1981) *Essays in Trespassing.* Cambridge: Cambridge University Press.

Hood, Christopher (1991) A public management for all seasons? *Public Administration* 69: 3–19.

Hull, Matthew S. (2012) *Government of Paper: The Materiality of Bureaucracy in Urban Pakistan*. Berkeley, CA: University of California Press.

Immergut, Ellen M. (1992) Health politics: interests and institutions in Western Europe, Cambridge: Cambridge University Press.

Islam, Mursaleena (2007) Health systems assessment approach: a how-to manual, *Health Systems Assessment Approach: A How-To Manual*. Submitted to the U.S. Agency for International Development in collaboration with Health Systems 20/20, Partners for Health Reform *plus*, Quality Assurance Project, and Rational Pharmaceutical Management Plus. Arlington, VA: Management Sciences for Health.

Jarman, Holly (2011) Collaboration and consultation: functional representation in EU stakeholder dialogues, *Journal of European Integration*, 33: 385–99.

Jarman, Holly (2014) *The Politics of Trade and Tobacco Control*. Basingstoke: Palgrave Macmillan.

Jessop, Bob (2007) Governance failure, in Mark Bevir (ed.) *Encyclopedia of Governance*. Thousand Oaks, CA: Sage, pp. 382–4.

Kaplan, Avril D., Dominis, Sarah, Palen, J. G., and Quain, Estelle E. (2013) Human resource governance: what does governance mean for the health workforce in low- and middle-income countries? *Human Resources in Health*, 11(6).

Kaufmann, D., Kraay, A. and Mastruzzi, M. (2010) The worldwide governance indicators: methodology and analytical issues. Policy Research Working Paper 5430. Washington DC: The World Bank. Available at: http://papers.ssrn.com/sol3/papers.cfm?abstract_id=1682130.

Kaufmann, Daniel, Kraay, Aart and Zoido-Lobaton, Pablo (1999) Governance matters. World Bank Policy Research Working Paper No. 2196. October. Washington, DC: The World Bank.

Kettl, Donald F. (2000) The transformation of governance: globalization, devolution, and the role of government, *Public Administration Review*, 60: 488–97.

Kickbusch, I. and Gleicher, D. (2011) *Governance for Health in the 21st Century: A Study Conducted for the WHO Regional Office for Europe*. Copenhagen: WHO Regional Office for Europe.

Kickbusch, I. and Gleicher, D. (2014) *Smart Governance for Health and Well-Being: The Evidence*. Copenhagen: WHO Regional Office for Europe.

King, A. and Crewe, I. (2013) *The Blunders of Our Governments*. London: Oneworld.

Kingdon, John W. (2003) *Agendas, Alternatives, and Public Policies*. New York: Harper-Collins.

Kirigia, Joses Muthuri and Kirigia, Doris D. G. (2011) The essence of governance in health development, *International Archives of Medicine*, 4: 11.

Kjaer, A. (2010) *Governance*. Cambridge: Polity.

Klitgaard, Robert E. (1988) *Controlling Corruption*. Berkeley, CA: University of California Press.

Klitgaard, Robert, Maclean-Abaroa, Ronald and Parris, H. L. (eds) (2000) *Corrupt Cities: A Practical Guide to Cure and Prevention*. Washington, DC: World Bank.

Labonté, Ronald (2010) Health systems governance for health equity: critical reflections, *Revista de Salud Pública*, 12: 62–76.

Lagomarsino, G., Nachuk, S. and Singh Kundra, S. (2009) *Public Stewardship of Private Providers in Mixed Health Systems: Synthesis Report from the Rockefeller Foundation-Sponsored Initiative on the Role of the Private Sector in Health Systems*. Washington, DC: Results for Development Institute. Available at: http://www.rocke fellefoundation. org/uploads/files/f5563d85-c06b-4224-bbcd-b43d46854f83-public.pdf.

Landwehr, Claudia and Böhm, Katharina (2011) Delegation and institutional design in health-care rationing, *Governance*, 24: 665–88.

Langlands, Sir Alan (2004) *The Good Governance Standard for Public Services*. London: Office for Public Management and the Chartered Institute of Public Finance and Accountability. Available at: http://www.coe.int/t/dghl/standardsetting/media/doc/Good_Gov_StandardPS_en.pdf.

Larmour, Peter (2012) Interpreting corruption: culture and politics in the Pacific Islands, *Interpreting Corruption: Culture and Politics in the Pacific Islands*. Honolulu: University of Hawai'i Press.

Le Grand, Julian (2007) *The Other Invisible Hand: Delivering Public Services Through Choice and Competition*. Princeton, NJ: Princeton University Press.

Levi-Faur, David (ed) (2012) *The Oxford Handbook of Governance*. Oxford: Oxford University Press.

Lewis, Maureen and Pettersson, Gunilla (2009) Governance in health care delivery: raising performance. World Bank Policy Research Working Paper (5074).

Leys, Colin, Heidenheimer, A., Johnston, M. and LeVine, V. (2002) What is the problem with corruption? in *Political Corruption: A Handbook*. New Brunswick, NJ: Transaction, pp. 59–76.

Lynn Jr., Lawrence J. (2011) The persistence of hierarchy, in Mark Bevir (ed.) *The Sage Handbook of Governance*. Thousand Oaks, CA: Sage, pp. 218–36.

Meijer, Albert and Schillemans, Thomas (2009) Fictional citizens and real effects: accountability to citizens in competitive and monopolistic markets, *Public Administration and Management*, 14(2): 254–91.

Mikkelsen-Lopez, Inez, Wyss, Kaspar and de Savigny, Don (2011) An approach to addressing governance from a health system framework perspective, *BMC International Health and Human Rights*, 11(1): 13.

Newman, J. (2001) *Modernising Governance: New Labour, Policy and Society*. London: Sage.

Omaswa, F. and Boufford, J. O. (2010) *Strong Ministries for Strong Health Systems*. New York: The Rockefeller Foundation. Available at: http://www.rockefellerfoundation.org/uploads/files/8819cca6-1738-4158-87fe-4d2c7b738932.pdf.

Ottersen, Ole Petter et al. (2014) The political origins of health inequity: prospects for change, *Lancet*, 383: 630–67.

Page, Edward C. (2006) The origins of policy, in Michael Moran, Martin Rein and Robert E. Goodin (eds) *The Oxford Handbook of Public Policy*. Oxford: Oxford University Press, pp. 207–26.

Page, Edward C. (2007) Middle level bureaucrats: policy, discretion and control, in Jos C. N. Raadschelders, Theo A. J. Toonen and Frits van der Meer (eds) *The Civil Service in the 21st Century: Comparative Perspectives*. Basingstoke: Palgrave Macmillan, pp. 152–68.

Page, Edward C. (2010) Accountability as a bureaucratic minefield: lessons from a comparative study, *West European Politics*, 33: 1010–29.

Page, Edward C. (2012) *Policy Without Politicians: Bureaucratic Influence in Comparative Perspective*. Oxford: Oxford University Press.

Page, Edward C. and Jenkins, Bill (2005) *Policy Bureaucracy: Government with a Cast of Thousands*. Oxford: Oxford University Press.

PAHO (2002) *Public Health in the Americas: Conceptual Renewal Performance Assessment and Bases for Action*. Washington, DC: Pan American Health Organization. Available at: http://www2.paho.org/hq/dmdocuments/2010/EPHF_Public_Health_in_the_Americas-Book.pdf.

Peters, B. Guy (2013) Toward policy coordination: alternatives to hierarchy, *Policy & Politics*, 41: 569–84.

Peters, B. Guy and Pierre, Jon (1998) Governance without government? Rethinking public administration, *Journal of Public Administration Research and Theory*, 8: 223–43.

Peters, B. Guy and Pierre, Jon (2004) Governance approaches, in Antje Wiener and Thomas Diez (eds) *European Integration Theory*. Oxford: Oxford University Press, pp. 91–104.

Peters, B. Guy and Savoie Donald D. J. (2000) *Governance in the Twenty-first Century: Revitalizing the Public Service*. Montreal: McGill-Queen's Press-MQUP.

Pollitt, Christopher (2007) New Labour's re-disorganization: hyper-modernism and the costs of reform – a cautionary tale, *Public Management Review*, 9: 529–43.

Sabel, Charles (2001) A quiet revolution of democratic governance: towards democratic experimentalism, in OECD *Governance in the 21st Century*. Paris: OECD, pp. 121–48.

Sabet, Daniel M. (2012) *Police Reform in Mexico: Informal Politics and the Challenge of Institutional Change*. Stanford, CA: Stanford University Press.

Saltman, Richard B., Duran, Antonio and Dubois, Hans H. F. (2011a) The evolving role of hospitals and recent concepts of public sector governance, in *Governing Public Hospitals: Reform Strategies and the Movement Towards Institutional Autonomy*. Copenhagen: WHO Regional Office for Europe on behalf of the European Observatory on Health Systems and Policies, pp. 15–35.

Saltman, Richard B., Duran, Antonio and Dubois, Hans H. F. (2011b) *Governing Public Hospitals: Reform Strategies and the Movement Towards Institutional Autonomy*. Copenhagen: WHO Regional Office for Europe on behalf of the European Observatory on Health Systems and Policies.

Savedoff, William D. (2011) Governance in the health sector: a strategy for measuring determinants and performance. World Bank Policy Research Working Paper Series.

Savedoff, William D. and Gottret, Pablo (eds) (2008) *Governing Mandatory Health Insurance*. Washington, DC: World Bank.

Scharpf, F. (1997) *Games Real Actors Play: Actor-Centred Institutionalism in Policy Research*, Boulder, CO: Westview Press.

Scharpf, F. W. (2009) Legitimacy in the multilevel European polity, *European Political Science Review*, 1: 173–204.

Schillemans, Thomas (2008) Accountability in the shadow of hierarchy: the horizontal accountability of agencies, *Public Organization Review*, 8(2): 175–94.

Schrag, Zachary M. (2010) *Ethical imperialism: institutional review boards and the social sciences, 1965–2009*. Baltimore, MD: Johns Hopkins University Press.

Seekings, Jeremy (2013) Is the South 'Brazilian'? The public realm in urban Brazil through a comparative lens, *Policy and Politics*, 41: 351–70.

Siddiqi, Sameen, Masud, T. I., Nishtar, S., Peters, D. H., and Sabri, B. (2009) Framework for assessing governance of the health system in developing countries: gateway to good governance, *Health Policy*, 90: 13–25.

Silberman, Bernard (1993) *Cages of Reason: The Rise of the Rational State in France, Japan, the United States and Great Britain*. Chicago: University of Chicago Press.

Smith, Peter C., Anell, Anders, Busse, Reinhard, Crivelli, Luca, Healy, Judith, Lindahl, Anne Karin, Westert, Gert and Kene, Tobechukwu (2012) Leadership and governance in seven developed health systems, *Health Policy*, 106(1): 3.

Stewart, Ellen (2013) What is the point of citizen participation in health care? *Journal of Health Services Research & Policy*, 18: 124–6.

Stoker, Gerry (1998) Governance as theory: five propositions, *International Social Science Journal*, 50: 17–28.

Sustainable Governance Indicators (2011) *Policy Performance and Governance Capacities in the OECD*. Bertelsmann Stiftung. Available at: www.sgi-network.org.

Thomas, Steve, Keegan, Conor, Barry, Sarah, Layte, Richard, Jowett, Matt and Normand, Charles (2013) A framework for assessing health system resilience in an economic crisis: Ireland as a test case, *BMC Health Services Research*, 13: 450.

Travis, P., Egger, D., Davies, P. and Mechbal, A. (2002) *Towards Better Stewardship: Concepts and Critical Issues*. Geneva: World Health Organization.

Travis, Phyllida, Egger, Dominique, Davies, Philip and Mechbal, Abdelhay (2003) Towards better stewardship: concepts and critical issues, in Christopher J. Murray and David B. Evans (eds) *Health Systems Performance Assessment: Methods, Debate and Empiricism*. Copenhagen: WHO Regional Office for Europe, pp. 289–300.

Tritter, Jonathan Quetzal and McCallum, Alison (2006) The snakes and ladders of user involvement: moving beyond Arnstein, *Health Policy*, 76: 156–68.

Tritter, Jonathan Quetzal, Koivusalo, Meri and Ollila, Eeva (2010) *Globalisation, Markets and Healthcare Policy: Redrawing the Patient as Consumer*. London: Routledge.

Tuohy, Carolyn Hughes (2003) Agency, contract and governance: shifting shapes of accountability in the health care arena, *Journal of Health Politics, Policy and Law*, 28: 195–215.

UNDP (1997) *Governance for Sustainable Human Development.* United Nations Development Programme. Available at: http://mirror.undp.org/magnet/policy.

Urbinati, Nadia and Warren, Mark M. E. (2008) The concept of representation in contemporary democratic theory, *Annual Review of Political Science*, 11: 387–412.

Vian, Taryn, Savedoff, William W. D. and Mathisen, Harald (2010) *Anticorruption in the Health Sector: Strategies for Transparency and Accountability.* Bloomfield, CT: Kumarian Press.

Warner, Carolyn M. (2007) *The Best System Money Can Buy: Corruption in the European Union.* Ithaca, NY: Cornell University Press.

Warren, Mark E. (2006) Political corruption as duplicitous exclusion, *PS: Political Science and Politics*, 39: 803.

Weale, Albert (2007) What is so good about citizens' involvement in healthcare? in Edward Andersson, Jonathan Tritter and Richard Wilson (eds) *Healthy Democracy: The Future of Involvement in Health and Social Care.* London: NHS National Centre for Involvement, pp. 37–44.

Weale, Albert (2011) New modes of governance, political accountability and public reason, *Government and Opposition*, 46: 58–80.

Weber, Max (1958) Bureaucracy, in H. H. Gerth and C. W. Mills (eds) *From Max Weber: Essays in Sociology.* New York: Galaxy, pp. 196–244.

Weber, Max (1978) *Economy and Society*, edited by Guenther Roth and Klaus Wittich. Berkeley, CA: University of California Press.

Wehler, Hans-Ulrich and Traynor, Kim (1985) *The German Empire, 1871–1918.* Leamington Spa: Berg.

Weisband, Edward and Ebrahim, Alnoor (2007) Introduction: forging global accountabilities, in Edward Weisband and Alnoor Ebrahim (eds) *Global Accountabilities: Participation, Pluralism and Public Ethics.* Cambridge: Cambridge University Press, pp. 1–23.

Wendt, David, Bouchet,Ya-Shin, Lin, Nanda, Lipika, Noriega, Shanthi, Rakhmanova, Nilufar and Searle, Sarah (2013) *Health System Rapid Diagnostic Tool.* Durham, NC: FHI 360.

WHO (2000) *The World Health Report 2000: Health Systems: Improving Performance.* Geneva: World Health Organization. Available at: http://www.who.int/whr/2000/en.

WHO (2007) *Everybody's Business: Strengthening Health Systems to Improve Health Outcomes: WHO's Framework for Action.* Geneva: World Health Organization. Available at: http://www.who.int/healthsystems/strategy/everybodys_business.pdf.

WHO Regional Office for Europe (2008) Stewardship/Governance of Health Systems in the WHO European Region, in WHO-EURO (ed.) *RC58/9.* Copenhagen: WHO: Regional Ofice for Europe.

WHO Regional Office for Europe (2012) *Health 2020: A European Policy Framework Supporting Action Across Government and Society for Health and Well-Being.* Copenhagen: WHO: Regional Ofice for Europe.

Williamson, Oliver E. (1981) The economics of organization: the transaction cost approach, *American Journal of Sociology*, 87: 548–77.

Williamson, Oliver E. (1996) *The Mechanisms of Governance.* Oxford: Oxford University Press.

Woods, N. (1999) Good governance in international organizations, *Global Governance*, 5: 39–61.

chapter three

Strategies for policy success: achieving 'good' governance

Denise F. Lillvis and Scott L. Greer

Health policy-makers are familiar with a common set of challenges that interfere with their mission – the unwillingness of some people to adopt new approaches to old problems, inadequate resources to initiate or maintain these approaches, and political considerations or pressures, to name a few. However, the stars occasionally align. A new idea is championed, resources are adequate and political winds bode well for success. And yet too often policies fail even in these ideal circumstances, due to weak governance.

The aim of this chapter is to present a set of strategies drawn from practical and scientific literature to use to promote good governance: improving how decisions are made and how authority is exercised in order to implement, sustain and reform policy. The emphasis of this volume is 'good enough' governance, not 'best' governance (Grindle 2004). This chapter provides quick, actionable overviews of the strategies that influence and generally seek to improve accountability, transparency, participation, integrity and policy capacity. It can be used to understand the costs and benefits of different schemes for improving the quality of governance; to identify changes that might be needed for a given policy to be effective and produce intended consequences; or to identify broad possible systemic improvements. Table 3.1 provides a list of all of the strategies covered in this chapter.

None of these strategies or tools is perfect. It is a cardinal sin of social sciences to compare an existing system with an abstract proposal; the main question is how alternative arrangements work (Williamson 1996: 196). Nor is pursuit of any of strategies to the maximum a virtue. They all have trade-offs such that too much of one can impede another and any of them can backfire or produce undesirable results. Context is key, and this chapter does not make any recommendations for that reason. The strategies are all presented in a positive and practical light, but not all will be beneficial in all contexts.

Strategies for transparency

Transparency occurs when the public is informed of decisions made by the government, as well as the process by which the decision was made. It is worth noting that, when contracting out government functions to the private sector, or devolving functions to local governments, transparency can suffer. Paul Light (1999) alludes to the 'shadow of government' created by privatizing or devolving functions, and suggests that there are instances in which a private contractor at the helm enables government to shift blame amidst failure or to avoid following administrative rules. With this in mind, the following strategies aim at improving transparency by giving responsibility and authority to investigate problems, mandating the provision of reports in order to track government activities and monitor progress, and enabling timely access to meaningful information about the government.

Watchdog committees and inspectorates

Watchdog committees and inspectorates are bodies established for the expressed purpose of detecting and exposing corruption. Structurally, the former is created as an independent organization, while the latter may be housed within an existing organization. The creation of internal entities signals to the public that the government is not only relying on outsiders to do this job. Rather, it is actively monitoring its own behaviour for serious violations. However, unlike the reliance of interest groups and others outside government, an internal operation to root out corruption needs resources and political support in order to be successful. Stapenhurst and Langseth (1997) stress that support, independence, authority and reputation are the necessary attributes of anti-corruption committees. These 'oversight bodies' need not just political, but also societal support to avoid being seen as an empty gesture toward integrity (Head 2012). Societal support is important, given that ethnic ties may run deep and hinder impartial judgement. And a culture that is hostile to such investigations will take time to accept, rather than undermine, institutional change (Grzymala-Busse 2010). Investigative bodies therefore need to be situated in favourable environs for them to have the desired effect. Further, they also need to be well-resourced financially and be comprised of skilled individuals (Head 2012). Combining the findings of Head with Stapenhurst and Langseth, the following is a list of necessary attributes:

- support from the highest echelons of government;
- independence to investigate any official;
- authority to access relevant materials and witnesses;
- reputation of having leaders with integrity;
- approval from societal members who have the power to undermine efforts; and
- resources to carry out investigations.

Without the above, oversight bodies will not be able to access the information they need to make determinations, and they will not be able to act upon their findings. Notably, it appears that oversight bodies help good democracies function better:

> It is perhaps a paradox that specialised integrity agencies work best in countries where accountability and transparency are already well incorporated

in public sector systems and where political leadership is concerned to support these values, rather than in countries where there is a huge gap between the formal rhetoric and actual practice of integrity.

(Head 2010)

Therefore, this is a strategy that operates best once accountability and transparency are addressed.

Oversight bodies should take advantage of advances in technology for information sharing and detection of problematic activity. As described in later pages, these entities should not just investigate; they should also report their findings to the public, including the press, and develop a communication strategy to make sure that information flows efficiently. Watchdog entities should include social media strategies in their investigating. Regular monitoring of Twitter, Facebook and similar applications may indicate problematic behaviour in its infancy but introduce new problems of personal privacy and human rights of employees as well as legal risk.

Reporting requirements

Reporting requirements ensure that public and private entities alike are aware that information sharing is mandatory. There should be a specific employee or group of employees charged with reviewing this information. With input from others, the report reviewer(s) will then specify the components to be included in these reports, as well as set the due dates for interim and final reports. Setting specific dates is important, as contractors and others have numerous entities competing for their time (see Whitford 2005, for a discussion about competing responsibilities and the US Environmental Protection Agency). Project-related components should include the aims that the organization set out to achieve, the strategies employed, and the results of the organization's efforts. Financial components should consist of the projected and actual budget, as well as a justification for over- and under-estimating expenses. The report should also assess the resources that went into the programme, such as the number of staff, a biography of the programme leaders and a description of the staff turnover during the programme period. Other components may include future plans for the continuation of the programme, or lessons learned about how to improve the programme. Ideally, the report should meet the standards of performance-based measurement (see below).

If an organization is collecting multiple reports from different entities, such as outside contractors, staff in charge of the reporting process should arrange for a technical assistance call to answer questions about the reports and provide a contact person who can address concerns. There may also be instances in which internal reports require a certain amount of technical assistance. This can be accomplished via a conference call or webinar, an in-person presentation, or on an ad hoc basis. The report will only be as useful as the clarity and relevance of the information it contains, so these investments in the quality of the report are crucial.

It is important for organizations to consider the time and effort necessary to complete the reports, as there is a trade-off between the resources used to complete the report and those that can be spent on programme implementation (see McCubbins and Schwartz 1984, for a theoretical overview). Some organizations specifically instruct contractors to include evaluation and reporting as a line item in their budget request for this reason. Additionally, reporting should be considered part of a larger evaluative strategy. Thus, if a yearly report is already in place, organizations should look to consultations and other forms of participation to glean additional information about their service providers.

Performance-based measurement

Performance measurement can be defined as the regular assessment of programme results and efficiency (Hatry 1999). One reason to use performance-based measurement is to determine whether government agencies and/or their contractors are keeping their promises to the public. A second reason is to indicate which programmes are working, which aren't, and why. These findings allow for learning across agencies and contractors, and provide justification for the discontinuation of non-optimal programmes.

Often, organizations create a 'logic model' at the beginning of the performance-based measurement process. The model allows an organization to map out the resources it has, how the resources contribute to the strategies, what the outcomes will look like, and what the 'ideal world' would look like if the outcomes were achieved. The components of the measurement process consists of the following (adapted from Hatry 1999):

- *Inputs* – the resources that can be devoted to the programme. This includes funding, staff, volunteers and materials.
- *Process* – the products or services to be provided; the strategies used to obtain the desired result.
- *Outputs* – a performance indicator that measures the amount of product or service provided, such as the number of home visits.
- *Outcomes* – a performance indicator that measures the desired result of the product or service, such as a change in behaviour or condition of participants.
- *Impact* – a visionary statement or broad societal outcome; it is often infeasible to directly link outcomes to impact.

By understanding how all of these components fit together, measures and standards can then be determined. This is not a job for one person; developing a logic model should involve multiple stakeholders who can provide advice on each of these components.

Freedom of Information provisions

Freedom of Information (FOI) provisions 'reflect a right of members of the public to access whatever (government held) information they wish' (Hunt and Chapman 2006, adapted from Hazell 1999). These provisions permit a member of the public to request any organization record, unless the government has prohibited the record from being shared. A process should be established by which an individual can request the record. For example, there may be a requirement that that the request be made in writing (e.g., a letter, online form, fax or email), include the name and contact information of the requestor, and describe as specifically as possible the type and format of information desired. In order to avoid burdensome requests, many organizations restrict requests to information only and do not provide data analysis (see for example, the US Department of Justice 2010). For examples of its use and effectiveness, see Hazell et al. (2010) and Holsen (2007). Citizens can use FOI, but it is much more common that sophisticated actors use it to challenge government decision – disappointed bidders for government contracts, journalists and campaigning NGOs are all frequent users of FOI. This is acceptable. The purpose of FOI is to encourage honesty and good decision-making by making it possible for outsiders to identify and challenge decisions. The risk is that it will be used to stall policy-making and will work to the advantage of narrow, monied interests.

Public information

Public information efforts on the part of government expand awareness about potential policy changes as well as policy decisions that have already been made. These efforts can take several forms, such as open meetings, annual reports and/or clarity regarding key personnel. It has become increasingly important for government entities to communicate directly with the people, as political debate can influence media coverage. For example, when a policy debate becomes more politically contentious, the media shifts its focus toward coverage of strategy and conflict, and away from substantive policy issues (Jacobs and Shapiro 2000). To counter this phenomenon, the government should aim to provide information that is factual, complete and timely (Gelders 2005). Government information is factual if it focuses on educating about policy content; it should not delve into a policy's political advantages or enter into the realm of propaganda. It is complete if it is clearly identifiable as government-sponsored information and also indicates the policy's status (e.g., a proposed change or a final decision). And it is timely if it proceeds in tandem with the steps in the policy process and gives the public a sense of what will transpire next. If the information is no longer useful to the public at the time it is revealed, it is not timely.

As mentioned by Gelders (2005), the use of government resources to inform the public about yet-to-be adopted policies can appear political regardless of factual content. Thus, organizations should pay particular attention to the wording of information provided about policy proposals. An organization should also plan ahead by mapping out 'worst case' scenarios if a communication error is made. For example, administrative staff should all be instructed to direct comments to a particular person. This assigned person should also be the first person to be contacted when it is discovered that communication has gone awry.

Strategies for accountability

Accountability can be defined as a social relationship occurring when one actor, such as a ministry, must inform another, such as an elected body, of certain

Table 3.1 Strategies for good governance

Strategy	Transparency	Accountability	Participation	Integrity	Policy Capacity
			Attribute		
Standards and codes of conduct		O	R	R	
Conflict of interest policies		O		R	
Competitive bidding	R	O			
Contracts		O		R	
Financial mechanisms		O		R	
Choice mechanisms		O	R		
Regulation strategies		O		R	
Organizational separation		O			
Watchdog committees and inspectorates	O			R	
Reporting requirements	O	R	R		
Performance measurement	O	R	R		
Freedom of Information provisions	O	R			
Public Information efforts	O	R	R		R
Client surveys			O		
Stakeholder forums	R		O		
Advisory committees	R		O		
Consultations	R	R	O		
Representation (elected or appointed)	w		O		

	Attribute				
Strategy	*Transparency*	*Accountability*	*Participation*	*Integrity*	*Policy Capacity*
Legal remedies			O	R	
Partnerships			O	R	
Internal audits				O	
Budget	R			O	
Financial audit	R			O	
Legislative mandate			R	O	
Clear organizational roles and purposes				O	
Personnel policies			R	O	
Intelligence on performance					O
Intelligence on process				R	O
Research and analysis capacity					O
Staff recruitment and retention				R	O

O: indicates that this is where the authors chose to organize the strategy
R: indicates that the strategy is also relevant to this particular attribute

actions, and can be punished for the failure to adequately inform. Thus, strategies to improve accountability focus on clarifying expectations and providing open lines of communication to report progress. The strategies below will assist in enhancing accountability at all levels of an organization.

Standards and codes of conduct

Standards and codes of conduct are important because they outline what is considered acceptable behaviour, as well as intolerable behaviour, within the organization. Furthermore, they form expectations for current employees as well as others who oversee the work of the organization. By establishing and publicizing such behaviours and expectations, a code makes deviant behaviour more apparent and therefore easier to address. This applies to deviant behaviour by superiors; it can help employees justify why they cannot take certain actions (see the section 'Conflict of interest policies'). While many employees find themselves in an institutional hierarchy and are expected to follow the instructions of their supervisor, there are instances in which discretion is provided. Standards and codes guide behaviour in these instances, calling attention to the effect actions will have on other employees or the constituencies served by the organization (for a general framework for standards of conduct from the corporate world, see Clark and Vranka, 2013: Section 3). Wording in these documents should state that employees must consider the impact that their behaviour will have on these groups prior to taking any discretionary action, as the employee is a representative of the organization.

Many professional organizations have example codes of conduct that can be adapted for a particular organization's purposes. In the programmatic realm, the Public Health Leadership Society in the United States provides a handout, *Skills for the Ethical Practice of Public Health,* that lists not just principles of ethics, but also skills that can be built to support the principles (Thomas 2004). In the public service realm, the Ethics Resource Center has published a guide, *Creating a Workable Company Code of Ethics* (2003), and the Council of Europe provides a 'Model Code of Conduct for Public Officials' (2000). In the event that an organization has already adopted these or similar codes, it may be time to revisit the codes and make them more relevant to job performance, such as asking employees to provide examples of how they followed the codes as part of their performance review. Or, it may be time to identify specific skills that underpin the codes and then train staff in these areas. Finally, it may be that the codes are outdated or ineffective, or need to be adapted to recognize the rights and needs of certain groups (see Gilman and Stout 2005: 86–98, for further discussion of code assessment). By revisiting current practices with stakeholder input, an organization is reinforcing its commitment to accountability by holding itself accountable to its employees and the individuals it serves.

In order for such codes to be successful, they require support as well as enforcement. As described above, involving employees and other stakeholders in code development and updating is important. For the best chance of success, code content 'should come from the bottom up' (Gilman 2005) and reflect the organizational culture or at least the norms to which an organization theoretically adheres. Second, codes should not be left to collect dust on a shelf; rather, they should be periodically revisited and all employees – not just new employees – should receive education and training relevant to the code. Third, employees should be assessed as to how well they follow the code and be recognized for their efforts. Fourth, in order to avoid punishing whistleblowers, the individuals in charge of code enforcement should be independent of the management hierarchy. Finally, employees should be made aware that there are appropriate consequences for violating the code (e.g., demotion), and that consequences will be applied reliably and consistently. Without enforcement and normative backing, a code of conduct (like a mission statement) is an extremely limited and even demoralizing tool.

Conflict of interest policies

Conflict of interest policies can help ensure that decision-makers are not motivated by private interest and instead consider the good of the organization and the individuals being served. They help to manage the multiple opportunities for self-dealing and self-serving behaviour that exist in health systems and that have been identified as the cause of waste in, for example, Cyprus and Greece. While, ideally, systems have the integrity and policy capacity to engineer out opportunities for abuse of positions, in practice, that is never wholly successful and so these policies are required at the organizational, professional and legal levels (Rodwin 2011).

Policies contain the following elements: interests to be disclosed, prohibited interests, type of employee who is subject to the policy, and the individual or organization to which the disclosure is made (Lo et al. 2000). Interests to be disclosed and prohibited interests include any instruments of financial gain, such as stocks, gifts or other income. Generally, organizations set a threshold amount above which they must report a conflict. The types of employees who are subject to the policy can range from a limited number of senior decision-makers to all staff. The policy may also ask individuals whether a family member has the potential to gain from their actions. Conflicts of interest may be filed with a supervisor; there may also be a committee that manages conflicts of interest.

This policy can be considered part of the enforcement mechanism for an established code of conduct, as organizational values often explicitly state that it puts the public good above private interests (Gilman and Stout 2005). When a conflict goes unreported, successful policies impose a sanction (or penalty), such as censuring, relocating or firing the employee.

Much like codes of conduct, conflict of interest policies should be periodically reviewed to make sure that they cover all relevant interests that can interfere with professional judgement. And it is also important to make sure that all staff are aware of the provisions and penalties contained within the policy. One study of clinical investigators at two US educational institutions found that less than half of those surveyed could accurately restate the institution's conflict of interest policy (Boyd et al. 2003). This was not due to a lack of available information, as the policy is located on the institutions' websites, nor due to a lack of enforcement, as they have designated specific staff for that purpose. Thus, these two mechanisms are not a substitute for more active education about conflicts of interest. The study mentioned that employees discounted the ability of a conflict to bias their judgement, suggesting that realistic scenarios may be a beneficial component of a training exercise. One other way to enforce conflict of interest is with stiff legal or other penalties, or extensive publicity; a few celebrated enforcement cases can get the attention of many others and make them consider their actions. As with codes of conduct, a conflict of interest policy must be enforced and related to the existing norms or it will become a possibly demoralizing dead letter.

Competitive bidding

Competitive bidding incorporates private sector principles of competition into the public sphere. Its goal is part financial, in that competition among providers can lead to lower costs and/or better service; it is also related to accountability, as it is easier to trace – and therefore deter – cronyism when there are multiple offers. In recent years, news stories abound regarding contracts being awarded following generous campaign donations or other benefits going to a member of a politician's family. As these are clear conflicts of interest (see above), competitive bidding reinforces other accountability efforts. Competitive bidding, with open and transparent procedures, does not solve all problems (Warner 2007) but it is hard to imagine another transparent, good value way while discouraging corruption to expend meaningful amounts of public money without it.

What makes a successful competitive bidding process? To deter the aforementioned cronyism, many individuals must be involved at all stages of the process. For example, if an organization is undergoing a strategic planning process, the individuals responsible for choosing a consultant via competitive bidding will likely be those on the strategic planning committee. As a first step, the committee will be responsible for drawing up a request-for-proposal (RFP) that describes the organization and the nature of the assignment, such as the specific needs, key deliverables, and desired timing from retention to completion. Additionally, the RFP should detail the parameters of the proposal. Applicants should provide information such as their understanding of the assignment, their approach to such assignments, a brief summary of relevant projects, a short biography of the staff involved, a detailed budget and, if necessary, whether their company has the requisite security or other government clearance needed to do the work. Supplemental material, such as a financial audit or proof of non-profit status, is also desirable. The RFP should also describe all of the steps involved in the bidding process. Then, the committee should decide whether to hold an open call for proposals, in which any company or individual can apply, or to limit the distribution of the RFP to certain, pre-screened applicants that have the capacity to provide the services needed. Prior to advertising the RFP, it is important to make sure that regulations governing the release of the RFP are followed (e.g., whether projects above a certain budget size must have an open process). Involvement of many employees at this initial stage ensures that every vendor has access to the same information and that a variety of vendors are aware of the opportunity.

After the RFP has been written and disseminated, the committee vets the applicants. Applicants should be evaluated objectively based on the following factors: the clarity and reasonability of their budget, the skills and expertise offered, the staffing management plan, and past experience (Stankevich et al. 2009). The committee may want to use a scoring system (e.g., whether the applicant fails, meets or exceeds the criteria) to rank applicants. Next, the top three or five applicants should be invited for a formal interview and/or presentation. The committee can use this meeting to ask any remaining questions, as well as assess the interest of the applicant. Observations from these meetings, as well as the rankings made in the prior stage, can then be used in any reports describing the progress and ultimate decision made by the committee. After an applicant has been chosen, the organization will enter into a contractual agreement to finalize the relationship. As the case studies by Lieberherr et al. in Chapter 7 show, as well as King and Crewer (2013) and Epstein (2013), introduction of competitive bidding can be very dangerous – the promise of better governance or effectiveness can be wiped out by the enormous governance challenges to doing and using it well. This is a high-risk tool with serious chances of failure, and one that can often be a cover for conflicts of interest and even corruption, though competitive bids are generally safer than non-competitive bids.

Contracts

Contracts can be used to ensure the efficient delivery of services by third-party contractors. As Salamon (1989) describes, contracts and other strategies change the function of government from acting as service provider to 'operating by remote control' and outsourcing to third parties. These third parties may include non-profits or non-governmental organizations (NGOs), private companies, and subnational governments such as local authorities. The challenge, then, is to make sure that the contracts are executed properly, and that policy objectives are reached once the money is in the hands of a third party (or, ideally, before; payment upon completion is always a powerful incentive). Contracts exercise control because there is often competition to secure one (see section on 'Competitive bidding') and awareness that the service provider can be replaced, should it fail to meet its goals prior to the expiration date (see, for example, Osborne and Gaebler 1992: 35–7).

Before entering into a contractual relationship, the individual or department that provides legal services to the organization should be contacted. It is good practice to have a template that all government contracts must follow; in novel areas of contracting (such as many PPPs), negotiating from blank paper frequently results in poorly resourced contractors agreeing to contracts with providers that are not good value. The contract will name the two parties, the organization and the third-party contractor, as well as a detailed offer of services (e.g., the amount to be paid, whether there are to be multiple payments, duration of the relationship, and a description of the services to be rendered by the contractor). The financial aspect of the exchange will need to be explicitly stated, especially if the organization chooses to tie the contract to the achievement of specific milestones. It is important to note that contracts, particularly contracts that have financial incentives, require management and monitoring. Thus, 'in-house' staffing needs should be assessed and addressed prior to entering into a contractual relationship.

A second meaning of contracting is to have contracts for performance between government bodies. This is both a mechanism used to work with regulatory and other agencies in many countries and a tool of intergovernmental relations in France (Gaudin 1999; Lascoumes and Le Gales 2007). These contracts, or agreements, are and should be softer than the ones signed with outside providers; their function is to enhance clarity and accountability by making it clear what one French government department will deliver with the money of another, or what an agency will be held accountable for doing in a year.

Financial mechanisms

Financial mechanisms such as pay-for-performance or performance-based payment, are often employed when governmental organizations contract with third parties. Such an arrangement requires that contractors provide evidence of outputs (e.g., number of patients enrolled in an exercise programme) and outcomes (e.g., percentage of patients who have reduced their blood pressure in the past year) toward specific objectives (e.g., to reduce the proportion of adults with hypertension). For additional information about these terms, see the section 'Strategies for transparency' below.

Payment is then based on when and/or the extent to which the agreed-upon targets are met. Targets and incentives should be chosen carefully, as it is inevitable that a contractor will try to 'game the system'. Gaming can be defined as focusing on only those programme aspects that are explicitly measured, or, simply put: 'hitting the target and missing the point' (Bevan and Hood 2006). In the example above, imagine if measurement was limited to outputs. What might happen? Contractors would have an incentive to enrol as many patients as possible, while spending less time getting the patients to achieve health goals. This is not to say that the outcome cannot be gamed as well, but it would be more difficult.

Choice mechanisms

Choice mechanisms hold organizations accountable by letting users 'vote with their feet' by giving the individuals using the service the opportunity to change providers if they felt they would get better value elsewhere (Hirschman 1970; for a sensible and sceptical view, see Schillemans 2008; Meijer and Schillemans 2009). One way to provide user choice is to award grants to multiple entities simultaneously, such as quasi-governmental entities, NGOs or private businesses. Grants are distinct from contracts, as they involve more than 'the purchase of specified goods and services' inherent in a contractual relationship (Salamon 1989: 9). Grants allow more discretion in achieving social outcomes and spending funds, such as in areas where the government has decided to devolve responsibilities. On the other hand, if a programme or service requires a close relationship between the provider and the government to monitor progress and provide technical assistance, a contract or cooperative agreement is preferred (Haider 1989).

The grant-making process is similar to the competitive bidding process, with the difference that multiple 'bids' will be accepted. Usually, for a specific social objective, one individual will be charged with disseminating an RFP and reviewing the applications. After an initial ranking of proposals is made, this individual will present his or her recommendations to a grant-making body comprised of senior managers. Following the presentation and a discussion of recommendations, final grant determinations will be made by the grant-making body. As described below in the 'Transparency' section, grantees should provide interim and final progress reports describing to what extent they have achieved the social objectives that were the purpose of the grant. If possible, standardized performance metrics will enable the organization to compare results across grantees and recognize high-performing grantees with grant renewal.

Regulation strategies

Regulation strategies align the incentives of all actors working in the same industry or sector by encouraging certain actions and discouraging others. Regulation is comprised of three necessary ingredients (adapted from Bardach

1989). First, it should begin with the adoption of governmentally approved rules that prescribe 'responsible' action. Second, regulations need to have some mechanism for detecting and then sanctioning those who fail to follow the regulations. Some of these methods of detection are covered in this chapter, such as watchdog committees, reporting requirements and stakeholder forums. Third, following detection, the sanction should be commensurate with the offence, and be able to be carried out consistently by the organization.

Regulatory strategies are best suited for organizations that have the autonomy to see that they are carried out. This ability is created by the organization's reputation for possessing expertise in the subject at hand, striving for efficiency in its operations, and/or positioning itself as a moral authority (Carpenter 2001). This positive view of an organization's reputation is then supported and perpetuated by politicians and the media. Ideally, regulations should be issued from this advantageous position to ensure that regulatory authority will not be circumvented. Otherwise, would-be regulators may find themselves outflanked by elected officials; that is, officials can pass a law stating that regulation of a particular activity can only be statutorily initiated. An organization's reputation can be strengthened by implementing a number of the strategies that appear in this chapter. For example, a reputation for expertise can be established by hiring skilled individuals, while efficiency can be communicated by publicly reporting information about the organization and employing the principles of performance management. Moral authority, at least from an administrative point of view, can be enhanced by establishing conflict of interest policies and codes of conduct. However, it may be difficult for some organizations to establish moral authority if citizens view regulatory activity as a ruse, given a prevailing public opinion that has a low level of trust in government.

One weakness of regulation is that it is an overt government action that may be interpreted as coercion by regulated groups. Thus, regulatory action may actually damage the cooperation that the regulator hoped to encourage. It can mobilize the regulated against the organization, which is why political autonomy is important in allowing the organization to carry out its work. There is also a permanent worry of 'capture', in which regulators become the servants of those they regulate. In such a scenario, a combination of more and less corrupt instruments (from bribes to hiring regulators to dinners to argumentation) allows industries to turn their regulators into bodies that inhibit competition and permit bad behaviour. It is, fortunately, possible to protect regulatory agencies against capture; there is no reason to believe, contrary to 'public choice' arguments, that capture is inevitable or even particularly common (Carpenter 2010). Good organizational integrity provisions for regulators, combined with intelligent accountability, can largely prevent capture (Carpenter and Moss 2013).

Organizational separation

Organizational separation is the process by which governmental units are disaggregated, with each part focusing on a particular product or service (Hood 1991). As described by Hood, one justification is to separate the 'provision' and 'production' employees, giving each function its own budget responsibilities. This is an approach often seen in the private sector, where research-and-development efforts are isolated from the production of a good so that management has a better sense for the resource demands (e.g., financing, staffing, etc.) and resulting output from each unit. This strategy can dovetail with other strategies, as organizational separation can help in establishing clear roles and responsibilities. In health systems, it frequently means creating separate agencies (or institutes) with specific responsibilities so that they may pursue their goals with more organizational flexibility and less political oversight than ministries (Pollitt et al. 2001; 2004).

There is a substantial literature on organizational separation, reflecting two decades in which the creation of independent bodies, agencies, 'quangos', 'institutes' and all sorts of other arm's-length public bodies with boards and contracts appeared to be the solution for a wide variety of problems. The theory was appealing, since it promised flexibility and good management in the agency, combined with accountability through a contract – just what economics ordered. Over time, disenchantment set in. While the creation of independent agencies is still a popular and effective policy tool, governments became aware of how information asymmetries, capture and a variety of problems meant that there was no guarantee that an agency with an appointed board or work programme would produce better outcomes (Smullen 2010: 3). Agencies were no panacea.

Strategies for participation

Participation enables those affected by policies to have access to decision-making and to feel empowered to make their voice heard. This access is generated by government institutions soliciting feedback from constituents, ranging from less formal expressions of opinion to more formal roles. Empowerment may involve directly reaching out to citizens, establishing representative bodies to provide feedback, or collaborating with other organizations that work with similar populations. The following are strategies to improve participation.

Client surveys

Client surveys are a good first step in obtaining feedback from constituents who are involved in or affected by government decisions or policy changes. Either surveys can be developed in-house, or an organization can retain the services of a management consulting firm for survey development assistance. Survey design can be quite complex and as such would require an entire chapter (or book) to cover the topic fully. Survey developers may face challenges writing questions and administering the survey. Those developing their own survey should first begin by determining what they want to know at the outset. This will help them write clear questions and improve response rates by not making the survey too long. Then, they should begin drafting questions based on this list. Good survey questions have the following attributes: they contain only one construct (avoid asking 'double-barrelled' questions), the intent is clear to the respondent, and answer choices are mutually exclusive and collectively exhaustive.

The next set of choices – how to administer the survey and how many to administer – depends on the survey budget. There are four main modes through which to administer a survey: internet, mail, phone and face-to-face. Internet surveying is perhaps the least expensive, while face-to-face is perhaps the most. Although it is virtually impossible to obtain a 100 per cent response rate, a study by Brehm (1993) found that face-to-face has the best rate, at 70 per cent. Internet and mail surveys tend to have lower response rates. For a review of additional problems that may arise in the survey design and administration process, see Krosnick (1999).

Stakeholder forums

Stakeholder forums are another way to obtain feedback from those who have a stake in an organization's programmes or policies. Such forums tend to be less structured than a survey, and offer a chance for two-way communication between staff and constituents. The purpose of such forums should be both to inform attendees of the various aspects of a programme and to obtain feedback about what is working well and what can be improved. For topics that may be sensitive, it is often preferable to administer a survey or to form an advisory committee. The feedback received will be most valuable if it is in regard to the policy or programme, rather than the inaccessibility of the facility, or the lack of food at lunchtime. Stakeholder forums are good recruiting grounds for volunteers and representatives. If an organization is looking to form an advisory committee, or if it needs additional members, individuals who attend a forum have signalled that they are willing to share their time and experiences. To that end, the organization should collect attendee names and contact information for follow-up.

Advisory committees

Advisory committees provide opportunities for more regular interaction between an organization and the individuals it serves. The right number of advisory committee members depends on an organization's needs, though a good start would be between 10 and 15 members. When establishing such committees, organizations should aim for broad representation across the programme or policy of interest. It is also good practice to set term limits, such that each member cannot serve for more than a certain number of years. Once again, it may vary depending on organizational need, but many organizations commonly limit membership to two three-year terms. Open positions should be publicly advertised on the organization's website, as well as the location of service, if applicable. Much like a board of directors, members of an advisory committee should receive an orientation prior to their first meeting. This should include a history of the programme(s), an introduction to any staff they may be in contact with, and other organization materials, such as a budget and by-laws (note, a description of the importance of by-laws appears in the section 'Strategies for integrity'). Some advisory committees will meet monthly or quarterly, while others may meet less often. If the committee is comprised of individuals who live far apart from each other, phone or Skype meetings may be more practical than in-person meetings. An agenda, sent out at least a day in advance, should anchor the meeting. This agenda will include the areas in which the organization desires feedback and may include specific questions or materials to encourage informed responses. Using this feedback to make decisions will also enhance the organization's transparency efforts (Transparency International 2004).

Consultations

Consultations are notice-and-comment procedures whereby the public can provide their perspective on proposed policy changes. Depending on the proposed change, consultations with the public may be required by law. They can be conducted via a public hearing, for which much of the above advice about stakeholder forums applies; they can also be conducted by soliciting written comments over a certain time period, such as 60 days. If an organization has the ability to do so, it can design an online form that has fields for requisite information, such as the commenter's name, address, the policy being commented on, etc. Additionally, individuals should also be able to submit their comments by traditional mail.

Participation from the public can yield useful suggestions for proposed regulations. However, when an organization is considering public feedback, it should not simply be a process of counting 'votes' for or against the change (US Department of Transportation 2012). Rather, it should weigh the evidence presented in the comments and assess whether it is sufficient enough to warrant a reconsideration of the policy change. Citizens may not understand that their comments are evaluated in this fashion; as such, in order for them to be as informative as possible, the soliciting organization should provide guidance as to what constitutes a 'good' comment. For example, an organization may want to state that comments providing evidence of their assertions will be more influential than brief statements of approval or disapproval. It can be all too easy for well-resourced interests to flood consultation processes with opinions that do not reflect popular opinion or new information.

Box 3.1 Balancing policy capacity and participation: NICE in the United Kingdom (Williams, see Chapter 8 in this volume)

The mission of NICE (National Institute for Health and Care Excellence) is to provide guidance on clinical practice guidelines and technology adoption, as well as promote evidence-based public health. Williams focuses on the Technology Appraisals Programme within NICE, which uses policy capacity strategies to ensure treatment cost and clinical effectiveness. According to Williams, the organization's technical capabilities are 'perhaps unsurpassed amongst technology coverage guidance bodies across the world'. Yet, NICE is also required to receive comments from organizations and individuals, including patients, prior to making decisions. While its mission supports effectiveness, patient participation shifts the focus to those who desire access to treatments that perhaps fall short of the effectiveness metric.

Official representation

Official representation through elected or appointed representatives institutionalizes constituent feedback. Similar to an advisory board, the number of members and the decision to impose term limits depend on the organization's needs. Representatives also require orientation, and the organization will need to set up agenda-driven meetings with a frequency that makes sense for the situation. In contrast to an advisory board, election requires that a voting mechanism be set up and appointment requires a greater vetting capacity.

Elections can be run through an online form or sent out via mail. For planning purposes, the response rate (i.e., the percentage of those solicited who actually voted) should be recorded. If response rates fall below a certain threshold, the organization may want to consider switching to a less resource-intense advisory board system.

Elections to specific health system organizations have been tried in a number of jurisdictions with health service systems, including Saskatchewan, New Zealand and latterly Scotland. The introduction of direct elections has been less consequential than policy-makers imagined; while elected health board members were usually not disruptive, unreasonable or the tools of interest groups, neither were the elections notably good at attracting attention or the resulting board relations with populations very different (Greer et al. 2012; Stewart 2012).

Legal remedies

Legal remedies to resolve disputes should be seen as a last resort, and should not be the only opportunity for constituents to gain notice. While there may be numerous variations of dispute resolution, the following are three variations that differ in their overall goals, publicity, and the extent to which the decisions are legally binding (adapted from Sohn and Ball 2012):

- *Mediation* – the goal is to privately find a compromise using a neutral mediator who guides both sides through the negotiation process; either party can walk away prior to reaching a resolution. The parties may choose to have legal representation.
- *Arbitration* – the goal is to privately determine the liability of each side and suggest an appropriate resolution, generally with legal representatives arguing before an individual arbiter or an arbitration panel. Arbitration occurs pursuant to an agreement that both sides will take a dispute to an arbitrator and the decision is usually binding.
- *Settlement negotiation* – the goal is to reach a binding decision regarding a settlement with both sides retaining legal representation.
- *Judicial action* – the goal is to publicly claim or deny a private wrong and to reach a binding judicial decision.

Note that a particular country's definition of the above terms may vary; as such, bureaucrats should consult with their legal representatives about the appropriateness of the above remedies. As governments rely on private contractors to provide public goods and services, the ability for arbitration to take place is necessary following the institution of competitive bargaining (as described by Coase 1960). One way that arbitration is binding is if legislation states that a settlement reached by arbitration must be carried out.

The variations also differ in terms of the time they take from initiation to decision, with judicial action usually taking longer than the other options. However, if the defendant has impetus to publicly clear his or her name, judicial action is likely preferred. For example, Sohn and Ball (2012) describe the current medical malpractice situation in the USA, in which physicians who settle privately have this fact recorded in a practitioner database, whereas those who clear their name in court do not. Thus, bureaucracies should keep in mind larger institutional incentives, such as being barred from competing for contracts if there is a settlement on record, that drive defendants and plaintiffs to court.

The variations discussed above require the injured party to have the funding and legal capacity to seek redress. Thus, it is easy to imagine a situation in which a large private contractor with a well-resourced legal team or health bureaucracy that has experience inside the courtroom is accused of wrongdoing by a disadvantaged individual or group. In these situations, a public court case may provide needed visibility in order for the disadvantaged group to obtain support from others. In a study of three state court cases in the USA, Songer et al. (2000) found that the additional support garnered by *amicus curiae* briefs levelled the playing field between the 'haves' and 'have nots'. Manning and Randazzo (2009) find that the 'have nots' enjoy more judicial success in the US Court of Appeals when the case pertains to health care and the government was the defendant. Of course, even groups that organize on behalf of the 'have nots' cannot address the needs of all of their constituents equally (see, for example, Strolovitch 2006). Therefore, programme managers within a bureaucracy should consider ways to reach out to voices that are not being heard, such as by inviting individuals to serve on advisory boards or lessen barriers to participation in stakeholder forums.

Choice mechanisms

Choice mechanisms provide another way for constituents to signal which aspects of an organization meet the needs of the public, and which do not. Much like providing choices to citizens about which contractor-provided programme to use, bureaucracies can allow individuals to participate by 'opting out' of their programmes and services. However, this is a poor strategy for participation and may actually stem from the bureaucracy's unwillingness to make tough decisions, such as discontinuing programmes or making necessary changes that have the potential to cause discomfort among long-time employees who have grown accustomed to the status quo.

Partnerships with other organizations

Partnerships with other organizations, such as citizen groups and NGOs that serve a similar population or policy area, can improve participation under certain circumstances. If an organization is perceived similarly to the partnering organization, or if the partnering organization is seen as even more favourable than the organization, it stands to benefit by partnering. Organizations should be wary of partnering with less reputable entities, as their own reputation may suffer. The comparability of reputations can be assessed by asking about other organizations in a participant survey (see above). Questions may include:

- What other organizations are involved in [policy area] in [location]?
- How trustworthy is [organization]? (Not at all, A little bit, Quite a bit, Very much)
- What distinguishes [organization] from the other groups working in [policy area]?

Prior to entering into a partnership, an organization should conduct an internal meeting where staff discuss what they hope to gain from the partnership, as well as identify any potential risks. These expectations and concerns should help inform a memorandum of understanding (MOU) that formalizes the relationship. An affiliated legal department may have sample MOUs; this department can also provide advice as to whether there is standard language that must be included in such a document. These documents may contain the following components (see for example, World Health Organization 2010):

- the organizational background of the partners, such as their mission and main programmatic activities;
- the goals of the collaboration;
- the resources being dedicated by each organization;
- the duration of the MOU;
- limits of the relationship, such as usage of names and logos by the partners;
- a plan for review and optional renewal of the MOU;
- the process should a dispute arise;
- the signatures of responsible parties.

Strategies for integrity

An organization has integrity if it creates reasonable expectations about its roles and responsibilities vis-à-vis society. It can therefore be damaged by unpredictable behaviour, such as ending a programme abruptly, engaging in irrelevant activities, or acting inconsistently in comparison to past decisions. Integrity is enhanced by strengthening financial, personnel and administrative management. The success or failure of integrity policies in large part depends on how they shape the incentives and ambitions of the people working at every level of the health system.

Internal audits

Internal audits can help an organization better understand where information needs to be shared more openly within an organization. Pockets of functions can exist that, when coupled together, affect the ability of an organization to detect resource management problems. One example is permitting a programme manager to purchase equipment and reconcile or take inventory of the account. Having one person in charge of multiple functions renders this part of the organization opaque – was the equipment actually purchased, and is it actually being used for the programme? Conducting an audit of how money flows through programmes will illuminate potential problems such as this. Failing to address these problems leaves the organization vulnerable to corruption, damaging its financial viability and reputation.

Budgets

A budget can also promote integrity by drawing attention to the financial underpinnings of the organization. Budgets are organized into revenues and expenditures, and generally cover a one-year time period often referred to as a 'fiscal year'. Fiscal years may not be based on a calendar year; for example, a fiscal year may start April 1, as in Canada, or July 1, as in Australia (note, a number of European countries' fiscal years do follow the calendar year). The revenue category represents the estimated amounts that the organization will receive in the coming year from taxes (e.g., via the federal government), user fees, and other sources. The expenditure category contains all of the outlays an organization is anticipating to make. This includes salaries, office rent, equipment, supplies, postage/shipping, travel, and anything else necessary to deliver programmes and services. While much of the revenue side of the budget is set, the organization may be able to estimate other aspects, such as user fees based on past year averages with an adjustment for inflation. Or fee revenue may need to be adjusted based on external factors, such as the local or national economy. Expenditure estimates can also be reasonably set based on actual expenditures averaged over prior years. Of course, if an organization is expanding or eliminating a programme, or setting up a new service, expenditures will need to be increased in these areas.

Creating accurate revenue and expenditure estimates requires that time and effort be invested in the budgeting process. Therefore, organizations should begin planning for the next fiscal year months in advance. Those drafting the budget should consult with others across the organization to make sure the budget reasonably anticipates any shortfalls or expansions. Once complete, estimated budgets can be used to communicate priorities throughout the organization, although transferring this information through multiple levels of a bureaucratic hierarchy can be a challenge (Carpenter 1996). For example, a high-performing programme can be rewarded by an increase in funding. However, in order for this signal to have the desired effect, the amount needs to be large enough to be noticed.

Financial audit

A financial audit can be conducted by contracting with an independent firm. The firm will review all of an organization's accounts, including revenues, expenditures, durable equipment and financial investments. They will flag problems that an internal audit might find and can make recommendations as to how to open up processes so that responsibility and power in one area are checked by someone else in another. Second, the firm will assess whether accounts have been reconciled properly and whether assets were appropriately depreciated. Finally, they will meet with the organization head and have him or her sign off on the resulting report, indicating that they were made aware of any issues found by the audit. Audits work well with budgets to identify financial issues in advance and enable the organization to be a predictable provider of services to society. Audits and budgets, if shared in a timely manner, can also contribute to transparency (see for example, Transparency International 2004).

Box 3.2 Transparency and policy capacity challenges: private finance initiative (see Lieberherr, Maarse and Jeurissen in Chapter 7 in this volume)

As the chapters in this volume describe, none of these governance tools can be adopted in isolation. While some tools involve trade-offs, where the virtues of one are vices for another, others must work in tandem to be effective. One example of this is the Private Finance Initiative (PFI) in the United Kingdom. PFI was designed as a contractual relationship between the government and private entities. The private entities usually consist of a mix of actors including a financial institution, a construction company and a service provider. In exchange for creating and maintaining public infrastructure projects, private actors receive a user fee from the government. The contract is attractive to the private actors because they are long-term and prohibitively expensive to terminate. They are attractive to the government because the fee is based on use, so the private actor is incentivized to provide good facilities to encourage usage. However, the contract alone was not enough to meet the PFI's goals to serve as a financing alternative and to improve value. Due to the 2008 financial crisis, the government had to put up the financing because a bank was not willing to invest. This is precisely where lack of transparency fits in: government investment in PFI does not appear on the balance sheet, meaning that the national debt should be higher than what is publicly reported. And, as the contracts are written in such a way that ensures investors' confidentiality, individuals who want to learn how much the government is investing must file a Freedom of Information Act request. Lack of policy capacity is also problematic, as staff turnover means that institutional knowledge about PFI is lost over time. New employees are not as familiar with the contracts and may not make the most informed decisions about the PFIs to maximize its goals. The authors also speculate that the lack of internal expertise leads to inflexible contracts, a hindered ability to monitor PFI performance, and a reliance on external consultants whose work cannot be adequately judged by the government employees receiving the consultants' advice. While contracts were put in place to ensure accountability, a lack of transparency and policy capacity hinders PFI governance.

Legislative mandates

Legislative mandates provide a clear justification to the public for why the organization is taking certain actions. Such directives provide political cover to organizations operating in sensitive areas. And they offer a viable option for citizens to voice their disapproval – the ballot box.

Clarity on organizational roles and purposes

Clear organizational roles and purposes can lessen confusion and make it easier for citizens to accept the legitimacy of the organization. When there is a general societal understanding of an organization's mission – what it is setting out to accomplish, for whom and how – it is clear why the organization exists and the unique role it plays. Once the organization's mission is elucidated, it should be transmitted throughout the organization, such as by putting it on the organization's website, annual reports and training manuals. Some management professionals recommend placing the mission at the top of every meeting agenda to serve as a constant reminder to current employees. Reinforcing the mission is beneficial in protecting the autonomy of an organization, as when employees and leaders know what they are supposed to be doing, for whom and how, they will be able to clearly delineate their jurisdiction. As a result, the organization can recognize threats to its autonomy if another organization encroaches on its 'turf' and make justifications as to why it should not engage in undesirable activities that fall outside of its mission (Wilson 1989). The former offence is also known as 'duplication of service', whereby two or more organizations serve the same function and, as such, create confusion for clients. The latter guards against valuable staff and funding from being reallocated to functions that do not serve the organization's core purpose.

As an organization seeks to improve the clarity of organizational roles and purposes, it may find that two or more functions no longer belong together. In these cases, organizational separation can help (see above).

Personnel policies

Within an organization, personnel policies can improve clarity regarding which individuals can and should be conducting what activities. This is a device to improve the quality and technical credibility of staff by reducing policies such as political patronage or nepotism, and can also be a tool to improve diversity by reducing informal barriers to hiring underrepresented groups. Such policies begin with hiring, where each open position announcement should have a clear job description. If job descriptions are not available for current employees, the organization should begin a process for drafting them. One option is to ask all current employees to write up their own job description, and have managers review it and provide feedback. An advantage of job descriptions is that it clearly delineates the responsibilities of each staff member and, as a consequence, lessens 'turf' battles between employees.

With these job descriptions in place, all employees should be given an annual performance assessment in relationship to the duties ascribed to them. The format of the performance assessment should be made known to all employees, along with a timeline for the review. On each aspect of performance, managers should rate their employees based on whether they fail, meet or exceed the aspects of their position in their job description. And suggestions for improvement should be made for those in the 'fail' category, such as trainings or workshops. For those who meet the standards, managers, in consultation with staff, should develop a performance improvement plan that will allow the staff to enhance their skills in areas of personal interest or organizational need.

Procedures

Procedures ensure that policies are consistently applied or followed, reinforcing management predictability and organizational sustainability. Staff are appreciative of the consistent application of procedures, such as approval for vacation days or other formal requests. Requests need not be on a paper form; rather, the information on them and the time it takes to evaluate them should be made known, such as in an employee handbook. Staff are more likely to feel fairly treated by an organization when procedures are formalized and when management follows these procedures (see Lamertz 2003, for a conceptual discussion).

Procedures also guarantee the sustainability of an organization in the event that employees leave or leadership changes. Thus, procedures should be in place to guarantee that records are kept for future review. One such example is a document or records management policy. Organizations should have clear rules for which documents must be kept and which electronic files must be stored, for how long and where. With regard to electronic files, it is important to schedule a regular back-up of certain files to a government-approved hard drive or online folder, such as every week or every month, depending on the organization's needs. A second example is taking meeting minutes. Minutes should be dated, record the names of those in attendance and their affiliation, include the results of any votes taken, and summarize each of the agenda items discussed. The minutes should then be stored in compliance with current document management procedures. These procedures strengthen the transparency of an organization, as it can more easily comply with Freedom of Information requests or provide needed documents to watchdog entities.

Another example of procedures that contribute to integrity is the management of board behaviour. Bureaucracies may rely on a board or municipal committee to exercise oversight or provide guidance when making strategic decisions. Much like unpredictable or inconsistent staff behaviour can harm the integrity of an organization, members of the board have the potential to hurt, as well as help, operations if they exhibit such behaviour. Thus, organizations often find it useful to adopt board procedures to guide the behaviour of members. Members can be informed of conduct expectations through the provision of written information, such as board by-laws. By-laws describe the purpose of the board and meeting frequency, set the minimum and maximum number of members, and state reasons for membership termination. These by-laws should be voted on by the board prior to their institution, and should be given to all new board members during their orientation. This way, new board members know what is expected of them and what will happen if they fail to act accordingly. Many organizations find it helpful to set a minimum number of meetings board members are expected to attend per year and automatically remove board members who fail to attend this number. Conflict of interest declarations are also good practice for members.

Strategies for policy capacity

Forecasting

Intelligence on performance is essential for strong policy leadership, as it enables the central policy-makers to identify problems and opportunities early and gauge consequences. To paraphrase an oft-repeated adage, organizations should prepare themselves for the unexpected, rather than continue to rearrange the deck chairs on the *Titanic*. They should engage in forecasting to understand the costs and benefits of adapting to shocks, such as how strikes, natural disasters, government reorganizations or economic crises will affect internal resources and public need. Forecasting provides managers with enough information to decide when to 'tweak' a programme and when to make major changes or discontinue the programme. When assessing how to adapt performance in the event of a shock, there are three phases: an anticipatory phase when leadership learns about the possibility of a shock; a responsive phase where the impact of the shock is being felt; and a readjustment phase when the shock is over (Meyer 1982).

Intelligence on process

Intelligence on process is essential for strong policy management, as it ensures that the organization can support policies with the necessary resources to complete day-to-day tasks. One obvious resource is funding, as the above strategy discussing the budget was merely an introductory step in financial management. As budgets represent estimated revenues and expenditures planned for the fiscal year, a second step is to review how these estimates compare with 'actuals' and to periodically assess the balance sheet. Comparing estimates and actuals allows organization leaders to understand how expectations at the outset of the year relate to the reality the organization is experiencing to date. Some organizations use sophisticated software to balance accounts and track expenditures; however, based on resources available, a simple spreadsheet application can suffice for smaller governmental programmes. Depending on the volatility of revenues and expenditures, the budget should be assessed quarterly, or even monthly. Managers can then determine whether the organization can fulfil its obligations for the rest of the year, or if cutbacks need to be made. Additionally, organizations can also use budget management to ensure that vendors and contractors are paid on time. And it can assist in monitoring how much is being spent on administrative expenditures as compared to direct programme expenditures. It can also be used to assess the performance of programme managers in appropriately allocating financial resources over time and to identify individuals who may need training in financial management. By improving budget processes, the organization can ensure the financial sustainability of its programmes.

Research and analysis capacity

Research and analysis capacity consists of the availability of trained staff who possess research-oriented skills and who are affiliated with a broader research community from which they can obtain advice and support. This capacity is field-specific (e.g., epidemiology, health education and communication, etc.), and is separate from research skills related to management or leadership, such as budget or threat analysis. It can assist a bureaucracy by creating programmes that respond to particular constituent needs or adapting programmes amidst unintended consequences. These staff can also provide technical assistance to other governmental organizations, perhaps via a collaborative agreement. These specialized employees can also assess the performance of outside contractors, as they have the expertise to evaluate the efficiency and effectiveness of contractor actions. To enable staff to effectively engage with other specialists in relevant fields, organizations should also adopt procedures that promote meaningful involvement of such specialists in policy formulation and recommendation. One such strategy is to hold adjunct meetings during the meetings of professional societies in order to obtain feedback.

With a clear sense of the current leadership, management, and research capacity of the organization, managers can then identify useful and/or necessary areas for improvement. The following strategies will assist organizations in enhancing the capacity of the bureaucracy.

Staff recruitment and retention

Staff recruitment and retention strategies provide the organization with the skills it needs to implement programmes and services successfully. Organizations should establish hiring procedures to improve the quality of the policy bureaucracy, where only those with publicly stated credentials will be considered for positions. Furthermore, applicants should be considered regardless of their background characteristics (e.g., ethnicity or gender) or their political ideology.

While some employees will have knowledge about the policy process in addition to their job-specific skills, other staff may need training to improve their technical policy capacity. For example, a doctor may be hired based on his or her clinical training, but may need to acquire additional policy skills. National or international organizations, such as NGOs, or universities, may offer programmes that can help provide such training. If an organization has adequate in-house capacity, it may want to consider assigning a few of its policy staff to write a 'how to' manual for those who lack a policy background. This manual can include specific examples of how the organization was able to benefit or was challenged by the policy environment and the lessons learned from these experiences.

Conclusion

The aim of this chapter was to provide a short and non-judgemental description of the strategies that frequently underlie attributes of good governance: accountability, transparency, participation, integrity and policy capacity. Adopting such strategies enables bureaucracies to better accomplish their mission by improving the foundations of decision-making and exercise of authority that are fundamental to the delivery of programmes and services. The chapters that follow in the rest of Part I provide readers with an expanded definition of good governance. In Part II, specific examples of these strategies will be provided in terms of pharmaceutical pricing regulation, the regulation of private insurance, and the public–private finance of health care services.

References

Bardach, Eugene (1989) Grants as a tool of public policy. in Lester M. Salamon, (ed.) *Beyond Privatization: The Tools of Government Action*. Washington, DC: Urban Institute.

Bevan, G. and Hood, C. (2006) What's measured is what matters: targets and gaming in the English public health care system, *Public Administration*, 84(3): 517–38. DOI:10.1111/j.1467-9299.2006.00600.x

Boyd, E. A., Cho, M. K. and Bero, L. A. (2003) Financial conflict-of-interest policies in clinical research: issues for clinical investigators, *Academic Medicine*, 78(8): 769–74.

Brehm, J. (1993) *The Phantom Respondents*. Ann Arbor, MI: University of Michigan Press.

Carpenter, Daniel, P. (1996) Adaptive signal processing, hierarchy, and budgetary control in federal regulation, *American Political Science Review*, 90(2): 283–302.

Carpenter, Daniel, P. (2001) *The Forging of Bureaucratic Autonomy*. Princeton, NJ: Princeton University Press.

Carpenter, Daniel, P. (2010) 'Confidence games: how does regulation constitute markets?' in Edward J. Balleisen and David A. Moss (eds) *Government and Markets*. Cambridge: Cambridge University Press, pp. 164–90.

Carpenter, Daniel, P. and Moss, David A. (eds) (2013) *Preventing Regulatory Capture: Special Interest Influence and How to Limit It*. Cambridge: Cambridge University Press.

Clark, William, H. and Vranka, Larry (2013) The Need and Rationale for the Benefit Corporation. White Paper. Version dated 18 January 2013. Available at: http://benefitcorp.net/storage/documents/Benecit_Corporation_White_Paper_1_18_2013.pdf.

Coase, R. H. (1960) The problem of social cost, *Journal of Law and Economics*, 3: 1–44.

Council of Europe (2000) *Model Code of Conduct for Public Officials*. Available at: http://www.coe.int/t/dghl/monitoring/greco/documents/Rec(2000)10_EN.pdf (accessed 7 October 2013).

Epstein, Wendy Netter (2013) Contract theory and the failures of public-private contracting, *Cardozo Law Review*, 22: 2211–59.

Ethics Resource Center (2003) *Creating a Workable Company Code of Ethics*. Washington, DC: Ethics Resource Center (www.ethics.org).

Gaudin, Jean-Pierre (1999) *Gouverner par Contrat: L'Action Publique en Question*. Paris: Presses de Sciences Po.

Gelders, Dave (2005) Public information provision about policy intentions: the Dutch and Belgian experience, *Government Information Quarterly*, 22: 75–95.

Gilman, Stuart, C. (2005) *Ethics Codes and Codes of Conduct as Tools for Promoting an Ethical and Professional Public Service: Comparative Successes and Lessons*. Washington, DC: World Bank. Available at: http://www.oecd.org/mena/governance/35521418.pdf (accessed 10 October 2013).

Gilman, Stuart, C. and Stout, Jeffrey (2005) Assessment strategies and practices for integrity and anti-corruption measures in the public service, in J. Bertok and E. Beth (eds) *Public Sector Integrity: A Framework for Assessment*. Paris: OECD.

Greer, Scott L., Wilson, Iain, Stewart, Ellen and Donnelly, Peter (2012) *Health Board Elections and Alternative Pilots: Final Report of the Statutory Evaluation*, Edinburgh: Scottish Government.

Grzymala-Busse, Anna (2010) The best laid plans: the impact of informal rules on formal institutions in transitional regimes, *Studies in Comparative International Development*, 45(3): 311–33.

Haider, Donald (1989) Grants as a tool of public policy, in Lester M. Salamon (ed.) *Beyond Privatization: The Tools of Government Action*. Washington, DC: Urban Institute.

Hatry, Harry, P. (1999) *Performance Measurement: Getting Results*. Washington, DC: Urban Institute Press.

Hazell, Robert, Worthy, Ben and Glover, Mark (2010) *The Impact of the Freedom of Information Act on Central Government in the UK*. Basingstoke: Palgrave Macmillan.

Head, Brian W. (2012) The contribution of integrity agencies to good governance, *Policy Studies*, 33(1): 7–20.

Hirschman, Albert (1970) *Exit, Voice and Loyalty: Responses to Decline in Firms, Organizations and States*. Cambridge, MA: Harvard University Press.

Holsen, Sarah (2007) Freedom of Information in the UK, US, and Canada, *The Information Management Journal*, 41(3): 50–5.

Hood, Christopher (1991) A public management for all seasons, *Public Administration*, 69: 3–19.

Kettl, Donald F. (2005) *The Politics of the Administrative Process*. Washington, DC: CQ Press.

King, Anthony and Crewe, Ivor (2013) *The Blunders of Our Governments*. London: Oneworld.

Krosnick, J. A. (1999) Survey research, *Annual Review of Psychology*, 50: 537–67.

Lamertz, K. (2002) The social construction of fairness: social influence and sense making in organizations, *Journal of Organizational Behavior*, 23(1): 19–37.

Lascoumes, Pierre and Le Gales, Patrick (2007) Introduction: understanding public policy through its instruments: from the nature of instruments to the sociology of public policy instrumentation, *Governance*, 20(1): 1–21.

Lawrence, R. and Shapiro, Robert Y. (2000) *Politicians Don't Pander: Political Manipulation and the Loss of Democratic Responsiveness*. Chicago: University of Chicago Press.

Manning, S. and Randazzo, K. A. (2009) Leveling the playing field? Litigant success rates in health-care policy cases in the U.S. courts of appeals, *Justice System Journal*, 30(3): 245–53.

McCubbins, Mathew and Schwartz, Thomas (1984) Congressional oversight overlooked? Police patrols or fire alarms, *American Journal of Political Science*, 28(1): 165–79.

Meyer, A. D. (1982) Adapting to environmental jolts. *Administrative Science Quarterly*, 27(4): 515–37.

Olson, Kristen (2013) Double-barreled questions, in Paul Lavrakas (ed.) *Encyclopedia of Survey Research Methods*. London: Sage. DOI: 10.4135/9781412963947. Available at: http://srmo.sagepub.com/view/encyclopedia-of-survey-research-methods/n145.xml

Osborne, David and Gaebler, Ted (1992) *Reinventing Government: How the Entrepreneurial Spirit Is Transforming the Public Sector*. New York: Penguin Group.

Pollitt, Christopher, Bathgate, Karen, Caulfield, Janice, Smullen, Amanda and Talbot, Colin (2001) Agency fever? Analysis of an international policy fashion, *Journal of Comparative Policy Analysis*, 3: 271–90.

Pollitt, Christopher, Talbot, Colin, Caulfield, Janice and Smullen, Amanda (2004) *Agencies: How Governments Do Things Through Semi-Autonomous Organizations*. Basingstoke: Palgrave Macmillan.

Presser, S. and Blair, J. (1994) Do different methods produce different results? In P. V. Marsden (ed.) *Sociological Methodology*. Cambridge, MA: Blackwell. pp. 73–104.

Rodwin, V. (2011) *Conflicts of Interest and the Future of Medicine: The United States, France and Japan*. Oxford: Oxford University Press.

Salamon, Lester M. (ed.) (1989) The changing tools of government action: an overview, in *Beyond Privatization: The Tools of Government Action*. Washington, DC: Urban Institute.

Smullen, Amanda Jane (2010) *Translating Agency Reform: Rhetoric and Culture in Comparative Perspective*. Basingstoke: Palgrave Macmillan.

Sohn, D. H. and Sonny Bal, B. (2012) Medical malpractice reform: the role of alternative dispute resolution, *Clinical Orthopaedics and Related Research*, 470(5): 1370–8.

Songer, D., Kuersten, A and Kaheny, E. (2000) Why the haves don't always come out ahead: repeat players meet amici curiae for the disadvantaged, *Political Research Quarterly*, 53(3): 537–56.

Stankevich, Natalya, Qureshi, Navaid and Queiroz, Cesar (2009) *Performance-based Contracting for Preservation and Improvement of Road Assets*. New York: The World Bank. Available at: http://www-esd.worldbank.org/pbc_resource_guide/Docslatest%20edition/PBC/trn_27_PBC_Eng_final_ 2005.pdf (accessed 26 July 2013).

Stewart, Ellen A. (2012) *Health Board Elections and Alternative Pilots: Literature Review*. Edinburgh: Scottish Government.

Strolovitch, Dara Z. (2006) Do interest groups represent the disadvantaged? Advocacy at the intersections of race, class, and gender, *Journal of Politics*, 68(4): 894–910.

Thomas, James (2004) Skills for the ethical practice of public health, *Public Health Leadership Society*. Available at: http://phls.org/CMSuploads/Skills-for-the-Ethical-Practice-of-Public-Health-68547.pdf (accessed 10 July 2013).

Transparency International and the UN Human Settlements Program (2004) *Tools to Support Transparency in Local Governance*. Nairobi: UN-HABITAT.

US Department of Justice (2010) *How to Make a FOIA Request*. Available at: http://www.foia.gov/how-to.html (accessed 5 August 2013).

US Department of Transportation (2012) *Rulemaking Process*. Available at: http://www.dot.gov/regulations/rulemaking-process (accessed 4 August 2013).

Whitford, Andrew, B. (2005) The pursuit of political control by multiple principals, *Journal of Politics*, 67(1): 29–49.

Wilson, James, Q. (1989) *Bureaucracy: What Agencies Do and Why They Do It*. New York: Basic Books.

World Health Organization (2010) Memorandum of Understanding for Collaboration between the World Health Organization, through its Regional Office for Europe and the International Network of Health Promoting Hospitals and Health Services, 2009–2012. Available at: http://www.euro.who.int/__data/assets/pdf_file/0003/134688/MoU_HPH_Network_2009-2012.pdf (accessed 31 July 2013).

chapter four

Measuring governance: accountability, management and research

William D. Savedoff and Peter C. Smith

This chapter reviews efforts to measure and compare governance arrangements and governance performance. The key objective is to consider how governance frameworks discussed elsewhere in the book can be translated into operational indicators, and how these might be used in decision-making processes. The chapter first explains why measurement and comparison of governance arrangements are an important undertaking. It then describes key governance measurement programmes developed by global agencies such as the World Bank, Transparency International and the Bertelsmann Foundation, followed by a consideration of specific efforts by WHO and others to develop governance measurement frameworks in the health sector. The chapter then discusses the challenges of measuring governance in the health sector, and offers a rudimentary framework for developing relevant metrics, based on the concepts of the structure, processes and outcomes of health governance. The chapter also discusses the need for metrics at different levels of analysis (national and local levels), and ends with a call for more systematic design and collection of indicators.

Why measure?

There are three fundamental roles for any measures of the nature and quality of governance in a health system:

1 As an *accountability* instrument, to assure patients, the public and all other stakeholders that there are arrangements in place to promote good quality services and efficient use of resources.
2 As a *managerial* instrument, to help governments, insurers and other relevant stakeholders ensure that services are delivered in line with intentions.
3 As a *research* instrument to help identify the governance arrangements that promote best use of scarce resources.

As an accountability instrument, governance indicators seek to assure stakeholders that relevant governance structures and processes are in place, and that they are functioning as intended. A limited approach would report on the existence of planning and budgetary arrangements, appropriate regulation of health professionals, audit and performance monitoring, and structures for complaints and redress. A more ambitious approach would measure the effectiveness with which these governance arrangements are functioning, for example, reporting on adherence to budgetary targets, regulatory failures, or levels of satisfaction with the complaints system. The choice of which governance arrangements to report should ideally be informed by evidence, and their existence should be considered necessary (but not sufficient) to secure good quality outcomes.

As a managerial instrument, governance indicators can be a diagnostic tool to understand the reasons for poor performance of a specific practitioner or organization or to act as a prompt for intervention before such performance arises. Retrospectively, indicators may help pinpoint why a problem has arisen and what corrective action needs to be taken. Prospectively, governance indicators can alert governments or strategic purchasers to weaknesses that should be monitored, perhaps prompting further precautionary investigation. Many such indicators might be the same as those relevant for accountability purposes but used in this case for direct managerial action, such as inspection to assess adherence to codes of practice or standards for external accreditation. The critical requirement is that the chosen indicators refer to aspects of governance that are known – from research evidence – to lead to improved performance, and that valid comparisons between institutions can be made using these indicators.

As a research instrument, governance indicators can be used to identify which aspects of governance are most effective in securing improved performance. Substantial debate remains over the effectiveness of many governance structures, such as professional regulation, patient engagement, provider inspection and public reporting. Collecting information on these structural features is necessary for research to inform these debates with evidence. The research knowledge of 'what works' in governance is at present rudimentary, and so it is important to inquire, experiment and learn. A fundamental concern is to ensure that such research identifies true causality and not mere association. Because of the technical difficulties of comparing complex health systems across countries, it is likely that the most reliable research will derive from analysing the impact of governance variations within particular health systems rather than making comparisons across different systems.

General governance indicators

In recent years, there have been many efforts to measure various aspects of general governance, reflecting the widespread growth of interest in the topic. The UNDP (2007) cites 35 initiatives, and mentions many others. These rarely relate specifically to the health system, and many refer to aspects of national governance that are only indirectly related to health system performance. Oman and

Arndt (2010) suggest four causes for the explosion of interest in measures of governance: (1) international investment; (2) the end of the Cold War; (3) failed policy reform; and (4) the rising influence of the 'new institutional economics'. Indicator systems currently in place focus mainly at the national level, and are predominantly aimed at governance in low- and middle-income countries. The Appendix at the end of this chapter discusses some of the governance indicator sources that are most commonly used and that are summarized in Table 4.1. This section briefly discusses these sources.

The *Worldwide Governance Indicators* are assembled annually by the World Bank for 215 countries, and report six domains such as Accountability, Rule of Law, and Regulatory Quality. The World Bank also produces an annual *Country Policy and Institutional Assessment* (CPIA), which is used as a basis for development resource allocations. Both are discussed in the Appendix to this chapter.

The *Bertelsmann Transformation Index* (BTI) analyses development and transformation processes toward democracy and a market economy through international comparison every two years, and offers metrics on performance of 128 developing and transition countries. The BTI measures the current state of democracy and the market economy, its evolution over the previous two years, and a country's more general quality of governance. It has three domains, relating to democracy, markets and management.

The *Sustainable Governance Indicators* initiative was developed as a complement to the BTI for OECD countries. It focuses on two broad areas: a *Status Index*, which examines the relative success of policies implemented in recent years, and a *Management Index*, which focuses on the efficiency and accountability of the underlying policy-making processes. Within these broad areas there are separate domains reflecting the quality of government and the extent to which it can be held to account.

Transparency International is a global coalition against corruption. It produces an annual *Corruption Perceptions Index*, which draws together data from a variety of sources to assess perceived levels of corruption in the public sector, from the perspective of business people and country experts. The methodology involves a statistical aggregation of 13 sources.

It is often unclear what countries can do to improve their scores on these broad governance indicators. For example, eligibility for Millennium Challenge Corporation grants depend on a country's CPIA scores, including a strict standard on corruption. However, the CPIA measures are both imprecise and unresponsive to reforms (Dunning et al. 2014). In response to such concerns, the World Bank has sought to develop *Actionable Governance Indicators* (AGIs) that is, indicators which not only serve to measure governance but guide policymakers as to what action they can take. Such indicators are more narrowly defined. They seek to offer information on specific elements of governance reforms, and draw together material from over 20 indicator sources, including those described above.

It is noteworthy to add that the initiatives described place different emphases on the three broad uses of indicators discussed earlier: (1) accountability; (2) management; and (3) research. For example, accountability is the prime use envisaged for the Transparency International Index and the Bertelsmann

Table 4.1 Sources of general governance indicators

Indicator set	Author	Website	Domains	Sources
Worldwide Governance Indicators	World Bank	http://info.worldbank.org/governance/wgi/index.asp	• Voice and Accountability • Political Stability and Absence of Violence • Government Effectiveness • Regulatory Quality • Rule of Law • Control of Corruption	30 various data sources
Country Policy and Institutional Assessment	World Bank	http://www.worldbank.org/ida/how-ida-resources-allocated.html	(a) economic management; (b) structural policies; (c) policies for social inclusion and equity; and (d) public sector management	Country experts and moderation
Bertelsmann Transformation Index	Bertelsmann Institute	http://www.bti-project.org/home/	*Assessment of Democracy Status* is measured in terms of five criteria, which in turn are derived from assessments made in response to 18 individual questions. *Market Economy Status* is based on seven criteria, which are based on a total of 14 individual questions.	Country experts use a codebook to assess the extent to which 17 criteria have been met
Corruption Perceptions Index	Transparency Institute	http://www.transparency.org/	Perceived levels of corruption in the public sector	Aggregation of data from 13 sources
Actionable Governance Indicators	World Bank	http://www.agidata.org/Site/Default.aspx		Twenty sources of governance indicators

indices. In contrast, the CPIA is used mainly for managerial purposes (the allocation of funds). Of all the sources, the World Governance Indicators and the Actionable Governance Indicators are probably most appropriate for research use.

These general initiatives also place different emphases on the five dimensions of governance put forward earlier in the book – accountability, participation, transparency, integrity and capacity. While all five of these dimensions are addressed by some of the initiatives, the initiatives particularly stress accountability, integrity and capacity, with perhaps less material relating to participation and transparency. This emphasis may simply reflect a greater comfort level dealing with ostensibly technocratic features – like institutional structures for managing fiduciary risks and establishing hierarchical reporting requirements – than more overtly political features, such as public oversight of government offices and explicit requirements for open access to government data.

Conceptually, these indicators are trying to capture very broad ideas about governance (e.g., democracy, integrity) at a national level. Their measurement tends to rely on expert surveys, which has the advantage of not requiring overly precise and reductionist definitions but the disadvantage of reducing reliability and precision (arising from inconsistency of judgements between different experts).

In developing governance indicators for the health sector, it is important to pay attention to all of the issues raised by the general governance measurement initiatives. This requires being explicit about how indicators will be used, whether for accountability, management or research. It requires attention to being comprehensive and balanced and not, for example, avoiding aspects of governance that are considered political, ideological or controversial, because governance is intrinsically involved with addressing social conflict. Finally, it is necessary to find ways to develop indicators that are both reliable and precise.

Governance indicators in the health sector

In spite of increasing discussion of health sector governance (and the associated concept of stewardship), relatively few efforts have got as far as assembling indicators on the nature and quality of governance in health. Consequently, no routine, regularly reported source of health sector governance indicators is available.

The WHO initiated a large-scale effort to generate quantitative measures for every aspect of a country's health system (WHO 2000; Murray and Evans 2003). Within this broad work programme, Travis et al. (2003) initiated a discussion of how to assess stewardship, listing a series of domains and subfunctions and proposing to measure each domain through a standard survey instrument administered to key informants. The domains identified in this work were:

- generation of intelligence;
- formulating strategic policy framework;
- ensuring tools for implementation: powers, incentives and sanctions;
- building coalitions/building partnerships;

- ensuring a fit between policy objectives and organizational structure and culture;
- ensuring accountability.

Though this work usefully disaggregated a number of governance features into measurable units and suggested promising avenues of measurement, it has, to our knowledge, never been operationalized.

Later, the World Health Organization (2008) published a toolkit that addressed the specific issue of developing indicators of good governance in the health sector. It follows the general approach of Kaufmann and Kraay (2008) in distinguishing between rules-based and outcome-based indicators. Rules-based indicators seek to measure whether countries have appropriate governance policies and structures in place. Outcome-based indicators seek to measure whether those structures and rules are being used effectively. They are summarized in Box 4.1.

Box 4.1 Indicators used in World Health Organization Governance Toolkit

Rules-based indicators

1. Existence of up-to-date national health strategy linked to national needs and priorities.
2. Existence of an essential medicines list updated within the last five years and disseminated annually.
3. Existence of policies on drug procurement which specify: (i) procurement of the most cost-effective drugs in the right quantities; and (ii) open, competitive bidding of suppliers of quality products.
4. TB: Existence of a national strategic plan for TB which reflects the six principal components of the Stop TB Strategy as outlined in the Global Plan to Stop TB 2006–2015.
5. Malaria: Existence of a national malaria strategy/policy which includes drug efficacy monitoring, vector control, and insecticide resistance monitoring.
6. HIV/AIDS: Completion of the UNGASS National Composite Policy Index Questionnaire for HIV/AIDS.
7. Maternal Health: Existence of a comprehensive reproductive health policy consistent with the ICPD action plan.
8. Child Health: Existence of an updated comprehensive, multi-year plan for childhood immunization.
9. Existence of key health sector documents, which are published and disseminated annually (such as budget documents, annual performance reviews, health indicators).
10. Existence of mechanisms, such as surveys, for obtaining timely client input on the existence of appropriate, timely and effective access to health services.

Outcomes-based indicators

1. Human Resources: Health worker absenteeism in public health facilities.
2. Health Financing: Proportion of government funds which reach district-level facilities.
3. Health Service Delivery: Stock-out rates (absence) of essential drugs in health facilities.
4. Health Service Delivery: Proportion of informal payments within the public health care system.
5. Pharmaceutical Regulation: Proportion of pharmaceutical sales that consist of counterfeit drugs.
6. Voice & Accountability: Existence of effective civil society organizations in countries with mechanisms in place for citizens to express views to government bodies.

Another contribution to assessing governance of health systems is found in material prepared for USAID by Islam (2007), who uses countrywide governance indicators together with indicators within the following five areas:

1 *Information/Assessment Capacity*: information available to decision-makers and a broad range of stakeholders on trends in health and health system performance and on possible policy options. Available information is used for planning and decision-making.
2 *Policy Formulation and Planning*: appropriate processes in place to develop, debate, pass and monitor legislation and regulations on health issues. The government planning process is functioning. There is consistency and coherence between health sector laws or plans and actual implementation.
3 *Social Participation and System Responsiveness*: involvement of a broad range of stakeholders (non-governmental organizations (NGOs) and representatives of various public sector actors) in understanding health issues and in planning, budgeting and monitoring health sector actions as well as the health system's responsiveness to the input of these stakeholders.
4 *Accountability*: existence of rules on publishing information about the health sector (e.g., plans, health data including health statistics, fee schedules); a functioning free popular and scientific press; functioning watchdog organizations; and consumer protection from medical malpractice.
5 *Regulation*: capacity for oversight of safety, efficacy, and quality of health services and pharmaceuticals; enforcement capacity for guidelines, standards and regulations; and perception of the burden imposed by excessive regulation.

Islam suggests 40 indicators to cover these five areas. They take the form of a series of qualitative 'questions' to explore the adequacy of governance arrangements. Although developed with low-income settings in mind, many of the questions can be translated to high-income countries.

Hansl et al. (2008) proposed a scheme for assessing governance of a subset of health systems, those relying upon mandatory health insurance. Their five dimensions overlap with those of Islam (2007), emphasizing coherent decision-making structures, stakeholder participation, transparency and information, supervision and regulation, and consistency and stability. Each dimension has associated features, and indicators that allow systems to be classified in ways that draw attention to imbalances or inadequacies. In this case, Hansl et al. (2008) demonstrate how the scheme can be applied by measuring governance in four countries: Chile, Costa Rica, Estonia and the Netherlands.

Lewis and Pettersson (2009) discuss what comprises good governance in health service delivery, and suggest a suite of governance performance indicators covering five areas:

1 budget and resource management, including issues such as budget process and budget leakages, payroll irregularities and inefficient procurement;
2 individual providers, including issues such as bribery, physician credentials, absenteeism and health worker performance;
3 health facilities, performance in areas such as length of stay, infection rates and patient satisfaction;
4 informal payments, in the form of illegal payments by patients to secure access to publicly provided services;
5 corruption perceptions by the public or officials.

The focus is on 'leakages' from the health system, often in other contexts conceptualized as inefficiencies, but in this case formulated specifically to highlight inefficiencies that appear to arise from weaknesses in governance arrangements.

Savedoff (2011) was commissioned by the World Bank specifically to identify governance indicators for the health sector that could be used as managerial tools – actionable governance indicators in the health sector – to address what Reid (2010) denotes as the 'missing middle'. Savedoff distinguishes between indicators that are useful as managerial tools because their interpretation is well understood (e.g., absenteeism) from indicators that are currently only useful for research because their implications are still not empirically established (e.g., the extent and nature of decentralization). The paper concludes with a set of proposed indicators based on their usefulness, completeness and feasibility (in terms of available data collection instruments).

Distinguishing structural, process and outcome indicators

Notwithstanding the acknowledged importance of good governance in promoting improved health system performance, it is sometimes difficult to identify indicators of governance that are in any sense distinct from conventional indicators of system performance, particularly measures of efficiency. For example, concepts such as health worker productivity (e.g., consultations per doctor) or use of facilities (e.g., inpatient length of stay) are conventional measures of performance. However, they can also be interpreted as indirect signals of the quality of governance in the organization under scrutiny, though there are of course many other potential determinants of such performance distinct from governance. If governance is an important determinant of such performance outcomes, then it is almost tautological, and not particularly helpful, to use such measures as a signal of the quality of governance. Rather, the intention should be to develop indicators of the specific contribution of governance arrangements to performance outcomes.

Savedoff (2011) makes the distinction between indicators of governance determinants from indicators of governance *performance*, to some extent reflecting the distinction between rules-based and outcomes-based indicators made in the WHO toolkit discussed above. He argues that it is relatively easy to identify indicators of governance *performance* such as levels of absenteeism or shares of counterfeit drugs in the market, because they are measures of problems with clear interpretations (e.g., it is better to have less absenteeism and fewer counterfeit drugs on the market). While these governance performance indicators are influenced by governance arrangements such as personnel policies and inspection procedures, the types of governance arrangements that enhance performance are not readily known. Thus, it is more difficult to formulate persuasive indicators of governance determinants because research has not established clear and reliable links between particular governance arrangements and health system outcomes. A key reason for the poorly understood links between governance and outcomes is precisely the complex nature of these systems and the fact that problems can derive from too much, too little or the 'wrong kind' of governance arrangements, as discussed in Chapter 2.

Measuring the type of governance in place therefore offers an important research resource, as it may help identify governance practices that lead to better performance. However, if such measures are also treated as normative indicators of performance, there is a risk of stifling innovation in managerial style, and advocating a single – possibly faulty – model of governance for the operation of the health system. In short, it is important to draw a careful distinction between measures of governance used for research purposes and those used for accountability or managerial purposes.

We propose three classes of governance measures, related to the structures, processes and outcomes of governance. This distinction has similarities to the structure–process–outcome paradigm regularly used to assess clinical quality (Donabedian 1988) and is, we think, more intuitive than the two-way classification proposed in Savedoff (2011). Measures of governance structure relate to the presence of governance arrangements: for example, in the form of an 'essential medicines' list. Process measures identify whether governance arrangements nominally in place are being implemented, such as enforcing rules to reimburse publicly only those drugs that are on an essential medicines list. Outcome measures explore whether the governance arrangements secure system performance improvements for example, that good-quality medications are increasingly available to and used by people who need them.

As an example, consider proposals to improve governance by increasing community participation. A related governance structure indicator might capture whether or not there is a democratic accountability mechanism in place, a process measure would indicate whether that mechanism offers citizens real choice and opportunity to express their views, and an outcome measure might indicate whether system behaviour changes as a result of democratic choices lead to better population health. Gray-Molina et al. (2000) implicitly make such a distinction when studying the impact of community participation on the performance of small Bolivian hospitals. They collected information about the existence of popular participation in hospital boards (structure), whether or not these boards were active as demonstrated by holding meetings (process), and whether more active boards influenced the prices paid for inputs and the extent of bribery (outcomes).

To illustrate the role and relevance of different types of indicator, Figure 4.1 (adapted from Savedoff 2011) shows the various influences on organizational performance. Governance 'determinants' can be interpreted as the *structures* of governance in place, while governance 'performance' reflects the *processes*. This in turn, along with many other factors, influences organizational performance (which can be considered the governance *outcome*).

This framework can in turn be used to examine the role of governance indicators in a specific context. Figure 4.2 illustrates some potential concrete indicators that could be used to report governance arrangements in primary care units. The framework first describes a governance structure that is hypothesized to influence processes and outcomes: in this case, whether local governments responsible for public primary health care facilities have local discretion to manage medical personnel. It then assesses the extent to which the local government uses this local discretion to discipline workers for unexcused absences, an indicator of how effectively the governance process is implemented. The governance outcome associated with this sequence would either be a direct measure of the share of workers who are absent from work without legitimate excuses, or the extent to which lower absenteeism is reflected in a larger number of consultations. It should in principle be feasible to place all potential governance indicators within this structure–process–outcome framework, and thereby identify gaps and redundancies in the indicator set.

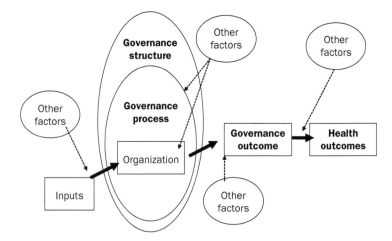

Figure 4.1 AGI Initiative Model of Governance Determinants

Source: Adapted by the authors from Reid (2010) and Savedoff (2011).

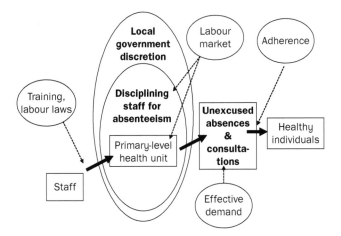

Figure 4.2 Illustration of governance structure, process and outcome

Source: Adapted from Savedoff (2011).

Deriving metrics from the governance framework

We maintain that indicators can be derived to populate almost any governance framework. To be useful, however, it is necessary to be clear when they are measuring structures, processes or outcomes and to distinguish when they are being used for accountability, management or research. The role of the framework is to indicate the purpose of any indicator – which aspects of governance it is seeking to capture – and therefore to help to choose the relevant metric, and then how to interpret and use it.

As an example, Table 4.2 summarizes governance indicators proposed by Lewis and Pettersson and the WHO Toolkit. It first categorizes them according to whether they address governance structure, process or outcome. The WHO toolkit is concerned mainly with the structures of governance. A useful question for these measures is whether evidence is available to demonstrate that improvements in these structural features are associated with improvements in processes or outcomes.

In contrast, Lewis and Pettersson (2009) propose a set of indicators with a mixture of focuses – four structural, three processes and eight outcomes. This mix is more balanced than the WHO toolkit, but in only a few cases is it possible to show linkages between the three levels. For example, governance structures associated with budget scrutiny, combined with processes assessed in terms of discrepancies between public funds budgeted for payroll and receipts by health care workers, may have an impact on illegal charges in facilities and irregularities in payroll. Other indicators in Lewis and Pettersson are less clearly related to one another.

In seeking indicators to operationalize the framework provided earlier in the book, Table 4.2 also provides a column that notes the extent to which a particular indicator addresses the five governance domains used in Chapter 2: accountability, participation, transparency, integrity and capacity. Many of the outcome indicators address integrity concerns, while the structure and process indicators

Table 4.2 Categorization of selected governance indicators

	Structure process outcome	*Accountability participation transparency integrity capacity*
Lewis and Petterson		
Indicators track budget credibility, comprehensiveness, transparency, execution, reporting, recording, and external audits and scrutiny	S	A, T, C
Discrepancy between public budgeted health funds and the amounts received by health providers	P	I
Irregularities associated with government payroll for health workers	O	I
Differences in prices paid for similar medical supplies/ equipment across health facilities	O	I, C
Frequency of illegal side payments/bribes influencing hiring decisions and of payments for particular assignments	O	I
Existence of licensing requirements and of continuing education programmes and their operation	S/P	T, C
Fraction of physicians or nurses contracted for service but not on site during the period(s) of observation	O	I
Types of incentives and accountability mechanisms facing public providers	S	A, C
Incentives and accountabilities in hospital payments	S/P	A, T, C
Average length of stay and bed occupancy rates	O	
Frequency of illegal charges for publicly provided health services	O	I
Fraction of households, experts or public officials perceiving corruption in health; relative ranking of health sector on corruption index	O	A, T, I
The Country and Policy Institutional Assessments (CIPA) for health	O	C
WHO toolkit		
Existence of up-to-date national health strategy linked to national needs and priorities	S	A, T, C
Existence of an essential medicines list updated within the last five years and disseminated annually.	S	A, T, C
Existence of policies on drug procurement which specify fair procurement and bidding processes	S	A, T, C

	Structure process outcome	Accountability participation transparency integrity capacity
TB: Existence of a national strategic plan for TB which reflects the six principal components of the Stop TB Strategy	S	A, T, C
Malaria: Existence of a national malaria strategy/policy which includes key control and monitoring elements	S	A, T, C
HIV/AIDS: Completion of the UNGASS National Composite Policy Index Questionnaire for HIV/AIDS	S	A, T, C
Maternal Health: Existence of a comprehensive reproductive health policy consistent with the ICPD action plan	S	A, T, C
Child Health: Existence of an updated comprehensive, multi-year plan for childhood immunization	S	A, T, C
Key health sector documents published and disseminated annually (such as budget documents, annual performance reviews, etc.)	P	A, T, C
Existence of mechanisms, such as surveys, to identify existence of appropriate, timely and effective access to health services.	P	A, T, C
Human Resources: Health worker absenteeism in public health facilities	O	I
Health Financing: Proportion of government funds which reach district-level facilities	O	I
Health Service Delivery: Stock-out rates (absence) of essential drugs in health facilities	O	I, C
Health Service Delivery: Proportion of informal payments within the public health care system	O	I
Pharmaceutical Regulation: Proportion of pharmaceutical sales that consist of counterfeit drugs	O	I, C
Existence of effective civil society organizations with mechanisms in place for citizens to express views to government bodies.	S/P	A, P, T, C

are more concerned with accountability, transparency and capacity. There are few indicators that directly address the nature or extent of participation.

Other chapters in the book elaborate on the five elements by giving examples of what we would term governance structures, such as conflict of interest policies under accountability or watchdog committees and inspectorates in the case of transparency. In each case, the discussion also elucidates governance processes and outcomes with attention to the fact that, depending on context and practice, similar structures can perform very differently. As just one example, Chapter 2 noted that participation is not an end in itself but rather a structure that affects governance outcomes like legitimacy, fairness and effectiveness (Fung 2006). So an assessment of particular governance structures – such as participatory budgeting, elections or advisory committees – needs to consider just how the processes function and whether their outcomes are favourable or not for health system performance.

Governance indicators at different levels of analysis

Good governance is required for numerous accountability and managerial relationships in the health system. However, the nature of such relationships varies greatly. To give some examples:

- For the government's accountability to citizens, it is likely that governance requirements will include transparent reporting to citizens, independent scrutiny of government performance by media, parliament and other commentators, and democratic processes that allow citizens to express their views.
- For the clinician's accountability to patients, governance requirements might include appropriate professional regulation concerning competence to practice, transparent reporting of performance, the ability to choose practitioner, and systems of redress that address complaints swiftly and effectively.
- For the provider organization's accountability to purchaser organizations, governance requirements include the existence of clear contractual obligations, adherence to budgets and volume and quality requirements, transparent reporting of performance, and the existence of appropriate sanctions such as removal of business.

This variation in the nature of governance arrangements suggests that – in addition to distinguishing between structure, process and outcomes – governance indicators should clearly distinguish the level of analysis at which they are directed (Savedoff 2008; 2011). For accountability to citizens, and to inform potential donors and investors, there is some argument for reporting on governance at the system level. Moreover, some measures of governance structure, such as the presence or otherwise of appropriate regulatory mechanisms, are the result of system-wide policy choices, and so can be reported only at the system level. However, for many purposes it will be more useful to report levels of governance at an organizational level, such as a local government, individual insurer or a health care facility, or even at the level of an individual practitioner. As well as being essential for managerial and research purposes, such reporting also indicates levels of variation in governance arrangements across the system as a whole.

It is also worth noting that it may be difficult to specify indicators of governance structures that are universally relevant across different health systems. Much will depend on the overall architecture of the health system. So, for example, if there is good public reporting of clinical outcomes within a health system, then it may be the case that some aspects of professional governance (such as licence to practise) may be less crucial than in systems where no such reporting is in place. This observation suggests that in many circumstances it will be the *portfolio* of governance arrangements, how they interact and how they are aligned with system objectives, that will determine governance effectiveness. Individual aspects of governance, such as quality inspection, may be functioning well, but their effectiveness will be blunted if they are not well aligned with other governance arrangements, such as provider licensing. Similarly, some governance requirements in a decentralized system might be quite different to those needed in a more centralized setting.

More generally, different institutional, legal and cultural contexts can give rise to needs for different types of health governance arrangements, and different interpretations of any variations (Savedoff 2008; 2011). One of the risks of prescribing certain normative requirements for governance is that it may ignore such local context.

Discussion

Whichever specific definition of governance is chosen, it will usually embrace the notion of 'steering' the health system towards a set of desired goals. The literature on the measurement of governance is extensive but mainly focused on low- and middle-income settings. In the health sector, the emphasis has been on governance infrastructure, in the form of the existence of certain basic planning and regulation instruments. Outcome measures of governance performance have focused on corruption and 'leakages' from intended resource flows. These issues are of course of profound importance in any health system. However, they reflect only part of the governance infrastructure needed to promote improved health system performance.

There are three broad uses for governance indicators: accountability, management and research. In their accountability role, indicators can serve to assure citizens and other stakeholders that proper governance arrangements are in place and are functioning satisfactorily. In their managerial role, indicators help identify weaknesses in specific organizations or parts of the health system, and suggest corrective actions. In their research role, indicators can help identify which aspects of governance are most effective in securing improved health system performance, and thereby inform appropriate governance reforms.

We have posited three categories of health governance indicators, based on structure, process and outcome. Structural indicators are most easily identified and correspond to the notion of rules-based indicators put forward by Kaufman and Kraay (2007). Such structural indicators are typically observed by their formal presence – the existence of representation on a board, a specific policy, or a legal right of access to information – rather than by their implementation. Of course they suffer from the risk that the nominal existence of an instrument may in practice be mere tokenism, which is why process indicators are essential. Process indicators are more difficult to formulate, but very informative, as they seek to indicate whether or not governance instruments are used as intended. Process indicators can be extremely useful for management decisions because they identify implementation failures that can be the focus of specific and direct problem-solving. Process indicators are also useful for research. There is no point in finding theoretical correlations between governance structures and health system performance without knowing whether the structural feature has functioned as intended, and understanding the reasons for any failure.

Finally, health governance outcome indicators are essential to all three uses of metrics. They are perhaps most important for accountability purposes, though they may be difficult to distinguish from more general efficiency measures that are also influenced by many factors other than governance. Governance outcome indicators are also important to management and research. Management of processes without attention to outcomes is clearly myopic. Research similarly should be guided by how these structural features, when implemented, have an impact on governance outcomes (such as absenteeism or productivity) and even, from there, to the ultimate ends of the health system – improved population health, universality and equity.

The collection and presentation of health governance indicators tend to be haphazard and opportunistic. Little discussion has been found on the vital distinction between normative indicators of good governance practice and descriptive indicators more suitable for research purposes. Furthermore, it is at times difficult to distinguish governance 'performance' metrics from general indicators of health system performance. We would argue that more thought should be given to the purpose and specification of indicators, and to identifying the specific contribution of governance arrangements to the performance of the health system.

A final crucial consideration is the level at which indicators are reported. Most of the work in this area has hitherto been concerned with broad-brush indicators at a national or system level. However, indicators are most useful at lower levels of analysis (devolved government entity, insurer, health care facility), particularly when used for managerial or research purposes. Variation in governance arrangements is easier to interpret within a system than between systems, and it can be strongly argued that more attention should be given to sub-national reporting.

Appendix

The Worldwide Governance Indicators are assembled annually by the World Bank for 215 countries and report six domains:

- Voice and Accountability
- Political Stability and Absence of Violence
- Government Effectiveness
- Regulatory Quality
- Rule of Law
- Control of Corruption

The data is derived from 30 individual data sources produced by a variety of survey institutes, think tanks, non-governmental organizations, international organizations, and private sector firms. See http://info.worldbank.org/governance/wgi/index.asp.

The World Bank also produces an annual Country Policy and Institutional Assessment (CPIA), which is used as a basis for development resource allocations.

The CPIA rates developing countries against a set of 16 criteria grouped in four clusters: (a) economic management; (b) structural policies; (c) policies for social inclusion and equity; and (d) public sector management and institutions. The criteria seek to capture key factors that foster growth and poverty reduction, while avoiding undue burden in the assessment process. The 2012 exercise used the following criteria:

A Economic Management
    1 Monetary and Exchange Rate Policies
    2 Fiscal Policy
    3 Debt Policy and Management
B Structural Policies
    4 Trade
    5 Financial Sector
    6 Business Regulatory Environment
C Policies for Social Inclusion/Equity
    7 Gender Equality
    8 Equity of Public Resource Use
    9 Building Human Resources
    10 Social Protection and Labor
    11 Policies and Institutions for Environmental Sustainability
D Public Sector Management and Institutions
    12 Property Rights and Rule-based Governance
    13 Quality of Budgetary and Financial Management
    14 Efficiency of Revenue Mobilization
    15 Quality of Public Administration
    16 Transparency, Accountability and Corruption in the Public Sector

Criterion 9 has two components: (a) health, including population and reproductive health, and nutrition as well as the prevention and treatment of communicable diseases such as HIV/AIDS, tuberculosis and malaria and (b) education, training and literacy programmes, including early child development programmes.

The CPIA is developed using a two-stage process. First, a small, representative sample of countries, drawn from all World Bank Regions, is rated. This is done using expert judgements from World Bank staff in the countries, regions and headquarters, and a subsequent moderation process. World Bank staff then rate the remaining countries using benchmark countries' scores as 'guideposts'. See http://www.worldbank.org/ida/how-ida-resources-allocated.html

The Bertelsmann Transformation Index analyses development and transformation processes toward democracy and a market economy through international comparison every two years, and offers metrics on performance of 128 developing and transition countries. The BTI measures the current state of democracy and the market economy, its evolution over the past two years, and a country's more general quality of governance. It has three domains, relating to democracy, markets and management.

Assessment of Democracy Status is measured in terms of five criteria, which in turn are derived from assessments made in response to 18 individual questions. *Market Economy Status* is based on seven criteria, which are based on a total of 14 individual questions. The *Management Index* focuses on how effectively policy-makers facilitate and steer development and transformation processes. It is the element of the BTI that is most directly relevant to health system governance, and examines the extent to which governments are consistent in pursuing their goals, use their resources wisely and effectively, and win broad consensus for their transformation goals. It is based on five criteria:

- level of difficulty
- steering capability
- resource efficiency
- consensus-building
- international cooperation

The indices are derived using a standardized codebook; country experts for each of the 128 countries assess the extent to which a total of 17 criteria have been met. A moderation process is then used to ensure consistency. See http://www.bti-project.org/home.

The Sustainable Governance Indicators initiative was developed as a complement to the BTI for OECD countries. It focuses on two broad areas: a *Status Index* that examines the relative success of policies implemented in recent years, and a *Management Index* that focuses on the efficiency and accountability of the underlying policy-making processes. Within these broad areas, there are separate domains reflecting the quality of government, and the extent to which it can be held to account. These two indices consist of 147 individual items, 82 of which are quantitative indicators derived from information collected from public data sources; the remaining 65 are qualitative assessments based on expert judgement. See http://www.sgi-network.org/index.php.

Transparency International is a global coalition against corruption. It produces an annual Corruption Perceptions Index that draws together data from a variety of sources to assess perceived levels of corruption in the public sector, from the perspective of business people and country experts. The methodology involves a statistical aggregation of 13 sources:

1 African Development Bank Governance Ratings
2 Bertelsmann Foundation Sustainable Governance Indicators
3 Bertelsmann Foundation Transformation Index
4 Economist Intelligence Unit Country Risk Ratings
5 Freedom House Nations in Transit
6 Global Insight Country Risk Ratings
7 IMD World Competitiveness Yearbook
8 Political and Economic Risk Consultancy Asian Intelligence
9 Political Risk Services International Country Risk Guide
10 Transparency International Bribe Payers Survey
11 World Bank – Country Performance and Institutional Assessment
12 World Economic Forum Executive Opinion Survey
13 World Justice Project Rule of Law Index

None of these sources reports scores for all countries, so a major analytic challenge is the treatment of missing data and the aggregation of data from different sources. The methodology underlying the index was subjected to independent analytic scrutiny, which led to revisions in 2012. See http://www.transparency.org. The World Bank has developed the concept of Actionable Governance Indicators (AGIs). These are indicators that focus on narrowly defined aspects of governance, rather than broad dimensions. They seek to offer information on specific elements of governance reforms, and draw together material from a number of over 20 indicator sources, including those described above. See http://www.agidata.org/Site/Default.aspx.

References

Arndt, C. and Oman, C. (2006) *Uses and Abuses of Governance Indicators*. Paris: OECD.

Baez-Camargo, C. and Jacobs, E. (2011) *A Framework to Assess Governance of Health Systems in Low Income Countries*. Basel: Basel Institute of Governance.

Donabedian, A. (1988) The quality of care: how can it be assessed? *JAMA*, 121(11): 1145–50.

Dunning, C., Karver, J. and Kenny, C. (2014) *Hating on the Hurdle: Reforming the Millennium Challenge Corporation's Approach to Corruption, MCA Monitor*. Washington, DC: Center for Global Development.

Fung, Archon (2006) Varieties of participation in complex governance, *Public Administration Review*, 66: 66–75.

Gray-Molina, G., Perez de Rada, E. and Yánez, E. (2000) Does voice matter? Participation and controlling corruption in Bolivian hospitals, in R. di Tella and W. Savedoff (eds) *Diagnosis Corruption: Fraud in Latin America's Public Hospitals*. Washington, DC: Inter-American Development Bank, pp. 27–56.

Hansl, B., Rahola, A., Gottret, P. and Leive, A. (2008) Good governance dimensions in mandatory health insurance: a framework for performance assessment, in W. D. Savedoff and P. Gottret (eds) *Governing Mandatory Health Insurance: Learning from Experience*. Washington, DC: World Bank.

Islam, M. (ed.) (2007) *Health Systems Assessment Approach: A How-To Manual*. Submitted to USAID in collaboration with Health Systems 20/20, Partners for Health Reform, Quality Assurance Project, and Rational Pharmaceutical Management, Arlington, VA: Management Sciences for Health.

Kaufmann, D. and Kraay, A. (eds) (2007) *What Are the Challenges in Developing and Applying Governance Indicators?* Washington DC: World Bank.

Kaufmann, D. and Kraay, A. (2008) Governance indicators: where are we, where should we be going? *World Bank Research Observer*, 23(1): 1–30.

Lewis, M. (2006) *Governance and Corruption in Public Health Care Systems*. Washington, DC: Center for Global Development.

Lewis, M. and Pettersson, G. (2009) *Governance in Health Care Delivery: Raising Performance*. Washington, DC: World Bank.

Murray, C. J. L. and Evans, D. (eds) (2003) *Health Systems Performance Assessment: Debates, Methods and Empiricism*. Geneva: World Health Organization.

Oman, C. P. and Arndt, C. (2010) *Measuring Governance: OECD Policy Brief 39*. Paris: OECD.

Reid, G. J. (2010) Actionable governance indicators: concepts and measurement, *AGI Initiative*, Washington, DC: World Bank. Mimeo available at: http://siteresources.worldbank.org/EXTPUBLICSECTORANDGOVERNANCE/Resources/286304-12354 11288968/AGIConceptsMeasurement.pdf.

Savedoff, W. D. (2008) Governing mandatory health insurance: concepts, frameworks, and cases, in W. D. Savedoff and P. Gottret (eds) *Governing Mandatory Health Insurance: Learning from Experience*. Washington, DC: World Bank.

Savedoff, W. D. (2011) *Governance in the Health Sector: A Strategy for Measuring Determinants and Performance*. Washington, DC: World Bank.

Travis, P., Egger, D., Davies, P. and Mechbal, A. (2003) Towards better stewardship: concepts and critical issues, in C. J. L. Murray and D. Evans (eds) *Health Systems Performance Assessment: Debates, Methods and Empiricism*. Geneva: World Health Organization.

United Nations Development Programme (2007) *A Guide To Governance Indicators*. New York: UNDP.

World Health Organization (2000) *The World Health Report 2000: Health Systems: Improving Performance*. Geneva: WHO.

World Health Organization (2008) *Health Systems Governance: Toolkit on Monitoring Health Systems Strengthening*. Geneva: WHO.

chapter five

Policy lessons for health governance

Scott L. Greer, Matthias Wismar,
Josep Figueras and Nikolay Vasev

Governance is a major factor determining what decisions are made and implemented. It shapes health politics and decisions in several different ways. It shapes the goals of actors through accountability, obliging them to think about how they will justify their actions. It gives the decisions greater or lesser transparency, making it easier or harder to predict and critique actions. It shapes the decisions and their implementation by setting rules of participation – who is in the room when the decision is made, and will they support the policy in practice? It shapes the decisions and their implementation through integrity measures, which can encourage clarity and probity or bureaucracy. And, finally, it encourages better decisions with better implementation, since policy capacity allows decision-makers to anticipate problems and identify options (and argue with lobbyists). In short, shaping governance shapes future decisions and their success.

Furthermore, governance can be analysed, problems identified, and its functioning improved. Chapter 3 and the case studies discuss the wide variety of policies that can be adopted by policy-makers who wish to make a change to the accountability, transparency, participation, integrity and capacity in their systems: the TAPIC framework. The context for focusing on policy lessons in this chapter is this TAPIC framework that has been more fully explained in previous chapters.

The TAPIC framework for governance

When there are policy failures – policies are adopted that should not have been, or good policies with adequate political and financial support nonetheless fail – these kind of situations point to a concern with governance. This book developed a framework, presented in Chapter 2, that identified five components of governance – transparency, accountability, participation, integrity and capacity – abbreviated as TAPIC. The framework emerged from a review of the extensive academic, professional and practical literature on governance, in health systems and in general; we found that it recurrently addressed these same five topics.

The purpose of the TAPIC framework is to identify components of governance, and then to go beyond it to identify the sources of actual or potential problems. If an unworkable policy is adopted, then its adoption might be a function of deficient governance, though it might also be a result of some other kind of political decision. If a workable policy is adopted, with political and adequate financial support and it encounters difficulties, then the problem is frequently to be found in governance.

Each component of governance, then, is a place to look for potential problems:

- Transparency is how and how much decisions and their grounds are made known.
- Accountability is explanation and sanction – who can effectively demand an explanation and sanction an action?
- Participation is the participation of those affected by a decision in the decision-making.
- Integrity is the establishment of non-corrupt, institutionalized organization.
- Capacity is policy capacity – the existence of expertise on policy formulation, implementation and evaluation.

A policy failure, whether it is an ill-advised policy or an unexpected failure of a sensible policy, can often be attributed to deficiencies in one of these five areas.

More is not always better. Each component of governance is an area to be investigated or addressed, and the governance of any health system should be considered in light of its specific circumstances. Poorly designed and managed transparency, accountability or participation can lead to bad outcomes, while poorly thought through integrity measures and investment in capacity can lead to waste and rigidity. Kyratsis' Chapter 12 makes this point particularly clearly. The components of governance in the TAPIC framework might all have positive connotations, but that does not mean that they are all to be endlessly increased.

Chapters 3 and 4 stressed these points. Chapter 3 presented a wide range of policy tools used to affect components of governance. Identifying the right policies for a given circumstance is an important and sensitive choice. Chapter 4, meanwhile, stressed the importance of context-sensitive and detailed measures of governance. Just as broad concepts like transparency or accountability must lead to specific policies, broad measures of governance are less helpful than specific ones that respond to local circumstances. The case studies in Part II use the TAPIC framework to address the challenges of making good health systems policies in a range of important areas.

The rest of this chapter distils lessons. It starts by showing how the case studies demonstrate the importance of governance in shaping markets, networks and hierarchies. It then moves from health systems governance to governance for health, showing how the TAPIC framework applies to broader policies for health. And, finally, it draws some lessons for policy-makers.

Governance and health systems

This section reviews key facets of health policy, drawing on the case studies to show how activities crucial to the operation of health systems are shaped by governance. Practically all health policies work through market-based, network or hierarchical policy tools such as outsourcing, contracting and competition (markets), intersectoral or professional governance (network) or direct administrative action such as provision by the government taxation.

Governance affects the ability of markets, networks and hierarchical organizations to contribute to healthy societies. A policy based on any of those instruments, from clinical governance to prospective payments to health technology assessment, can encounter governance difficulties.

Markets

Any health system is full of markets, from the market for health services to the market for labour to the market for devices and medicines. We often speak of markets as if they arise naturally. The Scottish economist Adam Smith spoke of a human propensity to 'truck and barter', and many policy initiatives are premised on the assumption that markets will develop if government retreats from regulation or supply. This is not the case. Markets are always embedded in governance and society (Polanyi 1944). Markets have been found to depend on governance as much as any other kind of health governance. At bottom, markets benefit from basic, society-wide attributes of governance such as property rights and the rule of law, and indirectly benefit from governance that leads to goods such as infrastructure, education and public health. The modern pharmaceutical industry, for example, is unimaginable without patent law and strict market access rules (as discussed by Cylus et al. in Chapter 9). Outsourcing and PFI industries, likewise, produce large multinational companies whose business models are unintelligible outside of particular public sector governance frameworks, as Lieberherr et al. discuss in Chapter 7. In health, the experience of markets without intensive governance has been somewhat dispiriting, for reasons well rehearsed by economists (Arrow 1963; Hammer 2003) starting with the information asymmetries that make governments, managers and especially patients unable to monitor professionals (Saltman et al. 2002).

The result is that markets in health have not just been intensely regulated in most countries. They have also frequently been the creatures of government. Insurance companies in the Dutch and Swiss systems, discussed by van Ginneken in Chapter 6, are tightly regulated and still have been distinctly unimpressive at cost control. Social health insurance systems such as the German one are even more tightly regulated; German health insurance funds are unable to compete on most things that a normal firm would, be it price, list of services, or price paid. The English NHS's market is almost entirely a creation of regulation and law – from the main purchasers, groups of doctors constituted by law, to the providers, most of which are publicly owned 'trusts', to the prices, which are set by the government, to the practice guidelines, set by NICE, there is almost nothing spontaneous. Like the Dutch financing market, the English provider market is what Rudolf Klein called a 'mimic market', a carefully engineered effort to make competitive pressures run in predesignated ways (Klein 1998; Greer 2016).

When governments relinquish direct control, and introduce profit motivations, they incur a variety of risks, and respond with tougher regulation to make the markets produce the 'right' answer. If the incentives cause unexpected results, itself often a failure of policy capacity or a flaw in the initial idea, then governments will often respond with still more regulation and changes to the incentives.

In other words, the working of markets in health depends on their governance. Even trying to manage the complexity of a system such as the Dutch or Swiss system requires a high level of investment in policy capacity. When working with private firms, such as the insurance companies in van Ginneken's Chapter 6, or the private infrastructure providers discussed in Chapter 7, it also requires a high level of integrity – both merit-based hiring policies geared to prevent corruption, and also strong and clear organizational missions so that regulators, HTA agencies and others can be clear about their purposes, as Williams makes clear in Chapter 8. Finally, accountability mechanisms must be clear, both so that regulators and purchasers are held accountable for good decisions, and so that private firms are accountable for something beyond their own commercial interests in their contracts, regulation and other mechanisms. As discussed below, it might also be simpler not to take on this particular governance challenge.

Regulation, in particular, is a challenge for health markets (Mossialos et al. 2001; Saltman et al. 2002). It can seem that we have either too much faith or too little faith in health regulation.

- *Too much*: The response of many policy-makers in different systems to a wide variety of problems, from poor quality to weak financial controls, has been the creation of new regulators and regulatory agencies (Majone 1994; Moran 2003). Introducing market mechanisms almost always comes with the introduction of regulators as older control mechanisms, such as professional associations or direct supervision by the health ministry, give way to semi-autonomous agencies whose job is to enforce good behaviour independently of politics.
- *Too little*: This use of regulators coexists with a firm, if often empirically unsubstantiated, conviction that regulators will eventually all be 'captured' by the regulated interests.[1] The free market liberal case for deregulation (one often echoed from the critical left) frequently starts with the argument that regulatory agencies are inevitably captured by their regulated sector, which generally has a more concentrated interest in the regulator than diffuse consumers, patients or people at large. The resulting assumption is that regulators will, rather than enabling the market, identify with the regulated industry incumbents, failing to curb rent-seeking and oligopolistic or monopolistic excesses while throwing up barriers to market entry and healthy competition.

This picture of regulatory politics is unattractive: global adoption of something that won't work. Unless we posit that policy-makers are deliberately creating dysfunctional, rent-seeking regulatory systems, a phenomenon that certainly exists, it is a paradox that needs to be addressed.

The solution to the paradox lies in the quality of governance, which the TAPIC framework can illuminate: the institutional design (accountability, integrity, participation and role) and policy capacity that can make a regulator an effective and rigorous part of a health system rather than an enabler of rent-seeking (Carpenter and Moss 2014). If the objective is to create a regulatory system that can turn more or less desirable private motivations into an effective force for health policy, then it is important that the regulatory process be transparent, that participation is both geared to information and useful for those who would challenge dominant interests, and that there are clear accountability mechanisms so decisions and their process are justified (Bianculli et al. 2015), strong integrity measures to prevent more or less sophisticated forms of corruption (including clear and public hiring guidelines and policies for controlling staff activities after they leave the organization), and capacity given to staff – not to consulting firms – capable of matching wits with regulated industries. Attention to those aspects of governance, and avoiding other governance problems such as defining participation uniquely to include industry or paying too little attention to subtler commercial influences (Adolph 2013), is likely to produce an effective and uncaptured regulator that can do its job well for the health system, public finances and society. The good news is that such effective regulators are plentiful; in many countries, there are established ways of creating effective agencies within local law and practice. The strength and effectiveness of regulators should largely be captured by the TAPIC framework, as we see in Chapter 9 by Cylus et al. and the similar situation of NICE, as discussed by Williams in Chapter 8.

Networks and coordination with society

Many policy areas, then, are too hard to address from the perspective of just one organization or sector. Health is a classic example: the causes of good and bad health spread across the whole of society. Even just within the public sector, effective health policy can involve schools, benefits systems, social work, police, labour regulation and environmental health. Public health advocates who point this out and try to influence all aspects of policy will generally be taken for dilettantes and disregarded by experts in other policy fields if they do not make a careful and politically sensitive approach (Fox 2003).

The term frequently used for this kind of intersectoral problem area is 'wicked issue'. A wicked issue involves a wide variety of policy areas and cannot be solved by one alone, and therefore involves coordinating among a variety of people and organizations with different interests, approaches and basic definitions of the problem (Rittel and Webber 1973). For example, serious mental illness among the homeless can be seen in quite different lights by a police officer, a psychiatrist and a social worker, let alone a variety of local politicians aware that the homeless rarely vote and are rarely popular. Addressing such wicked problems is widely regarded as a key task of governance, and failure to address them is a governance failure that can be remedied with approaches such as the 'whole of government' (Bevir 2012: 30–4).

In intergovernmental relations, discussed in Scott L. Greer's Chapter 10, coordination is particularly important and particularly difficult. In decentralized countries, resources, legal authority and money are dispersed among different units of government that each have their own priorities and interests. They are not accountable to each other in any simple way; as soon as a government has an electoral mandate of its own, that accountability must be considered and the tensions managed. Governance in such systems is therefore about managing tensions and multiple, conflicting, accountabilities, and making sure that needless conflict is avoided while channelling conflict. This means, among other things, transparency about intergovernmental relations, with broad outlines of legal authority, agreements and finances made as clear as possible. It also means investment in capacity (mostly meaning that officials are trained to understand federal issues), and participation of affected interests, which is especially an injunction against unilateral actions by a single government without discussion with other governments.

In the example of communicable disease control, very much a multi-level governance problem, complexity and cross-border coordination problems make the effective operation of networks crucial to transmitting the right kind of information, advice and resources, and compensating for inevitable gaps in capacity when there is an outbreak. This almost inevitably works through networks, as is implicitly recognized by the pattern that when countries reorganize their communicable disease control systems, they tend to create high-level agencies with scientific and technical resources that must work with a variety of local actors (Elliott et al. 2012; Greer 2012).

Public administration and organizations

Finally, there is an option that is still very popular in practice but often overlooked in practitioner and theoretical discussions of governance: running parts of a system directly, with public sector employees organized into hierarchies. There are two compelling reasons to do something directly with your own staff and resources (Coase 1937; Williamson 1981): flexibility and simplicity. Doing something directly is flexible because it does not require a contract, with all the delay and complexity and monitoring that can require. That is probably the reason that core communicable disease control capacity is usually public. Employees need to be available for whatever happens, and it is more efficient to have flexible permanent staff than to try to contract for different tasks during crises. Equally, the make versus buy calculus explains why so few organizations have their own in-house capacity for major construction projects. Since construction can be planned, it is better to buy construction when needed, benefit from competition among firms, and let them maintain the skills and equipment.

Doing something directly is also simpler: the costs of a transaction in contracting and monitoring can be very high and make demands on capacity and integrity that are not justified. A staff can produce other complexities, of course. Their accountability to the government that pays them can be limited by a variety of circumstances. Nevertheless, the reason to hire them is that doing something directly can still produce fewer demands on governance than other approaches. A national health service system has all the complexities of health care delivery, but at least has a simpler problem of market and financial governance than a more complex system.

Notwithstanding, public sector organizations have long histories of governance problems, often for obvious reasons. They can be too exposed to political influence and jobbery; or they can be too insulated from political oversight and, consequently, difficult to reform. Unlike dysfunctional firms in a market, they cannot simply fail and go out of business. Public organizations generally have a low mortality rate and governments are still more likely to persist. This persistence means that a public sector organization can stay dysfunctional for a long time if governance of that political regime does not create the kinds of accountability, transparency and participation mechanisms that allow leaders to force it to function and adapt well.

It is for that reason that so much governance research and writing focuses on the public sector: it produces such crucial goods for society, yet can be so difficult to discipline. The TAPIC framework, developed from literatures that often focus on the public sector, suggests a wide variety of tools to improve public sector resilience, performance and integrity; Chapter 3 discusses many of the practical actions policy-makers can take to improve public sector and organizational governance in pursuit of better and better-implemented policies for health.

What is most worth remembering here is that it can be tempting to focus on the governance problems of public sector organizations – such as rigid contracts that limit employee accountability, or weak capacity for policy-making and decision support, or lack of transparency about decisions – and become so frustrated as to want to simply replace public with private. While contracting for services from outside providers is often a good idea, simple privatization can replicate or exacerbate governance challenges. Private sector organizations are not immune to governance problems, and in fact are frequently less transparent and participatory than the public sector. In some areas, this might generate problems for service delivery. Contracting with them might seem like a way to avoid public sector governance problems, but it can put greater strain on public sector organizations. If a public sector organization's governance is too weak to build a building on time and on budget, why should we assume it will be strong enough to negotiate, implement and monitor a lengthy contract with a more capable contractor? The process of outsourcing and privatization, in fact, can increase opportunities for corruption by destabilizing existing integrity and accountability mechanisms. Privatization and public–private partnerships can cause a loss of accountability, transparency and participation without improving delivery, in large part because a market or a public private partnership, like a government agency, needs good governance to operate successfully.

From health systems governance to governance for health

The case studies in this book focus on the governance of health systems, but the issues in the TAPIC framework were by no means specific to health care systems. Governance of complex multi-sectoral issues such as food policy or accident prevention is even more complex than the governance of health systems (Barling et al. 2003; Bogdanor 2005). How does TAPIC apply, not just to governance of health systems, but to governance for health? This section outlines key ways in which the TAPIC governance framework sheds light on the policy challenges and solutions involved in producing intersectoral working and policies across multiple fields that support health.

Transparency

Transparency means that decisions, and their grounds, must be made clear. At a minimum, transparency means that health actors can identify the issues

Box 5.1 Lessons on transparency

- Inadequate communication of *clear and useful public information* on prices and insurance plans has been prohibitive to the facilitation of genuine health markets. Communication of prices, treatments and options has been subpar. Its impact is reflected in low rates of insured switching between providers, particularly in Switzerland (Chapter 6).
- Partners in PPPs may have different approaches to transparency. While public policy-makers seek to deliver *clear and useful public information*, private partners are focused on confidentiality, which gives them a competitive advantage but leaves citizens – and sometimes the policy-makers – in the dark (Chapter 7).
- NICE is often presented as an example for adequate transparency. It exercises *regular reporting* on its processes and decisions. NICE has used its website to disseminate *clear and useful public information*. It has emphasized the usage of Quality Adjusted Life Years (QALYs) in order to underline its evidence-based approach to decision-making (Chapter 8).
- External reference pricing (ERP) poses challenges to transparency in the pharmaceutical sector. *Regular reporting* on prices in other countries keeps third-party payers and consumers informed about the price they are paying, while it allows manufacturers to manipulate the prices in multiple systems at once (Chapter 9).
- Decreased transparency reduces actors' observability, it also benefits the latter, since it considerably impedes *performance managing/ reporting/assessment*. Thus, decreased transparency can allow or even encourage malpractice, corruption and bad governance in areas such as issues in the workforce, research, systems for allocating organs for transplants, and communicable disease control (Chapter 10).
- Lack of transparency during austerity could be interpreted as an indicator of malpractice. In the absence of *watchdog committees*, the population has no idea whether cost-cutting measures serve the interest of the public or of private actors. Coupled with deteriorating health care delivery, this can further erode public trust (Chapter 11).
- At health system level, a lack of *clear and useful public information* diminishes public trust in health care reform. Conflated with public fear of corruption and poor reform, loss of confidence in reform can seriously impede successful institutional reorganization (Chapter 12).

with which they must engage, and the areas where their arguments and evidence might work or meet with resistance. Transparency can also be employed against health, by delaying the inevitable moment of decision when there is political decision and discretion, so it is important that a demand for transparency does not result in sharing all the details of a decision-making process, or be able to challenge it. It is in nobody's interest to have policy-making grind to a halt, become biased towards well-resourced lobbies that can exploit 'transparent' procedures, or be pushed into the realm of winks, nods and poorly minuted meetings.

In health terms, transparency can make it clear when decisions are being made for or against health, and on good or weak health grounds. If it is clear, for example, how health and other public facilities are cited, and when a decision is being made, then it is possible to start combatting a tendency to locate hospitals on remote sites on the edge of town where the financial savings to the health system come at a cost of health accessibility. If it is clear when governments are meeting with industry representatives, then it is possible to document biases in public health policy-making (this is a particularly big issue in tobacco control). If examination of the grounds for decisions make it clear that health is not part of the decision-making process in a government agency, then it is possible to make that agency a target for mobilization, advocacy and political action.

Accountability

In principle, anybody responsible for financing health services has an interest in investing in good public health because prevention is typically much cheaper than cure. In practice, even those convinced of the benefits of prevention policies are often under budgetary and political pressure to focus on delivering health services.

Shifting accountability so that it promotes health across different sectors is both technically and politically difficult. Political difficulty, as usual, is a greater obstacle than technical difficulty. Politically, the problem is that key services, starting with health care but extending to all the other fields that shape health, already have their accountabilities. How are they to be made accountable for the protection and promotion of health when they are already accountable for something else? There are established techniques in most governments (McQueen et al. 2012; Greer and Lillvis 2014) such as coalition agreements, personnel changes, legislation, targets, plans, ministerial briefings, data reports, regular briefings to top ministers, budget plans, ministerial reorganizations, and interdepartmental committees and units.

Frequently, the problem lies in ensuring their immediate effectiveness – is there a demand for explanation backed by a sanction? – and then perpetuating it over time when there are different ministers and governments. The solution that policy-makers have frequently adopted is to change governance (McQueen et al. 2012). Directly, health can be promoted by entrenching it in administrative procedures. This means legislating health targets and regular updates (so it is clear who is accountable for hitting them), shaping legal 'proportionality' tests to incorporate the benefits of health (Jarman 2014), putting health ministries on the relevant committees, making budgets conditional on health targets, creating specific agencies and even merging or unmerging departments. There is promise in more ambitious ideas – health benefits could be incorporated into government accounting and budgeting processes, or health impact assessment made obligatory. These all try to entrench health in bureaucratic procedures.

Indirectly, the commitment to health can be aided by creating outside accountability, to people with health in mind. Public data releases, formal consultation procedures (if well managed, as per Chapter 3), and opportunities to challenge decisions in by ombudsmen or even in legal procedures are all ways to empower civil society. They can be, and frequently are, designed to empower business or other interests, but they can also work for health.

Direct measures make government internally accountable for health; indirect measures make it easier for outsiders with a concern for health to hold government to account for its actions. Both can be manipulated, but formally, and by appointment, governments can empower their health advocates to work across sectors (Greer and Lillvis 2014). Establishing accountability for health is crucial, but hard.

Box 5.2 Lessons on accountability

- When introducing provider and payer competition, *organizational separation* has significant consequences for ensuring accountability. A steep vertical separation between the actors can prevent effective communication of goals (as is the case in Switzerland), whereas operational proximity between the two can have adverse effects on codes of conduct (as is the case in the Netherlands) (Chapter 6).
- An example of a proper organizational separation with strong lines of accountabilities is the National Institute for Health and Care Excellence (NICE). NICE benefits from a clear *organizational separation* from the national government, but also from local implementing bodies. It has been subject to Audit Commission as well as House of Commons reviews, and its accountability record has been acknowledged (Chapter 8).
- Having said this, even very well-designed accountability relationships do not prevent conflict of values. Speeding up approval of new pharmaceuticals is crucial to suffering patients, but it also poses the threat of *conflict of interest*. Pharmaceutical companies in Mexico benefit from quicker approval of new medications, but impoverished patients don't. Incentives for faster approvals must above all seek to benefit the patients in order to avoid conflict of interests (Chapter 9).
- It is crucial to think about the mechanism for aligning interests. The case study on private finance initiative (PFI) illustrates how *conflict of interest policies* and unclear *contracts* can reduce accountability. Underspecified, lengthy contracts allow blame to be shifted between partners. And conflicts of interest are bound to occur, since public

authorities are interested in providing a service, whereas private actors primarily seek to make a profit (Chapter 7).

- *Delegated regulation* between federal and subfederal actors (in decentralized systems) raises intricate issues of accountability for the regional actors. If the central government's priorities differ from those of the regional population, regional actors find themselves facing a difficult situation. This has been the experience in Scotland and many Spanish regions (Chapter 10).
- This lesson is underlined by the critical role accountability relationships played in the economic and financial crisis. International *financial mechanisms* such as bailout agreements, required national health systems to cut costs, while the population expected them to maintain health care delivery. In this situation, national authorities must either cut benefits or deliver health care more efficiently. These two options represent their dual accountability to both international lenders, but also the domestic population. Chapter 11 provides an analysis of failing but also of solid accountability relationships.
- When undertaking a fundamental restructuring of the health care system, *laws that specify objectives, reporting and mechanisms* are crucial for the establishment of chains of accountability. If the former are not clearly stated, then tools, goals and effects dissipate, as they have in Bosnia (Chapter 12).

Participation

Participation is possibly the biggest challenge to governance for health. The basic reason is that shaping governance for health involves changing established policies and priorities in other fields, as diverse as urban planning, transport policy, food policy, education policy and, possibly most important, fiscal policy (White 2013). In each policy area there is likely to be an established set of players with their objectives – be they balanced budgets, rapid automobile travel or high mathematics test scores – and it is to be expected that they will not always appreciate an intervention by health specialists who will almost automatically look like amateurs in the field. Every item in the budget might affect health, but it would be unsound to draw the conclusion that everybody wants to think of themselves as doing health policy.

The question of why others should listen to health expertise and care about health issues, instead of their own politically validated goals and constituencies, is a question of participation. How can we engineer participation to produce a bias towards health? An Observatory study of relevant governance structures (McQueen et al. 2012) frequently focused on participation as a route to shaping decisions. One simple one is interdepartmental committees. At the bureaucratic level, many governments have a practice of formalized consultation between ministries; health ministries and health ministers should, if they do not already, strive to be on, and contribute to the work of, these committees (even at a price in political capital, budget or capacity). That is participation. Likewise, engagement with the public and civil society can be engineered to promote health; the wide variety of consultation mechanisms discussed by Lillvis and Greer in Chapter 3 can shape the extent of participation by those concerned with health. At the EU level, likewise, the formation of different consultative bodies have variable benefits for policy advocates inside and outside the EU institutions (Jarman 2011).

Box 5.3 Lessons on participation

- Lack of stakeholder forums and *consultations* has alienated insurers and providers in both Switzerland and the Netherlands. Decreased communications with stakeholders made the goals of reform politically sound, but empirically uncertain (Chapter 6).
- In Germany, there were no *consultations* of parliamentarians and civil actors. As a result, the greatest impediment to the Berlin Waterworks has been public disapproval, negative media coverage and an organized effort for the re-municipalization of the Waterworks (Chapter 7).
- NICE exemplifies *democratic innovations*, which has kept diverse actors involved, but has also underlined the difficulty in democratically negotiated agendas. The issue of research and resource allocation becomes ever more contested, as more participants are involved (Chapter 8).
- Avoiding *stakeholder forums* in pharmaceutical price negotiations benefits manufacturers at the expense of the patients. Public authorities should stand to gain efficiency, but they risk alienating the patients and isolating themselves (Chapter 9).
- In general, participation benefits good governance since it increases the input from concerned parties. There are, however, areas of high-level expertise (i.e., disease-specific surveillance networks) where *advisory committees* of technocrats constitute a better mode of governance than broad committees which include parties that have little to contribute but delay (Chapter 10).
- In the course of austerity measures, decision-makers face a difficult choice between involving patient organizations and the general public in policy-making. *Consultations* will involve social actors more actively, but it will also stall the process, which could agitate international partners looking for quick results (Chapter 11).
- Resource-poor systems, such as in Bosnia, can rely on international *partnerships* for support during fundamental institutional reorganization. Said support could, however, be heavily dependent on results, which accentuates efficient reform over local players' input. This could disenfranchise domestic actors (Chapter 12).
- Participation is not exhausted with the *consultations* of civil actors or patient organizations only. Involving practitioners and employees in the management of French health care providers has been an excellent way of including those most interested in the proper functioning of providers (Chapter 13).

Integrity

Integrity is a keystone of any effective policy, and that includes health policies and policies for health. It can be a charter for unlimited bureaucracy, but unless hiring and day-to-day operations restrain corruption and promote effectiveness, policies for health are often going to suffer. Integrity does not just mean anti-corruption measures, though they can be important (e.g., for highway safety, or programmes for disadvantaged populations who cannot always protect budgets

Box 5.4 Lessons on integrity

- The reorganization of public services, such as health care, along mar-ket principles, such as competition and efficiency, puts stakeholders' integrity into question. In Switzerland and the Netherlands, internal audits, but also *clear organizational roles and purposes* have been crucial in the context of market-oriented reforms (Chapter 6).
- In the case of the Berlin Waterworks, integrity was particularly under-mined due to the lack of distinction between public and private actors, specifically with regards to the role of the Senate. The absence of *clear organizational roles and purposes* resulted in an unconstitutional effectuation of the interest rate (Chapter 7).
- Lack of clear *legislative mandate* to address new developments in pharmaceutics (e.g., internet sales) threatens the integrity of national authorities. The necessity for further regulation of new forms of phar-maceutical fraud is endemically higher in low- and mid-income sys-tems, where the demand for cheaper drugs is higher (Chapter 9).
- Delegating the *legislative mandate* to regional actors in federal poli-ties does not automatically guarantee an increase in integrity. A pro-liferation of political levels/actors decreases concentration of power, but without a proper system of checks and balances it does nothing to increase integrity (Chapter 10).
- The abolition of established *procedures* could enhance the quicker effectuation of cost-cutting measures. Cutting corners, however is likely to be unpopular with the population, and risks alienating already unpopular decision-makers (Chapter 11).
- Public authorities' integrity in the course of reform processes in ethnic-ally mixed regions depends intrinsically on *clear organizational roles and purposes*. Where reforms are coordinated with international part-ners, the communication of clear roles and purposes is further compli-cated, as seen in Bosnia (Chapter 12).
- In Italy, the importance of *well-rewarded internal career trajectories* hindered the successful implementation of Clinical Directorates (CDs). Although CDs aimed at increasing accountability by closely involv-ing practitioners in the management of hospitals, the ill-defined pro-fessional prospects for participating in CDs disincentivized doctors (Chapter 13).

destined to help them). It also means a sense of mission and organizational coherence in each of the different parts of the system that can allow them to be more effective actors. This is both a management challenge, and a necessary part of any high-functioning system, since corruption saps organizational effectiveness.

In the specific case of broad public health and health in all policies, integrity matters because it affects the ability of government to take actions with costs

Box 5.5 Lessons on capacity

- In every reform, *intelligence on performance* and *process*, but also *research/analysis* capacity are going to condition the outcome. Policy capacity was concentrated in the centralized, arm's-length agencies in the Netherlands, whereas it was dispersed in the multi-level Swiss polity (Chapter 6).
- In the absence of domestic policy capacity, national bureaucracies may rely on international partners. However, in the case of Bosnia, poor decisions outsourced too many national competencies to international actors, who failed to factor in domestic particularities. This questions the applicability of international practices to the domestic environment (Chapter 12).
- In the United Kingdom, public authorities' lack of capacity with regards to PPPs has resulted in a competitive disadvantage during negotiations with their private partners. This shortcoming has decreased the government's ability to evaluate contracts and to find the most appropriate partners (Chapter 7).
- Finding adequate responses to the financial and economic crisis vis-à-vis the international lenders requires a lot of policy capacity. The productivity of agencies is dependent on the availability of properly *trained staff*. A greater division of tasks and competences between agencies must also be reflected in an appropriate allocation of human resources, otherwise the agencies would be overwhelmed, as is seen in the case of Greek ERP bodies (Chapter 9).
- One way to increase policy capacity is illustrated by the experiences from the United States Centers for Disease Control and Prevention, the French Institut de Veille Sanitaire, and the Dutch RIVM. In communicable diseases, policy capacity was drastically increased by *research/analysis* capacity in multiple fields concentrated in one agency where know-how and expertise can be shared between different experts (Chapter 10).
- The input of seasoned national bureaucrats who are acquainted with domestic institutional and legislative idiosyncrasies is critical. This is a lesson to be drawn from countries confronted with demands for austerity policies. *Procedures* to incorporate specialist advice are central to adopting and implementing successful austerity measures (Chapter 11).
- Greater emphasis needs to be placed on *intelligence on process* in health care providers. The successful execution of reform can benefit from an in-house driven reorganization effort, as it was in French hospitals (Chapter 13).

for economic actors and benefits for public health. Governments with short-term political appointees at the top are likely to lack integrity because those appointees are prone to reward their superiors, do favours for their potential future employers, and even profit from their position while they are in it. All of those are avenues for influence by monied interests who might not support public health policy.

Box 5.6 Road traffic accidents: an example

Road traffic accidents might make a very good indicator of governance.[2] Rather than focusing on process indicators such as hiring procedures or formal transparency, we can look at indicators of the outputs of governance, and road traffic accidents are a case with obvious health implications. It is no accident that Sweden, for example, is targeting zero road deaths while some other countries with weaker governance have extremely dangerous roads. Road safety comes about from a complex set of decisions by many actors, on different levels of government, with different backgrounds, and with different capacities and priorities. Aligning them on road safety is a governance achievement.

The TAPIC framework can show how. Transparency and capacity produce public data, which can enable a push for better road safety. For example, collecting information on accidents and mapping particularly dangerous areas can engage the public to participate while clarifying the kinds of problems that should be addressed. But data is not enough. The intersection of people, communities, cars, bicycles, laws, infrastructure and politics is extremely complex. Identifying good practice, developing good designs and policies, making legal changes, and encouraging and monitoring local actions all demand capacity. Accountability of highway agencies for safety, whether to local communities or to a well-informed central body, can lead to effective pressure to build safer roads – local communities often dislike dangerous intersections, and central agencies can target places and practices where road deaths are common. Accountability can be written into budgeting priorities, legislation and evaluation for road building agencies or co-financing schemes for roads, while transparency about road accidents can mobilize accountability to local voters. Integrity feeds into the ability to implement, both in terms of anti-corruption and in terms of a sense of job and mission (since the construction sector is famous for neither probity nor decisiveness). Strong and capable planning and contracting staff matter here, as do post-facto ombudsmen procedures, whistleblowers, an audit, an inspectorate and legal mechanisms to punish wrongdoing (e.g., substandard materials) and thereby discourage it in the future. Capacity also matters for writing codes on road design and meaningful vehicle maintenance; both can be powerful forces for safety or powerful forces for bureaucratic inertia or rent-seeking by road builders and mechanics.

Capacity

Finally, capacity matters. In a well-functioning government that wants to improve public health across fields, it might be one of the most important parts of health in all policies because understanding and participating effectively in broad policy-making is hard. Capacity means identifying opportunities to have an impact. It means having good arguments for sceptical budget-makers and people interested in other fields, including the ability to harness data and the ability to perceive and understand their interest group and partisan politics. It means having a sense of mission in the organization that aligns with its actual activities, and people with the requisite technical and political skills to participate in discussions across sectors.

Capacity does not mean the abstract ability to list ways other sectors could save the health system some money. That is both the easiest and the least effective thing to do.

Governance lessons

Governance shapes decisions and determines whether the decisions matter. It is set up to include or exclude people, to make some things easier and some things harder, to prioritize health or something else, and to prioritize the short or the long term. It makes some people accountable for specific goals, possible or not, and frees others from accountability.

Governance is about conflict management but it is not politics because it is about structures. It is about going beyond leadership and political will to shape the fates of future policy ideas – by building capable bureaucracies, setting rules of the game and entrenching specific patterns of policy-making, consultation and alignment. Long ago, governments set up agriculture ministries and patterns of engagement with farmers to protect the interests of large farming populations, large landowners and wartime food supplies. The existence of those ministries has shaped all subsequent food policies even as the power of those reasons dwindled. Long ago, the profession of public health was directed by donors towards laboratory science and microbiology rather than health systems or sanitary engineering (Fee 1987). Even if we now know that many victories for public health were won by health or water systems, the legacy in the form of a scientific focus in public health remains. So what governance decisions are we taking now that shape policy options for the future?

These lessons come from the literature review and case studies in this book;[3] they are aimed at anybody charged with policy issues that have a governance component. TAPIC is diagnostic and prognostic; it is about identifying governance problems in an area, as outlined in Chapter 2.

Governance matters

Each of the case studies shows the importance of governance, whether in performing vital functions such as communicable disease control and pharmaceutical safety managing complex interfaces between industry and medicine such as HTA, private insurance and PFI; or pushing forward important health policies such as hospital reform, primary care reform, or austerity. In each case the success or failure of intelligent-sounding policies rested substantially on governance, which can be clearly seen using the TAPIC framework. It is all too tempting as a policy-maker to focus on the idea without thinking about the machinery of government, or to underinvest in governance, or to see it as a set of bureaucratic impediments rather than see its potential benefits. But improving governance can be rewarding – and ignoring it can be dangerous to health systems and policies.

Choose policies appropriate to your system governance

There is a long history in health policies of inappropriate policy ideas being sold and sometimes adopted: overly complex policies, overly expensive policies or simply irrelevant policies are adopted and fail with greater or lesser consequences in the implementation (Vian and Bicknell 2013). Some policies require better governance than others. Policies with large amounts of money at stake, high levels of complexity, and clashing interests and incentives such as PFIs or insurance regulation are policies where there is a real risk of governance failing, and producing problems such as the Berlin water infrastructure PFI discussed in Chapter 7. We can call this governance risk: the extent that a policy depends on strongly and appropriately developed governance. It is highest for the most complex, indirect and networked policies with the least trust and highest stakes. It presents a case for simple policies that might be less elegant on paper but more likely to work in practice (also King and Crewe 2013: 221).

The solution to some of those policies might be to avoid them. There are other ways to finance infrastructure without a PFI, and few health systems try to produce universal coverage through private insurance mandates. Simpler policies than tax governance less might be wise. Dutch and Swiss finance, and English and German infrastructure PFIs are not unqualified successes; any government that suspects it has weaker governance than England, Germany, the Netherlands and Switzerland should proceed very carefully in deciding to choose policies so vulnerable to governance failures when there are simpler alternatives available. Simple policies that make less demand on governance might be recommended for all systems.

There are, however, some policies that are unavoidable – for example, licensing and purchasing pharmaceuticals and medical devices. Pharmaceuticals and medical devices have non-linear rewards (there is a huge difference between being licensed and listed for reimbursement, and not being licensed and listed), large amounts of money at stake, large companies with abundant resources of every kind, and a level of complexity unmanageable by few people. In other words, they are high-risk for governance, with a variety of obvious challenges to governance and high stakes (e.g., scandals) if the governance fails and an inappropriate or dangerous product enters the market. They are also unavoidable; modern health care needs medicines and devices. Consequently, the implication is that these areas should be intensively monitored, with high demands for transparency, constant use of strong accountability mechanisms by public authorities, and careful watch over participation to avoid domination of participation mechanisms by pro-industry interests that might bias decisions.

Governance is in the specifics

Governance as a word has too often been a synonym for haziness: an amalgam of government and avoidance, as John Kenneth Galbraith put it.[4] But useful thinking about governance is very practical: how should some component of governance be adopted and operate in a given circumstance? Chapter 3 reviews a wide variety of administrative and governance reforms and policies that strive towards better governance, and Chapter 4 complements it by showing the problems in broad-brush measures of accountability.

It is not enough, for example, to say that a medicines regulator, HTA agency, or even government is accountable 'to the people'. That is a moral objective rather than a practical statement about governance. Accountability happens through specific mechanisms: a regulatory agency can have an appointed board, be required to report to a legislature that oversees it and be subject to judicial review. Anybody can claim to be accountable to the public; the practical issue is to whom an actor must be accountable and how. Likewise, participation is a complex issue, with Chapter 3 listing mechanisms as diverse as consultations, polls and direct elections.

In short, it is not enough to have generic governance assessments. Rather it is better to focus on issues, problems and governance failures individually. Generic governance assessments all too often lead to generic policy implications. Therefore, we suggest using the TAPIC framework to assess a system from a problem-based starting point. That leads to the last point: governance is for a reason.

'Good governance' is not an end in itself

Governance can all too often seem like a panacea, but it is better to recognize it as tool. It is, at the broadest, one of the more effective tools for development and the preservation of a strong and effective health system (especially over time). Transparency, accountability, participation, integrity and capacity are components of the rule of law and effective policies that make for human and economic development. Likewise, even if spectacular feats have been achieved by regimes that impressed nobody with their participation, accountability or integrity, the money spent on bribes and ineptitude could still have been better spent. Stronger TAPIC measures generally promote a mixture of efficiency, resilience and effectiveness, and their effect seems to grow over time compared to regimes that do not incorporate them.

But there are two reasons why governance, beyond minimal order, is not an end in itself. First, it is all too easy to turn good governance into 'good-looking governance'.[5] Governance reform can become an arid, formalistic, box-ticking exercise, with formal budgeting or hiring or purchasing planning processes in law that have no bearing on reality, or formal markets and relationships between organizations that do not resemble the empirical reality (Andrews 2013).

Second, governance is also about mobilizing bias: designing institutions and procedures to shape policy decisions and implementation. A perfect case of this mobilization of bias in governance is in the Framework Convention on Tobacco Control (FCTC). Among its other provisions, the FCTC severely restricts government contact with the tobacco industry. In other words, it shapes participation so as to exclude the tobacco industry from tobacco control policy-making. That is because tobacco industry participation in tobacco control policy-making is antithetical to the narrow objectives of tobacco control and to the broader goal of health. Is it bad governance to thus restrict governance? No, it is good governance for health.

That is why governance is something that needs to be context-specific and oriented towards choosing and implementing good health policies. As the chapters in Part II show, governance has influenced a wide range of policies, including responses to the financial crisis and austerity.

Conclusion

At a presentation of this book's framework, a senior health policy-maker sketched out a problem: in one country, the chair of the parliamentary health committee also owned a large pharmaceutical business selling to the health sector, with predictable effects. What could this framework contribute to the solution of his problem?

The answer is simple: this book's framework, literature review and case studies supply the evidence that such a conflict of interest (a problem of accountability and integrity) is almost certainly undermining the ability of that health system to provide health for all. Perhaps the price for changing the situation, counted in lost opportunities for better health, is not worth paying. But the evidence we marshal here is that appropriate and extensive transparency, accountability, participation, integrity and capacity contribute to better health systems. The social sciences are notoriously inexact because all activity is ultimately local and everything is done by people with their own, complex motivations and ideas, but the five attributes we discuss here are building blocks of all health systems and can be used to make them better.

Notes

1   As Carpenter (2010) points out, an enormous body of literature assuming that regulators will be captured by the regulated, and turn into an instrument of rent seeking, sits on the improbable empirical base of a few, poorly executed, studies of US transport regulation in the 1970s. The political forces supporting this anti-regulatory focus in Chicago School economics are explored by Teles (2008). Edward Page's (2010) empirical work on policy-making in Europe likewise finds that worry about capture and bureaucratic self-interest is overstated; government officials tend to define their jobs

as service, which is unsurprising in systems with a reasonable level of integrity and accountability.
2   As pointed out by Matthew Andrews. See: http://matthewandrews.typepad.com/the_limits_of_institution/2013/11/ideas-for-post-2015-governance-indicators-focus-on-state-capability-or-governance-gaps.html.
3   Compare with the consonant conclusions of Charron et al. (2013).
4   Daniel M. Fox, personal communication, August 2014.
5   See Matthew Andrews, http://matthewandrews.typepad.com/mattandrews/2013/05/good-or-good-looking-governance-that-is-the-question.html.

References

Adolph, Christopher (2013) *Bankers, Bureaucrats, and Central Bank Politics: The Myth of Neutrality.* Cambridge: Cambridge University Press.

Andrews, Matt (2013) *The Limits of Institutional Reform in Development.* Cambridge: Cambridge University Press.

Arrow, Kenneth (1963) Uncertainty and the welfare economics of medical care, *American Economic Review,* 53(5): 941–73.

Barling, David, Lang, Tim and Caraher, Martin (2003) Joined-up food policy? The trials of governance, public policy and the food system, *Social Policy & Administration,* 36: 556–74.

Bevir, Mark (2012) *Governance: A Very Short Introduction.* Oxford: Oxford University Press.

Bianculli, Andrea, Fernàndez-i-Maròn, Xavier and Jordana, Jacint (2015) *Accountability and Regulatory Governance: Audiences, Controls and Responsibilities in the Politics of Regulation.* Basingstoke: Palgrave Macmillan.

Bogdanor, Vernon (ed.) (2005) *Joined-up Government.* Oxford: British Academy/Oxford University Press.

Carpenter, Daniel (2010) Confidence games: how does regulation constitute markets? in Edward J. Balleisen and David A. Moss (eds) *Government and Markets.* Cambridge: Cambridge University Press, pp. 164–90.

Carpenter, Daniel and Moss, David A. (eds) (2014) *Preventing Regulatory Capture.* Cambridge: Cambridge University Press.

Charron, Nicholas, Rothstein, Bo and Lapuente Gine, Victor (2013) *Quality of Government and Corruption from a European Perspective: A Comparative Study of Good Government in EU Regions.* Cheltenham: Edward Elgar.

Coase, Ronald H. (1937) The nature of the firm, *Economica,* 4(16): 386–405.

Elliott, Heather, Jones, David K. and Greer, Scott L. (2012) Mapping infectious disease control in the European Union, *Journal of Health Politics, Policy, and Law,* 37(6): 935–54.

Fee, Elizabeth (1987) *Disease and Discovery: A History of the Johns Hopkins School of Hygiene and Public Health, 1916–1939.* Baltimore, MD: Johns Hopkins University Press.

Fox, Daniel M. (2003) Population and the law: the changing scope of health policy, *Journal of Law, Medicine and Ethics,* 31: 607–14.

Greer, Scott L. (2012) The European Centre for Disease Prevention and Control: hub or hollow core? *Journal of Health Politics, Policy, and Law,* 37(6): 1001–30.

Greer, Scott L. (2016) Claiming authority over the English NHS, in Mark Bevir and R. A. W. Rhodes (eds) *Governance in Modern Britain.* London: Routledge.

Greer, Scott L. and Lillvis, Denise F. (2014) Beyond leadership: political strategies for coordination in health policies, *Health Policy,* 116(1): 12–17.

Hammer, Peter J. (ed.) (2003) *Uncertain Times: Kenneth Arrow and the Changing Economics of Health Care.* Durham, NC: Duke University Press.

Jarman, Holly (2011) Collaboration and consultation: functional representation in EU stakeholder dialogues, *Journal of European Integration*, 33(4): 385–99.

Jarman, Holly (2014) *The Politics of Trade and Tobacco Control*. Basingstoke: Palgrave Macmillan.

King, Anthony and Crewe, Ivor (2013) *The Blunders of Our Governments*. London: Oneworld.

Klein, Rudolf (1998) Self-inventing institutions: institutional design and the UK welfare state, in Robert E. Goodin (ed.) *The Theory of Institutional Design*. Cambridge: Cambridge University Press, pp. 240–55.

Majone, Giandomenico (1994) The rise of the regulatory state in Europe, *West European Politics*, 17(3): 77–102.

McQueen, David, Wismar, Matthias, Lin, Vivian, Jones, Catherine, St-Pierre, Louise and Davies, Maggie (eds) (2012) *Inter-sectoral Governance for Health in All Policies: Structures, Actions and Experiences*. Copenhagen: WHO Regional Office for European behalf of the European Observatory on Health Systems and Policies.

Moran, Michael (2003) *The British Regulatory State*. Oxford: Oxford University Press.

Mossialos, Elias, Mrazek, Monique and Walley, Tom (eds) (2001) *Regulating Pharmaceuticals in Europe*. Maidenhead: Open University Press.

Page, Edward C. (2010) Accountability as a bureaucratic minefield: lessons from a comparative study, *West European Politics*, 33(5): 1010–29.

Polanyi, Karl (1944) *The Great Transformation: The Political and Economic Origins of Our Time*. Boston: Beacon.

Rittel, Horst W. J. and Webber, Melvin M. (1973) Dilemmas in a general theory of planning, *Policy Sciences*, 4(2): 155–69.

Saltman, R. B., Busse, R. and Mossialos, E. (2002) *Regulating Entrepreneurial Behaviour in European Health Care Systems*. Maidenhead: Open University Press.

Teles, Steven M. (2008) *The Rise of the Conservative Legal Movement*. Princeton, NJ: Princeton University Press.

Vian, Taryn and Bicknell, William J. (2013) Good governance and budget reform in Lesotho Public Hospitals: performance, root causes and reality, *Health Policy and Planning*, 1–12.

White, Joseph (2013) Budget-makers and health care systems, *Health Policy*, 112(3): 163–71.

Williamson, Oliver (1981) The economics of organization: the transaction cost approach, *American Journal of Sociology*, 87(3): 548–77.

Part II

Sectoral case studies on health system governance

chapter

Governing competitive insurance market reform: case studies from the Netherlands and Switzerland

Ewout van Ginneken

Introduction: what is the policy?

Insurance competition is seen as a tool to improve efficiency in health care. In the European Union, several countries rely on insurance competition. These include Belgium, the Czech Republic, Germany, the Netherlands, Slovakia and Switzerland. All of these countries have systems that allow people to choose periodically among risk-bearing insurance funds (Van de Ven et al. 2013). In theory, health insurance competition can improve efficiency in administration and delivery: (1) if there is free consumer mobility between funds; (2) if insurers do not have incentives to select risks; and (3) if insurers are able to influence (and thus compete on) health service costs and quality (Thomson et al. 2013). The latter implies that insurance competition is not limited to the insurance market, but that also important supporting reforms in the health care purchasing market are needed that give insurers the tools to influence cost (e.g., selective contracting, negotiation on prices, contracting).

Introducing insurance competition frequently enters the political debate in many other European countries as well – often depending on which political parties are in power. Its appeal is understandable. It promises an efficient system based on competition, more consumer choice and innovation, a focus on quality and cost, combined with a smaller role for government. This chapter will focus on Switzerland and the Netherlands because these countries have been more explicit about pursuing competition in the system and went a step further in that they offer choices among private insurers (which in the Netherlands may make profits) and allow insurers to compete on premium level.[1] In both countries, establishing insurance competition through the introduction of 'managed competition' or 'consumer-driven health care' was expected to produce stronger insurers that could pressurize providers to be efficient and thereby slow the growth in health care spending. Other broad goals of the reforms were equity of access and solidarity.

This chapter will explore the Dutch and Swiss experiences regarding insurer competition and whether they have achieved their stated goals. Next, the chapter analyses the role that governance has played in some of its failures and problems before finishing with formulating some broad lessons for governance from these case studies.

Outcome of reforms: still work in progress

It is hard to define an outcome, because it can be argued that the reforms necessary to make insurance competition work, at least according to theory, are ongoing – even though reforms started in 1996 in Switzerland and 2006 in the Netherlands. The subsequent steps of establishing competition in the health care purchasing market – i.e., giving the insurers tools to influence the cost and quality of purchased care – is still work in progress in both countries. It is legitimate, however, to assess these reforms on their accomplishment as of today. This is especially relevant because some of the reasons behind the lack of progress directly relate to the nature of the reforms – i.e., their technical and political complexity and sometimes infeasibility. In the Netherlands, there is general agreement that the reforms are half of what they could be, but this also prompted an academic discussion as to whether the bottle is half-full or half-empty (Maarse and Paulus 2011; Bal and Zuiderent-Jerak 2011; Schut and Van de Ven 2011). It should be noted that the analysis below focuses on the broad goals of the reforms and not on several lower-level negative or positive outcomes.

Switzerland

The Swiss reform aimed to enhance equity of access to health insurance, to strengthen solidarity and to create incentives for organizational innovation and expenditure control (Thomson et al. 2013). Since 1996, Switzerland has required its residents to purchase and select one of the insurance policies sold in their canton (region) of residence. Every insurer can offer several 'basic' plans with standardized benefits; premiums are lower for plans with higher deductibles and managed care plans. Insurers may not reject applicants or earn profits on the basic plans. Premiums must be community-rated within cantons and may be adjusted for three age categories, but the insurer can charge different premiums for the same plan in other cantons. The cantons pay tax subsidies to compensate for those with lower incomes (OECD/WHO 2011; Van Ginneken et al. 2013).
On the whole, the aims of the reforms have not been met:

- Large premium differences within and between cantons threaten the equity of access. There is substantial variation in premiums across cantons because of differences in population health risks and provider costs among the cantons (Leu et al. 2009). What is more, premiums for the same basic plans also vary greatly within cantons. This is mainly caused by the rather crude risk adjustment system (which has been improved as per 2012). The federation expected that premium differences would slowly even out through converging risk pools because the insured are allowed to switch policies biannually.

However, switching rates have been relatively low – only 3–5 per cent per year (OECD/WHO 2011), although rates seem to have gone up recently (Okma and Crivelli 2013). One explanation for why few people switch insurers is that their willingness to switch plans declines while choices offered to individuals grows (Frank and Lamiraud 2009). Another is that people fear that their supplemental plan could become unaffordable if they have health problems but decide to opt for a different insurer for their basic plan (Kreier and Zweifel 2010; Beck 2011).

- Rising numbers of uninsured and defaulters have at times threatened equity of access to care. As the Swiss became individually responsible for selecting a policy and paying a monthly premium, and as premiums increased, the number of uninsured people increased. At the same time, the number of defaulters also rose. The Swiss federal government reacted in 2006 by allowing insurers to suspend people's coverage until they had paid their outstanding premiums. Yet the number of premium defaulters continued to grow, reaching 4.3 per cent of the population in some cantons (Crivelli 2010). The majority of defaulters had insufficient incomes to pay the premiums, but their incomes had been incorrectly estimated to be so high that they were ineligible for subsidies. After three years of debate, in January 2012 cantons began paying insurers 85 per cent of unpaid premiums on behalf of people with serious financial problems (OECD/WHO 2011).
- The system also did not provide a spur for organizational innovation. A growing number of insured individuals chose managed care products – such as physicians' networks, HMOs and call centres performing a triage function. Yet they have not had a major impact on the health system today. It is likely that managed care contracts are being underutilized by insurers to deliver innovative care approaches and drive improvements in the quality of care (OECD/WHO 2011). One explanation is that managed care contracts are known to attract people with good health for which innovative approaches would bring limited financial rewards for the insurer. Healthy individuals are more willing to opt for managed care plans than high risk individuals who have been reluctant to accept limitations in provider choice. Furthermore, they fear that access to needed health care would be rationed and lack confidence in managed care's ability to offer better quality care for those with substantial health needs or multiple chronic conditions. This development may further divide the insurance market according to health status and risks (OECD/WHO 2011). Moreover, since the risk adjustment formula continues to be relatively crude, health insurers miss an incentive to develop better disease and care management programmes. They fear attracting patients with chronic conditions for whom adequate compensation is not assured by the risk adjustment system – which increases the risk they are bearing.
- Although spending control was one of the aims of the reforms, Switzerland still has one of the most expensive systems today, expressed in US$ PPP, and is only surpassed by the USA and Norway (Norway is not shown in Figure 6.1) (see Figure 6.1). The gap with the OECD average has been slowly widening. Efficiency, which is often seen as a means to achieve cost control, is also lacking in the Swiss system. A recent report commissioned by the Swiss Academies for Arts and Sciences identified several causes for inefficiencies

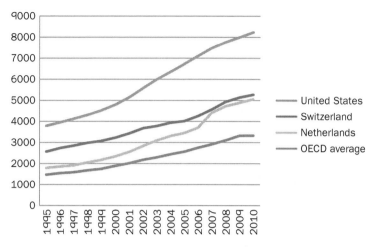

Figure 6.1 Total expenditure on health per capita, US$ purchasing power parity (1995–2010)

Source: OECD Health Data (2013).

in the system, including market failures, lack of regulation and lack of enforcement. These lead to perverse incentives for involved actors and inefficient structures (Trageser et al. 2012). The Swiss have realized that reforms involving the purchasing market will be needed to slow expenditure increases in health costs (Van Ginneken and Swartz 2012).

The Netherlands

In the Netherlands, policy-makers hoped that consumer choice of insurer would reduce the emphasis on government regulation of health care supply, increase efficiency through strategic purchasing and, ultimately, offer more affordable and more patient-driven health care (Thomson et al. 2013). In 2006, after almost two decades of preparation, the former sickness fund system, which covered about two-thirds of the population, and the voluntary health insurance system, for individuals above a certain income threshold, were unified, and a private market following the principles of managed competition was established. Residents are required to purchase insurance policies, and insurers must accept all applicants. Insurers must sell basic policies that cover a comprehensive set of benefits for acute care. Premiums for basic plans for acute care are lower for policies with higher deductibles, but only about 7 per cent of the population has chosen a higher-deductible plan (Vektis 2012). Furthermore, as in Switzerland, lower incomes are compensated for by tax subsidies. Whereas the Swiss largely left the purchasing market intact (collective negotiations between insurers and providers), the Dutch implemented new payment systems in which money follows the patient and costs were presented in a transparent manner. A newly developed diagnosis related group (DRG) system was to gradually facilitate free negotiations between insurers and providers, which would allow insurers to influence the cost of providers. Unlike Switzerland, the Netherlands permits people to buy insurance as members of a group, and 68 per cent of the population do so (Vektis 2012). To date, there is no evidence that insurers are using group contracts to select profitable risks, but the existence of identifiable sub-populations raises concerns about future risk selection (Commissie Evaluatie Risicoverevening Zvw 2012). All in all, and in contrast to Switzerland, the more sophisticated Dutch risk adjustment system has performed much better (Van de Ven et al. 2013). Insurers in the Netherlands are clearly engaged in robust premium price competition, resulting in relatively uniform premiums for the same plans (Leu et al. 2009).

Although some important gains were made in terms of patient-driven health care, most notably more choice and empowerment of patient groups (Van Ginneken et al. 2008) as well as decreasing waiting times, most of the broad goals of the reform have not been met:

- The complex Dutch model has required arguably more government intervention than the old model. More than seven years after its implementation, it has been a steep learning curve for all market players. Many short-term problems needed immediate attention. To name but a few, competition on premiums led to financial problems for many insurers; a wave of mergers resulted in just four insurers having 88 per cent of the market; excessive case-based payment system (DBC) tariffs led to overfunding of hospitals, which then had to be paid back; GP payments were delayed; GPs and medical specialists received more funding than anticipated; and the DBC system was too complicated and needed simplification. All of these problems had (and still have) to be dealt with on an ad hoc basis. On a positive note, although the demands on all actors have been high, the situation has never become chaotic (Van Ginneken et al. 2008). Some of these undesired effects are to some extent to be expected though it was hoped that the need for such ad hoc measures would gradually disappear when the system had developed.
- There also remains quite strong government involvement in purchasing and planning. Some commentators have argued that the government's role is expanding (e.g., Okma and Crivelli 2013), which is characterized by, for example, 'covenants' with the pharmaceutical industry on drug prices, reversal of pilots with free pricing for dental care, involvement with developing the Dutch DRG system (DBC-DOT), quality control and health technology assessment (HTA), new maximum tariffs for medical specialists (2010), and since 2012, a *de facto* return to budgets, albeit administered by the insurers. Others have expressed concern that the system would get stuck between a centralized system of state-controlled supply and prices and a decentralized system based on regulated competition providing insufficient incentives for provision of quality services and expenditure control (Werkgroep Curatieve Zorg 2010; Schut et al. 2013).
- Rising numbers of uninsured and defaulters may have at times threatened access to health care for vulnerable groups. On several occasions this has prompted additional regulation (e.g., actively tracing these individuals) before the trend could be reversed (Van Ginneken et al. 2013).

- The introduction of more competition in the hospital sector (e.g., allowing selective contracting, introduction of DRGs, allowing new specialized treatment centres) has had a mixed effect on cost efficiency. The reform has reduced prices of hospital care, but these gains were not translated into lower costs, but were compensated for by hospital care providers with higher volume of care (Schut et al. 2013).
- The reform has hitherto not led to cost containment in the care sector. On the contrary – total health expenditure rose more sharply after 2006 (Figure 6.1) and hospital volumes continued to grow. This has led to the decision to tighten government control on the budgets and introduce maximum tariffs for medical specialists. It is important to note, however, that a large share of this growth can be accounted for by the system for long-term care (AWBZ), in which the regionally dominant insurers organize care through care offices for the whole region. One explanation for the growing expenditures is that insurers have limited ability or interest in pressurizing providers to reduce their costs because the government controls most payments to providers. Furthermore, until 2012, health insurers did not have incentives to be competitive because of the ex-post compensation mechanism, which was necessary in the beginning of the new system to protect insurers for major financial risks. In 2012, however, the first step in dismantling these compensations was taken. But although further reforms have increased the percentage of negotiable hospital care to 70 per cent of hospital turnover and a simplified DBC-DOT system was implemented, it is clear that this is hardly the sort of market system envisaged at the onset of the reforms. Interestingly, since the 2010s, expenditures have been slowing and the volume of hospital care is stable or decreasing. It is likely the result of a mix of increased government control and more actively purchasing insurers (particularly pharmaceuticals). In 2014, the higher than legally required financial reserves that insurers were holding received a great deal of attention, especially after the expected premiums for 2015 were announced, which were on average almost 10 per cent higher than in 2014. Insurers argue that they need these reserves because they are bearing more risk, but several critics (the media, politics and consumer organizations) demanded that these reserves should be used to lower the 2015 premium.

Some of these experiences show similarities but some do not. The competitive nature as well as the design of the Swiss and Dutch insurance markets differs. The differences suggest that how competitive markets are designed, governed and regulated is critically important in achieving the objectives of the reforms.

What are the governance problems?

Main accountability relationships

The health care sector can be depicted as having three linked markets: health insurance; health care purchasing, and health care provision. Insurers, providers, and individuals all have roles in these three linked markets as purchasers,

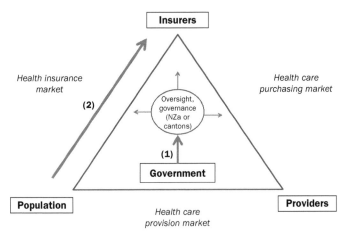

Figure 6.2 Main accountability relationships in insurance competition in the Netherlands and Switzerland

suppliers, or consumers. This analysis focuses on two broadly existing principal–agent accountability relationships. These are: (1) the government (principal) that has several arm's-length agencies (as in the Netherlands) or cantons (Switzerland) as agents to oversee the markets; and (2) the public as principal and the insurer/purchaser as agent (see Figure 6.2).

In the first, the government's role is to broadly provide oversight and regulations, most notably through the Health Insurance Act (Zvw) in the Netherlands and the Swiss Federal Health Insurance Law (KVG) in Switzerland, and to promote price and quality competition among insurers and among health care providers. However, the de facto enforcement lies with the Dutch Health Care Authority (NZa) and the Swiss cantons respectively. In the second, the insurer is expected to be the agent acting in the best interest of the people and act as prudent purchaser that also purchases on the basis of quality.

However, although a system of managed competition needs clear responsibilities, these relationships are not always as clear-cut as will be shown below.

Governance problems

Missing accountability relations

Chiefly in the Swiss system, accountability and definition of responsibilities pose a large and well-known problem. The system is characterized by a federal structure with a fragmentation of responsibilities across different players and governments. The fact that 26 cantons bear primary responsibility for adequate health care raises questions as the cantons wear multiple hats. They are at the same time owners of hospitals, providers, funders and regulators. It therefore comes as no surprise that Switzerland has one of the highest numbers of hospitals per population in the EU (OECD/WHO 2011). In addition, the many small insurers lack the expertise, authority, information or tools to effectively negotiate with providers. Furthermore, although the KVG can be seen as the first major federal initiative in Swiss health care, an overarching framework or health law was until very recently still lacking. This has been noted and criticized by two consecutive OECD/WHO reports (2006; 2011). Finally, for the first time the Swiss Federal government presented in 2013 a comprehensive national health strategy (*gesundheit2020*[2]). The strategy reaffirms the need for federal leadership in health policy to overcome the current governance fragmentation.

In 2014, a new report (*Commissie Borstlap*) was commissioned by the Dutch Minister of Health to look into the role and responsibilities of the NZa. A main recommendation was that it advocates splitting the regulatory tasks of the NZa from its implementation and enforcement tasks. Currently, the NZa sets the rules for the players (insurers, providers) in the health care markets and also enforces them. Moreover, the report criticized the ties between the Ministry of Health and the NZa as 'too close' and argued that there should be less mutual consultation on some key issues (advisory reports, granting subsidies). In April 2015, the Minister announced that they will follow the main recommendation of the report which should enter into force in 2017.

Although both the Swiss and Dutch governments require annual reports, they do not directly hold private insurers accountable. However, they do have high expectations in terms of access to care, planning provision, cost containment, innovation, and quality. If these are not met, it may be unclear what can actually be expected and done to achieve desired outcomes. Mostly, solutions are sought in putting in place the right incentives and regulation. But in the meantime, there has been a (probably necessary) reliance on existing institutions for monitoring and accountability (Smith et al. 2012). In the Netherlands, for example, the government clawed back overspending by hospitals through taxes, was heavily involved in purchasing (setting prices, developing DBCs) and had to reinforce budgeting in hospital care to counter the increases in care production. In Switzerland, the federal government finally adopted a new law (*Aufsichtsgesetz*[3]) in September 2014 to strengthen control over, and accountability of health insurers through a federal regulatory agency. This agency's competences, which overlap with some of the competences of the Dutch Health Care Authority (NZa), would assume this responsibility from the cantons.

Unlike, for example, Germany, Norway and England, clear setting of priorities for the health system against which the players are held accountable is missing in the Netherlands and Switzerland. Instead, priority-setting is left to arm's-length agencies in the Netherlands. This entails the risk of somewhat arbitrary choice of goals and a vulnerability to vested interests, while in Switzerland cantons are responsible, which may depart from national priorities (Smith et al. 2012; Widmer and Telser 2013).

Missing transparency

Making markets transparent through the provision of meaningful data is widely seen as a necessary precondition for a competitive insurance model (but arguably also any health system). The Swiss, and to lesser degree, the

Dutch governments have not been able to develop, provide or nurture enough meaningful information/performance indicators to make health markets more transparent and counter information asymmetry between (1) government and market actors; (2) purchasers and providers; (3) patients and providers; and (4) consumers and insurers (Schäfer et al. 2010; OECD/WHO 2011; Public Health Schweiz 2013). In theory, the government can use such information to make effective policy, the insurers can use it to become efficient purchasers, the consumer can use it to pick the most efficient insurance plan for their specific needs, while the patient can use it to choose a high quality provider.

Interestingly, the Dutch government-run website kiesbeter.nl has recently stopped providing information on insurance plans, arguing that there are enough independent websites to assist in this choice. A similar website in Switzerland (comparis.ch) is a private initiative. Whether these websites are entirely independent, as they are generally paid by commission, may not be so easy for the consumer to judge

So far, the developments to purchase on the basis of quality are limited and the development and availability of meaningful indicators have not had a serious impact on purchasing (van Ginneken and Swartz 2013). That said, quality has increasingly become part of the agenda and some Dutch insurers are increasingly using quality indicators, though, on the whole, this is quite limited. The data situation is worse in the Swiss cantons where data is not collected according to nationally standardized reporting requirements. In the Netherlands, a national quality institute was established to make quality visible for all market players but this is still work in progress (Van der Wees et al. 2014). Finally, there appears to be friction between the requirement for the (commercial) insurers and providers to provide their data and protecting their corporate knowledge.

Missing participation

At the highest level, both in the Netherlands and Switzerland, the market-oriented reforms have proven politically divisive. This means that depending on who is in power, the idea of insurance competition and the necessary supporting reforms are further implemented, slowed down, or, in various aspects, altered. The policy process is subject to political and legislative compromise, as well as stakeholder resistance, which makes the eventual shape of insurance competition uncertain (Van Ginneken and Swartz 2012). For example, in the Netherlands, the choice to opt for a system organized under private law – as opposed to a public law – was adopted by a coalition with a minimal mandate and very low approval rates and without support from the major opposition parties (Van Ginneken et al. 2008). Furthermore, the pace at which the market for hospital care was deregulated has been severely slowed down depending on who was in power. In Switzerland, the slow pace of reforms and regular debates on implementing a single payer also hindered progress. This is made more difficult because the reforms were implemented from a federal level (top-down) through adoption of the KVG. Yet the Swiss system has a bottom-up system based on cantons and consensus. This makes one wonder how far insurance competition is supported throughout all layers of the political system. Indeed, a study on how cantons regulate hospitals has shown that various cantons have acted against hospital competition (Widmer and Telser 2013), which is an important theoretical precondition for insurance competition as well.

Missing integrity

Missing integrity and fraud in the health system do frequently lead to media hypes in both countries. This seems especially the case in the Netherlands, where yearly premium and deductible rises have put not only insurers and providers, but also regulators under increased scrutiny. It could be argued that in a system that relies on market mechanisms, the likelihood that incentives are created which may conflict with the public interest is greater. Also the opportunity to enter the provider and insurance market and make a profit, if the legal framework allows this, could attract entities with questionable motives. The overarching question is thus, whether this is the result of misaligned incentives – understandable from the point of view of the provider – or missing integrity. Examples are numerous and include up-coding of DRGs, false declarations and risk selection (see Commissie Evaluatie Risicoverevening 2012; Trageser et al. 2012). Often medical specialists will argue that they are forced to engage in these practices to ensure quality of care, while an insurer may engage in risk selection, or risk putting themselves out of business. It underlines the need to invest in the removal of perverse incentives. In 2014, the NZa reported several hospitals to the authorities or penalized them after finding suspicious declaration behaviour, but also some insurers have reported fraud with declarations. Yet many criticize this as insufficient and estimate that fraud in health care is a much larger phenomenon and that more effective oversight and accountability mechanisms are needed.

In the Netherlands, a broader discussion on integrity in the semi-public sector, to which insurers, hospitals and, for example, educational institutions belong, has led to the setting up of a commission to explore drafting an ethical and professional code of conduct (Commissie Behoorlijk Bestuur 2013). This happened after several incidents where, for example, executives gave themselves large pay rises or took irresponsible investment risks with public funds. In general, the drive to economies of scale, which is a larger issue in the Netherlands than Switzerland, and mostly the result of market pressures, has led to a situation in which executives direct large nationally operating insurers or provider networks. This has increased the distance between the management and the field they operate in, which could lead to decisions that are not in the public interest.

Missing policy capacity

These reforms have been so complex that inevitably in certain sectors, the governments have underestimated the necessary requirements and have failed to govern effectively. In Switzerland, this is further complicated due to the federal structure. Its federal government does not have the levers to effectively manage and reform the system, which is also reflected in the slow pace of reforms.

Examples are manifold. Roles and responsibilities are still unclearly defined and conflicting, the risk adjustment system until recently remained too crude to effectively counter risk selection and large premium differences, while information systems are inadequate to make markets transparent. It is hoped that a much-needed framework and a federal level agency will prevent or alleviate some of these problems.

In the more centralized Dutch system, several arm's-length agencies were set up, reformed or assigned to facilitate and monitor the reforms. These include the Dutch Health Care Authority (NZa), the health inspectorate (IGZ), and a special agency that develops the case-based payment system (DBC-onderhoud). However, even though the institutional capacity was available, it was never able to prevent the unintended effects as described earlier in this chapter. To their credit, though much expected chaos, especially during the first years of implementation, this never occurred (Van Ginneken et al. 2008). In general, problems relate to the choice of design and system complexity, coupled with misaligned incentives as well as some governance failures, rather than missing policy capacity.

Finally, one could argue that there is insufficient policy capacity on the insurer side, which hinders effective strategic purchasing. Both in Switzerland and the Netherlands, a large role was envisaged for the insurer. However, it has become clear that insurers do not have the knowledge of hospital costs or quality of care, nor enough expertise and experience to negotiate effectively with hospitals (Aarden and Van Hoyweghen 2011; OECD/WHO 2011).

Lessons

Irrespective of the discussion whether the reforms are in progress or not, it seems that both the Dutch and Swiss governments have underestimated the technical and political complexity of implementing market-based insurance reforms while perhaps overestimating the promises of what such a model can do in terms of achieving some broad societal goals, most notably, cost containment. One could argue that this in itself is a governance failure. Moreover, some of the outcomes and problems so far have been exacerbated by governance difficulties, although in many cases worse outcomes have been prevented.

First of all, to a different degree, effective accountability mechanisms to govern insurance markets are lacking in both countries. This has led to a new law in Switzerland and public debate about the appropriate role of the NZa in the Netherlands. It underlines the need for clear definitions of the roles and responsibilities of the key players in the health system.

Second, both countries, Switzerland arguably more than the Netherlands, have failed to develop, provide or foster a broadly accepted set of meaningful quality indicators to make the health care markets more transparent for all players. This ideally would have led to better policy, stronger purchasing on the basis of quality (and not on price or volume), and more informed choice (of providers and insurance policies). In the Netherlands, almost a decade after the reform was introduced in 2006, limited initiatives on the insurer side show the use of some quality indicators for certain health services. The question is legitimate as to whether the governments perhaps trusted too much that insurers would take on this role (motivated by market forces) and whether they should have done more to support or require this development.

Third, missing public participation in adopting the reforms seems to be an issue in both countries, which is reflected in yearly discussions on the system and its costs and changes in the Netherlands and occasional referenda in Switzerland, as well as strongly differing views across the political spectrum and a different pace or direction of reforms when a new coalition assumes power.

Fourth, missing integrity has become a large public issue in the Netherlands, and to a lesser degree in Switzerland. It could be argued that market mechanisms increase the likelihood that incentives are created that may conflict with the public interest, which can have all kinds of unwelcome outcomes, including fraud. Better surveillance mechanisms are needed at all levels (including the insurers).

Fifth, the complexity of managed competition necessitates a comprehensive reform affecting all players in the health care system. This takes time and requires midcourse corrections, and can be expected to be a work in progress for many years to come, with uncertain outcomes. This requires strong institutions with sufficient policy capacity, ample technological capacity and timely available data. As seen in Switzerland, implementing a system that needs strong centralized steering and supervising institutions does not fit well with a decentralized bottom-up consensus-building system with electoral accountability and fragmented health markets. On a lower level, insurers probably still lack the policy capacity and expertise to be effective purchasers of care, though some developments are visible in the Netherlands.

Finally, though managed competition seems to be an attractive model, it remains an untested policy theory. Even if governments had managed to provide the best possible governance, outcomes would have been uncertain. Its theoretical blueprint is hard to implement due to the restrictive regulatory and political environment, as well as missing data. Furthermore, there seems to be a misunderstanding between the concept of 'efficiency', which is one of the goals of insurance competition, and the concept of 'cost containment', which is often an expectation held by policy-makers but is not necessarily a goal of insurance competition. At best, efficiency can be a means to achieve cost containment, but with the wrong incentives, efficiency gains are absorbed by the system and compensated for by higher production volume and supply-induced demand (as seen in both countries). Another important aim was quality of care, but this requires having a broadly accepted and published set of indicators. But whether such data can be developed at all is a legitimate concern. What the Dutch and Swiss systems are eventually developing into is hard to say at this point, but it will likely not be what the proponents of managed competition initially envisaged, and labelling these systems as such makes increasingly less sense. Countries interested in implementing insurance competition should take note of the Swiss and Dutch experiences.

Broader lessons

Introducing comprehensive reform cannot be considered without taking into account the existing legal and political structure and other possible missing preconditions also in terms of governance in a given jurisdiction for such a reform. In addition, *realistic* goals of reforms need to be explicitly stated by government and, depending on the system (e.g., market-based, electoral accountability), be translated into accountable priorities for the local level or arm's-length agencies. This will also require alignment of incentives and tools to enforce compliance if needed. Finally, it may be superfluous to say that countries should back up their decision-making processes with empirical evidence. Only then we can learn from experience, both negative and positive, from the past.

Notes

1 Also the German statutory system before 2009 allowed insurers to compete, albeit not on premium level (a flat rate), but on contribution level (a percentage of income).
2 See http://www.bag.admin.ch/gesundheit2020/index.html?lang=de.
3 See http://www.bag.admin.ch/themen/krankenversicherung/00305/06506/11597/index. html?lang=de.

Acknowledgement

The author wishes to thank Paul Camenzind, Luca Crivelli, Monika Diebold, Ab Klink and Madelon Kroneman, for helpful feedback on earlier drafts of this chapter.

References

Aarden, E. and Van Hoyweghen, I. (2011) Lessons from the Netherlands for the health and social care bill, *Lancet*, 377(9779): 1745.24.
Bal, R. and Zuiderent-Jerak, T. (2011) The practice of markets in Dutch health care: are we drinking from the same glass? *Health Economics, Policy and Law*, 6(1): 139–45.
Beck, K. and Risiko Krankenversicherung (2011) *Risikomanagement in einem regulierten Krankenversicherungsmarkt*. Bern: Haupt.
Commissie Behoorlijk Bestuur (2013) *Een lastig gesprek*. Available at: http://www. rijksoverheid.nl/documenten-en-publicaties/rapporten/2013/09/11/een-lastig-gesprek-advies-commissie-behoorlijk-bestuur.html.
Commissie Evaluatie Risicoverevening Zvw (2012) *Evaluatie Risicoverevening Zorgverzekeringswet* [Evaluation of risk adjustment in the Health Insurance Act], The Hague: Ministry of Health, Welfare, and Sport.
Crivelli, L. (2010) Swiss are back to (quasi-)universal coverage, *Health Policy Monitor* [serial on the Internet], April. Available at: http://hpm.org/ch/a15/1.pdf (accessed 4 March 2013).
Frank, R. G. and Lamiraud, K. (2009) Choice, price competition, and complexity in markets for health insurance, *Journal of Economic Behavior and Organization*, 71: 550–62.
Kreier, R. and Zweifel, P. (2010) Health insurance in Switzerland: a closer look at a system often offered as a model for the United States, *Hofstra Law Review*, 39(1): 89–110.
Leu, R. E., Rutten, F. F. H., Brouwer, W., Matter, P., and Rütchi, C. (2009) *The Swiss And Dutch Health Insurance Systems: Universal Coverage and Regulated Competitive Insurance Markets*, Jan. (Pub. No. 1220). New York: Commonwealth Fund.
Maarse, H. and Paulus, A. (2011) The politics of health-care reform in the Netherlands since 2006, *Health Economics, Policy and Law*, 6(1): 125–34.
OECD (Organization for Economic Cooperation and Development) (2013) *Stat Extracts: Health Expenditure and Financing* [Internet]. Paris: OECD. Available from: http:// stats.oecd.org/Index.aspx?DataSetCode=SHA (accessed 4 September 2013).

OECD/WHO (Organization for Economic Cooperation and Development, World Health Organization) (2006) *OECD Reviews of Health Systems: Switzerland 2006*. Paris: OECD Publishing, October 19.

OECD/WHO (Organization for Economic Cooperation and Development; World Health Organization) (2011) *OECD Reviews of Health Systems: Switzerland 2011* [Internet]. Paris: OECD Publishing, October 17.

Okma, K. G. and Crivelli, L. (2013) Swiss and Dutch 'consumer-driven health care: ideal model or reality? *Health Policy*, 109(2): 105–12.

Public Health Schweiz (2013) *Bessere Gesundheitsdaten für ein effizienteres Gesundheitswesen*. Available at: http://www.hausarztmedizin.uzh.ch/index/130816-Mani festGesundheitsdaten-D-def.pdf.

Schäfer, W., Kroneman, M., Boerma, W., van den Berg, M., Westert, G., Devillé, W. and van Ginneken, E. (2010) The Netherlands: health system review, *Health Systems in Transition*, 12(1): 1–229.

Schut, F. T. and Van de Ven, W. P. (2011) Effects of purchaser competition in the Dutch health system: is the glass half full or half empty? *Health Economics, Policy and Law*, 6(1): 109–23.

Schut, E., Sorbe, S. and Hoj, J. (2013) Health care reform and long-term care in the Netherlands. Economics Department Working Paper No. 1010. Paris: OECD.

Smith, P. C., Anell, A., Busse, R., Crivelli, L., Healy, J., Lindahl, A. K., Westert, G. and Kene, T. (2012) Leadership and governance in seven developed health systems, *Health Policy*, 106(1): 37–49.

Thomson, S., Busse, R., Crivelli, L., van de Ven, W. and van de Voorde, C. (2013) Statutory health insurance competition in Europe: a four-country comparison, *Health Policy*, 109(3): 209–25.

Trageser, J., Vettori, A. and Crivelli, L. (2012) Effizienz, Nutzung und Finanzierung des Gesundheitswesens, *Akademien der Wissenschaften Schweiz*. Available at: http://www.akademien-schweiz.ch/dms/D/Projekte-und-Themen/Medizin-im-Wandel/Roadmap_Gesundheitssystem.pdf.

Van de Ven, W. P., Beck, K., Buchner, F., Schokkaert, E., Schut, F. T., Shmueli, A. and Wasem, J. (2013) Preconditions for efficiency and affordability in competitive healthcare markets: are they fulfilled in Belgium, Germany, Israel, the Netherlands and Switzerland? *Health Policy*, 109(3): 226–45.

Van der Wees, P. J., Nijhuis-van der Sanden, M. W., Van Ginneken, E., Ayanian, J. Z., Schneider, E. C. and Westert, G. P. (2014) Governing healthcare through performance measurement in Massachusetts and the Netherlands, *Health Policy*, 116(1): 18–26.

Van Ginneken, E. and Swartz, K. (2012) Implementing insurance exchanges: lessons from Europe, *New England Journal of Medicine*, 367(8): 691–3. doi: 10.1056/NEJMp1205832.

Van Ginneken, E., Busse, R. and Gericke, C. A. (2008) Universal private health insurance in the Netherlands: the first year, *Journal of Management & Marketing in Health-care*, 1(2): 139–53.

Van Ginneken, E., Schäfer, W. and Kroneman, M. (2011) Managed competition in the Netherlands: an example for others? *Eurohealth*, 17(1): 23–6.

Van Ginneken, E., Swartz, K. and Van der Wees, P. (2013) Health insurance exchanges in Switzerland and the Netherlands offer five key lessons for the operations of US exchanges, *Health Affairs (Millwood)*, 32(4): 744–52.

Vektis (2012) Zorgthermometer: verzekerdenin beweging [Care thermometer: insured individuals on the move], *Zeist* (The Netherlands), Vektis (in Dutch). Available from: http://www.vektis.nl/downloads/Publicaties/2012/Zorgthermometer%20-%20Verze-kerden%20in%20beweging/.

Werkgroep Curatieve Zorg (2010) *Curatieve Zorg, Rapport brede heroverwegingen*, 11, The Hague: the Dutch Ministry of Finance.

Widmer, P. and Telser, H. (2013) Die Spitalversorgung im Spannungsfeld der kantonalen Spitalpolitik, *Studie im Auftrag von comparischen Polynomics*. Available at: http://fr.comparis.ch/~/media/files/mediencorner/medienmitteilungen/2013/krankenkasse/polynomics_spitalregulierung_13-08-20.pdf.

seven

The governance of public–private partnerships: lessons from the United Kingdom and Germany

Eva Lieberherr, Hans Maarse and Patrick Jeurissen

Introduction

This chapter analyses the provision of public services by means of public–private partnerships (PPP) from a governance perspective. Today, public sectors such as public health care, transport and defence frequently use PPPs. In this chapter we focus on a specific form of PPP where a private sector party enters a contractual agreement to jointly finance and operate public infrastructure with a public party. The relationship between the private and public sector parties is shaped by means of a long-term contract defining their rights and obligations. We discuss the governance of PPPs on the basis of two cases: the *Private Finance Initiative* (PFI) in health care in the United Kingdom and the *Berlin Waterworks* in Germany.

The two cases share two similarities. First, both feature a high degree of *asset specificity*, which can be described as the degree to which a resource (in our cases a hospital and water infrastructure) can be redeployed for alternative purposes. Asset specificity is high because both cases involve a durable investment in physical resources that cannot easily be reassigned for other uses. Second, both face the potential of *contract failure* (Epstein 2013): it may be difficult for the 'consumers' (patients and water users) to evaluate the quality of service provision (due to information asymmetry), which may lead to incentives for the service provider (with private actor involvement and hence a profit motive) to act opportunistically (e.g., saving money by providing lower-quality services).

Despite these similarities, our cases also involve several dissimilarities. Beyond involving different sectors (public health and water) in two diverging countries (the United Kingdom and Germany), the scope of the PPP also differs. In the PFI case, a private sector party manages the design, building, financing and operation of public infrastructure, and a public party pays for the use of the infrastructure by means of a periodic fee from the point at which the contracted facility is available for use. In contrast, in the PPP of the Berlin Waterworks, private actors buy ownership rights to 49.9 per cent of the already existing assets for the duration of the contract; the management and operations thus occur under joint ownership between public and private actors. Moreover, while the PFI involves an alleged transfer of risk from the public to the private actors, risk in the Berlin PPP case remains shared.

We chose these two contrasting cases because together they shed light on a range of governance challenges. Specifically, the PFI case illustrates transparency, accountability and policy capacity challenges, while the Berlin case informs us about participation and integrity governance difficulties. We first delineate the United Kingdom PFI case and then the Berlin case – defining each PPP, its objectives, outcomes and governance challenges.

The Private Finance Initiative (PFI)

The *Private Finance Initiative* (PFI) has its origins in Australia and the United Kingdom, where it was introduced in the early 1990s. Although at the time of its introduction it was heavily criticized by the Labour opposition, it was embraced by the Labour Government under premier Tony Blair, which took office in 1997. Labour rebranded PFI as a 'public – private partnership'. Since then, it has become an alternative model for the conventional model of capital funding of public infrastructure. In the past two decades PFI has been used to invest in many new hospitals and other health care infrastructures.

The basic idea of PFI is rather simple. A public sector party (e.g., a government department or a hospital trust) invites private contractors in a tendering procedure to design, build, finance and operate public infrastructure according to the output specifications set out by the public authority. When the contracted facility is available for use, the public authority pays a periodic fee to the private contractor in exchange for the use of the facility. No service means no fee for performance. The life-cycle of the contract is long: often 30 years or longer. The private sector party is set up as a consortium of private investors, known as a Specific Purpose Vehicle, which usually includes a finance company, a construction company and a service provider. The financing of the capital investment is generally provided by a combination of share capital and loan stock from the owners of the Specific Purpose Vehicle, together with senior debt from banks and bond-holders. Post-contractual changes during the life-cycle of the contract are possible. Termination of contracts is difficult, however, because the public sector party will be obliged to compensate the private sector party adequately. In fact, termination comes at a significant cost to the taxpayer.

In 2012, the government came up with a proposal to reform PFI by converting it into what was dubbed PF2. A key element of this reform was to allow the public sector to recover a share of the profits made by projects in the same way as private investors. In addition, investors with 'long-term investment horizons', including pension funds, were encouraged to participate in PFI-funded projects. This proposal was greeted with a great deal of scepticism, because it in essence meant that the government was lending money to itself and taking increased risk (HM Treasury 2012). Moreover, such measures in PF2 further blur the distinction between public and private, as the public actors can now become subject to a profit motive.

Objectives of PFI

PFI can be considered an instrument to achieve two main objectives. The first objective is to offer an alternative to the conventional way of capital funding by opening up private resources of capital funding for public infrastructure. Alan Milburn, the Labour Health Secretary in 1987, argued that 'when there is a limited amount of public-sector capital available, as there is, it's PFI or bust' (*The Guardian*, 4 September 1997). Edwards and her colleagues (2004) conceive the tapping of private capital as a macro-level objective of PFI.

The second, more micro-level, objective of PFI is to get more value for money. PFI is shaped as a contractual arrangement between a private sector party and a public authority designed to transfer project risks from the public to the private sector (Corner 2006). Underlying this is the assumption that the private sector partner is more capable than the public authority of understanding, controlling and minimizing the risks of large-scale public infrastructure projects. The profit motive should work as a powerful incentive to manage risks effectively. The involvement of banks in PFI should also minimize the risk for the public authority, because banks will only participate after an intensive due diligence procedure. There are various examples of successfully managed projects by the private sector party. Construction works are frequently mentioned in this respect. PFI thus implies the transfer of risk and the associated costs that would otherwise be borne by the public sector party. In sum, the central claim is that PFI generates more value for money and will save costs, which will ultimately lead to benefits for the taxpayer and consumer (House of Commons Treasury Committee 2011; hereafter cited as Treasury Committee).

Outcomes of PFI

Evidence indicates that PFI has not fulfilled the objectives of increased capital funding and value for funding. Due to the banks' unwillingness to get involved in the financing of PFI projects after the financial crisis in 2008, the government has had to support the use of PFI for investments by lending tax payers' money to private sector parties to enable them to invest under PFI. This was considered the only method to guarantee the continuation of the necessary investments in public infrastructure. In other words: PFI could not survive without government involvement in its financing. Alan Johnson, the Labour Secretary of State for Health, declared in 2009: 'PFIs have always been the NHS's "plan A" for building new hospitals ... There was never a "plan B"' (cited in Lambert 2010).

In addition, various agencies, including the National Audit Office (NAO) and the Treasury Committee of the House of Commons have hinted at a hidden objective of PFI. Following the definitions used in the European Standards of Account (ESA), investments under PFI remain off the balance-sheet in national accounts. The Treasury Committee estimated in this respect, that:

If all current PFI liabilities were included in the National Accounts, then ... the national debt would increase by £35 bn (2.5% of GDP). Therefore there has been, and continues to be, at least a small incentive to use PFI in preference to other procurement options, as it results in lower headline government borrowing and debt figures in comparison to other forms of capital investment.

(Treasury Committee 2011: 12)

Elsewhere the Committee seems more outspoken by saying that ESA 'creates incentives to use PFIs, rather than direct capital investment by departments' (Treasury Committee 2011: 56).

In relation to the aim of opening up private resources of capital funding, PFI has been widely used for investing in health care facilities for the NHS with NHS Trusts as the public contractor. However, the results are not impressive:

- The NAO has become increasingly critical of the assumed cost savings. It claims that the price of finance is significantly higher for PFI than for conventional borrowing on its own account (NAO 2011).
- Because hospitals are forced to prioritize their contractual payments, which can account for up to 10–15 per cent of their operating budget, 'all the other efficiency and productivity gains you need have to come out of only 85 or 90 per cent of your budget' (Edwards, cited in Timmins 2010).
- The substantial annual payment that the public sector party must pay may cause serious affordability problems. It may translate into job reductions and, as the British Medical Association claims, even distort clinical priorities. Shortcomings in design, construction and operation (which may be the result of an inappropriate description of the output requirements) may even jeopardize the lives of patients (McKee et al. 2006).
- The high costs for PFI hospitals may spill over to other hospitals because trusts may have fewer financial resources available for other (necessary) investments. For this and other reasons, Pollock (2012) writes: 'PFI, once trumpeted as the largest hospital building program, was in fact the largest NHS hospital and bed closure program.'

In contrast, the list of positive results is conspicuously short: there is evidence that PFI hospitals may do better than conventionally funded hospitals of similar age in terms of environmental ratings, cleanliness, and so on.

In relation to the second objective (value for money), the Treasury Committee (2011: 15) claims that 'private finance is invariably more expensive than direct government borrowing' (up to 3–4 per cent) and furthermore, that the gap between public and private financing has increased since the outbreak of the financial crisis. In another report, the Committee seems even more critical: 'A great deal of public money may have been misallocated or wasted' (Treasury Committee 2012: 3). It cites the Chancellor of the Exchequer who has said that the government 'shares some of the commonly identified concerns that PFI contracts can be too costly, inflexible and opaque' (Treasury Committee 2012: 3). The higher expenses of PFI projects are only warranted if these higher costs are outweighed by savings and efficiencies during the life-cycle of the projects. But this does not seem to be the case: 'the substantial increase in private finance costs means that the PFI financing method is now extremely inefficient' (Treasury Committee 2011: 18). In sum, there is ever more evidence that PFI contracts are very expensive.

Again, the list of positive results of PFI in terms of value for money is relatively short. Although missing hard evidence, the Treasury Committee suggests that the whole-life costs and innovation of PFI projects may be less than under conventional capital funding. However, savings may be realized by lowering the quality of the buildings delivered, which may result in rising maintenance and energy costs over the lifetime of the project (Treasury Committee 2011: 22–4).

Advocates claim that PFI projects score well in terms of time and budget. There is also some evidence for this. For example, the NAO reported that 69 per cent of the construction projects between 2003 and 2008 were delivered on time and 65 per cent were delivered at the contracted price (NAO 2011). However, these figures do not necessarily mean that PFI outperforms the public sector in this respect. Furthermore, additional charges may be written into the contract to absorb the costs of overruns (Treasury Committee 2011: 26–7).

PFI governance problems

In the previous sections we saw that there is a lot of controversy over the effectiveness and efficiency of PFI in terms of cost savings and value for money. In other words, there are serious concerns regarding the outcomes of PFI. In this section we examine the underlying governance problems of PFI, which have arguably contributed to these outcomes. We have found that particularly the lack of transparency, accountability and policy capacity have contributed to the above policy outcome concerns.

Accountability

An important cause of PFI's inability to increase the value for money is that accountability is weak, as the contract is supposed to transfer risks from the public authority to the private sector party, and the private actors are not held accountable. For example, the Treasury Committee concludes: 'Some of the claimed risk transfer may be … illusory – the government is ultimately accountable for the delivery of public services' (2011: 21). For this reason, it is very important to examine the transfer of risks carefully. Pollock, one of the most outspoken opponents of PFI, is of the opinion that, in spite of all the rhetoric, risks are in fact not transferred to the private sector (Pollock 2005). In addition, the following points include accountability challenges that have prevented the realization of the policy objectives:

- In PFI, public authorities become highly dependent on the private sector for the delivery of public services, for which the public actors remain accountable to the public at large. Questions of 'who is to blame' arise: e.g., who is to blame if the physical structure does not match the requirements of optimal patient treatment? Did the public sector party fail to adequately specify the performance requirements or did the private sector party opt for a less-than-optimal facility to save costs? What is clear, however, is that the public sector party cannot simply shift its public responsibility to the private sector party. The public at large will hold the public sector party responsible for the quality of the services delivered. In extreme cases, the public contractor may be forced to bail out the private contractor to guarantee the provision of services to its clients. This may impede cost savings.

- PFI contracts may include regulations that rebound the risk to the public sector party. Hence PFI can become more expensive than initially assumed.
- The objectives of PFI have also been undermined by the fact that the public and private sectors make use of different accounting procedures, which make it difficult to measure the financial performance of the contracts. A major issue in this respect is that PFI debts and assets are kept off the government's balance sheet, which gives a false impression of cost savings. The Treasury Committee warns that PFI should not be abused to keep the public debt artificially low: 'In the long term, the PFI arrangement will build up big commitments against future years' current budgets that have not even yet been allocated or agreed' (2011: 13).
- The lack of choice between alternatives minimizes the ability to choose the most efficient solution and thus restricts the ability to achieve value for money: the public authorities involved often offer no real funding alternative. The Treasury Committee reported in this respect that assessment procedures tend to be biased in favour of PFI.
- PFI is an inherently complex project. One reason for complexity is that issues may arise as to who is accountable for what during the project that often take 30 years or even longer. The contract may be less clear on these issues than assumed. Also note in this respect that a contract may be revisited and subjected to challenge during its term because of changing conditions. These factors may lead to increased transaction costs and impede the policy objective of value for money.

Transparency

The failure to achieve the goal of cost savings can be linked to the lack of transparency in PFI contracts, which may lead them to become expensive. The following transparency challenges may have contributed to the policy outcome concerns:

- The private sector party, known as the Special Purpose Vehicle, usually consists of many partners, subcontractors (often a sister of the contracting party) and so on. How the money flows within this network of partners is totally unclear. Ultimately, this lack of transparency can impede the policy objectives of cost savings and value for money, as the lack of clarity about the flow of money could lead to inefficient or illegitimate use of it.
- Contracts usually contain small print and clauses that may be vague and subject to differing interpretations. For instance, Swift (2012) reports about frequent interpretation problems as regards 'repeat ratchets', the penalties

incurred if targets are missed. Such interpretation challenges may impede policy effectiveness if enforcement (via penalties) cannot be sufficiently carried out.

- As regards the annual unitary fee that the public sector party contractor must pay to the private party contractor, it is unclear how much the public sector party must pay for the transfer of risks to the private sector party.
- Many PFI contracts are considered confidential for commercial reasons. The Freedom of Information Act has been used as a legal instrument to request openness for public scrutiny. For instance, in 2007, NHS Lothian was forced to disclose its contract with Consort Healthcare for the building and the maintenance of the Royal Infirmary of Edinburgh. Some 5000 previously unseen additional pages were discovered (Scottish Information Commissioner 2007). The lack of transparency about the contracts could complicate or cloud the degree to which public funding is employed in PFI, which could be a reason for the failure to achieve cost savings.
- The objective of cost savings has also suffered because the procurement procedure has been slow due to its lack of transparency. For this reason, the government recently announced some measures to improve transparency, including the introduction of an 18-month deadline for successful procurement.

Policy capacity

Public authorities often have limited in-house skills to make critical decisions and tend to be over-reliant on (very expensive) advisers, which may nullify cost savings. They may lack the skill and expertise to negotiate effectively with their smart commercial counterparts. There is also a risk to effective decision-making, if only a small number of post-holders have detailed knowledge of the contract and they leave the project. As a result, public authorities may fail to understand all the consequences of the PFI, and for that reason be unable to make decisions that foster the intended policy objectives.

The lack of good-quality data on costs and performance hinders the public sector parties' ability to monitor performance to drive efficiency and effectiveness improvements (Epstein 2013). For example, the Department of Health was unable to explain wide differences in catering costs. There is still evidence of poor governance and oversight of the project in the early stage. Evaluation and monitoring should therefore be strengthened in order to foster cost savings and value for money.

In considering 'getting better outcomes for less', NAO (2011) stresses the need for information on the range of contracts across the government, in particular as regards the number of contracts, the range of prices for similar items and the volume of business. Since there are nearly 50 professional buying organizations procuring similar goods and services in government, there is a risk that the government does not manage to get the best deal. What is needed is to share experience and build up expertise, also to make the government less dependent upon the expertise of external (and very) expensive consultants. Some progress has already been made, for instance, by the introduction of framework agreements and the development of benchmarks. However, the lack of this capacity may contribute to the inability to currently achieve the policy objectives.

There is a strong need for a coordinated approach to increase the public sector party's purchasing power to negotiate better contracts. NAO (2011) notes that such a coordinated approach may exist on the other side of the table: specialist investors are interested in a large number of PFIs in order to benefit from the economies of scale with no corresponding benefit to the public sector. This lack of policy capacity may have contributed to the general lack of flexibility in PFI contracts. Such contracts typically include specifications for a period of 30 years or even more. Post-contractual changes are possible but difficult to realize, if the private contracting party has little incentive to change the terms of a profitable contract. An efficient mechanism to solve emergent problems is not available and may force the public authority to bail out the private sector contractor to guarantee the continuity of public services. In this respect, the Treasury Commission (2011) also warns about an assessment bias in the comparison of the value for money to the conventional procurement option with funding provided by central government known as the Public Sector Comparator (PSC).

So far we have focused on the PFI in health care in the United Kingdom. In order to shed light on further governance challenges that may emerge in the context of public–private financing in the public sector, we now address the PPP of the Berlin Waterworks.

The PPP of the Berlin Waterworks

In the city-state of Berlin, Germany, the bankrupt State (the executive, made up of the Governing Mayor and up to eight senators with ministerial positions) entered an intended 29-year PPP with the private investors Vivendi (now Veolia) and RWE[1] in 1999, but the contract lasted only until 2013 (see below). The Waterworks is responsible for all infrastructure-related tasks: treating waste water and providing drinking water to citizens in Berlin, and to parts of the neighbouring constituent state of Brandenburg as well as managing rainwater drainage.

As shown in Figure 7.1, the private companies received 49.9 per cent of the Waterworks' assets for 1.7 billion Euros. While the State remained institutionally liable as the Waterworks' guarantor, it owned 50.1 per cent of the assets and served as a co-shareholder (Ochman 2005). For the actual implementation of the PPP, the Berlin Water Holding was created. While the Waterworks remains a public law institution, the private law Holding serves as its institutional owner with complete authority over the Waterworks' operational management (Passadakis 2006). Through the Holding, private actors – as 'silent partners' – could own and make capital investments in the Waterworks and conversely, could receive profits in the form of interest on the capital required for operations. Moreover, through this Holding, private actors could be responsible for the Waterworks' corporate management (Ochman 2005).[2] Termination of this contractual agreement was difficult, as the public sector party was obliged to compensate the private sector party.

The PPP of the Berlin Waterworks was the second largest privatization in the European water sector – after England and Wales (Beveridge and Hüesker

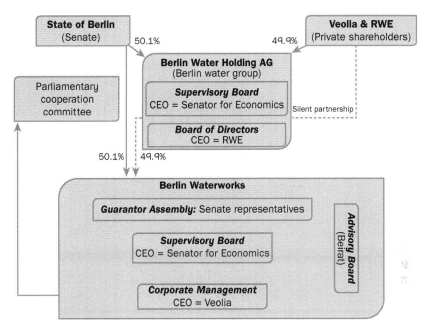

Figure 7.1 The PPP of the Berlin Waterworks

Source: Lieberherr et al. (2012).

2010). In addition, this PPP was an example of the German privatization model with *shared* ownership and financing between public and private actors and with regulation via *supervisory* boards. This serves as an alternative privatization model to the commonly known English model of divestiture and the French model of delegation: i.e., concession and lease within a public ownership frame (Moreau-Le Golvan and Breant 2007).

Objectives of the PPP

The aim of the PPP in Berlin was to attract sufficient private capital so as to effectively operate the Waterworks: e.g., meet investment, drinking water and resource protection mandates (Lieberherr et al. 2012). In addition, a key aim set out in the contracts (signed between the State and shareholders) was to generate profit through increased efficiency (Oelmann et al. 2009). Ultimately, the aim can be described as attracting private capital so as to effectively provide water services to achieve public acceptance in the city-state of Berlin.

Outcomes of the PPP

The outcomes of the PPP have been mixed. On the one hand, the Waterworks has been operating effectively in terms of fulfilling investment mandates as well as generating profit for the private shareholders albeit not for the State. Studies indicate that the Waterworks exceeded its investment mandate of a minimum of 2.56 billion Euros from 1999 to 2009 (Hüesker 2011; Oelmann et al. 2009). Simultaneously, the private shareholders have received their promised 11 per cent rate of return since 1999 (Oelmann et al. 2009). Interestingly, the latter two outcomes are linked: as demonstrated by the following quote, particularly the private shareholders have had a direct incentive to invest: 'Opponents of the PPP always think that the private investors restrict investments … The private shareholders rejoice about every Euro that is invested [in the assets] because they can then re-invest this Euro and make a profit' (Interview 1.1 in Lieberherr 2012). The drinking water objectives have also largely been achieved: while the water quality is considered high and the Waterworks complies with the legal standards, there have been some pollution incidents; yet no reported public health incidents (Lieberherr 2012).

On the other hand, the Waterworks has achieved mixed results in terms of resource protection: the Waterworks increasingly failed to meet the effluent wastewater standards and the Berlin Water Authority reported that it was difficult for it to implement projects and legal mandates to safeguard resource protection under the PPP (Lieberherr 2012). However, the effectiveness of the PPP has been most significantly impeded by the low public acceptance. The push and impact of such discontent have been manifested through public protests, negative press and the creation of a citizen organization focused on the re-municipalization of the Waterworks. According to a survey by the *Berliner Morgenpost* newspaper, the majority of citizens (67 per cent) support the re-municipalization of the Waterworks as well as of gas and electricity (Fahrun 2010). Specifically, the successful 2011 popular initiative to make the partial privatization contracts public can be regarded as an indicator of public dissatisfaction with the current governance mode (Lieberherr 2012; *Der Tagesspiegel* 2011). Spurred on by the popular initiative, the Waterworks was re-municipalized in 2013 at the expense of the state which had already forfeited its profit-share in the early years of the PPP (in this chapter we only assess the outcomes up until 2012, prior to the re-municipalization).

Berlin Waterworks Governance Problems

Two critical factors affecting the outcomes of the PPP are: (1) a participation deficit; and (2) a lack of integrity.

Participation

The low public acceptance was largely due to the exclusive policy-making of the PPP, involving select senators, private consultants and representatives from the private shareholders (Beveridge 2010). Decision-making occurred without collective discussion and approval of a larger body of actors, e.g., the Parliament or civil society (Lieberherr et al. 2012). The parliamentarians were excluded from decision-making about the contractual agreements, and generally had limited influence on the PPP (Lieberherr et al. 2012). In addition, there was public outrage due to extra-legal contracts that were made behind closed doors and were secret to the public and the Parliament (until the Autumn of 2010, when they became public due to public pressure) (Hüesker 2011; Moss and Hüesker 2010).

In addition, the water users in Berlin did not have direct access to, and influence on, decision-making concerning the Waterworks, neither through the Parliament nor through public voting; thus, they could not influence substantive decisions on how the Waterworks spent its money and which projects it implements. The only democratically authorized body *in*directly involved in decision-making was the Senate – co-shareholder with Veolia and RWE – through its *representation* in the supervisory boards. A senator was the chairperson of both supervisory boards and the private investors were in the minority in these bodies, as shown in Figure 7.1.

The public also disapproved of the extra-legal contracts that weakened the Senate's ability to influence decision-making and *de facto* the democratic control instruments were not found to be used (Lieberherr 2012). The Senate could not make decisions without the approval of the private actors (Beveridge and Hüesker 2010). Moreover, all decision-making about the Waterworks – including about the PPP arrangement – required the approval of all shareholders, as defined in the extra-legal contracts (Lieberherr 2012). The advisory board – shown in Figure 7.1 – was supposed to provide a public interest voice within the Waterworks' decision-making structure. This body was comprised of diverse actors including representatives from the lower house of Parliament, industry and the Chamber of Commerce in Berlin, the Environment Department of the State of Brandenburg and various other governmental and civil societal associations. Yet the advisory board had a limited amount of influence, as it was only able to advise the corporate management and supervisory boards regarding tasks relating to the general public interest.

Integrity

The lack of integrity was another key factor affecting the negative outcomes of the PPP. A primary reason for the lack of effectiveness was that the process of economic enforcement as well as the public and private roles became blurred in the context of the PPP. Indeed, the Senate became its own regulator: as Berlin is a city-state, it is a two-tiered system, the Senate (and its departments) simultaneously became regulator and majority shareholder of a for-profit organization. A key element here is the development of the interest rate. Following a constitutional court ruling in 1999 declaring the initial interest rate as unconstitutional for a provider of services of general public interest, representatives from the Senate Finance Department and the private shareholders revised the interest rate calculation (profit margin) in such a way that it in effect became the same rate (ca. 8 per cent) (Heiser 2010; Hüesker 2011). In other words, the 'unconstitutional' interest rate was implemented. As background information for this manoeuvre: the Senate had obliged itself to ensure that the shareholders received their profit margin which initially led the state to forfeit its profit-percentage, until the interest rate was high enough (Consortium Contract, §23.7, 'Profit Guarantee' clause).

The effect of this interest rate on the Waterworks was a fixed profit percentage within its tariff system that has been borne by the water users: 21–22 per cent of all proceeds were allocated to the shareholders – half to the State of Berlin and the other half to the private shareholders (Berliner Wasserbetriebe 2007).

In addition, the high interest rate and rate of return regulation led to incentives to increase the asset base, and invest more, because this increased the interest rate (Lieberherr 2012). Accordingly, there are arguments that investments were not made based on actual needs. Data indicate that the large sums that were invested today might not have been necessary. A report argues that large-scale investments were necessary in Berlin in the early 1990s, due to the unification of water utilities in East and West Berlin (Oelmann et al. 2009). Yet with today's state-of-the-art infrastructure, it became questionable whether large investments were necessary per se (Lieberherr 2012). What might matter more than lump-sum investments is where, how and for what investments were made, e.g., it was found that investments for resource protection were lacking (Lieberherr 2012).

Furthermore, the above interest rate has been borne by the water users (since 2003) via a rise in water prices (between 22 and 25 per cent since 1999). The rise in water prices was a key factor influencing the low public acceptance and the eventual process of re-municipalization (Fahrun 2010; Hüesker 2011).

Conclusion

We have analysed two cases – PFI in United Kingdom health care and the Berlin Waterworks – of PPPs for public service provision from a governance perspective. In both cases we find governance challenges that negatively affect the intended policy objectives. Overall, these cases serve as different examples of PPP in diverging contexts. Within this 'least similar' design we have found governance challenges in both. The cases also share the challenge of high asset specificity and contract failure. Moreover, in both cases, the long-term contracts are difficult to terminate, and come at a significant cost to the taxpayer, as the state must compensate the private sector actors. These factors can be regarded as contributing to the governance challenges.

A key challenge shared by both cases is the ability of the government to generate a profit in public service provision in the context of a PPP. In the United Kingdom, this is the stated objective of the PF2 and, in Berlin, it was implemented via the extra-legal contracts linked to the PPP. This led to a blurring of public and private motives in both cases, as the respective governments also became subject to a profit motive. In addition, despite the alleged risk transfer from public to private sector actors in the context of PFI, the government ultimately remains responsible for safeguarding the provision of public services in both cases – be it public health care or water.

We have also found key governance dimensions that differed between the cases. In the United Kingdom PFI case, we found that a lack of accountability, transparency and policy capacity play a central role in the failure to achieve cost savings and value for money. To offset the lack of transparency and the hidden incentives to choose PFI over other capital investment measures, the Treasury Committee in the United Kingdom has strongly recommended the application of International Financing Reporting Standards (IFRS). Yet the issue still has not been settled. To strengthen policy capacity, NAO lists various proposals and scientific reports, reports of the House of Commons Treasury Committee, and other public or private agencies have contributed a great deal to the stock of knowledge on how to deal with PFI. But the availability of intelligence does not guarantee that it is properly used in practice, which may be currently impeding the achievement of efficiency and effectiveness.

We set forth the argument that PFI is not in itself a bad idea, but that in order to be successful in achieving policy outcomes, a very careful accountability structure should be set up, which pays special attention to the risk transfer, avoiding regulations that rebound the risk to the public sector party. In addition, the accountability structure (who is responsible and held accountable to whom) should be very clearly and explicitly formulated in the contract. Also, as policy capacity matters, emphasis should be placed on developing the skills and expertise of public actors. Indeed, as noted above, progress has already been made in this regard, through framework agreements and benchmarks.

In the Berlin Waterworks case, we found that the governance challenges of low participation and integrity have a negative effect on the outcomes of the PPP. The lack of civil societal participation as well as the blurring of roles regarding economic regulation and interest rate development, have arguably led to the mixed policy outcomes and the current re-municipalization. Indeed, the dual role of the Senate as economic regulator and shareholder meant that the PPP model might lack the necessary integrity to achieve the policy outcomes. The PPP arguably led to a 'double institutionalization of a profit-orientation' (Moss and Hüesker 2010: 38): on the one hand, policies became measured according to whether they meet commercial interests of private shareholders. On the other hand, the State, now as the majority shareholder of the for-profit Waterworks has had a strong incentive to orient policies towards profit opportunities rather than towards social and environmental needs.

In response to the lack of participation and integrity in Berlin, civil society groups put pressure on the Parliament to take action against the Senate and the PPP, with lawyers arguing that the Parliament can 'force the State of Berlin to act against the partial privatization of the Berlin Waterworks', because the contractual obligation of the Senate's 'Profit Guarantee' to the private investors "'violates the Parliament's" budget law' (EUWID 2011: 1). Moreover, the parliamentary elections in 2011 were regarded as playing a pivotal role in the future of the Waterworks (Lieberherr et al. 2012). This civil society pressure culminated in the re-municipalization of the Waterworks in 2013.

In sum, by improving the integrity by clarifying the roles of the Senate as well as making the policy-making process more open to at least the Parliament, the Berlin PPP could have been more successful in achieving its policy outcomes, and a re-municipalization could have been avoided. Indeed, the lack of re-regulation to clearly separate the role of the Senate in Berlin by, for example, implementing a sector-specific regulator is remarkable, because such privatization processes are often coupled with re-regulation so as to foster integrity

(Menard 2009; Peterson et al. 2009). Indeed, a comparative analysis of other cases of privatization, such as in England and Wales, with the Berlin case, indicates that the re-regulation and the system of semi-independent regulators is a decisive factor influencing the policy outcomes (Lieberherr 2012).

Drawing lessons from the two cases on PFI in health care in the United Kingdom and the Berlin Waterworks, we argue that the strengthening of specific governance dimensions could foster the achievement of the intended policy outcomes. While the factors of assets specificity and contract failure cannot be changed in these cases of health care and water infrastructure, the governance dimensions of accountability, transparency, policy capacity, participation and integrity can be adapted in order to offset information asymmetry and opportunistic behaviour. Certain dimensions of governance failure of PPP projects, such as lack of participation and transparency, may serve as preconditions for private actor involvement. However, we make the argument that by adapting governance, PPPs may be successful: for example, re-regulation can have a positive effect on policy outcomes (see Peterson et al. 2009). We have given some indications of how these can be adapted both top-down (government (re-)regulations, implementing sector-specific regulations, reporting standards, etc.) and bottom-up (civil society initiatives, representative and direct democratic means).

Together these two cases of PFI in the United Kingdom and the Berlin Waterworks in Germany shed light on a whole range of governance challenges. They illustrate that governance challenges are both case- and context-specific. By gaining insight into the challenges in specific cases, we can then glean insights to apply to similar cases in the respective sectors.

Notes

1 Veolia Environment is a French multinational environmental service corporation. RWE Aqua is a German multinational energy and water service corporation. Another company, Allianz, was also initially a shareholder but later withdrew.
2 The 1999 Partial Privatization Law enabled this delegation of the Waterworks' management to an external legal entity (Ochman 2005). However, this Holding model is considered 'atypical' because it has more entrepreneurial rights than usual and has complete authority over the Waterworks, as the Holding is responsible for the operational management (Lanz and Eitner 2005).

References

Berliner Wasserbetriebe (2007) *Grundlagen der Tarifkalkulation* (Vol. 9/2007 1.000, pp. 1–20). Berlin: Berlinerwasser.

Beveridge, R. (2010) A politics of inevitability: the privatisation of the Berlin Water Company, the global city discourse and governance in 1990s Berlin. Doctoral thesis, Newcastle University, Newcastle, UK.

Beveridge, R. and Hüesker, F. (2010) Privatisation and the de-politicisation of water policymaking: the partial privatisation of Berliner Wasserbetriebe. Paper presented at the CFP Politics Beyond the State: Transformations of the State between De- and Repoliticisation, Bremen.

Corner, D. (2006) The United Kingdom Private Finance Initiative: the challenge of allocating risk, *OECD Journal on Budgeting*, 5(3): 37–53.

Edwards, P., Shaoul, J., Stafford, A. and Arblaster, L. (2004) *Evaluating the Operation of PFI in Roads and Hospitals*. Association of Chartered Certified Accounts (ACCA), Research Report no. 84.

Epstein, W. (2013) Contract theory and the failures of public-private contracting, *Cardozo Law Review*, 6: 2211.

EUWID (2011) Experten halten juristische Anfechtung der BWB-Wasserverträge für möglich, *EUWID Wasser und Abwasser*, 39: 1–2.

Fahrun, J. (2010) Kartellamt ermittelt gegen Berliner Wasserbetriebe, *Berliner Morgenpost*, 7 December.

Heiser, S. (2010) Gewinne marsch!, *Die Tageszeitung*, 31 October.

HM Treasury (2012) *Government's New Approach to Private Finance*. London: HMSO.

House of Commons Treasury Committee (2011) *Private Finance Initiative: Seventeenth Report of Session 2010–2012*. London: The Stationery Office Limited.

House of Commons Treasury Committee (2012) *Private Finance Initiative: Government, OBR and NAO Responses to the Seventeenth Report from the Committee: Twenty-fifth Report of Session 2010–12*. London: The Stationery Office.

Hüesker, F. (2011) *Auswirkungen von Privatisierungen auf die Gemeinwohlfähigkeit des Daseinsvorsorgestaates – untersucht am Fall der Wasserbetriebe des Landes Berlin*. München: Oekom Verlag.

Lambert, V. (2010) The pros and cons of PFI hospitals, *The Telegraph*, 10 March.

Lanz, K. and Eitner, K. (2005) *WaterTime Case Study: Berlin, Germany*. Hamburg: European Commission, pp. 1–30.

Lieberherr, E. (2012) Transformation of water governance and legitimacy: comparing Swiss, German and English water supply and sanitation service providers. Doctoral thesis, Swiss Federal Institute of Technology, Lausanne.

Lieberherr, E., Klinke, A. and Finger, M. (2012) Towards legitimate water governance? The partially privatized Berlin waterworks, *Public Management Review*, 14(7): 923–46. DOI: 10.1080/14719037.2011.650056.

McKee, M., Edwards, N. and Atun, R. (2006) Public-private partnerships for hospitals, *Bulletin of the World Health Organization*, 84(11): 890–6.

Menard, C. (2009) From technical integrity to institutional coherence: regulatory challenges in the water sector, in C. Menard and M. Ghertman (eds) *Regulation, Deregulation, Reregulation: Institutional Perspectives*. Northampton, MA: Edward Elgar Publishing, Inc., pp. 83–108.

Moreau-Le Golvan, Y. and Breant, P. (2007) Organisation and financing models of the drinking water sector: review of available information on trends and changes, *Techneau*, January: 1–31.

Moss, T. and Hüesker, F. (2010) *Wasserinfrastrukturen als Gemeinwohlträger zwischen globalem Wandel und regionaler Entwicklung – institutionelle Erwiderungen in Berlin-Brandenburg Interdisziplinären Arbeitsgruppen IAG Globaler Wandel – Regionale Entwicklung* (Diskussionspapier Vol. 4). Berlin: Berlin-Brandenburgerische Akademie der Wissenschaften, pp. 32–41.

NAO (National Audit Office) (2011) *Lessons from PFI and Other Projects: Report by the Comptroller and Auditor General*. London: NAO.

Ochman, D. (2005) Rechtsformwahrende Privatisierung von öffentlichen Anstalten: Dargestellt am Holdingmodell zur Teilprivatisierung der Berliner Wasserbetriebe. Doctoral thesis, Universität Bochum, Bochum.

Oelmann, M., Böschen, I., Kschonz, C. and Müller, G. (2009) *10 Years of Water Services Partnership in Berlin: An Assessment of the Public-Private Partnership between the State of Berlin, RWE Aqua and Veolia Wasser*. Berlin: wik Consult, pp. 1–34.

Passadakis, A. (2006) The Berlin WaterWorks: from commercialization and partial privatization to public democratic water enterprises, in S. Wagenknecht (ed.) *Berlin* and Brussels: *Vereinigte Europäische Linke/Nordische Grüne Linke, Europäisches Parliament*, vol. 10, pp. 1–49.

Peterson, T., Klauer, B. and Manstetten, R. (2009) The environment as a challenge for governmental responsibility: the case of the European Water Framework Directive, *Ecological Economics*, 68: 2058–65.

Pollock, A. (2005) *NHS Plc: The Privatisation of Our Health Care*. London: Verso Books.

Pollock, A. (2012) How PFI is crippling the NHS, *The Guardian*, 29 June.

Scottish Information Commisioner (2007) Scottish Information Officer orders release of NHS Lothian PFI contract. News release, 24 October.

Swift, N. (2012) Why PFI contracts need to be more transparent, *Guardian Professional*, 29 June.

Der Tagesspiegel (2011) Berliner Volksentscheid erfolgreich Senat soll Wasserverträge offenlegen, *Der Tagesspiegel*, 13 February.

Timmins, N. (2013) Spending squeeze to hurt hospitals the most, *Financial Times*, 22 January.

chapter eight

The governance of coverage in health systems: England's National Institute for Health and Care Excellence (NICE)

Iestyn Williams

Introduction

Government programmes to restrict the use of medicines in public systems are fraught with risk, and rarely increase the political capital of their architects. While 'success' in this endeavour is likely to provoke accusations of rationing, unsuccessful strategies can exacerbate spending and service variation levels. It is little wonder then that formal government policy has customarily been marked by its absence (Blank and Burau 2007). In recent times, delegation and devolution of responsibility for decision-making have emerged as the dominant policy approaches, and national coverage advisory bodies are now a common feature of OECD health care systems. However, the governance arrangements of these bodies differ substantially, with attendant implications for both the policy formation process and the implementation of this into practice. This chapter examines the governance of coverage policy in health care. It presents a case study of the National Institute for Health and Care Excellence (NICE), the body that issues guidance on coverage of health care interventions to the English NHS. The chapter begins by contextualizing and describing the work of NICE and in particular its Technology Appraisals Programme. This is followed by an analysis of the governance dimensions of NICE, and how these have shaped outcomes in terms of policy implementation and impact. Although NICE emerges as something of a success story from the analysis presented, a number of persistent tensions and challenges are identified, the resolution of which is perhaps beyond the remit of the Institute itself.

The context: understanding coverage policy

Although the focus here is on publicly funded health care, coverage decisions are taken both in systems where private insurance is prevalent and in those dominated by government programmes. In the US Medicare, Medicaid, the Children's Health Insurance Program, the Department of Veterans Affairs, as well as private insurance and managed care organizations all have some responsibility for coverage decision-making. Systems with a stronger central planning function, such as the United Kingdom, assign greater responsibility to statutory bodies, whereas non-profit insurance agencies carry prime responsibility in countries such as Germany and the Netherlands. Coverage decision-making can be administered at levels ranging from the organizational (e.g., the hospital formulary) to the macro governmental, and can include positive listing of sanctioned interventions or negative listing of those not approved for reimbursement.

The intended implications of coverage at the policy implementation stage are that treatments not covered are withdrawn from the menu on offer to patients and patient cohorts. In this respect, technology coverage can be an important mechanism for the rationing of health care. However, coverage is more commonly presented as a means of solving problems of access and service inequality, through standardized assessment of the effectiveness and cost effectiveness of interventions. The evidence required for such assessment has given rise to Comparative Effectiveness Research (CER), Health Technology Assessment (HTA) and Cost Effectiveness Analysis (CEA). Increasingly the dominant OECD approach to supply of such evidence is through specially created guidance-producing bodies set up as advisers to health ministries. However, significant variation exists in the levels of autonomy and responsibility assigned to these. For example, while some do issue advice, others produce *de facto* policy decisions that are binding on subsystems (Landwehr and Böhm 2011). However, despite the ubiquity of these arrangements, we know relatively little about how the distinctive features of coverage bodies interact with contexts to shape policy implementation and outcomes (Flinders 2009; Williams 2013).

The policy: NICE and coverage in the English NHS

In 1999, the United Kingdom Labour Government established the National Institute for Clinical Excellence (NICE) , later to become the National Institute for *Health* and Clinical Excellence and, later still, the National Institute for Health and *Care* Excellence. These name changes reflect an expansion in the NICE's role and remit to include evidence-based reviews of public health and social care interventions, alongside its original brief to produce guidance on investment in new health care technologies and guidelines for clinical practice. Following the most recent NHS reforms, NICE has been granted the status of a non-departmental public body.

The programme of NICE work that has generated most interest has been the Technology Appraisals Programme. The appraisals function is performed by four branches of a committee consisting of experts and advocates appointed by NICE. For each proposed intervention the committee receives an independent evidence review in the form of a formal assessment of a new technology relative to a comparator and with benefits measured against cost. The committee also considers submissions from parties ranging from the sponsor of each technology considered to patient representatives and expert bodies. The committee convenes to discuss the evidence and listen to further testimony from clinical and patient representatives before producing provisional and final determinations. At its most definitive, this guidance will either recommend the routine use of the technology in all appropriate clinical situations, or will recommend that the NHS not adopt the technology. Alternatively, guidance will recommend restricted use, for example, in certain patient categories only or as part of ongoing research (Raftery 2001).

The stated policy aim of NICE is to reduce unacceptable variations in service quality and access. However, NICE coverage decisions are based on the twin criteria of clinical and cost effectiveness which implies a second policy aim: to restrict access to only those interventions that represent value for money. Despite its counter-claims, therefore, NICE might reasonably be considered a mechanism to support health care prioritization and rationing (Klein 2010).[1] The NICE approach is made possible by an explicit delimiting of decision criteria. For example, issues of affordability and implementation of decisions taken are deemed to be beyond the core remit of the Appraisals Committee, leaving them to focus on evidence of effectiveness and cost effectiveness.

Perhaps the most unique feature of NICE technology appraisals, when compared to HTA bodies elsewhere, is their compulsory status: appraisal recommendations are binding on local NHS payers and funding for approved technologies must be made available within 90 days of publication. NICE is therefore not just an embodiment of coverage policy in the English NHS but also a policy-making body in and of itself. The centrally mandated status of NICE guidance therefore forms a major plank of the government's strategy for coverage policy implementation.

The outcome: appraising NICE

The NICE model of technology coverage policy has received widespread and sustained critical attention. Two fundamental aspects of output perhaps best illustrate the extent of NICE's success as a vehicle for coverage policy. The first is the degree to which NICE recommendations are adopted by local systems, and the second is the extent to which this adoption has brought about the intended benefits in service access and quality. Before touching on each of these, it is perhaps worth noting that the survival of NICE for 14 years, and for the foreseeable future, might itself be regarded as something of an achievement. The Institute may have a mixed profile at home but overseas is regularly held up as an example of good practice (Kerr and Scott 2009). What's more, four Westminster governments have concluded that NICE's work is not just necessary but should be expanded in terms of both the volume and range of guidance it produces.[2] This is despite repeated reform of virtually every other aspect of the system, and at least one attempted 'bonfire of the quangos' (Flinders and Skelcher 2012). In the highly inflammatory area of health care coverage, this longevity is notable and perhaps owes something to NICE's willingness to evolve and develop over time.

Implementation rates

The status of NICE appraisals and guidance – and therefore the relationship of the Institute with government, local payers and industry – has been subject to change. In line with most equivalent bodies, NICE initially made recommendations which the wider health system was encouraged but not obliged to implement. However, early national evaluations showed implementation rates to be poor (Sheldon et al. 2005). Low take-up of NICE guidance triggered a government directive compelling implementation within three months, with extensions only granted by the Secretary of State. Despite this, implementation and compliance rates remain something of a problem. Formal requests to extend the implementation period have been made in relation to approximately 10 per cent of guidance, and studies tracing implementation of specific technologies suggest that variability has not been substantially reduced (Price et al. 2012; Harvey 2013). More recently, NICE recommendations regarding discontinuation of treatments have also suffered from low rates of take-up (Chamberlain et al. 2013).

Impact

NICE has undoubtedly increased the level and volume of evidence used to support investment decisions in key areas of NHS activity. In this respect it can be seen to have moved health care further in line with an evidence-based model of policy and practice, and to have reduced geographical variation – the so-called 'postcode lottery'. However, notwithstanding problems of implementation, a number of other aspects of NICE's impact have been questioned. For example, a House of Commons Select Committee (2007) report criticized the delay in access to treatments caused by the lengthy nature of the appraisals process. In response, the Institute has launched a parallel 'single technology appraisal' process designed to generate swifter recommendations. A key difference of this new programme is that the evidence base is supplied primarily by the manufacturer of the intervention (NICE 2009). This brings NICE closer to the model of bodies such as the Scottish Medicines Consortium (Cairns 2006).

A second issue relates to the potentially distorting effect that NICE appraisals can have on local clinical priorities. An Audit Commission report – along with the aforementioned Select Committee review – noted that NICE appraisals have an additive effect on NHS spending (Audit Commission 2005; House of Commons Select Committee 2007). As a result, commissioners of services at the local level have been forced to divert funds from other treatments for which there is no NICE guidance (Buxton 2006). Arguably, this unintended effect has a negative impact on service quality, while also delaying implementation, as Fearnley et al. (2012: 559) note:

> The reality is that funding to allow acquisition of new equipment and staff training must be obtained through savings elsewhere. The need for structured training and assessment of personnel involved in the use of new technology is clearly an additional obstacle to rapid implementation.

NICE and the governance of coverage policy

Despite its achievement, then, NICE's appraisals programme has not been an unqualified success and this next section considers elements of governance as a means of examining why this might be the case.

Accountability

The delegation of guidance production to non-majoritarian national HTA bodies can be understood as an example of 'agencification', that is, the structural disaggregation of statutory bodies from government ministries. In the area of health care coverage, organisations such as NICE have become integral to policy formation, albeit within the constraints and parameters set down by government. Accountability for processes and outcomes is therefore important, especially where guidance is binding on subsystems. This places NICE in a complex inter-organizational relationship in which it is both agent – with the government as principal – and principal – with local implementing bodies as the agent. The latter relationship has proven most difficult to negotiate, as is discussed below. NICE's primary relationship of accountability is to its sponsor department within national government, via the NICE board and senior management team. However, the Institute has a higher level of relative autonomy from government than national HTA agencies in most other OECD countries. Indeed, demonstration of this independence to outside parties has become integral to the Institute's legitimacy.

NICE operates a conflicts of interest policy for directors, employees, collaborating bodies, chairs of advisory committees, and employees, which precludes financial relationships with industry (Steinbrook 2008). Furthermore, the clinicians, professional groups, academics, and patient and public representatives that make up the branches of the appraisals committees are independent from and not employed by NICE (Sorenson et al. 2012). Alongside these arrangements, NICE has invested heavily in the procedural dimensions of its appraisals process. In particular, NICE aims to meet the conditions of 'accountability for reasonableness'. This framework, formulated by Daniels and Sabin (1998) in the context of US managed care coverage decision-making, seeks to increase legitimacy and acceptance for decision-making and is made up of four conditions, described here by Syrett (2003: 135):

> Decision-making should be characterised by public accessibility of decisions and their rationales (the 'publicity' condition), by predication upon principles and evidence that are considered relevant to the fair distribution of healthcare resources (the 'relevance' condition), by the existence of mechanisms for dispute resolution and revision of decisions in light of new evidence (the 'appeals' condition) and by the existence of systems of voluntary or public regulation to ensure that the other conditions are met (the 'enforcement' condition).

Further discussion of how NICE seeks to maximize publicity and relevance is provided below. To date, the combination of accountability mechanisms and processes implemented by NICE appears to have enabled it to be robust to challenge both through its internal appeals process and in the courts (NICE 2004; Raftery 2006; Syrett 2008). As noted, NICE has also been subject to Audit Commission and House of Commons reviews, both of which identified areas for development while acknowledging the overall soundness of NICE's operations.

Transparency

In comparison to other coverage bodies, NICE has been found to be unusually proactive in publicizing its processes and decisions (Landwehr and Böhm 2011). Alongside its considerable national media profile, the Institute points to ongoing enhancements to its website designed to make information easily accessed and understood (Sorenson et al. 2012). NICE publishes Appraisal Committee minutes and both preliminary and final guidance on its website, and final guidance is made available as a technical report, a summary report and as a patient information document. NICE was one of the first HTA bodies to make available a formal appeals mechanism and remains rare in allowing individuals other than manufacturers of the technology to launch an appeal (Stafinski et al. 2011).

Observational studies of NICE appraisal decision-making have noted how the rules governing committee deliberation – especially in the absence of compelling evidence – have at times been somewhat opaque (Williams et al. 2007). Conducting deliberations behind 'closed doors' has been shown to enable decision-makers to project a misleading appearance of certainty and precision to outside audiences (Chambers 2004). NICE's recent move to hold board, advisory committee and appeals panel meetings in public directly addresses this perceived failing of transparency. The rationale provided indicates the Institute's awareness of the transparency dimensions of governance:

> Holding committee meetings in public supports the Institute's commitment to having processes for developing guidance that are rigorous, open and transparent. It allows consultees and stakeholders to understand the basis for the acceptance or rejection of the various forms of evidence that are considered and illustrates how the committees take account of the evidence submitted by stakeholders and consultees.

> (www.nice.org.uk, accessed 30 December 2013)

There is somewhat less transparency with regard to the process of agenda-setting for NICE. Topic selection is determined through a combination of means but final responsibility rests with the Department of Health. This relative lack of transparency (compared to other stages of the appraisal process) is symptomatic of a relationship with government which at times threatens to undermine NICE's legitimacy. For example, the Ministry of Health has on occasion intervened in the 'territory' of NICE by recommending the availability of technologies before NICE has ruled on them, apparently in an attempt to court public opinion (Harding 2005).

A further source of transparency derives from NICE's aspiration to an evidence-based approach to decision-making and its commitment to comparative economic evaluation presented, where possible, using Quality Adjusted Life

Years (QALYs). This has formed an important component of NICE's defence against complaints of unfairness and unreasonableness in its determinations (Williams 2013). However, it has also been weakened by the apparently arbitrary grounds for deciding what constitutes a satisfactory level of cost effectiveness. There has been some confusion over whether NICE operates a cost effectiveness threshold above which new technologies are not funded. NICE itself has indicated that it is inclined to 'accept as cost effective those interventions with an incremental cost effectiveness ratio of less than £20,000 per QALY' (NICE 2007). The House of Commons review picked up on the theme of the threshold, suggesting that this was unsupported and requires independent validation:

> The affordability of NICE guidance and the threshold it uses to decide whether a treatment is cost-effective are of serious concern. The threshold is not based on empirical research and is not directly related to the NHS budget.

> (House of Commons Health Select Committee 2007: 7)

Perhaps in recognition of this weakness, NICE does not treat the threshold as fixed, and characteristics of the patient population can lead NICE towards more lenient treatment of expensive interventions (Stafinski et al. 2011). However, this flexibility arguably compromises transparency and on occasion – for example, in relation to the NICE ruling on Beta Interferon and glatiramer acetate as treatments for multiple sclerosis – has laid the Institute open to claims of capture from either the Department of Health or industry (Klein 2006).

Participation

NICE has increased and improved the avenues for participation in its appraisals during its time-in-life. Interested parties have opportunities to become involved at multiple stages in the appraisals process as a result of the phased dissemination of information. Comparisons suggest that NICE is rare in its acceptance of unsolicited presentations from any quarter, and the extent of its stakeholder consultation in general (Stafinski et al. 2011). NICE currently convenes a Partners' Council to discuss strategic challenges with stakeholders from industry, the NHS and academia and works closely with industry in the scoping phase of assessment (Sorenson et al. 2012). It has also created a Citizens' Council which deliberates on social value dilemmas relating to age, disease severity, equity, and so on. This Council consists of 30 members of the public and these exclude representatives of lobbying organizations (Sorenson et al. 2008).

In these ways, NICE has developed its participative mechanisms to a point where it is held up as an example of innovation. However, participation remains constrained and is traded off against other drivers and imperatives. A particular challenge for NICE is the breadth of groups affected by its appraisals guidance – including patients and patient groups, citizens, professional groups and manufacturers and industry. In its decision rules, NICE clearly proceeds on a predominantly technocratic basis, in line with HTA agencies across the OECD. However, its parallel mechanisms for participation can be accused of invoking inconsistent forms of rationality in the pursuit of politically acceptable decision-making (Cheyne and Comrie 2002). The former draws on the instrumentalism that is compatible with a normative economic approach and the latter promotes dialogue and democracy as an end in itself (Fleck 1992; Fischer 2003).

The tension between evidence and participation is one that can be negotiated but perhaps not resolved by bodies such as NICE. Clearly the organizing assumption of the Institute's work is that fairness and legitimacy are best served through the objectivity of an evidence-based approach rather than the more traditional 'special pleading' of winners and losers in the policy process. However, this has proved to be a necessary but insufficient step to attainment of defensible determinations, and the requirements to consider social values have increasingly been recognized. This poses problems because, as Evans (1997) notes, definitively held public values are hard to pin down. This complexity has led some to posit an 'irreducible pluralism' preventing attainment of a unified normative stance (Schlander 2008: 535). Of course NICE is not alone in navigating these tensions. Elsewhere the rise of HTA does not appear to have brought about a de-politicization of explicit priority setting, and many HTA agencies merely feed into a broader process of pluralistic bargaining over resource allocation (Oliver et al. 2004). By contrast, NICE's primary approach is medico-economic and this sets considerable constraints on the extent to which devolution and deliberation in decision-making can be pursued.

Integrity

NICE appears to conform to required standards of integrity in terms of how it recruits and manages employees, as well as how it spends its budget and inducts committee members. Efforts have been made to clarify and explain the Institute's role and mission, and potential for agency role duplication has been addressed through merger with bodies such as the Health Development Agency and the National Prescribing Centre.

Policy capacity

NICE's technical capability and resource are perhaps unsurpassed among technology coverage guidance bodies across the world. The multiple appraisals process affords the committee a *de novo* systematic review and economic evaluation for every technology under review, and in-house resources for any additional analytical work required. The committees include individuals with high levels of expertise in the methodologies employed in the evidence-analysis process, such as, for example, decision modelling, health economics and public health.

Other areas of policy capacity have proven less robust and have been targeted for improvement. In particular, the implementation gap that emerged in the early years of NICE has been addressed in a number of ways. This includes integration of NICE guidance adoption into NHS regulatory and performance management regimes, and financial incentives and payment systems. For example, the NHS Quality and Outcomes Framework, which is used to assess the performance of health care providers, applies clinical indicators derived from NICE guidance. Furthermore NICE-approved treatments are expected to be automatically added to local formularies and access to these is considered a patient entitlement under the NHS Constitution (NICE 2012). NICE has also developed an implementation programme to support guidance adoption (Sorenson et al. 2012). This includes: targeted dissemination of guidance; active engagement with implementing organizations within and outside of the NHS; development of awareness-raising educational materials and implementation tools, and evaluation of uptake. A full evaluation of these activities is beyond the scope of this chapter. However, the wider literature on technology adoption would suggest that these explicit knowledge dissemination strategies require accompanying tacit knowledge exchange work if they are to reap significant benefits (Williams and Dickinson 2010).

There are also broader issues of alignment that constrain the success of NICE as a means of shaping coverage policy in the English NHS. Chapter 2 of this volume states that policy capacity is the *ability to develop policy that is aligned with resources in pursuit of societal goals*. We have already seen that NICE guidance has had an additive effect on NHS spending. In the early period of NICE's life, this was offset to some degree by incremental uplifts in government spending on health care. However, the current period of stagnant spending and budgetary shortfalls threatens to intensify the financial dilemmas created by NICE rulings. The Institute recognizes this problem and has responded by increasing activity in the area of disinvestment. However, there is a dearth of evidence on how to tackle disinvestment in an English NHS context. This is despite the growing consensus that decommissioning is something of an 'Achilles' heel' for health care systems which has been characterized as local health communities often becoming 'stuck with the old and overwhelmed by the new' (Elshaug et al. 2007). In response, attempts have been made to generate lists of existing practices for discontinuation including NICE's 'do-not-do' database (Garner et al. 2013). In support of this work, research has focused on the application of clinical evidence and economic analysis to the process of candidate identification, principally through the reorientation of Health Technology Assessment (or 'reassessment') (Leggett et al. 2012; Shepperd et al. 2013). NICE is at the heart of this work, for example, through development and evaluation of its own disinvestment tools and resources in the South-West Peninsula (Flynn and Gericke 2012). Overall, therefore, NICE continues to be at the forefront of developments in technology coverage policy and practice but remains in the short term somewhat out of step with the financial landscape inhabited by those affected by its work.

A second area of potential misalignment relates to the social value principles embodied and propagated by NICE. In consideration of the participatory aspects of the governance of NICE, we noted the potential for disjuncture between a utilitarian decision rule (i.e., QALY maximization) and wider social values. This tension also impinges on the policy capacity of NICE. For example, Coast (2004) concludes that adoption of cost effectiveness analysis as the primary lens through which decisions are viewed results in a reliance on methods incommensurate with societal values. These include the rule of rescue (whereby life-saving interventions are seen as paramount) and respect for individual human dignity (Jagsi et al. 2004). To these can be added values of equity and distributive justice as well as the 'precepts of access and treatment on which the NHS is founded' (Syrett 2003: 742). From NICE's perspective, procedures are viewed as valuable only when they can demonstrate positive outcomes, however, as Calnan and Ferlie (2003: 186) note, it has become increasingly recognized that 'patients, professionals and managers ... value intermediate outcomes or aspects of process as much as final clinical outcomes'. The commitment of NICE to a utilitarian approach to evaluation therefore raises further governance obstacles.

Lessons and conclusion

Overall, then, NICE, and its appraisals programme in particular, can be seen as unique and ground-breaking while at the same time facing challenges resulting directly from the policy strategy which brought it into being. This is an important point to stress as NICE cannot be blamed for the pressure it has placed on health service budgets, since it was the government that decided its advice should be mandatory for the English NHS. This unusual inter-organizational relationship – no other national guidance body of this kind is granted policy-making powers – is at the heart of the controversy that occasionally surrounds NICE rulings. However, as an agent of government, NICE has proven to be indispensable to successive administrations and has both amended its practices and expanded its remit over time. Although, on occasion, accusations of illegitimate external influence have been made, in general, NICE's accountability arrangements have proved to be robust to challenge. The Institute is at pains to demarcate where its responsibilities end and those of government begin, although again this demarcation has not always been fully accepted by external parties. Put simply, NICE performs relatively well in governance terms, and appears to grasp the implications of its unusual status within the United Kingdom coverage landscape. In particular, the mandatory status of NICE guidance has been the catalyst for heightened attention to aspects of accountability, transparency and participation. In this regard, the main lessons from the NICE experience are that granting real 'teeth' to national coverage bodies implies in turn the need to invest generously in areas of evidence, analysis, involvement and publicity.

For these reasons, the NICE model is necessarily expensive. And there are other factors to consider before adopting a similar approach to coverage policy-making elsewhere. Although the English NHS has in recent times incorporated some quasi-market mechanisms and practices, it remains comparatively centralized in its structures and operations. Standards and policy objectives are set by government and an embryonic central commissioning body ('NHS England') looks like becoming a powerful corrective to the rhetoric of increased devolution (Walshe 2012). For these reasons the NHS is perhaps still more redolent of a traditional bureaucracy than it is of a networked, decentralized constellation of actors and forms (Newman 2004). This makes the NICE model a more plausible means of controlling practice than it would be elsewhere. Somewhat paradoxically – i.e., despite strong governance arrangements and a compatible structural context – the experience of NICE has nevertheless uncovered important limits to top-down approaches in coverage policy. There are ongoing questions to be asked about the (cost) effectiveness of investing responsibility for increasing uptake of guidance to the Institute itself. It is unrealistic to expect national coverage bodies to be able to transform and align wider system conditions or to bring disparate and competing civic values and beliefs into line – this surely should be the work of governments. In the face of these more fundamental tensions, there are limits to what even NICE can achieve. Overall, then, the example of NICE perhaps illustrates that good governance alone is not enough; even when governance processes and arrangements are highly developed, policy in controversial areas such as technology coverage is likely to remain contested.

Notes

1 By contrast, for example, in the USA, the Patient Protection and Affordable Care Act prohibits consideration of cost effectiveness in US federal coverage decision-making.
2 NICE does not give official advice to NHS Scotland and its guidance is not mandatory for health care organizations in Wales.

References

Audit Commission (2005) *Managing the Financial Implications of NICE Guidance.* London: Audit Commission.
Blank, R. H. and Burau, V. (2007) *Comparative Health Policy*, 2nd edition. Basingstoke: Palgrave Macmillan.
Buxton, M. J. (2006) Economic evaluation and decision making in the UK, *Pharmacoeconomics*, 24(11): 1133–42.
Cairns, J. (2006) Providing guidance to the NHS: the Scottish Medicines Consortium and the National Institute for Clinical Excellence compared, *Health Policy*, 76: 134–43.
Calnan, M. and Ferlie, E. (2003) Analysing process in healthcare: the methodological and theoretical challenges, *Policy and Politics*, 31(2): 185–93.
Chamberlain, C. A., Martin, R. M., Busby, J., Gilbert, R., Cahill, D. J. and Hollingworth, W. (2013) Trends in procedures for infertility and caesarean sections: was NICE disinvestment guidance implemented? NICE recommendation reminders, *BMC Public Health*, 13: 112.
Chambers, S. (2004) Behind closed doors: publicity, secrecy, and the quality of deliberation, *Journal of Political Philosophy*, 12: 389–410.
Cheyne, C. and Comrie, M. (2002) Enhanced legitimacy for local authority decision making: challenges, setbacks and innovation, *Policy and Politics*, 30(4): 469–82.
Coast, J. (2004) Is economic evaluation in touch with society's health values? *British Medical Journal*, 329: 1233–6.
Daniels, N. and Sabin, J. (1998) The ethics of accountability in managed care reform, *Health Affairs*, 17(5): 50–64.
Elshaug, A. G., Hiller, J. E., Tunis, S. R. and Moss, J. R. (2007) Challenges in Australian policy processes for disinvestment from existing, ineffective health care practices, *International Journal of Technology Assessment in Health Care*, 4: 23–8.
Evans, J. G. (1997) The rationing debate: rationing health care by age: the case against, *British Medical Journal*, 314: 820–2.

Fearnley, R. A., Bell, M. D. D. and Bodenham, A. R. (2012) Status of national guidelines in dictating individual clinical practice and defining negligence, *British Journal of Anaesthesia*, 108(4): 557–61.

Fischer, F. (2003) *Reframing Public Policy: Discursive Politics and Deliberative Practices*. Oxford: Oxford University Press.

Fleck, L. M. (1992) Just health-care rationing: a democratic decision-making approach, *University of Pennsylvania Law Review*, 140(5): 1597–636.

Flinders, M. (2009) Theory and method in the study of delegation: three dominant traditions, *Public Administration*, 87(4): 955–71.

Flinders, M. and Skelcher, C. (2012) Shrinking the quango state: five challenges in reforming quangos, *Public Money and Management*, 32(5): 327–34.

Flynn, H. and Gericke, C. A. (2012) Accelerating the adoption and diffusion of disinvestment initiatives: is a NICE way the right way? *The Lancet*, 380: S38.

Garner, S., Docherty, M., Somner, J., Sharma, T., Choudhury, M., Clarke, M. and Littlejohns, P. (2013) Reducing ineffective practice: challenges in identifying low-value health care using Cochrane Systematic Reviews, *Journal of Health Services Research and Policy*, 18(1): 6–12.

Harding, M. (2005) Hewitt, Herceptin and the £100 million bill PCTs can't afford to pay, *Health Services Journal*, December.

Harvey, G. (2013) Evidence-based innovation in practice: experiences from health care and implications for the future, in S. P. Osborne and L. Brown (eds) *Handbook of Innovation in Public Services*, Cheltenham: Edward Elgar, pp. 461–77.

House of Commons Health Select Committee (2007) *The National Institute for Health and Clinical Excellence*. London: Stationery Office.

Jagsi, R., DeLaney, T. F., Donelan, K. and Tarbell, N. J. (2004) Real-time rationing of scarce resources: the Northeast Proton Therapy Centre experience, *Journal of Clinical Oncology*, 22(11): 2246–50.

Kerr, D. J. and Scott, M. (2009) British lessons on health care reform, *New England Journal of Medicine*, 261: e21.

Klein, R. (2006) *The New Politics of the NHS: From Creation to Reinvention* (5th edition). Oxford: Radcliffe Medical Publishing.

Klein, R. (2010) Rationing in the fiscal ice age, *Health Economics, Politics and Law*, 5(4): 389–96.

Landwehr, C. and Böhm, K. (2011) Delegation and institutional design in healthcare rationing, *Governance: An International Journal of Policy, Administration and Institutions*, 24(4): 665–87.

Leggett, L., Noseworthy, T. W., Zarrabi, M., Lorenzetti, D., Sutherland, L. R. and Clement, F. M. (2012) Health technology reassessment of non-drug technologies: current practices, *International Journal of Technology Assessment in Health Care*, 28(3): 220–7.

Newman, J. (2004) Modernizing the state: a new form of governance? in J. Newman (ed.) *Remaking Governance: Peoples, Politics and the Public Sphere*. Bristol: The Policy Press.

NICE (2004) *The Legal Implications of NICE Guidance*. London: NICE.

NICE (2007) *The Guidelines Manual*. London: NICE.

NICE (2009) *Guide to the Single Technology Appraisal (STA) Process*. London: NICE.

NICE (2012) *Good Practice Guide: Developing and Updating Local Formularies*. London: NICE.

Oliver, A., Mossialos, E. and Robinson, R. (2004) Health technology assessment and its influence on health-care priority setting, *International Journal of Technology Assessment in Health Care*, 20(1): 1–10.

Price, S. J., Whittle, I. R., Ashkan, K., Grundy, P. and Cruickshank, G. (2012) NICE guidance on the use of carmustine wafers in high grade gliomas: a national study on variation in practice, *British Journal of Neurosurgery*, 26(3): 331–5.

Raftery, J. (2001) NICE: faster access on modern treatments? Analysis of guidance on health technologies, *British Medical Journal*, 323: 1300–3.

Raftery, J. (2006) Review of NICE's recommendations, 1999–2005, *British Medical Journal*, 332: 1266–8.

Schlander, M. (2008) The use of cost-effectiveness by the National Institute for Health and Clinical Excellence (NICE): no(t yet an) exemplar of a deliberative process, *Journal of Medical Ethics*, 34: 534–9.

Sheldon, T. A., Cullum, N., Dawson, D., Lankshear, A., Lowson, K., Watt, I., West, P., Wright, D. and Wright, J. (2005) What's the evidence that NICE guidance has been implemented? Results from a national evaluation using time series analysis, audit of patients' notes, and interviews, *British Medical Journal*, 329.

Shepperd, S., Adams, R., Hill, A., Garner, S. and Dopson, S. (2013) Challenges to using evidence from systematic reviews to stop ineffective practice: an interview study, *Journal of Health Services Research and Policy*, DOI: 10.1177/1355819613480142.

Sorenson, C., Drummond, M. and Kanavos, P. (2008) *Ensuring Value for Money in Health Care: The Role of HTA in the European Union*. Copenhagen: WHO Regional Office for Europe on behalf of the European Observatory on Health Systems and Policies.

Sorenson, C., Drummond, M. and Chalkidou, K. (2012) Comparative effectiveness research: the experience of the National Institute for Health and Clinical Excellence, *Journal of Clinical Oncology*, 30(34): 4267–74.

Stafinski, T., Menon, D., Phillipon, D. J. and McCabe, C. (2011) Health technology funding decision-making processes around the world: the same, yet different, *Pharmacoeconomics*, 29(6): 475–95.

Steinbrook, R. (2008) Saying no isn't NICE: the travails of Britain's National Institute for Health and Clinical Excellence, *New England Journal of Medicine*, 359: 1977–81.

Summerhayes, M. and Catchpole, P. (2006) Has NICE been nice to cancer? *European Journal of Cancer*, 42(17): 2881–9.

Syrett, K. (2003) A technocratic fix to the 'legitimacy problem'? The Blair government and health care rationing in the United Kingdom, *Journal of Health Politics, Policy and Law*, 28(4): 715–46.

Syrett, K. (2008) NICE and judicial review: enforcing 'accountability for reasonableness' through the courts? *Medical Law Review*, 16: 127–40.

Walshe, K. (2012) Lansley's legacy, *British Medical Journal*, 345: e6109.

Williams, I. (2013) Institutions and health care rationing: the example of health care coverage in the English National Health Service, *Policy and Politics*, 41(2): 223–39.

Williams, I. and Dickinson, H. (2010) Can knowledge management enhance technology adoption in healthcare? A review of the literature, *Evidence and Policy: A Journal of Research, Debate and Practice*, 6(3): 309–31.

Williams, I., Bryan, S. and McIver, S. (2007) Health technology coverage decisions: evidence from the N.I.C.E. 'experiment' in the use of cost-effectiveness analysis, *Journal of Health Services Research and Policy*, 12(2): 73–9.

nine

Understanding the role of governance in the pharmaceutical sector: from laboratory to patient

Jonathan Cylus, Olivier Wouters and Panos Kanavos

Introduction

Pharmaceuticals are a major component of total health care expenditure in Europe, and a key driver of overall spending growth. In 2011, per person spending on medicines ranged from 280 PPP$ in Estonia to 673 PPP$ in Greece (Figure 9.1). As a share of total health expenditure, pharmaceutical spending varied from 6.8 per cent in Norway to 34.6 per cent in Republic of Moldova. A recent study of data from the Health Survey for England found that half of women and 43 per cent of men regularly take prescription drugs (National Statistics Health Survey for England, 2013 (2014)). The demand for and spending on pharmaceuticals are expected to continue to grow due to ageing populations, rising income levels, increasing costs of developing new technologies, and evolving public perceptions of acceptable standards of health care (Bodenheimer 2005a; 2005b; 2005c).

Given the high costs and the large number of actors involved in the pharmaceutical sector, it is important that decision-makers play a strong steward-ship role to ensure that patients have access to high-quality medicines, and that health systems receive good value for the money they spend. In keeping with the main objectives of national health policies and national pharmaceutical policies, decision-makers must be able to ensure equitable access (i.e., availability and affordability), good quality (i.e., safety and efficacy) and rational use (i.e., clinically sound and cost-effective use) of medicines, while balancing concerns over financial sustainability (WHO 1988).

In this chapter, we examine how good governance is a necessary component of a well-functioning pharmaceutical sector. First, we briefly describe the complex process of how pharmaceutical products travel from the laboratory bench

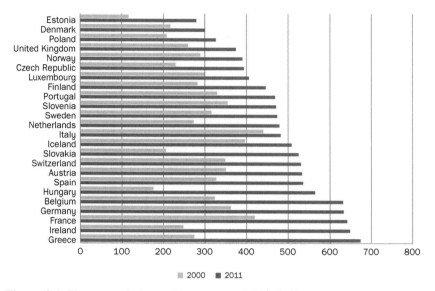

Figure 9.1 Pharmaceutical spending per capita PPP$ (2000 and 2011, selected European countries)

Source: WHO Health for All database (2013); data for other EURO53 countries not available.

to the patient's bedside. At each stage in the life-cycle of a drug there is the potential for governance to play a crucial part in determining whether the goals of the health system are met. We focus on selected stages of this process and highlight some of the areas where governance may be most relevant.

Pharmaceutical products: from the lab bench to the patient's bedside

The path of pharmaceutical products from the laboratory bench to the patient's bedside consists of several stages: research and development (R&D), marketing authorization, market access (i.e., pricing, reimbursement, and coverage), distribution to pharmacies, and, finally, dispensing of medicines to patients (Figure 9.2).

The life-cycle of medicines starts long before drugs are available to patients in consumable forms. In the R&D stage, manufacturers first conduct pre-clinical studies – either in vitro (e.g., cell cultures) or in vivo (i.e., animals) – to identify new molecular entities that may confer therapeutic benefits. Manufacturers then apply for patents on these entities, which grant a minimum of 20 years of intellectual property rights in accordance with World Trade Organization (WTO) agreements. Patents protect the originator manufacturer's invention, reward creativity and socially beneficial innovation, and preserve incentives for future R&D. In most WTO Member States, the 20-year period starts when the patent application is filed.

After filing for a patent, manufacturers conduct clinical trials on human subjects to satisfy the safety, efficacy, and quality criteria of regulators – e.g., the

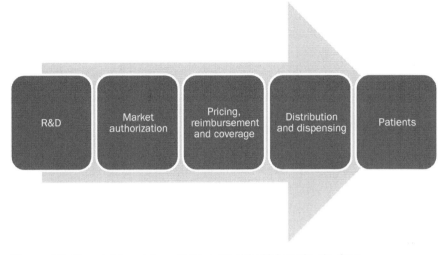

Figure 9.2 From lab bench to patients: a simplified life-cycle of a drug

European Medicines Agency (EMA) in the EU and the Food and Drug Administration (FDA) in the United States – to obtain marketing authorization. The R&D process typically lasts between seven and 12 years. In the EU, supplementary protection certificates can prolong the 20-year nominal patent term to ensure sufficient returns on investment for manufacturers.

After obtaining marketing authorization, drugs can be made available on the market. Manufacturers of in-patent drugs enjoy monopoly positions, or quasi-monopoly if therapeutic substitutes are available, and they set prices that maximize profits within the confines of national regulatory frameworks (i.e., pricing and reimbursement regimes). Patents generally allow manufacturers to price a medicine higher than its marginal production cost, particularly for medicines that offer significant improvements over existing treatments. To ensure continued innovation in the pharmaceutical industry, prices above the cost of production are necessary to compensate for the substantial R&D costs incurred by the originator manufacturer. It also encourages manufacturers to undertake high-risk R&D in therapeutic areas with historically high failure rates during clinical trials (e.g., oncology and orphan drugs).

While a robust intellectual property framework is necessary to stimulate innovation, it is also important to protect payers (i.e., governments and insurers) from excessive pharmaceutical spending that could reduce patient access to medicines. Various supply- and demand-side policies have been devised to contain pharmaceutical costs. Supply-side policies target manufacturers, while demand-side policies target physicians, pharmacists, and patients. The two types of policies play complementary roles.

Supply-side policies include the pricing, reimbursement and coverage of medicines. Pricing strategies differ across countries, ranging from price controls to free pricing; in some countries, payers procure generics through tenders. In many countries, medicines are also reimbursed at different rates. Increasingly, payers who finance health care have pursued formal arrangements with manufacturers to share the financial risk associated with paying for new medicines when there is uncertainty surrounding the clinical effectiveness or cost effectiveness. In the EU, health technology assessments (HTAs) increasingly inform reimbursement and coverage decisions (Box 9.1). Depending on the country, one of two groups conduct HTAs – payers or advisory agencies that provide recommendations to payers (e.g., the National Institute for Health and Care Excellence (NICE) in the United Kingdom).

Box 9.1 Types of value assessment used by HTA agencies

---

(1) Value assessment with economic analysis

Cost-effectiveness analysis compares the costs and health benefits of a drug to those of a therapeutic alternative. The therapeutic alternative may be the best, cheapest, or most common treatment; it may also be no treatment. A drug is considered cost-effective compared to the alternative if it provides (a) the same clinical effect at a lower price, or (b) a better clinical effect at the same price or lower. A drug is considered possibly cost-effective if it provides a better clinical effect at a higher price; in these cases, the reimbursement decision depends on the agency's willingness-to-pay threshold. The threshold represents the maximum price that the health system is willing to pay for an additional unit of health benefit.

(2) Value assessment without economic analysis

In some instances, HTA bodies do not consider economic data when assessing the value of a drug: the HTA outcomes inform coverage decisions, but the reimbursement prices are set independently. For example, the French HTA agency – the National Authority for Health (HAS) – assesses the value of a drug based on its clinical benefits (relative to existing alternatives).This is done in two steps. First, the agency evaluates the 'overall clinical benefit' of the medicine. Second, the agency compares the clinical benefits of the drug to those of available treatments. The drug is ranked on a five-point scale according to its 'level of improvement of the clinical benefit' (ASMR), where I and V correspond to major and no improvement' in therapeutic benefit, respectively. The HTA agency only recommends that a drug be reimbursed if it provides meaningful improvements in clinical benefit (usually ASMR I, II, or III) or cost savings. The reimbursement price is then set by a separate agency based on the ASMR score.

Medicines that gain market access must still pass through the pharmaceutical distribution chain, composed of manufacturers, wholesalers, and retailers, before reaching patients. The wholesalers generally serve as middle men between manufacturers and retailers. At each stage of the distribution chain, the sellers (e.g., manufacturer to wholesaler, or wholesaler to pharmacist) mark up the prices. In most high-income countries, the supply chain is heavily

Table 9.1 Selected governance issues in the pharmaceutical sector

	Accountability	Transparency	Participation	Integrity and fraud	Policy capacity
Marketing authorization	✓			✓	
Pricing		✓			✓
Risk-sharing agreements		✓	✓		✓
HTA		✓	✓		✓
Distribution chain	✓	✓		✓	

regulated to ensure the affordability and availability of medicines. Patients obtain medicines from pharmacists, usually after receiving prescriptions from physicians. Policy-makers often try to influence prescribing and dispensing behaviour through various financial and non-financial incentives. These efforts can be coupled with public awareness campaigns to promote the rational use of medicines by patients (e.g., increase demand for generics).

Governance in the pharmaceutical sector

The complex interactions between multiple stakeholders coupled with uncertainty about the economic and clinical value of new medicines, could leave the pharmaceutical sector vulnerable to poor governance. This may in turn comprise the objectives of the health system. We examine selected stages of the pharmaceutical sector from a governance perspective and apply the five elements of the governance framework outlined in Chapter 1: accountability, transparency, participation, integrity and fraud, and policy capacity (Table 9.1). The following discussion is not exhaustive and aims to illustrate areas where governance plays an important role in the pharmaceutical sector.

Marketing authorization

Market authorization is the first regulatory hurdle for manufacturers: they must demonstrate that their products are safe, efficacious, and of a high quality. In the EU, where the EMA evaluates whether these criteria are met, marketing authorization approval does not guarantee that patients will have unfettered access to new drugs. Instead, payers – or agencies that act on their behalf – decide whether to cover or reimburse a new drug. Therefore, it is more appropriate to explore governance issues at this stage in countries where medicines are not generally paid for by the public sector or by third-party payers. In such settings, marketing authorization plays a direct role in access to medicines.

Accountability

In all countries, regulators should serve the interests of patients: the role of the regulator is to ensure that only drugs which comply with regulatory criteria and that are fit for human consumption receive market authorization. Yet, although regulators are primarily concerned with the quality, efficacy and safety of medicines, some of these agencies also aim to ensure timely access to medicines by rapidly approving new medicines. This fourth objective could be consistent with the notion of regulator accountability to patients. Yet in settings where medicines are not commonly added to the benefits package following market authorization, increasing the quantity of drugs that are authorized may inadvertently serve the interests of pharmacies and manufacturers, potentially forming a pseudo line of accountability between regulators and the industry.

In Mexico, for example, the Federal Commission for the Protection against Sanitary Risks (COFEPRIS) – the national regulatory body that is in charge of regulating pharmaceutical products, among other responsibilities – is tasked with reviewing the clinical trial evidence for new medicines. On the basis of this evidence, COFEPRIS decides whether or not to approve medicines. In an effort to speed up the approval process for originator medicines, as well as generic counterparts, COFEPRIS has set duration targets for the review process; the agency has even outsourced elements of the approval process to external entities, including private companies.

COFEPRIS has had unprecedented success in speeding up the marketing authorization process, and as a result has rapidly expanded the number of medicines that are available in Mexico. However, these efforts might serve the interests of the pharmaceutical industry rather than poor households who are in need of medicines, since marketing authorization does not mean that a product is covered by public insurance scheme benefits packages. New medicines approved by COFEPRIS may therefore be unobtainable for the poor, and an added expense for households that are able to afford them (Fundación Mexicana para la Salud 2011); this is especially of concern given the proliferation of physicians' offices located within pharmacies themselves, which induces increased demand.

Although COFEPRIS likely views itself as only accountable to patients, to successfully meet its objectives and strengthen its accountability to patients, better coordination and collaboration between regulators and payers are needed to ensure that the patients in need of medicines are able to access them. Otherwise, regulators may unintentionally protect the commercial interests of local generic manufacturers, and not generate commensurate gains for patients.

Integrity and fraud

In low- and middle-income countries – and, to a lesser extent, in high-income countries – weak governance of marketing authorization can lead to issues with the quality of medicines. The International Criminal Police Organization

(Interpol) recently estimated that 30 per cent of all medicines in low- and middle-income economies are counterfeit or of inferior quality; in some African countries, the figure may exceed 50 per cent (Cockburn et al. 2005). Weak regulatory oversight may enable fraudulent manufacturing. The growth in internet sales of medicines (e.g., e-pharmacies) and the lack of adequate regulation of online distribution channels have catalysed this issue. There have been calls for greater efforts to curb these global trends, including collaboration between key international stakeholders such as the World Health Organization, Interpol, and the UN Office of Drugs and Crime (Mackey and Liang 2013).

Pricing

Pricing policies vary across Europe. The most common pricing policy in Europe is external price referencing (EPR) (Leopold et al. 2012). EPR sets a domestic price based on the prices in a basket of countries (e.g., the average or minimum price in the basket). Some countries, such as France, use EPR to verify that they are not overpaying for medicines but not to actually determine prices.

Transparency

Opaque processes in EPR can undermine system credibility, increase the likelihood of erroneous or inappropriate regulatory outcomes, and prevent the sharing of experiences and ideas across settings. EPR schemes are usually transparent, but can differ across various dimensions, including (1) the legal framework; (2) the pricing methodology; (3) the frequency of price revisions; (4) the appeals process for stakeholders; and (5) the risk management strategy to handle logistical issues, such as the unavailability of a drug in a comparator country or exchange rate fluctuations. To promote transparency in EPR, most pricing authorities do not consider discounted or rebated prices in other countries when formulating their own prices.

Transparent EPR rules, however, can also have undesirable consequences. If EPR is widely used by payers across countries, prices are effectively linked across markets. Price changes in one country can have a sizable effect on prices in another. As the reference countries in the EPR basket are publicly available, manufacturers may attempt to game EPR systems. To manipulate prices across countries, manufacturers can first launch drugs in countries that are likely to accept high prices. Manufacturers can then launch in the remaining countries that reference the high prices of the initial launch countries. There is growing evidence of both launch sequencing and launch delays, although most studies are unable to isolate the effect of EPR on firm strategies (Danzon et al. 2005; Kyle 2007; Kanavos et al. 2010). Manufacturers may also try to reduce price transparency across markets to maximize profits: for example, by offering confidential rebates or discounts so that countries are unable to capture these transactions in EPR schemes.

Policy capacity

It is challenging to compare drug prices across countries, as drugs often differ across countries in terms of names, package sizes, dose formulations and strengths. If prices are revised frequently, it can be resource-intensive and time-consuming to obtain prices in the reference countries. In the Czech Republic, for example, 65 full-time employees run the system. Greece, on the contrary, is understaffed, with only a few employees managing the EPR scheme (Kanavos et al. 2010). It is unclear, however, how to determine the optimal amount of resources that countries should dedicate to running their EPR system.

Risk-sharing agreements

Regulators increasingly enter into risk-sharing agreements to hedge against uncertainty about the budget impact, clinical effectiveness, and cost-effectiveness of medicines at the time of market entry. In general terms, payers grant manufacturers favourable prices and reimbursement rates in return for achieving financial (e.g., price-volume agreement) or outcome targets (e.g. effectiveness evidence) (Ferrario and Kanavos 2015).

Transparency

The conditions of risk-sharing agreements are usually negotiated confidentially between manufacturers and competent authorities. A non-transparent process is desirable by manufacturers, so that negotiated prices do not become the market prices paid by all payers; manufacturers may be more willing to accept lower prices if they are not concerned that the negotiated prices will be referenced by other payers through EPR. The agreements therefore need to remain confidential to allow each party to bargain successfully. However, the lack of transparency can lead to price discrepancies due to differences in market share or negotiating capabilities among payers. For example, opaque risk-sharing agreements may result in poorer, smaller countries with worse negotiating power paying higher prices than wealthy, larger countries.

Participation

Manufacturers and payers enter into risk-sharing agreements; all other institutional stakeholders are excluded. Notably, patients – who may bear some costs out-of-pocket – are not privy to the details of these negotiations. This can mean that drugs which are highly valued by patients and patient advocacy groups might not end up being those for which prices are negotiated.

Policy capacity

These schemes are in their infancy and have proved difficult to implement. There are challenges in performance measurement and enforcement that need to be addressed (Raftery 2010; Neumann et al. 2011). The agreements can also result in substantial transaction and implementation costs. For example, many countries lack the infrastructure to collect and monitor the relevant outcomes.

Health technology assessment

With scarce resources for health, governments need to invest in goods and services that deliver the best value for money. To help meet this challenge, various EU Member States have used HTA systems to evaluate new, expensive medicines, as well as highly consumed drugs.

Transparency

Despite the purported objectivity of HTA processes, coverage decisions can be controversial. Evidentiary requirements differ between HTA bodies, with limited or no justification for the criteria used by each system (Box 9.2). If a new drug is not covered by a health system, or covered only for a limited population, both patients and manufacturers will want to understand the reasons behind this decision (Nicod and Kanavos 2012). HTA criteria and outcomes should therefore be transparent and publicly accessible. Many review bodies are members of international networks and societies, which promote the harmonization of HTA processes and exchange of best practices across Europe and globally. National and international cooperation among assessment groups can enhance the transferability, accountability and transparency of HTA processes.

Box 9.2 The evidentiary requirements of HTA bodies

- *Austria, Norway and the Netherlands*: These countries collect and validate manufacturer data. Manufacturers are required to submit evidence based on a systematic review, as well as a summary of published and unpublished data.
- *Sweden and the United Kingdom*: Perform the systematic review in-house or outsource to an independent entity; HTA bodies may or may not review manufacturer data.
- *Finland, France and Switzerland*: Systematic reviews are preferred but not required. Assessments are based primarily on the clinical trial data provided by manufacturers.

Source: Adapted from Sorenson et al. (2008).

Participation

Stakeholder involvement in the generation and assessment of the evidence is central to the HTA process. An inclusive process can enhance the overall assessment, lead to greater objectivity and transparency, reduce the number of appeals, and encourage the implementation of recommendations and guidelines. Most HTA bodies involve various stakeholders, including carers, the general public, health and social care professionals (e.g., physicians, pharmacists, and pharmacologists), other health organizations, local government officials, health economists, industry representatives, and patient advocates. In some countries, stakeholders are heavily involved (e.g., the United Kingdom), while in other countries they are barely involved (e.g., Canada) (Morgan et al. 2006).

Participation in the HTA process can take many forms, such as helping to select comparator drugs or clinical outcomes of interest, commenting on reports, and appealing against recommendations. Topic agendas are often set by national authorities, such as Ministries of Health, or by expert committees affiliated with an HTA body. Various stakeholders may submit topic suggestions or comment on priorities. While selection criteria differ across review bodies, these criteria typically include health benefit, disease burden, resource impact, innovation capacity, clinical and political relevance, and feasibility of assessment. Manufacturers typically generate and submit models to HTA agencies. Most agencies review these submissions themselves, although some agencies (e.g., NICE) ask external organizations to independently review the data. A participatory approach allows stakeholders to maintain a role in the market access process, but mitigates the influence of lobbyists on drug coverage decisions.

Integrity and fraud

As HTA agencies do not receive patient-level data, they must rely on manufacturers to submit accurate data. A rigorous process with high standards of evidence is crucial to ensuring the political sustainability of a HTA scheme (Morgan et al. 2006).

Additionally, the HTA process consists of two general components: the assessment and appraisal of evidence. The assessment consists of an evaluation of the data by an expert panel. The aim of the panel is to review the submitted evidence and interpret the results, as well as the degree of uncertainty in the findings. The subsequent appraisal leads to a coverage decision. These two stages are carried out by separate committees to promote the integrity of the process. A scientific committee usually conducts the assessment to avoid a purely technocratic process and to separate the technology assessment from rationing decisions. In some cases, the coverage decision is only a recommendation to another authority that makes the ultimate decision, which enhances process integrity (Morgan et al. 2006).

Policy capacity

To meet their objectives, HTA agencies must have sufficient capacity to collect the data, evaluate the evidence, and disseminate the information. The composition of the scientific and appraisal committees influences the rigour and validity of HTA evaluations. A comprehensive group of individuals with complementary skills is essential (e.g., pharmacology, medicine, health economics and financial administration).

The different roles of HTA agencies lead to different review durations. Some bodies only negotiate the reimbursement rates and prices, while others also promulgate clinical guidelines (Cairns 2006; Morgan et al. 2006; Drummond 2009). For example, the assessments in France usually take a couple of weeks, while reviews in Sweden and the United Kingdom often last longer than one year. Several agencies have introduced 'rapid reviews' to produce more timely information to decision-makers and the public. For example, NICE now conducts 'single technology appraisals' to provide a quicker channel than its standard technology assessments.

Distribution chain

Poor governance can influence the pharmaceutical distribution chain: for example, by compromising the dispensing practices of pharmacists. Sub-optimal dispensing, such as giving patients needlessly expensive medicines, can arise due to asymmetry of information between payers, such as social insurers or patients, and pharmacists.

Accountability

Pharmacists yield considerable market power in the absence of price differences between comparable drugs (e.g., generics). Wholesalers and manufacturers therefore provide discounts to pharmacies, which incentivizes pharmacists to dispense the products with the largest differences between the reimbursement and discount prices. Pharmacists accountable to their own bottom line may prioritize private profits over the well-being of patients and dispense medicines with the highest margins.

Transparency

While there are legislated limits on the discounts wholesalers and manufacturers may offer pharmacies, the level and scope of discounts are kept confidential. This is a potentially inequitable pricing mechanism due to the lack of transparency, especially if the negotiation skills of wholesalers and pharmacists vary. The prices may therefore not correspond to the quality of services provided.

Integrity and fraud

There is evidence that the discounts in some countries exceed legally permissible levels. This results in reimbursement rates that are too high and that generate excessive profits for wholesalers and pharmacists. In France, for example, the maximum discount limit is 2.5 per cent and 10.74 per cent for originator and generic products, respectively. In a study of the French generic market, however, it was found that while discounts are related to prices, the discounts regularly exceed the government ceilings; the discounts may be as high as 70 per cent of the wholesale price (Kanavos and Taylor 2007). In the United Kingdom, there are no restrictions on the discounts negotiated between manufacturers, wholesalers, and pharmacists. However, the large differences between the discount and reimbursements prices – often as high as 60 per cent – generate substantial profits for distribution chain actors; this reduces the cost-saving potential of generics for payers and patients. In response to discounting practices, the United Kingdom government now reviews pharmacy margins and tries to 'claw back' excessive profits (Kanavos and Taylor 2007).

Reflections on the governance framework

The potential for problematic governance issues exists in many parts of the pharmaceutical sector. Poor governance is a serious concern which can lead to low-quality medicines being approved and high prices being paid for drugs that do not offer commensurate therapeutic value.

We find that different parts of the governance framework are most relevant at various stages in the life-cycle of a drug. Some of the governance elements, such as transparency and policy capacity, are cross-cutting issues in the pharmaceutical sector that affect multiple stages. However, the pursuit of more transparency to improve governance in all instances may be misguided. As described in the case of managed entry agreements, too much transparency could have a detrimental effect on negotiating capabilities. Good governance is not necessarily a monotonic function where 'more is better'. For example, greater policy capacity in the form of more skilled personnel may be needed to improve the functionality of under-staffed HTA agencies, but too many staff may lead to decreasing returns to scale.

There are also possible interactions between elements of the framework that we have not explored. Again in the case of risk-sharing agreements, while transparency is not desirable in general, the presence of some degree of transparency may not be problematic as long as payers are effective negotiators (i.e. strong policy capacity). Without an understanding of 'how much is too much' for each dimension of the framework, as well as how different elements of the framework may substitute for, or exacerbate other elements, it is difficult to make a proper assessment of whether and how to improve governance.

Overall, the framework successfully indicates where there is the potential for governance problems in the pharmaceutical sector. Further work is needed to translate the awareness of the role of governance into performance evaluation or policy action.

References

Bodenheimer, T. (2005a) High and rising health care costs. Part 1: seeking an explanation, *Annals of Internal Medicine*, 142(10): 847–54.
Bodenheimer, T. (2005b) High and rising health care costs. Part 2: technologic innovation, *Annals of Internal Medicine*, 142(11): 932–7.
Bodenheimer, T. (2005c) High and rising health care costs. Part 3: the role of health care providers, *Annals of Internal Medicine*, 142 (12): 996–1002.

Cairns, J. (2006) Providing guidance to the NHS: the Scottish Medicines Consortium and the National Institute for Clinical Excellence compared, *Health Policy*, 76(2): 134–43.

Cockburn, R., Newton, P. N., Agyarko, E. K., Akunyili, D. and White, N. J. (2005) The global threat of counterfeit drugs: why industry and governments must communicate the dangers, *PLoS Medicine*, 2(4): e100.

Danzon, P. M., Wang, Y. R. and Wang, L. (2005) The impact of price regulation on the launch delay of new drugs: evidence from twenty-five major markets in the 1990s, *Health Economics*, 14(3): 269–92.

Drummond, M. F. (2009) More haste, less speed? The emerging practice of HTA in the United Kingdom, *Euro Observer*, 11(1): 9–10.

Ferrario, A. and Kanavos, P. (2015) Dealing with uncertainty and high prices of new medicines: a comparative analysis of the use of managed entry agreements in Belgium, England, the Netherlands and Sweden, *Social Science & Medicine*, 124: 39–47.

Fundación Mexicana para la Salud, A. C. (2011) *Trabajando por la salud de la población. Propuestas de política para el sector farmacéutico. Versión para el diálogo.* Available at: http://www.funsalud.org.mx/eventos_2011/trabajando%20por%20la%20salud/Doc%20PolPublSFarm%20vFDigital%20060511.pdf.

Kanavos, P. and Taylor, D. (2007) Pharmacy discounts on generic medicines in France: is there room for further efficiency savings? *Current Medical Research and Opinion*, 23(10): 2467–76.

Kanavos, P., Nicod, E., Espin, J. and Van Den Aardweg, S. (2010) *Short- and Long-term Effects of Value-based Pricing vs. External Price Referencing.* European Commission, Directorate General Enterprise.

Kyle, M. K. (2007) Pharmaceutical price controls and entry strategies, *The Review of Economics and Statistics*, 89(1): 88–99.

Leopold, C., Vogler, S., Mantel-Teeuwisse, A., De Joncheere, K., Leufkens, H. and Laing, R. (2012) Differences in external price referencing in Europe: a descriptive overview, *Health Policy*, 104(1): 50–60.

Mackey, T. K. and Liang, B. A. (2013) Improving global health governance to combat counterfeit medicines: a proposal for a UNODC-WHO-Interpol trilateral mechanism, *BMC Medicine*, 11(1): 233.

Morgan, S. G., Mcmahon, M., Mitton, C., Roughead, E., Kirk, R., Kanavos, P. and Menon, D. (2006) Centralized drug review processes in Australia, Canada, New Zealand, and the United Kingdom, *Health Affairs*, 25(2): 337–47.

National Statistics Health Survey for England, 2013 (2014) Available at: http://www.hscic.gov.uk/catalogue/PUB16076.

Neumann, P. J., Chambers, J. D., Simon, F. and Meckley, L. M. (2011) Risk-sharing arrangements that link payment for drugs to health outcomes are proving hard to implement, *Health Affairs*, 30(12): 2329–37.

Nicod, E. and Kanavos, P. (2012) Commonalities and differences in HTA outcomes: a comparative analysis of five countries and implications for coverage decisions, *Health Policy*, 108(2): 167–77.

Raftery, J. (2010) Multiple sclerosis risk-sharing scheme: a costly failure, *BMJ*, 340.

Sorenson, C., Drummond, M. and Kanavos, P. (2008) *Ensuring Value for Money in Health Care: The Role of Health Technology Assessment in the European Union.* Copenhagen: WHO Regional Office for Europe on behalf of the European Observatory on Health Systems and Policies.

World Health Organization (1988) *How to Develop and Implement a National Drug Policy.* Geneva: WHO.

ten

Intergovernmental governance for health: federalism, decentralization and communicable diseases

Scott L. Greer

One of the most basic attributes of the governance of health systems is the role and powers of different governments. Many countries have decentralized health systems to directly elected regional and local governments (Saltman and Bankauskaite 2006; Saltman et al. 2007; Adolph et al. 2012; Costa i Font and Greer 2013). German and Austrian *Länder* play a role in public health, Belgian regions also play a role in hospital finance and planning, while Canadian provinces, Spanish and Italian regions and the United Kingdom's three devolved administrations run almost every aspect of their health systems. Local governments in almost every country have health roles and functions. And while some federations are old, decentralization of health policies to elected governments has been a trend almost everywhere, with little evidence of recentralization (Hooghe et al. 2010). The result is the phenomenon of multi-level governance, in which governance is the interaction of governments at local, regional, state and European, if not international levels (Hooghe and Marks 2003). Their collective ability to interact productively determines whether the outcomes are good for people and health systems.

The number, roles, and relationships of governments involved in health policy naturally shape the governance of health care, and thereby the quality of, cost of, and access to the health system. Decentralizing can produce more responsive, democratic, efficient, equitable systems – or needless friction, poor coordination, subscale organizations and weakened health systems. The difference, a difference on which the advisability of decentralization and the success of health systems in the world's many decentralized countries, rests on governance. Can the governance of politically decentralized health systems allow them to reap the benefits and overcome the costs?

Decentralization means two things (Agranoff 2004).[1] One is self-rule: the ability of a given unit such as a province, state, or region to govern itself and do things differently. The other is shared rule: rule through the interaction of different governments and their ability to influence each other when, for example, German *Länder* can vote in the German federal Upper House. They pose different kind of opportunities and challenges for health systems governance. Self-rule can create diversity, competition, experimentation, adaptation, democracy and learning, but can also create races to the bottom or empower deviant elites and behaviour. Shared rule can mean coordination and solidarity or vetoes and blockage. These challenges, and their opportunities, extend to the European Union, which is building shared rule systems atop the self-rule of old states.

It is crucial to note the difference between decentralization to elected general purpose governments, which is known as political decentralization, and decentralization within the state apparatus, e.g., to regional offices such as the French Regional Health Agencies (Adolph et al. 2012; Jones 2013). Elected general purpose governments include most local governments as well as Italian regions, Spanish autonomous communities, Austrian or German *Länder*, Belgian communities and regions, Canadian provinces, devolved administrations in the United Kingdom, or states in countries such as Australia, Brazil, Mexico and the United States. The key difference is that political decentralization involves politicians – not appointed board members, civil servants, or others who are accountable to the central minister, but elected politicians with their own coalitions, accountability, legitimacy and priorities. Managing regional offices is one thing, albeit frequently difficult; negotiating with politicians whose ambitions, legitimacy, and priorities do not match is another (Greer and Massard da Fonseca 2015). Muddying the distinction makes it almost impossible to understand the dynamics of intergovernmental relations.

Political decentralization: a benefit with costs

Decentralization of health care has presumptive advantages that political scientists have discussed extensively, often in the context of evaluating the many decentralization proposals that international organizations and political entrepreneurs put forth so confidently. The putative advantages of decentralization include (Treisman 2007: 11–14; also Costa-i-Font and Greer 2013):

- *administrative efficiency*: decentralization makes it easier to adapt to local peculiarities and preferences;
- *competition*: governments forced to compete for people and investment will produce more efficient public services;
- *fiscal incentives*: governments that must raise their budget from the local area will have incentives to produce better economic growth;
- *democracy, accountability and participation*: with shorter principal–agent links, better information about local conditions, and more opportunities to participate in a smaller area, voters will be able to more effectively participate in and control their government;
- finally, and in many cases most importantly (Stepan 1999), decentralization is often adopted as a way *to manage tensions* and keep together multinational countries that otherwise might split up. When decentralization in a country like Belgium or Spain is criticized, it is fair to ask: what is the alternative?

These benefits, which are by no means guaranteed, also come with costs, and those are the costs that governance must address while also maximizing the odds that it reaps some of the benefits:

- *lack of economies of scale*: there is no guarantee that democracy, competition, information and efficiency all will come together. The participatory virtues of easy access to politicians or voters' presumptive ability to observe the quality of government fit badly with the size of many regional health care systems, notably such big governments as Ontario or Andalucia.
- *differing accountabilities*, which produce different priorities: political decentralization means that voters have several governments, each with a different electorate and political world. There is no guarantee that the city of Barcelona, the Generalitat of Catalonia, and the government of Spain will have the same policy priorities, but every one of them has electoral legitimacy as a democratically elected government.
- *coordination and alignment problems*: differing accountabilities and priorities combined with imperfect economies of scale both demand coordination and make it more difficult. How would two adjacent governments with different organ donation and allocation policies agree to share?
- *lack of competition or destructive competition between jurisdictions*: there are (largely theoretical) arguments extolling the virtues of intergovernmental competition (Tiebout 1956), but in practice the conditions for intergovernmental competition are almost never met, and the benefits are therefore rare (Treisman 2007).
- *intergovernmental politics*: politicians deal in credit and blame, seeking the former and avoiding the latter (Weaver 1986). They will frequently have incentives to push blame for unpopular policies (taxes, service reductions) onto other levels of government, and take the credit for even events in which they played no part. This can naturally interfere with coordination; if every regional politician can get credit for establishing a high-technology medical centre, it is likely that the country will end up with too many high-technology medical centres.

The quality of governance is, in large part, its ability to surmount these problems and make it easier to reap the possible benefits of decentralization (Agranoff 2004). In other words, how can we improve health systems by improving governance in intergovernmental relations?

Intergovernmental relations refers to the full range of interactions between governments on different levels of territory (Wright 1982; Agranoff 1999; Trench 2006; 2007; Greer and Trench 2010). It means both the mechanisms of shared rule and the interactions that come about when there is interaction between the policies of different self-ruling units.

It is a classic case of a policy area where there is no chance of attaining 'good governance' and stopping; there is always room for improvement and there is always a need to adapt as the politics, roles, challenges and roles of governments evolve. A system that works perfectly with one set of politicians will need adjustment when another arrives. A system that operates well in one policy area might not operate well in another. A politician will see a problem or opportunity and destabilize something, or politicians will mobilize against each other, or politicians will club together to obscure an embarrassment. The governance should adapt to changes, and there will always be disappointments in a system that tries to constrain and clarify the actions of democratically elected politicians. We should put a premium on governance that accepts political and policy conflict, intergovernmental competition and bureaucratic friction, and tries to reap benefits. Over time, we can hope that good intergovernmental relations governance can shift incentives in political systems, so that politicians have reason to compete within sensible limits,[2] opt for coordination and alignment when they can, and manage tensions when they pursue different policies.

Strengthening governance to reap the benefits of decentralization

This section examines the way that intergovernmental governance might be improved. It first identifies a largely irresolvable problem: conflicting and manipulatable accountabilities. Short of constitutional changes such as abolishing tiers of elected government, such conflicting accountabilities are here to stay, and politicians will continue to have incentive to manipulate them in pursuit of credit and avoidance of blame. One should never assume that a central, or federal, government is more competent or less corrupt than a regional or local government, or vice versa. The competence and integrity of any polity depend on the extent of political competition, the vibrancy of the public sphere, the quality of integrity measures including the police, the attention and combativeness of the media, and other outside factors.

Likewise, there is no case for assuming that decentralization produces beneficial competition, accountability, transparency or participation; rather, those attributes must be built into the governance of decentralization. As Treisman notes of efforts to connect decentralization with public administration, 'Some of the conditions required for successful decentralization are actually benefits that decentralization is itself supposed to produce' (Treisman 2007: 280).

There are two basic features of political decentralization that challenge health systems governance. One comes with shared rule, the extra complexity that political decentralization creates. There is not just a government, there are also intergovernmental relations. Even in the best-organized systems, it is not always clear where money is going, or who does what, or what the overall priorities are (frequently, there are no overall priorities). Politicians with different strategies, parties and accountabilities must somehow collaborate to produce a high-functioning system, but we must accept the conflicts that come about between democratically elected governments.

The other feature stems from self-rule. It is the risk of deviant, or bad, behaviour. Decentralization or federalism can empower local areas where the quality of governance – be it its integrity, capacity, transparency, participation or accountability – is flawed. Good governance of decentralized polities demands mechanisms to preserve those across a larger number of governments, which will have all the natural variation in politics that can be seen in a country.

In both cases, the threat is to good overall coordination or alignment. Good governance can contribute, along with political incentives, to coordination and alignment in pursuit of useful objectives. It can encourage leaders to share objectives and pursue them effectively in the complex systems of decentralized or federal states. Lack of coordination or alignment diffuses effort, can lead to waste, and sometimes paralyses or degrades systems entirely.

Throughout, the section focuses on the organization of public health, specifically the organizations focused on communicable disease control in the EU, which increasingly also occupy themselves with the epidemiology and control of non-communicable diseases. Communicable disease control is a useful way to examine the different challenges of governance because it demands that so many different actors work together, from doctors and epidemiologists to states and the WHO (Bashford 2006; Lakoff and Collier 2008; Weir and Mykhalovskiy 2010; Greer and Mätzke 2012, Greer 2013). It is spread across multiple levels of government (Adolph et al. 2012). Local governments are often first responders in outbreaks and responsible for day-to-day services and inspection that do much to prevent outbreaks; regional governments are often formally responsible for public health, and often have a role in operating or regulating health providers; and central governments tend to have resources (such as laboratory and rapid response capacity). If the three do not collaborate effectively, preparation, prevention and management can all go badly wrong. Effective communicable disease control is also dependent on collaboration within and across the health sector: with primary care doctors and health care facilities for vaccination and surveillance; with increasingly visible security and emergency management agencies that bring their own approaches to public health; and with a range of other organizations whose participation can be necessary, such as veterinary medicine and schools. There was only a short period in history, roughly from the antibiotic revolution to the appearance of AIDS, when we could regard communicable disease control as a specialist technical area that did not need to interest the rest of us. Like most of public health, it always has and always will be intersectoral and intergovernmental. So good governance means that, no matter the good or bad incentives to alignment or coordination that exist in a country's politics, the system promotes alignment and avoids paralysis or crisis. That means its governance is important, and a good window through which to see the effects of good or bad intergovernmental governance.

Accountability

We do not lose much nuance if we state the challenge of intergovernmental relations thus: political decentralization creates multiple, contradictory accountability relationships that present a challenge for governance and good health system performance.

What does it mean to say that conflicting accountabilities create a governance challenge? The basic problem is that in a system with multiple governments delivering health systems, the governments are accountable to both voters and to each other. Is the Scottish government accountable to Scottish voters who elected it, or the 'UK taxpayers' (Connolly et al. 2010: xiv) who give it a good portion of its budget? Does the Spanish framework law on health and the redistributive formula that finances health services in poor Extremadura give the Spanish government a say over how Extremadura uses that money? Governments, when they do not raise all of their own money in taxes, are accountable to both their voters and their paymasters, who are frequently other governments. There is no reason to expect that the United Kingdom government and the Scottish government, or the Extremaduran and Spanish governments, will all agree on the right way to run health services. The result, phrased in the language of principal–agent analysis, is an agent with two principals (voters and another government) that both have weak oversight.

There is something of a contradiction between two normative economic principles here. On one hand, the objective of carrying out tasks at the lowest possible level that can internalize externalities means that it is efficient to organize delivery at a lower, regional or local level, and centralize finance at the level of the largest jurisdiction in order to have a larger risk pool (Boadway and Shah 2009; Adolph et al. 2012). This calls for either centralized financing (e.g., in nationwide social insurance funds such as found in Germany and Belgium, or the US Medicare system) or for large budgetary allocations to regional governments that deliver health care (as in Spain, Italy, or the devolved United Kingdom). It has the further benefit of equalizing access to health care and other aspects of the welfare state; what is the point of a country if it does not try to equalize the health care due a newborn across its whole territory (Banting 2006)? Even if equity is not an objective of policy-makers, the experience of the Eurozone highlights the problems that can arise in a monetary and fiscal union that lacks significant transfers.

On the other hand, economic theories that attempt to incorporate politics tend to argue for making regional and local governments accountable by giving them taxing responsibilities; if they are spending somebody else's money, then they will be irresponsible, while if they spend their own taxpayers' money, they will be sensible because the voters will supervise them and they will have to compete for mobile factors of production. Rather than having some federal government oversee and subsidy poorer areas, they should be forced to be accountable to their voters. Both arguments are plausible, both arguments are easily justified by many examples, and yet they are in conflict. One says to have finance at the largest possible level, and the other says to have it at the smallest possible level.

The result is a mass of confusions (Greer 2006; Papadopoulos 2010) that appears to invalidate the ambitious claims made for accountability as a policy mechanism (e.g., Flood 2003, as well as much of the fiscal federalism literature reviewed in Costa i Font and Greer 2013). Voters can almost always find better ways to use their time than understanding multi-level governance. They typically are not aware of which government delivers which service, and are impaired in their ability to reward and punish politicians (Kettl 2008). Politicians have an incentive to strategically collect credit and blame in ways that might or might not actually reflect their actions. Even experts have trouble sorting out the different mechanisms that finance and control health systems in the different systems.

The result is also, properly viewed, an excess of accountability. A regional government is accountable to voters, who elect it, but also accountable to the central state government, which gives it more or less constricting mandates and more or less conditional finances. Viewing a regional government as accountable to deliver services on behalf of a larger government is usually just as empirically wrong as viewing it as an autonomous and unconstrained actor accountable only to its voters. Adding in other accountability, whether it is to report health events under the IHR to the WHO, to comply with EU law, or to satisfy bond-holders, makes the situation more difficult to model. Adding in the ability of politicians to muddy credit and blame, and the lack of interest voters usually show in such issues, makes it still more difficult. Finally, the practice of inter-governmental relations (or EU politics, or international negotiations) has a way of reducing the transparency and accountability of decisions – politicians log-roll and negotiate in private, with voters largely unaware and excluded (Simeon and Cameron 2002).

One obvious solution is to simplify accountability by recentralizing, but this rarely works in practice. It is difficult to abolish a tier of elected governments, as seen in the rarity of such an action. Putting more constraints on them, or chan-ging their financing, might change their incentives but still leaves the multiple accountabilities intact, and might give their politicians extra incentive to blame somebody else for problems. In a rare case of abolition, Margaret Thatcher abolished the large municipal governments of the United Kingdom (such as the Greater London Authority) and thereby demonstrated that the result was not simplicity. The successor regimes proved to be astoundingly complex webs of compacts, authorities, and offices that carried out the old governments' func-tions, but without the transparency or electoral accountability (Pimlott and Rao 2002; Travers 2004).

In communicable disease control, multiple manipulatable accountabilities show up best in the persistent underinvestment that plagues the sector. Under-investment in trained staff, laboratory capacity, surveillance systems, inspec-tion capacity, coordination capacity and research are all regular complaints. Such intergovernmental shirking is a sign of weak accountability to those who prefer not to suffer infectious disease. One systematic research project found a plethora of complex and hazy organizational structures in the EU Member States and a remarkable number of 'competent bodies' whose competence could be questioned (Elliott et al. 2012; Mätzke 2012). If nobody is clearly in charge of keeping us free from avoidable communicable diseases, then will anybody take necessary measures? Likewise, even if the 'competent bodies' list has been rationalized, as it subsequently has, does that automatically mean they are more competent to speak for and act in their Member States?

It is all too easy for each level of government to underinvest, responding to the probabilities of a catastrophe and the probabilities that some other level of government will be able to solve the problem for them. In the developed West, outbreaks of communicable disease are relatively rare, temporally and geographically. It is easy for politicians to calculate that they will not person-ally be held accountable for failures. Even in systems with more serious and frequent communicable disease problems, evading blame is not impossible (particularly for diseases associated with stigmatized populations). For local and some regional governments, the solution has often been to impose central requirements and duties on them, but that is not always politically possible and the imposition of a requirement does not always mean its fulfilment. As with most areas of health policy, it is easy to say that the central health ministry should have a coordinating role and some hierarchical superiority, but it is not always the case that the health ministry has the resources, coordinating skills, capacity, credibility or legal authority sufficient to merit the role.

A more durable solution takes two steps. The first is to have relatively clearly understood roles for different governments and organizations as to who is accountable for a given task, and to then ensure that the adequate resources are available. This is easier said than done, because so much of the response to health threats, including communicable diseases, involves extensive coordination between different organizations. Making it clear what different governments do – and mechanisms to hold them accountable, such as clarity about obligations in framework laws – can clarify accountability and avoid subsuming communicable diseases into the broader complexities of multi-level democracy. That is not a banal or simple thing to do. It is often in the interests of all politicians to obfuscate. As Treisman (2007: 81) notes,

> Rules do not become unclear by chance or by oversight of the designers: they are deliberately obfuscated by the players. Both local and central governments have reason to blame the other for their own failures and claim credit for the others' successes. The public collaborates in blurring the rules because [it may] pressure the center to provide remedies.

The second, which falls outside conventional legal and economic theory but has an impressively good evidence base, is to rely on networks of specialists charged with similar responses who can be held accountable by different actors for their outcomes, and have incentive to learn (Sabel and Simon 2006). If a given, delineated, network is held responsible by everybody, including voters and politicians on different levels, then we can avoid many of the problems of hierarchical accountability. In the case of communicable disease control, the many disease-specific surveillance networks that preceded and became part of the ECDC are nice examples of stable networks focused on a given issue that surmounted theoretically (and legally) insurmountable barriers to coordination (Greer 2012).

Capacity

If the key problem of intergovernmental relations is the complexity of arrangements, then a key area of investment is the capacity to foresee, avoid, and manage problems. Expertise in intergovernmental relations and finance, like expertise in European Union policy (Greer 2010), is relatively inexpensive, but can have a profound effect on the effectiveness of coordination and the frequency of intergovernmental failures (Greer and Trench 2010). A relatively centrally located small unit with information can monitor government activities for potential intergovernmental pitfalls, though such units tend to introduce tension because they care about 'diplomatic' issues of intergovernmental politics, while health ministries tend to care more about substantive policy, and will often trade off a principle of federalism for a useful new programme. Over time, an entire bureaucracy can also develop an understanding of intergovernmental coordination, as is the case in many long-standing decentralized and federal countries such as Germany and Canada. Spain, for example, underwent a long learning process during the 1980s and 1990s in which its politicians and civil servants learned ways to coordinate and manage conflict – not by avoiding conflict, which is inherent in democratic politics, but by avoiding undesired conflict (Börzel 2002; Colino 2010). One example of good Spanish intergovernmental practice is its internationally well-regarded organ donation and transplant system, which is often regarded as a case study in bioethics but which should really be seen as a case study in successful coordination and capacity (Box 10.1).

Box 10.1 Why capacity matters: organs in the United Kingdom and Spain

Spain's organ transplant system is widely regarded as a model, with a combination of widely available cadaver organs and efficient allocation that almost every other system fails to achieve (Matesanz et al. 1994; 1995; Miranda et al. 1999).[3] It combines two policies: the ethically and politically interesting one of presumed consent (in which all people are assumed to be willing to donate organs, and must opt out if they do not wish to donate), and, two, a highly effective intergovernmental system for collecting and distributing organs, including a specific agency and an intergovernmental council of regional governments (which control the actual health systems). Often regarded as a triumph of Spanish intergovernmental coordination, the latter system allows the country's different governments to allocate organs by agreed criteria of need.

In Wales, meanwhile, the Welsh Assembly Government sought to adopt the policy of presumed consent from Spain, but failed to also adopt the Spanish attention to intergovernmental relations. The result was a Welsh legislative proposal that had a number of salient flaws. These included: it was not clearly within the powers of the Welsh Assembly Government, it took no notice of the existing United Kingdom-wide agency for managing organ transplants and donations, and it failed to consult with the United Kingdom government (whose consent was necessary). Above all, operating a presumed consent regime in Wales while remaining integrated into a United Kingdom-wide transplant system led to the philosophically debatable prospect of a massive export of Welsh organs to the rest of the United Kingdom or of an effort to create Welsh autarchy in organs.[4] It does not speak well of the Welsh process, notably the policy capacity that might have identified such problems, or the mechanisms of participation (which did not consult crucial organizations such as UK NHS Blood and Transplant).

The lesson is that the Welsh project, an attractive approach to a serious problem that was in line with the distinctive social policy approach of the Welsh government, was derailed by a simple lack of capacity and participation – of preparation, consultation and legal analysis. More broadly, it suggests that there are two lessons to be learned from Spain. There is its legally and bioethically interesting policy of presumed consent. There is also, however, its much more mundane lesson: in a complex operation involving organizations from the hospital to the Spanish central state, well-organized policy capacity, with skilled designers and a transparent decision-making process in which all the relevant governments participate, is necessary to make the process function.

In the case of communicable disease control, the creation of the European Centre for Disease Control and Prevention, in Stockholm, is an effort to create relevant coordinating capacity at the EU level, in order to overcome coordination failures that occur with any cross-border outbreak as well as to build scientific and coordinating capacity in the member states. This is a function that EU agencies frequently fulfil. While they generally lack executive authority (Hervey 2012), they can use their capacity to promote networks, shared understandings, and shared knowledge in areas as distinctive as civil aviation safety, electric utilities regulation and air traffic control (Sabel and Zeitlin 2010; Rittberger and Wonka 2011). Furthermore, the small number of staff in such hubs might have limited capacity to carry out microbiological investigation or field epidemiology, but they can become knowledgeable about the Member States' organization: the capacities, limitations, and people involved. In principle, the competent bodies that connect the EU and Member State organizations also develop expertise in the organizational aspects of communicable disease control, of understanding the various organizations involved and the people and rules that operate them.

Within states, there are a variety of techniques used to improve capacity for intergovernmental and intersectoral coordination (often resembling the ones in McQueen et al. 2012). The most popular current solution is to incorporate high-level functions, including microbiology, field epidemiology capability, research, and international connections into a single agency: the United States Centers for Disease Control and Prevention, but also the French Institute de Veille Sanitaire, the Dutch RIVM, the Robert Koch Institute in Germany, and Public Health England (which inherits the old Health Protection Agency). Health ministries are also natural homes for this kind of expertise; they can know where resources and responsibilities lie and how to activate them. Another is to have coordinating committees or centres, which are often subsumed under the relatively new language and conceptual framework of 'health threats' or 'health security', which in turn connects public health threats with terrorism, natural disasters, and other such major emergencies (Fidler and Gostin 2008; Lakoff and Collier 2008). Introducing military or emergency response agencies and thinking into public health can radically improve resources and capacity to act in an emergency. Governments tend to use emergency management structures in case of large events such as pandemic influenza, which creates a whole new set of coordination issues, sometimes involving security agencies that are not accustomed to coordination with other, civilian, agencies (Botoseneanu et al. 2011). It can also distort public health by, for example, designing surveillance systems that overreact in a way that might make sense if every public health issue were a sign of terrorist attack but does not in the context of limited epidemiological resources (Fearnley 2008).

Perhaps the most effective form of coordination comes through technical and professional networks, which are less cumbersome than the bureaucratic or legally bound hierarchical approaches, and which are quite capable of standardizing definitions and codes of good practice (professional education and training, viewed through this lens, is a process of standardizing people's responses, as doctors, epidemiologists, or whatever else). The problem is its creation, discovery, and reliability – lack of institutionalization means flexibility, but also makes any given network vulnerable to personnel changes, resource constraints, or reorganization. Delegation to semi-formal groups, such as expert committees, high-level groups (as in the EU, de Ruijter 2014) or agencies that work closely with technical experts is a solution that allows governments to sustain and hold experts accountable.

Transparency

The next attribute that can help us out of the problem is transparency about how programmes work. It can be surprisingly difficult to work out intergovernmental accountability arrangements or financial flows, or accountability relationships, or even basic questions of who does what. A simple study examining publicly available data on which diseases are reportable in different EU Member States did not just find wide diversity in procedures and diseases; it also found that such obvious information, which should be public if it is to be useful to those who should be reporting, was largely hidden and demanded a high level of informal diplomacy (Reintjes 2012). This kind of secrecy is deplorable, but all too common. Most organizations default to secrecy and self-protection and neither governments nor international organizations nor health agencies nor emergency managers nor soldiers are exceptions.

There are general benefits to democracy and legality in transparency; and there are more specific benefits to health systems in multi-level democracies. First of all, it is easier to advocate for policies, and learn lessons, when it is clear which governments are doing what, with what money and legal authority. For example, one of the problems in the Spanish health system has long been delayed payment of various kinds, including to the central government in the form of social security payments. This has hidden structural deficits in regional health systems, which became a serious problem after 2010, and also meant that the public presentation of intergovernmental financial negotiations or health budgeting was very difficult to understand as it involved credits and debits that did not exist in public (Gray 2014). The Spanish sovereign debt crisis was not caused by health systems' accounting, but the interlocking crises of regional and central government finances were exacerbated by such problems (Rodden 2005; Labrador 2007; Greer 2010; Repullo, Chapter 11 in this book). Likewise, the four health systems of the United Kingdom have made no efforts to produce comparable data and are in fact producing less comparable data over time, which means that it is difficult to see (or defend) the benefits of different funding levels (Timmins 2013; Bevan et al. 2014). On the other hand, when there are shared standards, or public data, it can create an incentive for governments to compete with each other to improve the quality of their services (Dupuy and Le Galès 2006; Wallner 2009, 2012; Elliott 2013).

Second, transparency makes shirking and corruption more difficult and might improve performance by making outside critique easier. If it is impossible to examine comparative data, or learn about the performance of organizations, and to examine their activities in expenditures and hiring, then it is easy for them to govern badly.

Shirking and unrecognized poor performance are a problems in many important but low-profile areas of health policy, including workforce issues, research, organs, and communicable disease control. It can be made worse if governance includes units that are badly governed in themselves, such as the single-party, low-integrity local or regional governments that appear in many countries. If it is hard to work out who does what (Elliott et al. 2012), which diseases are notifiable (Reintjes 2012), or what influenza pandemic preparations countries have made (Mounier-Jack and Coker 2006), then it is hard to comment on them or develop a means of improving them, or even work out whether there are adequate preparations and allocation of responsibility. The creation of the ECDC, as with so many other EU initiatives (notably organs and blood, but also registers of rare diseases), has forced Member States to at least identify competent bodies and formulate procedures to make their competent bodies more competent. It also creates mechanisms by which to hold networks accountable in the broader political arena. If the ECDC and competent bodies need to think about how their performance will look to various audiences, then they have the incentive to promote effective problem-solving. Visibility and responsibility are key to accountability, and there are a variety of ways to achieve them, which all benefit from transparency.

Participation

Participation, in the framework of this book, is not so much a normative objective as it is a condition for improved governance. Because it focuses on affected parties, it means that policies in multi-level health systems should always be discussed with involved local and regional governments. They might have information that will be useful to implementation; their support might be necessary for implementation; and even when governments are opposed on some issues (and direct public attention there), they can often negotiate on others.[5] In the worst case scenario, consultation alerts policy-makers to potential opposition at the price of denying them the element of surprise. At any rate, the focus here is on intergovernmental participation: if governments share rule, they should participate in the marking and implementation of decisions if they are to work.

Approaches to intergovernmental participation in decisions take two broad forms. One focuses on high-level law and politics. There have been a variety of efforts to promote intergovernmental coordination, most of them essentially trying to promote information exchange and coordinated planning: a 'no surprises' politics. Such agreements often entrench existing norms, especially among civil servants, but also tend to fall prey to politicians' own incentives, whether they are to solve crises with quick actions or make dramatic moves that give them credit for popular policies (Trench 2006). Politicians tend not to want to feed their favourite projects into bureaucratic machinery that is better at blocking than taking action, and still less into the capricious, low-trust and leaky machinery of intergovernmental relations (Savoie 2010). Conflicting accountabilities and politicians' strategies for managing them mean that consultation will not always work, and will often work least well in the areas of the highest profile political issues where governments disagree (Page 2005). On the other hand, low-salience areas, and low-conflict areas, can work relatively well when left in the hands of bureaucracies that have the capacity to carry out intergovernmental consultation. The result should be fewer actions carried out without regard to their advisability.

While political conflict and blurring of credit and blame are inevitable aspects of life under decentralization, there are many effective mechanisms for intergovernmental communication and coordination around the world and in the European Union. Typically, they take the form of more or less formal networks that bring together technical specialists from the relevant governments (Sabel and Zeitlin 2010). In these areas, neither specialists nor generalists see the value of high-level participation and are willing to delegate to relatively stable networks of technical experts. Disease-specific surveillance networks are a good example in communicable disease control; many such international networks have a good record of standardizing case definitions, data sources, and other components of surveillance (Elliott 2013).

Integrity

Finally, integrity – organizational coherence and the basic Weberian virtues of a professional, non-corrupt bureaucracy – makes almost any structure work better. Structures permeated by corruption and clientelism generally have reduced effectiveness and are particularly poor at providing expensive, service-intensive services like health, or politically difficult services like inspection over time. This is the case for decentralization; decentralization seems at least as likely to benefit from integrity as integrity from decentralization.

While integrity is often put forward as a reason for decentralization, the evidence that it will do so is not good. The argument essentially runs as follows: decentralization will produce intergovernmental competition which produces pressure for efficiency, greater transparency since voters can more easily watch their rulers which produces efficiency, and greater participation, since voters can more easily control their representatives which produces efficiency. Unfortunately, these mechanisms are all very spotty and never automatic; not only might competition, transparency and participation not appear, the voters and politicians might make different calculations (there are a variety of reasons why local machine politics and persist and can even be popular). Against theoretical virtues, such as shorter lines of accountability to citizens, intergovernmental competition, or better information, we must counterbalance the low profile, representational biases, and complex institutional contexts of decentralized institutions. There are simply too many ways that decentralization can fail to deliver improvements, or make it easier for popular local governments to engage in corruption, or even facilitate local authoritarian behaviour (Gibson 2013; Mickey 2013).

The challenge of integrity has nothing specific to intergovernmental relations. It amounts to the proposition that all levels of government would benefit from the good practice discussed in Chapter 3 and by theorists of the modern state since at least Max Weber. Multi-level polities are no more virtuous and organized than any others; they just present the extra challenge of policing behaviour in more governments. This means, in many cases, shared civil service structures, independent auditing agencies and courts with jurisdiction over many governments, strong ombudsman and whistleblowing procedures, broadly applicable transparency legislation such as freedom of information, and open budgeting data that allows outsiders to monitor contacts and expenditure.[6] None of these are distinctive to decentralized or federal countries, but they bear the extra burden of preventing locally deviant behaviour by enforcing good standards of public administration, taking advantage of information about violations, and producing broadly accessible data that lets outsiders identify problematic jurisdictions.

Conclusion: strengthening intergovernmental governance

The basic problem of political decentralization is that it deliberately multiplies accountabilities, giving tiers of government accountability to their local voters as well as the central state. This can both confuse accountabilities and make coordination more difficult. The benefits of monitoring, responsiveness, competition, innovation and so forth are uncertain. But while decentralization might not be as advisable as its many proponents suggest (Gerring et al. 2005; Treisman 2007; Gerring and Thacker 2008), in many countries it is a fact, and its management is part of good governance for health systems. Recentralizing or decentralizing policies within an existing federation might have costs or benefits, but they are unlikely to undo the fundamental complexity that comes with multi-level democratic governance.

This chapter has focused on the specific health governance challenges that come with intergovernmental relations. Intergovernmental relations makes accountability harder, in theory and in practice, by creating multiple conflicting lines of accountability and by empowering politicians at all levels to blur them in pursuit of credit and avoidance of blame. This can, in health policy, lead to shirking in crucial areas such as communicable disease control as well as poor coordination and deployment of resources. Sometimes this must just be accepted; if every provincial government wants an expensive medical research centre regardless of its rationality, that is a mistake for them to make. But there are also many successful professional networks that can depoliticize areas of policy, particularly areas with a low political profile, and develop standards that are effectively binding, so even if every province wants to have sub-standard heart transplant facilities, there are professional associations and regulators that can step in.

If there is inevitably a level of competition, obfuscation and political contestation in decentralized systems, such that simple models of accountability fail to work, then a simple way to improve their governance is to make the small investments necessary to improve intergovernmental relations capacity: training policy-makers in the complexity of intergovernmental relations and the tools used in any given country, and establishing the small units that can manage intergovernmental relations effectively.

Another way to improve governance is to enlist outsiders: NGOs, the media, even the occasional interested citizen. Integrity and transparency are difficult enough to maintain within any organization, but maintaining them across a web of organizations is naturally still harder. Transparency allows any interested party, from the political opposition to journalists to academics to international NGOs the opportunity to police government activities. Measures such as transparency, and all the other policies that assist in the creation of integrity, are especially important because the demonstrated capacity of decentralization and federalism to obfuscate things in even countries with high integrity is much greater than its capacity to improve the integrity of health systems. In particular, integrity and transparency measures are necessary because smaller units are quite prone to deviant behaviour.

Perhaps the most theoretically unlikely, but empirically common, successes are when networks of experts with responsibility and expertise that span different governments are formally or informally held responsible by making things work. Sabel and Zeitlin laid out the ideal situation for them to work. They work best in areas where there are agreed challenges, no agreed answers, and a bad outcome should nothing be done (Sabel and Zeitlin 2007). Communicable diseases is a good case of such a policy area; the threat of failure (and the career consequences for those seen to have failed) is dramatic, and is a good incentive for the very diverse people involved in communicable disease control to puzzle together and take measures they regard as binding. This is vastly more practical and possible than trying to create hierarchies of legal power, and takes the tendency of communicable disease control to rely on interpersonal networks as a strength rather than a crutch. Hierarchies ultimately underpin network governance, but they need not be the main or only tool.

Decentralization can reap benefits, and is often a deservedly unquestioned aspect of politics, but it opens up both the possibility of local deviant behaviour and an almost automatic confusion of accountability. The effects are visible in many areas of health systems, from uncoordinated investment (which has opportunity costs) to weak communicable disease control systems (which can cost lives) and local corruption or incompetence: some decentralized units are cleaner and more competent than their central governments, but others are not. This means that health systems governance in decentralized countries must focus on improving both the systemic aspects – transparency, intergovernmental participation, capacity to cope with a complex system of powers and responsibilities and accountability that spans governments – and have an appropriate level of transparency and integrity to the complexity and possibility of bad behaviour at every level. Politics and health policy are always complex, but decentralization produces certain forms of complexity that must be managed if health systems are to achieve their potential.

Notes

1   Questions of what is federal, or confederal, or unitary, are better left to lawyers; for purposes of policy analysis, these categories are less helpful than direct analysis of finance and law (Greer and Massard da Fonseca 2015).

2   There is a case for competition in low taxes or high social investment; there are also, however, cases of destructive competition such as bidding wars for investment that show little or no sign of producing, as against moving, investment.
3   For the key documents of the programme, see http://www.ont.es/publicaciones/Paginas/Publicaciones.aspx.
4   See Alan Trench's analysis at http://devolutionmatters.wordpress.com/2011/11/09/the-welsh-government's-plan-for-organ-donations-in-wales and his contribution to the parliamentary documentation of the Welsh Affairs Committee: 'Welsh Affairs Committee Sixth Special Report Proposed Legislative Competence Orders relating to Organ Donation and Cycle Paths, Annex C', available at: http://www.publications.parliament.uk/pa/cm201011/cmselect/cmwelaf/896/89606.htm. The Welsh Assembly Government withdrew the requests due to a constitutional change that made the specific legal instrument needless, but the Welsh Affairs Committee published submissions to its inquiry on the subject. See http://www.parliament.uk/business/committees/committees-a-z/commons-select/welsh-affairs-committee/inquiries/parliament-2010/organ-donation-lco/timeline.
5   This dynamic is presently visible in the implementation of the Affordable Care Act in the United States, where the states present an uneven map of collaboration and resistance to the policy, with different effects on policy and people who lack access to health care (Jones and Greer 2013).
6   The website www.recovery.gov is a notable example of budgetary transparency that probably helps to explain the low level of malversation in the US$800 bn 2009–2012 American Recovery and Reinvestment Act budget, which was spread across thousands of governments and focused in notoriously corruption-prone areas such as construction.

References

Adolph, Christopher, Greer, Scott L. and Massard da Fonseca, Elize (2012) Allocation of authority in European health policy, *Social Science Medicine*, 75(9): 1595–603.
Agranoff, Robert (1999) Intergovernmental relations and the management of asymmetry in Spain, in Robert Agranoff (ed.) *Accommodating Diversity: Asymmetry in Federal States*. Baden-Baden: Nomos.
Agranoff, Robert (2004) Autonomy, devolution and intergovernmental relations, *Regional & Federal Studies*, 14(1): 26–65.
Banting, Keith G. (2006) Social citizenship and federalism: is the federal welfare state a contradiction in terms? in Scott L. Greer (ed.) *Territory, Democracy, and Justice*. Basingstoke: Palgrave Macmillan.
Bashford, Alison (ed.) (2006) *Medicine at the Border: Disease, Globalization and Security, 1850 to the Present*. Basingstoke: Palgrave Macmillan.
Bevan, Gwyn, Karanikolos, Marina, Exley, Josephine, Nolte, Ellen, Connolly, Sheelah and Mays, Nicholas (2014) *The Four Health Systems of the United Kingdom: How Do They Compare?* London: Health Foundation and Nuffield Trust.
Boadway, Robin and Shah, Anwar (2009) *Fiscal Federalism: Principles and Practice of Multi-Order Governance*. Cambridge: Cambridge University Press.
Börzel, Tanja (2002) *States and Regions in the European Union: Institutional Adaptation in Germany and Spain*. Cambridge: Cambridge University Press.
Botoseneanu, Anda, Wu, Helen, Wasserman, Jeffrey and Jacobson, Peter D. (2011) Achieving public health legal preparedness: views on public health law threaten emergency preparedness and response, *Journal of Public Health*, 33(3): 361–8.
Colino, César (2010) Understanding federal change: types of federalism and institutional evolution in the Spanish and German federal systems, in Jan Erk and Wilfried Swenden (eds) *New Directions in Federalism Studies*. London: Routledge.

Connolly, Sheelagh, Mays, Nicholas and Bevan, Gwyn (2010) *Funding and Performance of Healthcare Systems in the Four Countries of the UK Before and After Devolution.* London: The Nuffield Trust.

Costa i Font, Joan and Greer, Scott L. (eds) (2012) *Federalism and Decentralization in European Health and Social Care.* Basingstoke: Palgrave Macmillan.

Costa i Font, Joan and Greer, Scott L. (2013) Territory and health: perspectives from economics and political science. In Joan Costa i Font and Scott L. Greer (eds) *Federalism and Decentralization in European Health and Social Care.* Basingstoke: Palgrave Macmillan pp. 13–44.

de Ruijter, Anniek (2015) A silent revolution: The expansion of EU power in the field of human health: a rights-based analysis of EU health law and policy. PhD in Law. University of Amsterdam.

Dupuy, Claire and Le Galès, Patrick (2006) The impact of regional governments. In Scott L Greer (ed.) *Territory, Democracy, and Justice: Regionalism and Federalism in Western Democracies.* Basingstoke: Palgrave Macmillan pp. 116–138.

Elliott, Heather A. K. (2013) European Union information infrastructure and policy. In Scott L Greer and Paulette Kurzer (eds) *European Union Public Health Policies.* London: Routledge pp. 36–50.

Elliott, Heather, Jones, David K. and Greer, Scott L. (2012) Mapping infectious disease control in the European Union, *Journal of Health Politics, Policy, and Law*, 37(6): 935–54.

Fearnley, Lyle (2008) Redesigning syndromic surveillance for biosecurity. In Andrew Lakoff and Stephen J. Collier (eds) *Biosecurity Interventions: Global Health and Security in Question.* London: Routledge pp. 61–88.

Fidler, D. P. and Gostin, L. O. (2008) *Biosecurity in the Global Age Biological Weapons, Public Health, and the Rule of Law.* Stanford, CA: Stanford University Press.

Flood, Colleen, M. (2003) Galvanizing publicly funded health care systems through accountability. In Peggy Leatt and Joseph Mapa (eds) *Government Relations in the Health Care Industry.* Westport, CT: Praeger pp. 49–76.

Gerring, John and Strom, C. Thacker (2008) *A Centripetal Theory of Democratic Governance.* Cambridge: Cambridge University Press.

Gerring, John, Strom, C. Thacker, and Moreno, Carola (2005) Centripetal democratic governance: a theory and global inquiry, *American Political Science Review*, 99(4): 567.

Gibson, Edward L. (2013) *Boundary Control: Subnational Authoritarianism in Federal Democracies.* Cambridge: Cambridge University Press.

Gray, Caroline M. (2014) Smoke and mirrors: how regional finances complicate Spanish-Catalan relations, *International Journal of Iberian Studies*, 27(1): 21–42.

Greer, Scott L. (2006) Conclusion: territorial politics today. In Scott L. Greer (ed.) *Territory, Democracy and Justice: Regionalism and Federalism in Western Democracies.* Basingstoke: Palgrave Macmillan pp. 257–275.

Greer, Scott L. (2010a) Territorial politics in hard times: the welfare state under pressure in Germany, Spain, and the United Kingdom. *Environment and Planning, C, Government & Policy*, 28 (3): 405–419.

Greer, Scott L. (2010b) Standing up for health? Health departments in the making of EU policy, *Social Policy and Administration*, 44(2): 208–24.

Greer, Scott L. (2013) Catch me if you can: communicable disease control. In Scott L Greer and Paulette Kurzer (eds) *European Union Public Health Policy: Regional and Global Trends.* London: Routledge pp. 141–155.

Greer, Scott L. and Massard da Fonseca, Elize (2015) Decentralization and health systems governance, in *Palgrave International Handbook of Healthcare Policy and Governance.* Basingstoke: Palgrave Macmillan.

Greer, S. L. and Mätzke, M. (2012) Bacteria without borders: communicable disease politics in Europe, *Journal of Health Politics, Policy and Law*, 37(6): 815–914.

Greer, Scott L. and Trench, Alan (2010) Intergovernmental relations and health in Great Britain after devolution, *Policy and Politics*, 38(4): 509–29.

Hervey, Tamara (2012) The role of the European Court of Justice in the Europeanization of communicable disease control: driver or irrelevance? *Journal of Health Politics, Policy, and Law*, 37(6): 977–1000.

Hooghe, Liesbet and Marks, Gary (2003) Unraveling the central state, but how? Types of multi-level governance, *American Political Science Review*, 97(2): 233–43.

Hooghe, Liesbet, Marks, Gary and Schakel, Arjan (2010) *The Rise of Regional Authority: A Comparative Study of 42 Democracies*. London: Routledge.

Jones, David K. (2013) France. In Joan Costa i Font and Scott L. Greer (eds) *Decentralization and Federalism in European Health and Social Care*. Basingstoke: Palgrave pp. 208–227.

Jones, David K. and Greer, Scott L. (2013) State politics and the creation of health insurance exchanges, *American Journal of Public Health*, 103(8): e8–e10.

Kettl, Donald F. (2008) *The Next Government of the United States: Why Our Institutions Fail Us and How to Fix Them*. New York: W W Norton & Company.

Labrador, José R. Repullo (2007) Gasto sanitario y descentralización:? Saldrá a cuenta haber transferido el INSALUD? *Presupuesto y Gasto Público*, 49: 47–66.

Lakoff, Andrew and Collier. Stephen J. (eds) (2008) *Biosecurity Interventions: Global Health and Security in Question*. New York: Columbia University Press.

Matesanz, R., Miranda, B. and Felipe, C. (1994) Organ procurement in Spain: impact of transplant coordination. *Clinical Transplant* 8(3 Pt 1): 281–6.

Matesanz, R., Miranda, B., Felipe, C. and Naya, M.T. (1995) Organ procurement in Spain: the national organization of transplants. In *Organ Shortage: The Solutions*. Berlin: Springer pp. 167–177.

Mätzke, Margitta (2012) Commentary: The institutional resources for communicable disease control in Europe: diversity across time and place, *Journal of Health Politics, Policy, and Law*, 36(1): 967–76.

McQueen, David, Wismar, Matthias, Lin, Vivian, Jones, Catherine, St-Pierre, Louise and Davies, Maggie (eds) (2012) *Inter-sectoral Governance for Health in All Policies: Structures, Actions and Experiences*. Copenhagen: WHO Regional Office for Europe on behalf of the European Observatory on Health Systems and Policies.

Mickey, Robert (2013) *Paths Out of Dixie: The Democratization of Authoritarian Enclaves in America's Deep South*. Princeton, NJ: Princeton University Press.

Miranda, B., Fernández Lucas, M., De Felipe, C., Naya, M., González-Posada, J. M., and Matesanz, R. (1999) Organ donation in Spain. *Nephrology Dialysis Transplantation*, 14(suppl. 3): 15–21.

Mounier-Jack, S. and Coker, R. J. (2006) How prepared is Europe for pandemic influenza? Analysis of national plans, *The Lancet*, 367(9520): 1405–11.

Page, Edward C. (2005) Joined-up government and the civil service. In Vernon Bogdanor (ed.) *Joined-Up Government*. Oxford: Oxford University Press/British Academy pp. 139–155.

Papadopoulos, Yannis (2010) Accountability and multi-level governance: more accountability, less democracy? *West European Politics*, 33(5): 1030–49.

Pimlott, Ben and Rao, Nirmala (2002) *Governing London*. Oxford: Oxford University Press.

Reintjes, Ralf (2012) Variation matters: epidemiological surveillance in Europe. *Journal of Health Politics, Policy, and Law*, 37(6): 955–65.

Rittberger, B. and Wonka, A. (2011) Introduction: Agency governance in the European Union, *JEPP*, 18(6): 780–9.

Rodden, Jonathan A. (2005) *Hamilton's Paradox: The Promise and Peril of Fiscal Federalism*. Cambridge: Cambridge University Press.

Sabel, Charles F. and Simon, Herbert (2006) Epilogue: accountability without sovereignty. In Gráinne De Búrca and Joanne Scott (eds) *Law and New Governance in the EU and the US*. Oxford: Hart.

Sabel, Charles F. and Zeitlin, Jonathan (2007) Learning from difference: the new architecture of experimentalist governance in the European Union, *European Law Journal*, 14(3): 271–327.

Sabel, Charles F. and Zeitlin, Jonathan (eds) (2010) *Experimentalist Governance in the European Union: Towards a New Architecture.* Oxford: Oxford University Press.

Saltman, Richard B. and Bankauskaite, Vaida (2006) Conceptualizing decentralization in European health systems: a functional perspective, *Health Economics, Policy and Law*, 1: 127–47.

Saltman, Richard B., Bankauskaite, Vaida and Vrangbaek, Karsten (eds) (2007) *Decentralization in Health Care.* Maidenhead: Open University Press.

Savoie, Donald J. (2010) *Power: Where Is It?* Montreal and Kingston: McGill-Queens University Press.

Simeon, Richard and Cameron, David (2002) Intergovernmental relations and democracy: An oxymoron if there ever was one? In Herman Bakvis and Grace Skogstad (eds) *Canadian Federalism: Performance, Effectiveness, and Legitimacy.* Toronto: Oxford University Press pp. 278–295.

Stepan, Alfred (1999) Federalism and democracy: beyond the U.S. Model, *Journal of Democracy*, 10(4): 19–34.

Tiebout, Charles M. (1956) A pure theory of local expenditure, *Journal of Political Economy*, 64: 416–25.

Timmins, Nicholas (2013) *The Four UK Health Systems: Learning from Each Other.* London: Nuffield Trust.

Travers, Tony (2004) *The Politics of London: Governing An Ungovernable City.* Basingstoke: Palgrave Macmillan.

Treisman, Daniel, S. (2007) *The Architecture of Government: Rethinking Political Decentralization.* Cambridge: Cambridge University Press.

Trench, Alan (2006) Intergovernmental relations: in search of a theory. In Scott L. Greer (ed.) *Territory, Democracy and Justice: Regionalism and Federalism in Western Democracies.* Basingstoke: Palgrave Macmillan.

Trench, Alan (2007) *Devolution and Power in the United Kingdom.* Manchester: Manchester University Press.

Wallner, Jennifer (2009) Beyond national standards: reconciling tension between federalism and the welfare state, *Publius*, pjp033vl

Wallner, Jennifer (2012) Political structures, social diversity, and public policy comparing mandatory education in Canada and the United States, *Comparative Political Studies*, 45(7): 850–74.

Weaver, R. Kent (1986) The politics of blame avoidance, *Journal of Public Policy*, 6: 371–98.

Weir, Lorna and Mykhalovskiy, Eric (2010) *Global Public Health Vigilance: Creating a World on Alert.* London: Routledge.

Wright, Deil Spencer (1982) *Understanding Intergovernmental Relations.* Monterey, CA: Brooks/Cole.

chapter eleven

Austerity: reforming systems under financial pressure

José R. Repullo

Introduction

The austerity measures introduced in Europe, as a response to the economic and fiscal crisis that began in 2008, show a shift in focus from the previous concerns on the internal sustainability of public health care systems towards an effort to reduce the weight of health expenditures on budgets and national economies (shifting from sustainability to austerity). It is possible to debate the intent and intelligence of any policy, but austerity is a fact in much of Europe. Austerity policies, adopted in many cases by governments under heavy financial pressure, have driven the reduction of public expenditures and created a challenge for the health sector: how can health systems save public money without affecting mortality and morbidity, and without damaging the functioning and quality of the services provided by the public health care system?

The ideological perspectives of governments shape the goals of austerity, but the ability of developing good quality governance could make a fundamental difference in devising and implementing austerity policies. This chapter identifies two patterns of austerity: (1) the *wise* version of austerity, which is capable of mobilizing the instruments of good governance to get value for money; and (2) the *thoughtless* version of austerity, which is unable to advance beyond the imposition of financial cutbacks and downsizing of supply and services.

The TAPIC framework shows how governance encourages wise or thoughtless austerity policies. Good governance patterns should arouse the confidence of citizens and patients and the cooperation of doctors and other health personnel, through good accountability, transparency and participation, while having integrity and policy capacity of government to allow clever and long-term transactions among different actors. The absence of those good governance capacities (or the weak political will to apply them) could lead to linear, turbulent and disjointed cuts made to obtain quick and neat savings of public money.

An analytical framework is proposed to assess the pattern of governance as applied to austerity policies. Further research must be done, both to identify the specific country responses, and to evaluate the connection between 'wise' austerity and better outcomes, in terms of maintaining the effectiveness, increasing the efficiency and strengthening the internal sustainability of health care systems. Nevertheless, the conceptual analysis confirms the relevance of good governance principles to efforts to construct and sustain effective health systems.

Economic crisis and austerity policies

The economic crisis

Since 2008, Europe has had major economic problems: recession, weak economic growth and unemployment, also with a low likelihood of a new and sustainable period of social and economic development. This troubled environment is affecting European countries in different ways. In particular, Portugal, Italy, Greece and Spain (and also Ireland) have suffered from a more serious recession, unemployment, deficit and debt (Sapir 2006). They are consequently key cases for understanding the governance of austerity for better or for worse.

Structural problems behind the 2008 economic and fiscal crisis are beyond the remit of this chapter. Nevertheless, globalization and deregulation plays an important role, rearranging wealth and growth among different worlds, regions and economies. Therefore, the maintenance of the so-called 'European Social Model' in times of flat growth rates means an additional effort at solidarity and a major challenge to put in place reforms for the efficient running of the state.

Nevertheless, the pattern of macro-economic policies in the Euro-zone has been less ambitious and reformist, giving a clear priority to quick fiscal stabilization: balancing budgets mainly at the expense of reducing expenditures was the dominant response in the Euro-zone. This dominant strategy is being criticized, even within the IMF (Blanchard and Leigh 2013) due to the unexpected level of GDP freezing produced by sharp drops in public expenditure: ("fiscal multipliers" were substantially higher than implicitly assumed by forecasters). However, for at least five years, cost cutting has been the basic medicine prescribed to all, but especially to those countries with major problems in public deficit and sovereign debt (Greece, Ireland, Portugal, and Spain).

From sustainability to austerity

The rapid economic growth of public expenditure in welfare services, but particularly in health care (well over the increase of GDP) between 1997 and 2007, raised concerns about its sustainability. Extrapolation of demand-side factors (ageing population, changing public demands, needs, preferences, etc.) and supply side ones (technology, innovations, etc.) in OECD countries have led to a worrying forecast (de la Maisonneuve and Martins 2013). A stream of proposals, coming from researchers and policy advisors, addressed the need for structural changes in the welfare services (technology, organization, incentives, role of users, etc.) to make them 'internally sustainable' and efficient: both productive and allocative efficiency (doing things right, and doing the right things) were seen as essential strategies to maintain the equity and quality of healthcare services for citizens; reconfiguration of services, information, funding mechanisms, health-related behaviour, and accountability play a key role in efficiency (Smith 2012).

Unfortunately the good economic situation and the myopic nature of conventional policy-making had the effect of leaving the unpopular changes for the future and the enjoyment of the political advantages of expanding structure and services now: it is always difficult to go against path dependency, though much more so in affluent times. Another particularly troublesome element in some countries was the speculative nature of a good part of the economic growth (housing bubbles), where most analysts advised unsuccessfully to implement counter-cyclical policies.

When the financial crisis arrived, it was inevitable that countries would have to leave the comfortable path, and the new political scenario gave more power and initiative to authorities to lead the transformation. It should have also brought the opportunity to put sustainability onto the main agenda of the changes being made. But in many countries what in fact happened was the subtle and progressive substitution of 'sustainability' for 'austerity' in the political discourse. In a very short time, the language of structural reforms gave way to a claim for radical changes that would make expenses fall into line with falling public revenues; there was no room for specific measures to improve the service. As in moments of a ship capsizing catastrophically, all the attention was focused on rescuing the system (reducing deficit and debt); equity concerns simply vanished, as well as the former aspiration for universalism.

The polysemy of austerity

'Austerity' is a word with many meanings, and that seems essential to its current success in policy-making. For example, in Spanish, the word '*austeridad*' conveyed the meanings of a severe, sober, and simple behaviour, which closely fitted the moral standards. The idea of prioritization and waste avoidance makes the term very attractive for political purposes, and avoids using other pejorative terms like trimming, cutting, thinning, or divestment. Something similar can be said regarding the term in English,[1] Portuguese (*austeridade*[2]), Italian (*austerità*[3]) and Greek (λιτότητα[4]). Multilanguage semantics reinforces the use in global politics; the merit of the word seems to be its unusual positive appeal in many languages, which makes it easier for it to wrap up unpopular measures.

Nevertheless, the practical use of the term 'austerity', in the European 2008 crisis, has been to put a name to policies aimed at cutting social costs for two reasons: to balance public expenditure deficits (at the expense of raising revenues) and to attend to other priorities (mainly financing the bail-out of the bank system). This implies a growing semantic contradiction and tension between the formal definition and the real meaning. In fact, austerity policies allow an overall more inequitable redistribution of wealth.

The former contradiction has biased the understanding of the term: the most 'positive' meaning (making savings at the expense of unnecessary actions or expenses) has turned, in many countries, into distrust in the ability of governments to discriminate between the fundamental and the superfluous, and in

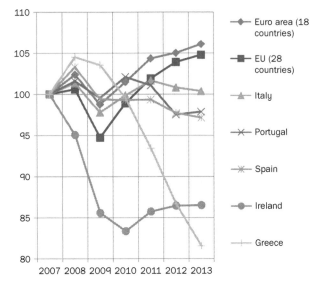

Figure 11.1 GDP at market prices (current prices), evolution EU-28, Euro-zone and selected EU countries: 2007=100

Source: Eurostat, Statistic Database http://epp.eurostat.ec.europa.eu/portal/page/portal/national_accounts/data/main_tables.

despair at the lack of results in controlling the deficit, the increase in debt, the rise of unemployment, and the relapse after 2012 of the economic downturn in quite a lot of European countries; the stagnation is particularly visible in the Mediterranean countries (see Figure 11.1).

Regarding welfare sectors, it is remarkable that the formal political commitments of the EU are quickly forgotten under hard financial pressures, as medical profession representatives and other personalities of four countries complained (Ireland, Portugal, Spain and Greece) (*Open Letter to European Political Leaders and Health Authorities* 2013).

Moreover, it seems that a more negative and critical meaning has emerged: austerity equals 'linear cost-cutting', or even worse: influential and wealthy elites are not substantially affected, leaving the workers and the poor people to carry the weight of the budget adjustment. Also the 'external' component of the policy (the EU, the ECB, the IMF and Germany, exerting a closer and tougher influence) was perceived as the key driving force behind the austerity policies. External influence, and even the perception of such external influence, ultimately weakens countries' sovereignty and adds to the devaluation of the national parliaments and national politics.

Ideological understandings behind austerity

Different understandings of austerity, according to political ideology and preferences, can be found: social-democrats (who have avoided whenever possible the term austerity), points to the pragmatic, incrementalist and reformist adaptation of the welfare state, while liberal-conservatives point to downsizing the public sector to limit the role of the state. Those two versions of austerity are not always seen as conflicting; short-termism and the extreme financial pressures can make both left and right end up combining them through pragmatism to create a blended and ambivalent understanding of austerity. The preponderance of the ministries of economy and finance helps to impose this blended and ambiguous vision on the main agenda. The confluence of both approaches hides the adversarial nature of those two quite different ideological understanding of 'austerities'.

Social-democrats and left-wing parties, supporting in normal times rise in expenditure to improve equity and quality of services, see austerity in the coordinates of changing the welfare state for its sustainability: reforming public service is the main challenge to do more with the same (or even with less). Several anti-crisis agendas were proposed in 2009 and 2010 in different countries; in the health care systems there are a number of relevant documents with a high degree of concordance in the proposed structural changes (Appleby et al. 2010, Bernal et al. 2011, *Relatório de Primavera 2013: duas faces da saúde*, 2013). The rationale of this continuous improvement strategy is that there is fat that can be removed to 'save' the muscle and bones of the body; there are low or null value-added interventions that can be disinvested to gain effectiveness elsewhere. The financial crisis gave a momentum to policies aimed at tackling well-diagnosed problems of the health care system. Government has the clout to implement necessary reforms, having the authority and power to make changes, there is room for governance to play its role: implementing a set of policy objectives and initiatives into real changes on the ground; and in doing so minimizing the social stress and costs.

Conservatives, liberals, and right-wing parties follow a different and more radical vision of austerity: the underlying rationale is the downsizing of the public economy in favour of individual responsibility, including now the 'sacred land' of health care. From this provective, it can be acceptable to set a high level of savings in the public budget, combined with fostering the entrance of markets into the financing, insurance and provision of health care. This is expressed as 'conditional solidarity' of the state, a new social contract where individuals are committed to pursue healthy living, or even further, the creation of 'super-empowered individuals' in competitive markets (*Sustainable Health Systems: Visions, Strategies, Critical Uncertainties and Scenarios*, 2013). The basic story in this vision emphasizes that the generosity of society, providing universal subsidies and services, is not compatible with the new stringent times. In the public health care sector, the main effect is the challenging of universalism (well defined by McKee and Stuckler 2011).

In between those two versions, some authors, like Saltman and Cahn (2013), challenge the classical universalism, on the basis that the state budget will not cope with growing demand and innovation. They propose a 're-structuring' alternative, which points to (1) shifting a substantial part of the costs of care from the state to the individuals; (2) simplifying the regulation of government (making it less costly); (3) encouraging and supporting patients and relatives so they produce more self-care and lay care; and (4) asking employers to provide care for their workers cheaper than conventional existing primary care

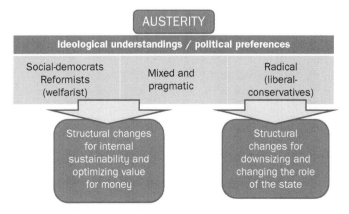

Figure 11.2 Ideological understandings of austerity

services. On the foundations of this proposal is a change in the social contract between citizens and government, to maintain the 'core' of social insurance.

The former approach takes into account some of the problems of growing demand (medicalization of discomfort and troubles) and lack of control over the supply side (technology industry and its influence on doctors, organizational problems, and weaknesses of alignment between professionals and the public interest), but the key messages are aimed at the demand side (to be stopped by co-payments and benefit exclusions), and that seems to place the re-structuring closer to the vision of the above-mentioned radical changes that have recently taken place across many countries in Europe. Some left wing parties, in Southern Europe in particular, contend that there is indeed a need for radicalism, but in the opposite direction of Treasury or market radicalism: income re-distribution, prevention, community action, knowledge management, new public service management, and good governance.

In Figure 11.2 these alternative visions are depicted: in this chapter we will concentrate on the reformist or pragmatic approach, to analyse whether the willingness or ability to develop good governance could make a difference to achieving the improvement goals. It would be much more difficult and complex to study in terms of good governance principles and dimensions the more radical and intentional option of withdrawal of the state from its traditional functions and responsibilities.

The outcomes of health austerity policies in the reformist approach

It can be generally agreed that the fate or general purpose of austerity in health is to stabilize or reduce health care costs without reducing effective services or altering the health of populations. It might be more complicated to disaggregate it into more specific goals, but three levels of outcomes (dominant, satisfying and complementary) could be defined:

- *Main (dominant) goal*: obtaining the intended and marked savings of public expenditures; in other words, to reach the stabilization or reduction of expenditure according to the macro-economic scenario and goals devised for the health sector.

- It is quite easy to measure this goal, as it is also of the utmost importance to the dominant agent in the government decision-making: the Treasury Ministry, and also the EU and Euro-zone authorities (especially when bail-out conditionality exists). Key indicators will be constructed around the public health care expenditure. Portugal's memorandum of and clearly stated the reductions in the public health expenditure, and it includes a wide set of specific policies to save money in the health system (objective 2013: 375 million € health care savings) (*Portugal: Memorandum of Understanding on Specific Economic Policy Conditionality*, 2012); in the case of Spain, with only a partial bail-out of the banking system, the objectives of expense reduction are defined within the Programme of Stability of the Government (objective 2016 – health expenditure to be downsized into 5.4 per cent of GDP) (*Programa de Estabilidad del Reino de España 2013–16* 2013).
- *Secondary (satisfying) goal*: The main goal must be reached without a significant and severe adverse effect on the health of the population. Scandals of mortality or severe morbidity are the limit of the unacceptable effects of the austerity policy, though acceptability might vary between countries, and with the length of the austerity period.
  - In the short term, the main health indicators (mortality and morbidity) are not able to show changes attributable to the economic crisis, or to specific policies to face the crisis (in general or in the health care and social services); the time-lag usually takes years to show the damages. Nevertheless, the severity and the extent of the Greek crisis and austerity policies began to show adverse outcomes on health (Kondilis et al. 2013).
  - Other measures of throughput or indicators of use (consultations, discharges, operations, procedures, waiting times) may be worsened, but it can be claimed that there is no real impact on outputs or outcomes.
- *Complementary goals*: maintaining the core effectiveness, safety, quality of the system and the satisfaction with the services, but reducing their scope, depth and breadth. Some contractions of the health care services can be performed by authorities (though frequently hidden and denied if questioned): temporal streamlining (investment, training, research), delays or cuts in non-essential services (waiting times, symptomatic drugs, etc.), overloading providers (less time with patients and quicker processing of patients), cost-sharing of ancillary or complementary services, less expenses in promoting accessibility (or covering home care), exclusion of benefits for some groups of people ("health tourism" immigrants, etc.)
  - Many savings in health services do not produce short-term visible effects on mortality or morbidity, but the erosion of the effectiveness, quality, safety, satisfaction, accessibility and waiting times happens gradually. However, confidence in this strategy is quite politically risky: it is very difficult to prevent a major problem arising from silent and pervasive streamlining (see Stafford Hospital scandal in the United Kingdom (*Stafford Hospital: Q&A* 2013), and the death of a Senegalese immigrant in Mallorca

of tuberculosis although it could be better described as severe adverse effect) (Manresa 2013).

- The progressive reduction of scope, depth and breadth of services can be also accepted if the ideological references are finally changed (the already mentioned 'radical' approach to austerity).

Therefore, the best outcome of a reformist austerity policy in health care would be the accomplishment of marked cost containment, allied to the maintenance or rise (not to mention improvements) of health and health care indicators, and the limitation of damage in terms of: (1) the erosion of services; (2) the decapitalization of assets; and (3) the demoralization of employees. The main issue to be addressed in this chapter is whether the application of good governance principles and dimensions makes a difference in the achievement of the best outcomes for austerity policies in health care.

The TAPIC framework as applied to health care austerity

The application of tools related to the TAPIC framework in governance requires willingness to use such tools (political knowledge, confidence, commitment and talent), and also the ability to put them into practice and manage the implementation. What is clear is that many instruments will not be available, they could be time-consuming to acquire, or they have cultural obstacles to import; in other words, the lack of those good governance instruments makes it impossible to use them. Therefore, willingness and availability are the two elements to be considered in the application of good governance policies. In Table 11.1, the five dimensions in the TAPIC framework are shown, and a gradient from good (left side) to poor (right side) shows the specific applications of the five dimensions to the 12 assessment categories.

Accountability is the first dimension, and must be applied at the macro-institutional level, and at the meso-micro level of health care organizations (centres and units providers of health care).

The crucial question in *institutional accountability* is to determine who plays the role of 'principal' in the multiple and intricate agency relationships of the health sector. The main duality of 'principals', that is, the duality of citizens (tax-payers) or patients (users), must be properly aligned and managed: the agents of these principals play on essential role: political elites and economic authorities versus doctors and health authorities.

To find a good outcome maybe it would be better to empower health authorities to harmonize citizens' and patients' visions: creating a fluid relationship between political and social organizations, and setting up a stable and honest relationship with the mass media. Regarding priorities, it is essential to protect those populations who are poorer and frailer, and to consider the opportunity cost of health expenditures, regarding actions in other social services; intelligent trade-offs should be possible to minimize the effect of crisis in welfare and in health (e.g., food supplement for children at schools). Authorities must also be accountable for the adverse effects of their austerity policies, and that means preparedness, openly monitoring undesirable outcomes, acting promptly

Table 11.1 Governance dimensions applied to austerity

Accountability	
Good	*Poor*

MACRO LEVEL-Institutional: Who is the principal? Which discourse prevails?

Citizens + Patients (aligned and harmonized) National Health Authorities take the lead.	**National + International political elites-networks** Economic Authorities and agencies take the lead
Priorities... preventing damages: Savings + Adverse Effects (combined)	**Constricted prioritizing** Savings + economic growth

MESO LEVEL - Organizational: Purchaser–Provider split (gap)

Narrowing gap: accountable–open rationing	**Widening gap:** Blind rationing + blame providers if problems

Transparency	
Good	*Poor*

Open access *Wide set of data and information available*	**Closed access** Selective disclosure of cooked data
Easy comparison Benchmarking easy and quick (self-comparison)	**Difficult comparison** Lack of data and confidence in official sources

Participation	
Good	*Poor*

Taking risks and delegate to the front line: empowerment and confidence in front line agents / social-patients organizations	**Classical Executive Managerialism** Centralized and distrust approach for quick and dirty cost-containment
Emphasis on clinical management and alliance with professionalism	**Reconsidering and limiting the role of doctors:** managerialist approach to incentives

Integrity	
Good	*Poor*

Clear, open and stable rules of the game Delegation to front line units and evaluation by end-results	**Changing and discretionary rules, and ambiguity** Tough input control + more autonomy for local rationing + procedural sanctions if scandals
Clear role for Principles Coherence, values and exemplarity of management and managers	**Clear domain of Utilitarianism (Consequentialism)** Match to assigned goals (expenditure) as dominant virtue (ends justify means)

(Continued)

Table 11.1 Governance dimensions applied to austerity (*Continued*)

Policy capacity	
Good	*Poor*
Requirements for intelligence	**Up - Down needs no requirements**
Asking for enough time and space for devising and implementing good policies	Assume disciplined adaptation to quick and radical budget cuts
Activate institutional intelligence	**Replace internal intelligence if reluctant**
Enhancing internal policy-making technostructure	Use consultancy if civil servants are reluctant
Combine different time-frames	**Overwhelming priority to immediate targets**
Ability to work in different terms (short–mid–long)	Short-term dominant (low-hanging apples)

to minimize the harmful effects, and being open-minded to reconsider specific austerity policies when their application is harmful.

But there are barriers for open accountability: neo-elitist approaches are always possible; it seems easier to bring a limited group of political elites together to formulate pacts, endorsed and supported by multilateral organizations, and based on the argument of pragmatism and lack of other options. A more extreme option could be to assign the leading role to economic authorities and external agents which stick to the letter of the bail-out agreements ('the troika' team who visit to assess the accomplishment of the Memorandum of Understanding commitments). Lack of support from the public can be compensated with populist-led components, such as passing the burden of guilt to the 'parasites of the welfare state' (immigrants, unemployed, subsidized families, etc.). If there are adverse effects, the easiest way is to ignore or minimize its importance as 'anecdotal events', or blame 'incompetent' local implementation.

In the *organizational accountability* section, the main challenge is to determine how distant from the health authorities the health care services must be placed: the purchaser–provider split creates a gap that can be narrowed or widened. In tough times it is probably wiser to bring all the agents closer and united under a well-defined agenda and clear and open access contracts (accountable and open rationing). The more opportunistic alternative should be to put more distance between authorities and providers, giving them more autonomy (foundation or private status), and more open and discretionary contracts (e.g., based on unconditioned capitation) to play the game of externalization of the services, therefore putting the central authorities far from the guilt and damages in case of problems (blind rationing?).

Transparency is the second dimension, and includes consideration of the information provided to the public, and its honesty, reliability and validity. Good governance means complete and balanced information, including the budget savings in question, but also the risks and adverse effects of these; and also, if applying the principle of open access, good governance would involve putting into the public domain a chunk of information regarding expenditure and performance of centres and services (which is an opportunity for impulse benchmarking and self and control), and allowing a wide, quick and specific problem identification and problem solving.

On the contrary, in non-transparent governance, austerity tends to limit the scope of information, stressing only the economic targets, and provide biased data; moreover, focusing on a small number of fiscal indicators of interest to international organizations and bond markets can lead to reporting problems ranging from slight manipulation to clear deceit.

Participation is the third governance dimension, in which authorities can play different roles in the design and application of austerity policies. The managerial style can be hierarchical (i.e. command and control), or participatory. In particular, then, the approach to doctors is crucial because of their role in allocating resources and making decisions.

A participatory and consensual approach will create an alliance of policy-makers with health managers and professionals. Only by delegating authority, confidence, competencies, and discretionary margins to front-line services will this allow them to act selectively to convert rationing into rationalization. That means generalizing clinical management experiments and supporting them with a knowledge-management policy at the national level while disinvesting in inefficient practices and changing the balance of services and priorities. Patients and social groups need to play a stakeholder role, despite their likely opposition to any service cuts (including those traditionally provided but not 'evidence-based'). Participation brings procedural legitimacy to the decision-making process, and very frequently enriches and enlarges it.

Despite these advantages, it is easy to fall in the trap of leaving participation aside and opting for being more hierarchical and executive. It is not easy to implement participation in tough times, and so it seems to be more practical to try 'quick and dirty' inquiries to feed the formal participation requirements, practising a more authoritative and expeditious style. The lack of confidence in the end results of involving doctors in 'rationing' may lead to reconsidering the role of the 'clinical management' experiments, in favour of close managerial control of professionals (focus on use of resources and aggregated activity, and volume-based incentives).

Integrity is the fourth dimension; it deals with the conditions for preserving honesty and alignment with the general interest (that is, the interest of both citizens and patients, who are the real 'principals'). It might be better to reform the control rules and means, in a coherent and well-explained way, to focus on forward-looking accountability rather than constantly reducing the discretion (and therefore eroding the morale and development) of staff. But integrity also plays a crucial role in the support for and legitimacy of managers, and the application of value-based management.

Against this dimension is the trend of central authorities to take over and change the rules very frequently (exceptionalism); there is a lack of coherence in control rules and means: on one hand, authorities ask front-line managers to achieve financial objectives using their local autonomy (relaxing the accomplishment of formal rules and means); but, on the other hand, if problems arise, the same authorities will lead the claim of strict application of formal procedures and sanctions.

And, the fifth dimension is the *policy capacity* of governments: the key issue in times of crisis is whether there is time, place and space to put intelligence to work into well-designed austerity policies for health care.

The activation and the good performance of institutional intelligence requires sufficient time, and the objectives of reducing spending should be moderate, medium-term and predictable. Given this, it is essential to reinforce the role and means of the core groups of civil servants who provide high-level assessment to politicians.

Policy-making and implementation are difficult amidst turbulence and changing agendas and restrictions imposed on the health sector. Policy-making has to overcome difficulties in the day-to-day interaction between politicians and senior officials (the technical policy-makers). If an adversarial relationship with the internal techno-structure appears, politicians may opt to contract out to external consultancy support; this practice might erode the core policy capacity of the Ministry of Health and the health care agencies. Short-termism and improvisation could easily replace competent and strategic policy-making. The use and abuse of temptingly easy-to-apply measures (cutting salaries, employment, investments, etc.) are like taking the low-hanging apples: when the upper-level apples need to be collected, alliances are impossible, and structural changes remain out of the scope.

Two patterns of governance: wise (enlightened) and thoughtless (crude)

We have just seen the five dimensions of governance in the TAPIC framework as applied to austerity policies, and 12 assessment categories have emerged. Good and poor governance could be analysed not only as the level of accomplishment of those 12 elements, but as patterns of integrated response. This method can be useful for connecting governance with the already mentioned outcomes of an austerity policy. In Figure 11.3, good governance performance leads to a pattern called 'wise austerity', and poor governance to another called 'thoughtless austerity'. The conceptual hypothesis of the relationship between wise and thoughtless austerity and their positive and negative outcomes is described below.

The bottom part of Figure 11.3 depicts the diminishing returns of expenditure to health; it shows the popular 'flat part of the curve medicine' representation: the x-axis shows health expenditure of countries (or volume of services), while the y-axis represents the attained level of health (life expectancy usually adjusted by disability or quality). This concept, well popularized by Fuchs (2004), is born in times of rapid growth of health expenditures, and highlights the reduction of marginal returns of health utilities as the money spent on health increases. The traditional lesson for developed countries (living in the 'flat part of the curve') was therefore not to do more of the same, but to find new strategies to improve health; another conclusion was to be aware of the opportunity costs of allocating funds to health care as compared to other services (some of them, like education, poverty subsidies or social services, will produce valuable welfare, and in some cases should bring as side effect a real impact on health).

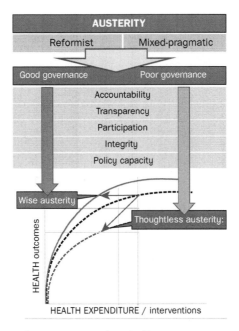

Figure 11.3 Patterns of governance and austerity

But the same argument can be read in the reverse sense in wealthy countries: if only a bit of health impact can be achieved with a lot of money, it might be easy to cut a great amount of expenditure with almost no impact on the population's health. This would be a very promising strategy, if it were possible to drive back into the past by the same road on which we arrived at the present. But the way we have added up resources and innovations (people, technologies, investment, benefits, etc.) is somehow irreversible by its own nature.

In other words: if health expenditure goes down (back along the x axis), a *wise and enlightened downsizing* should allow a system to maintain the health level of the population through the mobilization of a wide set of integrated managerial, public health and clinical resilient strategies. Alternatively, a *thoughtless and crude downsizing* will search for quick and neat savings of public money, based upon linear, turbulent and disjointed cuts; and the problem with externally-driven and indiscriminate applied cuts is the destruction of assets and the end to the system's capability to produce appropriate and needed services. Therefore, it can be said that the technical fate of an excellent austerity policy should be to follow the 'wise downsizing' pattern, which in fact means moving to the other curve of the health production function: not doing more of the same, but doing new and different things, and doing less of other ineffective or harmful things.

One particularly clear example is public health; as Morgan (2013) states: 'Disinvestment in public health is always a possibility given the often long-term nature of its benefits, but this becomes more acute in times of austerity and public sector cuts.' Thoughtless downsizing is usually myopic and is not aware of the rationality and future savings that health promotion and protection and disease prevention can bring.

The conceptual connection between a wise austerity pattern and positive outcomes intended by austerity policies can be explained as follows:

- *Cost containment* can be better reached by removing inappropriate services, but only physicians helped by accurate knowledge can differentiate and reduce them; new movements rooted in evidence-based medicine, like the British 'do not do' or the American 'choosing wisely' point in that direction. Also, realigning the contractual relationship between health systems and professionals is a clear *accountability* measure that could be implemented. Knowledge management, created and delivered by intelligent organizations with mid-term vision, needs a good deal of *policy capacity*.
- *Preventing mortality and morbidity side effects* of cost containment also requires intelligence (*policy capacity*), specially to devise inter-sector strategies to reduce the burden of disease, but also active monitoring of problems: that means *transparency* and not hiding bad news. In addition, *accountability* to society imposes the obligation of being prepared and acting promptly on health problems.
- Working with scarce means is annoying and difficult; *preventing the erosion of services* (volume, appropriateness, quality, etc.) requires an allowance for local decision-making: more autonomy to clinicians would empower doctors and enhance the operational dimension of *participation*. But acceptance of restrictions benefits from the *transparency* which allows citizens or patients to observe and assess the relative effort of all hospitals and services. *Accountability* reinforced through clever contracting with hospitals and clinical departments (*policy capacity*) gives a foundation for running the services in stringent times.
- *Willingness of health personnel* to participate in these strategies depends heavily on their commitment to the public service: *integrity* expressed by setting out clear rules of the game and through the exemplarity and legitimacy of institutional leaders is essential for the whole set of measures, and especially for the recruitment of clinical leaders to make the public health care service resilient and sustainable.

Conclusion: good governance through wise austerity, could lead to resilient and sustainable public health care systems

Even though a strategy of 'thoughtless austerity' in some countries can reduce public expenditure, and time will finally bring a new period of GDP growth and creation of employment, the post-crisis society will reemerge being less equitable, with weaker social capital, and not so healthy and wealthy.

Moreover, these countries will have yet to face the challenge of internal sustainability, because linear cost-cutting of health resources will have probably damaged the operation of services, and delayed the necessary structural reforms in health care.

Applying good governance principles and means is a promising strategy to help in facing short term financial nightmares, while building the future of a more rational, effective, human and austere medicine, within an efficient, safe and satisfactory health care services, and a public health system that is able to prioritize and coordinate actions, programmes and networks. Quality of government is the key variable to put those ideas into practice.

Research on the influence of principles, dimensions, instruments, or patterns of good governance in the improvement of public interventions in welfare services and health will be essential in the future; it can provide evidence about the impact of good governance on desired outcomes; and if this evidence is robust, it will lead to improving the role of government, giving new tools for contracting and running public services.

In the worst case scenario, if European countries have to face a long cycle of slow growth, wise austerity measures in health can play a major role in reshaping planning and managing the health care systems to guarantee the universal access of all citizens to effective and good-quality services.

Notes

1 Including also ascetic or abstinent dimensions. Dictionary.com: http://dictionary. reference.com/browse/austere.
2 Includes lack of make-up and ornament. Infopedia: http://www.infopedia.pt/ lingua-portuguesa/austeridade;jsessionid=5NTAoManIJXnpsbYuqRuyQ__.
3 Refers also to solemnity or severity of manners. Dizionario Italiano: http://www. grandidizionari.it/Dizionario_Italiano.aspx.
4 Limiting to the few and essential. Dictionary of Modern Greek. http://www. greek-language.gr/greekLang/modern_greek/tools/lexica/triantafyllides/search.html?lq=%CE%BB%CE%B9%CF%84%CF%8C%CF%84%CE%B7%CF%84%CE%B1&dq=.

References

Appleby, J., Ham, C., Imison, C. and Jennings, M. (2010) *Improving NHS Productivity: More with the Same Not More of the Same.* London: The King's Fund.
Bernal, E., Campillo, C., González, B., Meneu, R., Puig-Junoy, J., Repullo, J. and Urbanos, R. (2011) La sanidad pública ante la crisis. Recomendaciones para una actuación pública sensata y responsable, *Documento de debate de la Asociación de Economía de la Salud.*
Blanchard, O. J. and Leigh, D. (2013) *Growth Forecast Errors and Fiscal Multipliers,* Available at: http://www.imf.org/external/pubs/ft/wp/2013/wp1301.pdf
De La Maisonneuve, C. and Martins, J. O. (2013) *Public Spending on Health and Long-term Care,* http://www.keepeek.com/Digital-Asset-Management/oecd/economics/public-spending-on-health-and-long-term-care_5k44t7jwwr9x-en
Fuchs, V. R. (2004) More variation in use of care, more flat-of-the curve medicine, *Health Affairs-Millwood Va/ Bethesda Ma*, 23, VAR-104.
Kondilis, E., Giannakopoulos, S., Gavana, M., Ierodiakonou, I., Waitzkin, H. and Benos, A. (2013) Economic crisis, restrictive policies, and the population's health and health care: the Greek case, *American Journal of Public Health*, 103(6): 973–9.
Manresa, A. (2013) Hospital chief fired over illegal immigrant's tuberculosis death. Available at: http://elpais.com/elpais/2013/05/23/inenglish/1369308282_724474.html.

McKee, M. and Stuckler, D. (2011) The assault on universalism: how to destroy the welfare state, *BMJ*, 343.

Morgan, A. (2013) The benefits and challenges of evidence based public health: the experience of the National Institute for Health and Care Excellence. *Gaceta Sanitaria*, 27(4): 287–9.

Open Letter to European Political Leaders and Health Authorities (2013) Available at: http://www.nsph.gr/files/009_Oikonomikon_Ygeias/Open%20letter_v2%20.pdf.

Portugal: Memorandum of Understanding on Specific Economic Policy Conditionality (2012) Available at: http://www.portugal.gov.pt/media/557075/3r-mou-20120315.pdf.

Programa de Estabilidad del Reino de España 2013–16 (2013) Available at: http://serviciosweb.meh.es/APPS/DGPE/Textos/Progest/progest.pdf.

Relatório de Primavera 2013: duas faces da saúde (2013) Available at: http://www.observaport.org/rp2013.

Saltman, R. B. and Cahn, Z. (2013) Restructuring health systems for an era of prolonged austerity, *BMJ*, 346.

Sapir, A. (2006) Globalization and the reform of European social models, *JCMS: Journal of Common Market Studies*, 44(2): 369–90.

Smith, P. C. (2012) What is the scope for health system efficiency gains and how can they be achieved? *Eurohealth*, 18(3): 3–6.

Stafford Hospital: Q&A (2013), Available at: http://www.bbc.com/news/health-21275826.

Sustainable Health Systems: Visions, Strategies, Critical Uncertainties and Scenarios (2013) Available at: http://www3.weforum.org/docs/WEF_SustainableHealth Systems_Report_2013.pdf.

chapter twelve

Issues of governance in implementing complex policy innovations: lessons from primary health care reforms in Estonia, and Bosnia and Herzegovina

Yiannis Kyratsis

Introduction

This chapter analyses the family medicine-centred primary health care reforms in two Eastern European transition countries, from a governance perspective. The reforms comprised a complex policy innovation for the host health systems, involving coherent policy plans for multi-level, system-wide change (Atun et al. 2006; 2007). This chapter discusses governance issues of such complex health policy plans for reforms on the basis of two cases: the primary health care reforms in Estonia and in Bosnia and Herzegovina (BiH).

The two cases share similarities. In the aftermath of the Second World War until the early 1990s, both countries were members of communist (Estonia of the Soviet Union) or socialist (BiH of the Socialist Republic of Yugoslavia) federal states. Prior to reforms, the health systems in both countries were characterized by hospital-centred, specialist-led models of health care. Both countries introduced similar plans for health system reforms with the aim of transitioning from specialist to family medicine-led (FM) primary health care (PHC) (see Box 12.1). They both also featured a high degree of political will in introducing the reforms, while international organizations (the World Health Organization and the World Bank) supported the governments in both countries with technical assistance through pilot projects and financial support (primarily in Bosnia and Herzegovina).

Box 12.1 Definition of Primary Health Care (PHC) and Family Medicine (FM)

The term primary health care has been widely used since 1978 when its fundamental importance was recognized by the World Health Organization in the Alma Ata Conference (WHO 1978). In the same year, the US Institute of Medicine identified the four core components of good primary health care as accessibility, comprehensiveness, coordination, and continuity of care.

PHC may be generally viewed as: (1) a set of activities; (2) a level of care; (3) a strategy for organizing health services; and (4) a philosophy that underpins the entire health system (Vuori 1986). As a system, primary care can be conceptualized as consisting of three interlinked levels: structure, process and outcome (Kringos et al. 2010). The *structure* comprises three dimensions: (1) governance; (2) economic conditions; and (3) workforce development. The primary care *process* consists of four dimensions: (1) access; (2) continuity of care; (3) coordination of care; and (4) comprehensiveness of care. The *outcome* of a primary care system includes three dimensions: (1) quality of care; (2) efficiency of care; and (3) equity in health (Kringos et al. 2010:3). An adaptation of the structure dimensions was used to map the elements of the reforms for the focal countries that are summarized in Tables 12.1 and 12.2.

Family medicine comprises an integral part of PHC, but the terms are not synonymous. The role of the family physician (also called general practitioner, family doctor or FM specialist), as identified by the World Organization of Family Doctors (WONCA 2002), is to manage key processes within health systems, including: (1) first contact care, which is accessible at the time of need; (2) continuing care, which focuses on the long-term health of a person, not on the short-term duration of the disease; (3) comprehensive care, providing a range of services appropriate to commonly encountered health problems in the population; and (4) coordination, by which the family physician acts to coordinate other specialist services which the patient may need.

Despite these similarities, the cases also involve several dissimilarities. The two focal countries differ in their respective history, culture, geography, population and size. The governance arrangements and policy contexts of the reforms also differ. Bosnia is home to what is most arguably one of the world's most complicated systems of health governance, also experiencing unsettling political transition. Bosnia and Herzegovina declared independence from Yugoslavia on 1 March 1992, resulting in a civil war with severe casualties, which was ended with the signing of the Dayton Peace Accords in late 1995. The Accords resulted in an extremely complex system of government, which has made health governance extremely challenging. Bosnia and Herzegovina comprises two entities: the Federation of Bosnia and Herzegovina, and Republika Srpska and a multiethnic self-governing administrative unit the Brčko District. The Federation is predominantly Bosniak (Muslims) and Bosnian Croat (Catholics), and is further administratively divided into ten cantons; the Republika Srpska is Bosnian Serb (Orthodox). The health system structure in Bosnia also follows the above administrative structure, resulting in 13 ministries of health in a country with a population of 3.8 million (one federal and 10 cantonal ministries in FBiH; one ministry in RS; one ministry in Brčko District). In contrast, the small Baltic state of Estonia with a population of 1.3 million did not experience an armed conflict during transition. However, the country experienced one of the most significant deteriorations in health indicators of all European transition countries in the 1990s (Jesse et al. 2004; Lai et al. 2013). Unlike Bosnia, successive coalition governments in Estonia in the last two decades have had a clear strategic vision of integrating the country into Western political and economic structures. Estonia joined the European Union and NATO in the spring of 2004 and adopted the Euro currency in January 2011. Regarding the health context for the introduction of the family medicine-centred PHC reforms, Estonia had to radically restructure the Soviet *Shemasko* and *san-epid* system in which the PHC infrastructure was underdeveloped. In contrast, BiH as a member state of Socialist Yugoslavia, retained some primary health care structures, such as the primary health centres (*Dom Zdravlje*) and the system of public health institutes.

These two contrasting cases were chosen because the same reform idea was implemented with diverse levels of success across the two country settings: Estonia is widely considered one of the most successful cases in implementing such complex health system reforms in Europe (Koppel et al. 2003; Atun et al. 2005a; 2006; Kringos et al. 2013), while Bosnia and Herzegovina experienced considerable challenges in implementation (Atun et al. 2005a; 2007; Kringos et al. 2013). In addition, due to dissimilar structural health system elements and reform trajectories, the two cases shed light on a range of governance challenges and lessons to be learnt. I first delineate the Bosnian case and then the Estonian – defining the policy reform objectives, outcomes and governance issues in each of the cases. Prior to this discussion I outline the context for the launching of PHC reforms in European transition counties.

The family medicine-centred primary health care reforms in European transition countries

In the 1990s and early 2000s, newly independent countries in the former Union of Soviet Socialist Republics (USSR), the Socialist Federal Republic of Yugoslavia and former communist countries in Central and Eastern Europe (CEE) attempted to implement health care reforms that reorganized the national health systems with the *aim of strengthening primary health care* (Rechel and McKee 2009). In the context of post-communist transition, the reforms were triggered by the legacy of accumulated unsolved problems on social matters – including health – on the one hand, and added problems caused by the social disruption due to transition on the other.

Even prior to transition, a remarkable gap in life expectancy between Eastern and Western Europe was already evident (Bobak and Marmot, 1996; WHO, 1997). In the communist European states, the decline in avoidable mortality had been slower compared to the West during 1970s and 1980s (Boys et al. 1991).

This discrepancy was even more striking when considering evidence for the male population (Murray and Lopez, 1997). Superimposed on these longer-term trends of declining health, the transition had an added negative effect on the health of the population of these countries (Saltman et al. 1997; McKee 2004). Overall, life expectancy in many transition countries decreased even further, particularly as death rates among young men became higher than in the past (Velkova et al. 1997). The effects of transition were better handled by some countries and in particular the countries in CEE, the three Baltic States and Slovenia (McKee 2004; Nolte et al. 2004). More favourable starting conditions, stronger social cohesion, better infrastructure, greater exposure to the international scientific and policy community were some of the factors which explain the divergent success outcomes for the latter group of countries (McKee 2004).

The worsening health indicators owing to transition emerged as an additional burden for the already stressed health systems in the European transition countries. The tendency for economic liberalization in the wider society also affected the health sector and led to an inclination for the removal of centralized state control and in some cases the rapid introduction of unregulated competitive markets in health care (Preker and Feachem 1995). The health systems of most transition countries were in a rundown state. Commonly encountered challenges involved issues of *overcapacity, undercapitalization* and *inefficiency* at the health system-level (Goldstein et al. 1996; Staines 1999). These chronic problems rendered the transition health systems financially unsustainable, particularly given the rising costs of pharmaceuticals and new medical technology, the investment needed to counter the results of years of suboptimal capital investment, the relatively high staffing levels, and the wider economic pressures that existed especially during the last years of socialist administration and early transition. Thus, one of the greatest challenges of the transition era for the countries in the region has been the quest for sustainable financing of the health service.

Additionally, the health services provided were of low quality, characterized by poor responsiveness to patients' needs, and use of outdated clinical practices delivered by poorly motivated health professionals (Figueras et al. 2004). Health sector funding decreased as a percentage of the national budget, and then during transition as the general economy deteriorated (Bozicevic et al. 2006). In sum, the health systems of the transition countries were undercapitalized and labour-intensive, characterized by overcapacity and low efficiency (Kornai and Eggleston 2001; Bozicevic et al. 2006).

Launching the reforms

Against this social and economic background, high public expectations for health care services had to be met by transition governments in a climate of economic decline and low public sector institutional capacity. Fundamental changes were needed to address the inherent chronic health system inefficiencies and the additional challenges that had emerged during transition. Since the early 1990s under the influence of international aid agencies and particularly the World Bank (World Bank 1987; 1993), the majority of transition countries formulated a number of policy responses to cope with the aforementioned chal-lenges. The objectives of these policies were in general threefold: (1) to improve the health of the population; (2) to restore macroeconomic balance in health systems (World Bank 1987); and (3) to improve the institutional capacity of the health sector (World Bank 1993; Preker and Feachem 1995).

The first policy objective included policies to raise the standards of living, to promote healthier life-styles, to protect the environment, and to enhance the effectiveness of preventive and curative health services (Preker and Feachem 1995). The second set of policies focused on measures: (1) to control public expenditure through cost containment policies and the introduction of non-budgetary sources of health care financing; (2) to expand consumer choice, diversify supply of services, and improve productivity of health personnel; and (3) to improve risk pooling (World Bank 1987; Preker and Feachem 1995). The third set of policies included measures to design and adopt new legislation, to strengthen the physical and managerial infrastructure of institutions, and to reorient and upgrade the training of personnel (World Bank 1993; Preker and Feachem 1995).

Within the above policy framework, national governments in most transition countries, with the support of international agencies, promoted health systems reforms characterized by a strong emphasis on primary health care and the model of family medicine. Research evidence and increasing health policy con-sensus internationally conclude that developing a strong primary health care is increasingly seen as contributing to more efficient, equitable and cost-effective health systems (Starfield 1994; Kringos et al. 2010; 2013a, 2013b). A number of published systematic reviews, cross-national and country-level studies demon-strate considerable benefits of health systems based on strong primary care (Engstrom et al. 2001; Atun 2004a; Starfield et al. 2005). Health systems that are centred on PHC have better population health outcomes and higher patient satisfaction. Access to strong primary care is believed to reduce at least some of the adverse health effects of social inequalities associated with the differ-ential distribution of income and resources (Shi et al. 1999; Shi and Starfield 2000). Also, health systems with strong generalist-led primary care orientation (as opposed to those which emphasize hospital care) tend to be more pro-poor, more accessible, and have more equitable distribution of health outcomes (Starfield 1998; Starfield and Shi 2002). They also tend to be more efficient and effective, with lower demand for specialist-led hospital care, less hospi-talization and diminished risk of inappropriate diagnostic investigations or medical interventions (Roberts and Mays 1998). Finally, strong primary care is associated with improved functioning of the health system since it promotes more prevention, but also better referral, continuity, and coordination of care (Casanova and Starfield 1995; Macinko et al. 2003).

The case of Bosnia and Herzegovina

The reforms in Bosnia and Herzegovina (BiH) comprised plans for multi-fac-eted change in the health sector reflecting the adoption of major legislative and health policy initiatives, such as the Laws on Health Care and Health Insurance, and the Strategic Plans for Reform in both entities in the late 1990s and early 2000s. The reforms aimed for significant modifications in the organization, delivery, financing, clinical, and regulatory systems, which were more prominent in the country's pilot sites.

Objectives of the reforms

With the end to the war in 1995, the Ministry of Health (MoH) in the Federation (FBiH) and the Ministry of Health and Social Welfare in the Republika Srpska (RS), with support from international and multilateral aid organizations,[1] initiated health reform initiatives to reorganize the BiH health system as part of the post-war reconstruction and development programmes (World Bank 1996; Cain et al. 2002; EC 2008). Establishing a strong primary health care (PHC) level based on the concept of family medicine comprised a central pillar in these efforts, which was aimed particularly at improving the health system's efficiency and access to health services (RS-MoHSW 1997; FMoH 1998).

Sporadic attempts to introduce a family medicine-centred model of care delivery in PHC commenced in the mid-1990s in the form of pilot projects, the most prominent being a pilot initiative in the capital, Sarajevo, in 1996, under the aegis of the Federal MoH with funding from the Italian government and the involvement of UNICEF, which, however, failed. The governments in both entities undertook more systemic reform efforts through the adoption of the Health Care and Health Insurance Laws, in 1997 (FBiH) and in 1999 (RS). Through amendments in the Health Care Laws in 2000, family medicine (FM) was officially recognized as a medical specialty, signalling the beginning of the health system-wide implementation of the PHC reforms in BiH. The World Bank Basic Health Project that commenced in May 1999 comprised the first large-scale health policy intervention to pilot the FM-centred PHC reforms in selected demonstration sites in both entities (World Bank 1998). The most innovative elements of this transformational policy plan along the health system's functions are summarized in Table 12.1.

Outcomes of the reforms

Evidence indicates that despite significant progress, the implementation of the reforms have not fulfilled the policy objectives. The reforms were first introduced in pilot sites in both entities in 1999–2000. Within four years of the introduction (2000–04), family medicine teams covered 24 per cent of the population in both entities (Atun et al. 2005b). In 2005, the World Bank launched the Health Sector Enhancement Project (HSEP) aiming among other objectives at the full scaling up of the FM-centred reforms in BiH by 2010 (World Bank 2005). Parallel initiatives carried out by other international and multilateral agencies have complemented the HSEP activities. As illustrated in Figure 12.1, by 2008, in a period of eight years, the FM model covered approximately 55 per cent of the population in the country. As indicated in Figure 12.1, in 2001 there were 44 family

Table 12.1 Innovative elements of the FM-centred PHC reforms in BiH

Health System Organization	*In FM pilots:* • FM-centred PHC system instead of specialist-led PHC organized in Primary Health Care Centres (*Dom Zdravlje*) and Polyclinics • Enrolment of patients with FM practices for the first time • User choice of family doctor with enrolment • Appointment system for clinical consultation *Across BiH health system:* • Separation of planning, purchasing and provision functions
Financing	*In FM pilots:* *Payment systems for family medicine teams:* • *Federation:* weighted capitation instead of fixed salaries • *RS:* combination of weighted capitation, performance bonus and allowance for accreditation instead of fixed salaries *Across BiH health system:* • Capitation formula for regional and institutional allocation of resources in contrast to historical line budgeting *Compulsory Health Insurance at sub-national level:* • Creation of Health Insurance Funds in RS and Brčko • District Cantonal Health Insurance Institutes in the Federation
Human Resource Generation	• FM recognized as a Medical Specialty for the first time • Independent *University Departments* established with Cathedras (Chairs) in FM • *FM Associations* created in both RS and FBiH • PHC nurses trained in FM becoming Family Nurses (FNs) • Training of FM team members primarily in PHC Centres instead of training occurring exclusively in hospitals as in the past for GPs and PHC nurses
Service Provision	*In FM pilot areas:* • Unified provision of PHC services instead of the fragmented Yugoslav PHC model that delivered services according to age, gender, occupation, type of illness of users • More patient-centred instead of disease-centred models of care • Health promotion and illness prevention services provided by FM Teams • Family Physicians (FPs) trained as specialists instead of being mainly unspecialized General Practitioners (GPs) • Expanded scope and content of service for FPs and FNs as compared to GPs and PHC nurses • Introduction of evidenced-based guidelines in the clinical practice for FM teams

physicians, by 2004 this number had reached 336, and in 2008 1,172, while the number of family nurses during the same period increased from 143 to 419 and 1,657 respectively.

The adoption of the FM-centred model was often contested and sometimes strongly debated by local health administrators, local politicians and narrow

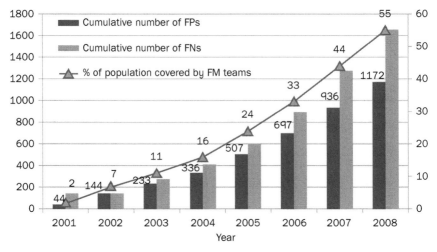

Figure 12.1 Family medicine adoption in BiH

Source: Queen's University Canada Family Medicine Development Project (2008).

specialists, especially paediatricians and gynaecologists. Pockets of high resistance corresponded with the distribution of 'traditional' and 'reform-averse' communities in the eastern parts of the RS and among those cantons in the Federation where political consensus between inter-ethnic communities was difficult to achieve. FM has achieved a rather strong academic basis at university level in both of the country's entities. While education and training activities (primarily involving retraining narrow specialists as family physicians) have been producing significant numbers of trained family physicians, the latter are not always able to practise according to the principles of FM. This is primarily due to the reality that governance arrangements did not always align organizational and financial structures with the changes promoted by the reforms. Outside the pilot areas and the associated reform-advanced regions, the health system in Bosnia and Herzegovina continues to function mainly according to pre-reforms principles.

Governance problems

In the previous sections we saw that although there has been significant progress in implementing the reforms in a number of pilot regions, there was also controversy on the reforms' perceived effectiveness by key actors in the health system. The implementation of the reforms did not result in system-wide change and health system reconfiguration as espoused by the health policy plans. This section examines the underlying governance issues, which have arguably contributed to these reform outcomes. In particular, it is argued that the lack of accountability, participation, organizational integrity and policy capacity contributed to the above policy outcome of sub-optimal implementation and enactment in practice of the family medicine model.

Accountability

The following points include accountability challenges that have impeded the successful implementation of the policy objectives:

The reforms comprised an inherently complex project. They embraced multi-faceted and simultaneous interventions that were introduced at multiple levels of the health system, involving multiple stakeholders. Due to the complicated health governance structure in the country, an additional reason for complexity was that issues arose on who was accountable for what during the implementation of the primary health care reforms.

The transition from the old specialist-led PHC delivery model to the FM-centred organizational practice advanced in a 'fragmented' mode, within 'pilot silos' since the two systems – the pre-reform PHC and the FM-centred model – were often running in parallel and this arrangement created confusion for the system actors (clinicians, policy-makers, patients and the public) regarding the roles and responsibilities in the execution of action plans and the delivery of clinical services.

In the Strategic Plans adopted by both entities in the late 1990s, it was specified that the citizens entitled to social insurance could register with a named family physician and they were given the right to choose a family medicine team (RS-MoHSW 1997; FMoH 1998). In 2001 there were 44 FPs, by 2004 this number had reached 336 and in 2008 1172, while the number of FNs during the same period increased from 143 to 419 and 1657 respectively. Family medicine was recognized as a medical specialty in 2000 through amendments to the 1997 Law on Health Care in FBiH, and the respective 1999 Law in RS. FM teams, comprising a FP and one or two family medicine nurses, became the basic building blocks for the provision of PHC services in the pilot regions in both entities, also undertaking a gatekeeping role in the health system (partial gate-keeping since a number of narrow specialists could still be accessed directly). Nonetheless, with the exception of municipalities in the pilot sites, the organization of PHC service delivery has remained largely unchanged. *Dom Zdravlje* (PHC Centres) that have not yet adopted the FM model, still deliver health care services segmented by age, gender, and type of illness according to the Yugoslav health model, hindering the development of a holistic and continuous model of care according to the principles of FM.

Along with the creation of a Federal Ministry of Health and ten Cantonal Ministries in FBiH, one Ministry of Health and Social Welfare in RS and one MoH in Brčko District, Health Insurance Funds and Public Health Institutes were also founded, following the same distributional pattern across sub-national administrative units. The complex governance structure resulted in a higher need for oversight and coordination between health system levels and among institutions, hampering inter-organizational collaboration in the implementation of comprehensive policy plans.

In pilot areas, the FM teams signed contracts directly with the *Dom Zdravlje* or through them with the newly created Health Insurance Organizations – the Health Insurance Fund (HIF) in RS, and the Cantonal Health Insurance Institutes (CHIIs) in FBiH. Implementation progress in the financing of FM teams outside few advanced pilot sites (e.g., the municipalities in Kladanj in the FBiH Canton of Tuzla and in Laktasi in RS) has been very limited and the lack of financial incentives and associated earmarked budgets has prevented the clinical teams from enacting the expectations of the new model in clinical practice. Furthermore, standards in the form of duties and role expectations for family medicine teams at the level of PHC Centres were rarely effectively set up, often creating frustration and confusion for FM teams; in addition, the application of contractual sanctions was often applied only by holding FM teams to account while failures to meet contractual expectations by the Insurance Funds were often violated, thus undermining accountability relationships.

Indicators and targets often did not accompany national health strategies and policy documents adopted in the country so that progress in health system reform implementation could not be monitored effectively. In particular, policy documents rarely included detailed action plans that described activities, finances and responsible institutions for overseeing and monitoring implementation.

In the case of the uptake of the centrally planned PHC reforms, there was an inherent inability to transform policies and laws into effective action. The *Dom Zdravlje* (PHC Centres) are under municipal authority. Their autonomy, a legacy of the socialist system, results in the Ministries having little direct influence on the management policy at the *Dom Zdravlja* level, a governance arrangement that arguably greatly contributed to delaying the implementation of the reforms and consequently the uniform translation of policy plans into action (Cain et al. 2002).

Transparency

The following transparency challenges may have contributed to the policy outcome concerns. A World Bank (2000) country report highlighted the complicated, expensive, ineffective and inefficient public administration in Bosnia and Herzegovina as a whole. The document reported that the war had eroded the integrity of public institutions and the rule of law, resulting in the formation of weak public institutions and an ethnically fragmented political environment, which leaves space for corruption and rent seeking.

Transparency international index ranks BiH as low compared with other countries in Europe – the country is ranked 80th in the 2014 country index compared to 26th position for Estonia. Bosnia and Herzegovina's weak legal framework is vulnerable to corruption due to the country's post-war divisive political context.

There is lack of transparency and accountability due to a complex legal framework, which also reflects governance issues in the health sector. Especially in the Federation, regulatory and supervisory control has been insufficient to counter the complex accountability structure. The operational planning and execution of the reform plans had been substantially hindered by a lack of sufficient baseline information, for example, on available population information (no census has been conducted since the war despite substantial internal displacement of the population), or on financial and human resources. The lack of good-quality data on policy costs and performance evaluation further hindered the ability to monitor the implementation progress and allow close monitoring of planned efficiency and effectiveness improvements in the health system.

A related issue is that there has been little transparent decision-making. Very limited information on policy decisions is made publicly available, and the public's understanding of decisions and the decision-makers is rather restricted. This was evident in the case of FM-centred primary health care reforms.

Widespread corruption is considered a major reason for tax and health insurance contribution evasion in the country (Cain et al. 2002; Atun et al. 2005b). This has had negative consequences for the financial stability of the new model that is structured on health system financing through social insurance.

Policy capacity

Ministries of health, health insurance funds and health care providers lacked the management capacity and the technical infrastructure to implement the reform plans. Issues of policy capacity deficit were more evident in the Federation where the need for inter-cantonal coordination was very high.

Public authorities in BiH had limited in-house skills to make critical decisions and tended to over-rely on international advisers, which did not allow for adequate contextualization of the reforms to the particularities of the extremely complex governance environment in the country. As a result 'political ownership' of the reforms was low.

The FM institution-building efforts of the coalition of PHC reform proponents in BiH drew largely on the financial, technical and political support external to the country agencies and organizations. Technical support for clinical training and capacity building in family medicine was primarily provided by the Canadian Queen's University, with academics and educators coming to the country from Kingston, Ontario, and financial support was provided by the Canadian International Development Agency.

At a policy level, the World Bank comprised a key ally of family medicine proponents in the country. The World Bank exercised a direct and significant political influence on the governments in both entities, advocating regulatory and political support for the FM-centred reforms. Technical assistance was provided in physical infrastructure re-building projects, in efforts to update health technology infrastructure, in drafting legislation and strategic policy documents, and in health management capacity building in collaboration with Imperial College London. The World Bank additionally financed large-scale demonstration projects to increase the observability of the policy innovation and promote the FM concept in both entities.

Participation

The reforms comprised a top-down approach to change with local views often not taken into account, which contributed to the slow implementation with a lack of perceived ownership of the reforms by local institutions, and limited local participation by municipalities who owned the Primacy Health Care Centres (Kyratsis 2010).

Bosnia and Herzegovina has been highly dependent on external aid after the end of the war, and therefore was more influenced by transnational policy. As a result, the country introduced policies and legislation prescribed or promoted by the transnational institutions upon which it depended. In the case of the PHC reforms, such were primarily the World Bank and secondarily the World Health Organization.

Decision-making occurred after limited collective discussion and approval by a large body of health system actors. As a result, the reforms were perceived as being imposed by the health administration and the international organizations, particularly the World Bank (Kyratsis 2010). Hence the FM-centred PHC model met resistance from various actors; strong resistors were especially narrow medical specialists (such as gynaecologists and paediatricians working in PHC, the Health Care Unions, and academics in internal medicine), local politicians who had a sense of ownership, the political control, and feelings of the continuing heritage of the old model, and finally the administrators of the PHC Centres who felt threatened in giving away administrative power (Atun et al. 2007; Kyratsis 2010).

In areas around the country where the new model had not been introduced, there was low public acceptance of the policy innovation, largely due to the above actors influencing people's perception on the acceptability of the new model. A prime example of an early implementation failure due to limited participation of key local actors combined with micro political factors was the failure of the pilot reform in the municipality of Trebinje in eastern RS.

The weak role of the FM academic community and professional associations in BiH, and their limited participation in the national policy debate, were other contributing factors that shaped the outcome of the reforms' implementation. For example, a negative development for many clinicians on the ground was that physicians who specialized in FM through a three-year residency programme had the same status, remuneration and job description with non-specialists family physicians who had been retrained in short-duration Programmes of Additional Training. The policy urge to increase the numbers of practising family physicians created a two-tier system of FPs on the ground with different levels of expertise, but without commensurate recognition of skill differentiation. Such developments de-incentivized the early enthusiastic adopters and deterred subsequent physicians from residency training in FM, thus undermining the development of FM as an independent medical discipline.

Associations of Family Doctors were created in 2000 in both entities and were accepted in 2002 to membership of WONCA Europe (The World Organization of National Colleges, Academies and Academic Associations of General Practitioners/Family Physicians). However, the FM associations have neither succeeded in getting established as powerful actors in the health care arena, nor have they been influential and effective at intervening in health policy decision-making in BiH. The role and influence of narrow specialists have remained central in PHC even after the introduction of the FM-centred reforms.

Finally, one of the greatest negative consequences of the war was the weakening of bonds of trust between communities and individuals in the country. The lack of trust resulted in political intolerance and exclusion from collective decision-making, and the health policy arena was not immune. Such developments increased challenges to co-ordination of care across sub-national levels and often within health system levels of care.

Organizational integrity

The administrative structure in the country and particularly the delegation of power to the ten cantons in the Federation have resulted in deficiencies and fragmentation in administrative and governance systems, and inadequate inter-cantonal and inter-entity cooperation. The same fragmentation is reflected in the organizational arrangements of BiH health system, which resulted in a complex operational environment and weak health care institutions (Cain et al. 2002; Atun et al. 2005b). The lack of organizational integrity there-fore, affected the implementation progress of the reforms since the adoption decision and subsequent implementation often took the form of tactical politi-cal games.

In localities where the adoption of the FM-centred PHC reforms was rapid and implementation successful, there was synergistic action between local, central and external-international stakeholders. Prime examples of success-ful assimilation of the model were found in the municipality of Laktasi in RS and Tuzla Canton in FBiH, which exhibited collaborative action by PHC Centre directors, the cantonal authorities in Tuzla, the municipal authorities in both localities, the health insurance agencies, the FM academic educators and local trainers, and the international agencies who contributed to the development of clinical, managerial, educational, and physical infrastructure.

In the Federation of BiH, the administrative segmentation and the pres-ence of many stakeholders with veto power amplified the challenges and complexities of implementing the reforms. Political 'tactical issues' and 'ten-sions' in the ethnically mixed cantons such as the Herzegovina-Neretva can-ton in the south, where the two communities of Bosniaks and Bosnian Croats have been struggling for symbolic equal representation at all levels of the decision-making process, further exacerbated these challenges. On the other hand, in the canton of Tuzla – the largest population canton with approxi-mately 500,000 citizens and home to the third largest city in BiH – the adop-tion of the model was successful with approximately 60–70 per cent of the population being covered by FM teams by 2008. The initiative was strongly backed by the cantonal authorities, local governments and Tuzla's FM uni-versity department.

Following independence in 1992 and during the armed conflict until the end of 1995, financing of the health service was predominately budget-based and split into three systems corresponding to the newly emerged ethnic communities that controlled different parts of the country's territory: Bosnian Muslims, Bos-nian Croats, and Bosnian Serbs (Ljubic and Hrabac 1998). In the post-conflict context, budget funding was replaced with a mixed financing system, based on the introduction of mandatory health insurance complemented with budget transfers from the state at the level of entity, canton and local government. The re-introduced health insurance-based system was officially adopted in FBiH in 1997 following the enactment of the Health Insurance Law and in RS in 1999 through the adoption of a similar law.

In the reformed health system, allocation of funding to PHC institutions changed from budgets to simple per capita formulas of insured persons in each institution's service area. Additionally, both entities have specified in law that 40 per cent of the revenues of the Cantonal Health Insurance Institutes and the RS-Health Insurance Fund (which come predominantly from health insurance contributions) should be allocated to PHC (RS HIF 2001). The payment method of PHC providers also changed. A simple per capita payment system has been successfully introduced in the demonstration sites to remunerate FM teams in both entities – the municipalities of Kladanj and Lukavac in FBiH, and the municipalities of Laktasi and Doboj in RS. Since 2004, the per capita model has been weighted by age and in RS it additionally includes a performance-related element for health promotion and disease prevention activities.

The case of Estonia

In the early 1990s, to overcome the weaknesses of the Semashko model, which characterized the Estonian health system during the Soviet era, the Ministry of Social Affairs (MoSA) launched health system reforms, including the establishment of compulsory health insurance and the development of a strong PHC. Prior to independence, the Estonian health system had a curative focus and was characterized by an extensive hospital network and a highly fragmented system in primary health care, comprising mainly specialist-led polyclinics (for adults, women, and children, and specific infectious diseases such as tuberculosis) and dispensaries. These reforms are discussed here.

Objectives of the reforms

The prime objectives of the reforms were to curtail rising health care costs and improve the health of the Estonian population, mainly through the implementation of a FM-centred model in PHC, encompassing aims for improved service quality with emphasis on health promotion and disease prevention (World Bank 1995). The FM-centred PHC reforms in Estonia comprised complex and multi-faceted changes in the health system inherited from the Soviet era. As in the case of Bosnia and Herzegovina, they involved modifications in the clinical systems, the organization, financing, regulation and delivery of health services. The main elements of the reforms across important health system functions are summarized in Table 12.2.

Outcomes of the reforms

The adoption and implementation of the new family medicine model in Estonia were widespread and universal within the country's health system. In a period of just six years from the launch of the relevant legislation in 1997, the FM-centred reforms were fully scaled up and by 2003 the whole population was enrolled with a family physician and since then, family physicians have been the sole providers in primary care in both rural and urban areas (Boerma 2003; Hakansson et al. 2008).

Table 12.2 Innovative elements of the FM-centred PHC reforms in Estonia

Health System Organization	• Family physician-centred PHC system instead of specialist-led polyclinics • Family physicians as independent private contractors with significant organizational autonomy in the health system • Enrolment of patients with FM practices for the first time • User choice of family physicians with enrolment • Separation of planning, purchasing and provision functions
Financing	• Bismarck-like health system: mandatory health insurance instead of the centralized tax-based Semashko model • Mixed payment systems for family physicians: capitation, FFS, allowances, performance bonus instead of fixed salaries • Capitation formula for regional allocation of resources
Resource Generation	• FM recognized as a medical specialty • Independent university-based FM department established • FM Association created that actively promoted FM to become a distinct profession
Service Provision	• Unified provision of PHC services instead of the fragmented polyclinics-based model of care (disease-gender-age specific care) • Patient-centred instead of disease-centred model of care • Health promotion and disease prevention services provided by FPs • FPs trained as specialists instead of unspecialized district Physicians in the Semashko model • Expanded scope of service and role for FPs

In 2006, the number of family physicians totalled 853, and in 2008 grew to more than 900, accounting for about 20 per cent of the total number of physicians in the country (Koppel et al. 2003). The percentage of family physicians over the total number of physicians grew from 14.3 per cent in 1993 to 18.3 per cent in 1998, against an average of respectively 29.8 per cent and 27.4 per cent for the European Union countries (Lovkyte et al. 2003) (Figure 12.2). In Estonia, all physicians working in primary care were progressively retrained in FM, thus eliminating the Semashko primary care segmented specialization from medical training programmes. The retraining programmes targeted former district paediatricians, gynaecologists, district physicians and internal medicine specialists. The Estonian Society of Family Doctors was founded in 1991. Estonia was the first post-socialist country to create an independent Family Medicine Department in the Medical Faculty – at Tartu University in 1992 – and to recognize FM as an independent medical specialty in 1993.

Initial resistance to the reforms emerged in the capital city, Tallinn, where the adoption of the FM-centred PHC model was delayed for almost three years. The main resistors in the capital city were the heads of the polyclinics, the politicians from the Socialist Party – the major opposition party in the late 1990s – local politicians and the local health administrators. Despite these obstacles, the reforms were rapidly rolled out, covering a significant part of the country by 1998, and in 1999 pilot projects were initiated in Tallinn with support from the World Health Organization Country Office. These pilot projects in the capital

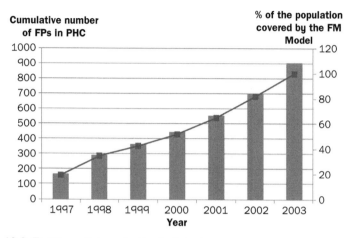

Figure 12.2 Family medicine adoption in Estonia

Source: Estonia Social Sector in Figures (2006).

acted as a 'Trojan Horse' in the area where the highest levels of resistance had been experienced (Atun et al. 2006). A shift in local politics, with a new mayor supportive of the reforms in 2000, provided the final push for the countrywide implementation of the reforms.

Following the adoption of the 1991 Health Insurance Act, the Semashko tax-based system of health system financing was replaced by a system based on health insurance. Earmarked contributions for health insurance were collected and pooled by the newly created Sickness Funds, which operated as non-competing, regionally-based entities. In 1994, a Central Sickness Fund with initially 22 and later 17 regional offices was created and a per capita formula for regional allocation of funding was also introduced. In 2001 the Estonian Health Insurance Fund (EHIF) with its four regional branches was established as a public-owned independent legal entity replacing the pre-existing Sickness Funds. By the end of 2003, 94 per cent of the population was covered by the health insurance scheme (Jesse et al. 2004).

In sum, within only 12 years since the country had regained its independence in 1991, Estonia had managed to fully diffuse the FM-centred PHC reforms, while most post-Soviet countries faced serious delays in introducing and scaling up similar complex policy changes. Estonia adopted a uniform organizational model across the country, which was a radically new system in contrast to the pre-existing Soviet model.

Governance issues

Critical factors affecting the implementation outcomes of the reforms are discussed in the following sections in terms of two governance functions that were central to such developments: *participation* and *integrity*.

Participation

Unlike the case of Bosnia where the reforms were externally driven, in Estonia, there were local – within the country context – and internal – from within the PHC – actors who initiated the change. Those actors were experienced physician clinicians and academics who were involved in the early stages of policy design and implementation. The FM-centred PHC reforms therefore, were initiated and led by clinicians who were influential opinion leaders within both the medical and academic communities. Physicians maintained control over the process and content of change and therefore feelings of 'policy ownership' were high.

The academic clinicians, even from the early planning stages of the reforms, assumed a pivotal role and maintained it throughout the whole process. Particularly during the early and most delicate phase of the reforms, these opinion leaders leveraged their professional recognition as experienced clinicians and the legitimacy that derived from their academic role to introduce the principles of the innovative model to both the policy and medical circles. They used their links to the international FM academic community to familiarize themselves with the new discipline, and acquired practical knowledge of the new model through training abroad, which they later introduced into the Estonian health system.

In Estonia, radical changes were implemented very rapidly. Even though there was initial resistance to change, key actors from both the clinical and policy levels aimed at synthesizing conflicting opinions through discussions and alterations to plans, with the aim of reinforcing the change rather than impairing it.

Organizational integrity

The implementation of the 1991 Health Insurance Act and the 1994 Health Services Organization Act, and the amendments of those Acts in 2002 separated planning, purchasing and provision functions within the Estonian health system. Strategic planning was retained by the MoSA; purchasing and contracting were delegated to the newly established Sickness Funds and later to the EHIF, while PHC service provision was handed over initially to polyclinics and later to autonomous family medicine practices who were legally recognized as private enterprises in contractual relationship with the Fund. The reforms transformed the pre-independence heavily centralized Semashko health system to a more decentralized Bismarckian-like model of care based on health insurance.

In 1997, changes in health regulations through the introduction of a Ministerial Decree mandated all Estonian citizens to enrol with FPs. Users were also given the right to choose their personal FP for the first time. The Health Services Organization Act 2002, approved by the parliament, verified the above provisions and established family physicians as private, independent legal entities and the main providers of care in PHC.

In Estonia, stakeholders have embraced the new ideas and practices associated with family medicine coherently. The reforms were particularly successful in engaging the physicians; the status of family physicians as independent private entrepreneurs as demarcated in the reforms protected their professional autonomy, and helped them to construct an independent professional identity and a legitimate new medical role (Kyratsis 2010).

The introduction of FM specialist training and the development of contracts with the EHIF significantly broadened the scope of services provided by FPs in PHC. Health promotion and disease prevention services became increasingly available through FM practices. In the late 1990s, evidence-based clinical guidelines were introduced, encouraging FPs to care for cases previously managed by narrow specialists. Since the mid-1990s, to improve the quality and uniformity of PHC provision, more than 100 treatment guidelines have been developed and introduced in collaboration with the EHIF and the Estonian Society of Family Doctors (Atun et al. 2005a). The unified generalist-led FM model replaced the fragmented polyclinics model of care delivery according to age, gender and type of disease.

The collective decision-making process for the reforms in primary care aimed at designing a realistic reform and getting it implemented rapidly. Estonia pushed for a more radical and comprehensive change. In Estonia, the primary care reform was part of an overall plan to change the health care system that was consistently pursued over the years; this resulted in the reconfigured health system being compact and coherent. The primary care reforms were structured in a very comprehensive way, so that, over time, the 'whole system bundle' changed consistently. The new medical role was introduced, but policy change also included adjustments in the legal status of the FM practices, the financial mechanisms, coordination with other levels of care, and service delivery structures. Following an integrated approach to policy change allowed stability in the system, and created clear demarcation of relationships with the other levels of care, therefore increasing the legitimacy of the new model.

Conclusion

Two cases have been analysed – Bosnia and Herzegovina, and Estonia – of primary care reforms from a governance perspective. In both cases there were governance challenges that positively or negatively affected the realization of the intended policy. Overall, these cases serve as differing examples of reforms in diverging contexts delineating dissimilar governance issues that influenced the outcome of complex policy initiatives. These factors can be regarded as contributing to the governance challenges.

The Estonian case was an example of successful adoption and implementation of a complex policy innovation, with rapid spread across the country, resulting in revolutionary change in the health system. The Bosnian case was moderately successful in the degree of change achieved, facing considerable challenges in scaling up the FM-centred PHC model outside pilot sites, while both the old and the new system co-exist in patchy developments across the country.

Estonia managed to rapidly implement revolutionary reforms in health financing by adopting a completely different system compared to the pre-existing Semasko model. The new financing arrangements rolled out rapidly, and were characterized by the gradual integration of sophisticated resource allocation formulas and performance payment mechanisms for service providers. BiH also adopted substantial structural changes in financing and performance payment systems, but these were delimited primarily to the pilot sites. Estonia has adopted more radical structural changes in service provision, such as the introduction of numerous guidelines and protocols, has enhanced the clinical role of FPs, and has implemented unified service provision in PHC, achieving a considerable shift in service provision from secondary to primary care. BiH, in contrast, has adopted moderate changes in service provision.

I selectively discussed key governance dimensions that differed between the two cases. In the Bosnian case, lack of *accountability, transparency,* low *participation* and organizational *integrity* played a central role. In the Estonian case, the governance issues of strong *integrity* and *participation* are argued had a positive effect on realizing the policy outcomes. Together these two cases shed light on a range of governance challenges shaping the introduction of *complex policy innovations* in diverse contexts. They illustrate that governance challenges are both case- and context-specific, though useful insights can be generated that apply to similar cases in international health systems.

When national and local governance dynamics aligned, as was the case in Estonia, the change was rapid and radical, while in the case of BiH where there was incongruence among national, sub-national and local governance arrangements, the observed policy realization was limited and sub-optimal in achieving the aims of the reform.

Estonia accomplished a very clean-cut, comprehensive reform, while in Bosnia the approach was more fragmented and piecemeal, which resulted in creating parallel health systems. Public agencies in BiH had limited in-house skills to make critical decisions and tended to over-rely on international advisers, thus limiting the 'political ownership' of the reforms. The complex and fragmented organization and regulatory frameworks in Bosnia also proved to be a barrier to implementation. The complex governance structure resulted in higher need for oversight and coordination and the implementation of comprehensive policy plans faced insurmountable difficulties. As a consequence, the reform failed even in local contexts where system improvement and change seemed to be perfectly feasible. In those contexts, funding, technical knowledge, infrastructure and trained human resources were available. In sum, by improving the integrity via clarifying the roles of key actors and the relationships between institutional structures, as well as making the policy-making process more open to wide participation, the reform could have been more successful in achieving its policy outcomes.

Given the historical trajectory and stronger PHC infrastructure in BiH compared to Estonia, the country would arguably be a more likely candidate to adopt the complex policy innovation. Estonia, however, had a much longer way to go, but did manage to go the full distance; it counts today as a country of strong PHC (Kringos et al. 2013b). Drawing lessons from the two cases, therefore, it is argued that the strengthening of specific governance dimensions could foster the achievement of the intended outcomes of complex policy initiatives.

Note

1   Agencies such as the World Bank, the World Health Organization and the United Nations family of assistance agencies, the Canadian (CIDA), Swiss (SDC) and

Japanese (JICA) International Development and Co-operation Agencies, the European Union (especially through the PHARE program), the International Committee of the Red Cross (ICRD) and others.

References

Atun, R. A. (2004a) *What Are the Advantages and Disadvantages of Restructuring a Health Care System to Be More Focused on Primary Care Services?* Copenhagen: WHO Regional Office for Europe's Health Evidence Network (HEN). Available at: http://www.euro.who.int/document/e82997.pdf.

Atun, R. A. (2004b) *Estonia PHC Evaluation Project Final Report: Advisory Support to PHC Evaluation Model.* WHO Regional Office for Europe, December

Atun, R. A., Ibragimov, A., Ross, G., Meimanaliev, A., Havhannasiyan, S., Cibotaru, E., Turcan, L., Berdaga, V., Kyratsis, I., Jelic, G., Rados-Malicbegovic, D., Grubac, Z., Kadyrova, N., Ibraimova, A. and Samyshkin, Y. A. (2005a) *Executive Summary: Review of Experience of Family Medicine in Europe and Central Asia* (in five volumes): volume I. Washington, DC; World Bank. 32354-ECA.

Atun, R. A., Kyratsis, I., Jelic, G., Rados-Malicbegovic, D., Grubac, D. and May, Z. (2005b) *Review of the Experience of Family Medicine in Europe and Central Asia: Bosnia Herzegovina* (in five volumes): volume III. Washington, DC: World Bank. 32354-ECA.

Atun, R. A., Menabde, N., Saluvere, K., Jesse, M. and Habicht, J. (2006) Introducing a complex health innovation: primary care reforms in Estonia (multimethods evaluation), *Health Policy*, 79: 79–91.

Atun, R. A., Kyratsis, I., Jelic, G., Rados-Malicbegovic, D. and Gurol-Urganci, I. (2007) Diffusion of complex health innovations: implementation of primary care reforms in Bosnia and Herzegovina, *Health Policy and Planning*, 22: 28–39.

Bobak, M. and Marmot, M. (1996) East West mortality divide and its potential explanations: proposed research agenda, *British Medical Journal*, 312: 421–5.

Boerma, W. G. W. (2003) *Profiles of General Practice in Europe: An International Study of Variation in the Tasks of General Practitioners.* Amsterdam: NIVEL.

Boys, R. J., Foster, D. P. and Jozan, P. (1991) Mortality from causes amenable and non-amenable to medical care: the experience of eastern Europe, *British Medical Journal*, 303: 879–83.

Bozicevic, I., Rechel, B., McKee, M., Favaro, D., Iliev, D., Suhrcke, and June, M. (2006) *Health and Economic Development on South-Eastern Europe.* Copenhagen: Council of Europe Development Bank and the Regional Office for Europe of the World Health Organization.

Cain, J. et al. (2002) Health Care Systems in Transition: Bosnia and Herzegovina. Copenhagen: European Observatory on Health Care Systems, 4 (7).

Casanova, C. and Starfield, B. (1995) Hospitalizations of children and access to primary care: a cross-national comparison, *International Journal of Health Services*, 25(2): 283–94.

Engstrom, S., Foldevi, M. and Borgquist, L. (2001) Is general practice effective? A systematic literature review, *Scandinavian Journal of Primary Health Care*, 19: 131–44.

Federal Ministry of Health of Bosnia and Herzegovina (1998) Strategic health system plan for the federation of Bosnia and Herzegovina, Sarajevo.

Figueras, J., McKee, M., Cain, J. and Lessof, S. (2004) Overview, in J. Figueras, M. McKee, J. Cain and S. Lessof (eds) *Health Systems in Transition: Learning from Experience.* Copenhagen: The World Health Organization on behalf of European Observatory on Health Systems and Policies.

Goldstein, E., Preker, A. S., Adeyi, O. and Chellaraj, G. (1996) *Trends in Health Status, Services, and Finance: The Transition in Central and Eastern Europe.* Technical Paper No. 3. Washington, DC: The World Bank.

Hakansson, A., Ovhed, I., Jurgutis, A., Kalda, R. and Ticmane, G. (2008) Family medicine in the Baltic countries, *Scandinavian Journal of Primary Health Care*, 26: 67–9.

Jesse, M., Habicht, J., Aaviksoo, A., Koppel, A., Irs, A. and Thomson, S. (2004) *Health Care Systems in Transition: Estonia*. Copenhagen: WHO Regional Office for Europe on behalf of the European Observatory on Health Systems and Policies.

Koppel, A., Meiesaar, K., Valtonen, H., Metsa, A. and Lember, M. (2003) Evaluation of primary health care reform in Estonia, *Social Science and Medicine*, 56: 2461–6.

Kornai, J. and Eggleston, K. (2001)*Welfare, Choice, and Solidarity in Transition: Reforming the Health Sector in Eastern Europe*. Cambridge: Cambridge University Press.

Kringos, D., Boerma, W., Hutchinson, A., Van der Zee, J. and Groenewegen, P. (2010) The breadth of primary care: a systematic literature review of its core dimensions, *BMC Health Services Research*, 10: 65.

Kringos, D., Boerma, W., Bourgueil, Y., Cartier, T., Dedeu, T., Hasvold, T., Hutchinson, A., Lember, M., Oleszczyk, M., Rotar Pavlic, D., Svab, I., Tedeschi, P., Wilm, S., Wilson, A., Windak, A., Van der Zee, J. and Groenewegen, P. (2013a) The strength of primary care in Europe: an international comparative study, *British Journal of General Practice*, 63(616): e742–50.

Kringos, D., Boerma, W., Van der Zee, J. and Groenewegen, P. (2013b) Europe's strong primary care systems are linked to better population health but also to higher health spending, *Health Affairs*, 32(4): 68–94.

Kyratsis, I. (2010) Diffusion and adoption of complex health innovations: the case of family medicine-centred primary health care reforms in five European transition countries. Doctoral thesis, Imperial College of Science Technology and Medicine, Imperial College Business School.

Lai, T., Habicht, T., Kahur, K., Reinap, M., Kiivet, R. and van Ginneken, E. (2013) Estonia: health system review, *Health Systems in Transition*, 15(6): 1–196.

Ljubic, B. and Hrabac, B. (1998) Priority setting and scarce resources: case of the Federation of Bosnia and Herzegovina, *Croatian Medical Journal*, 39(3) (September).

Lovkyte, L., Reamy, J. and Padaiga, Z. (2003) Physicians' resources in Lithuania: change comes slowly, *Croatian Medical Journal*, 44(2): 207–13.

Macinko, J., Starfield, B. and Shi, L. (2003) The contribution of primary care systems to health outcomes within Organization for Economic Cooperation and Development (OECD) countries, 1970–1998, *Health Services Research*, 38(3): 831–65.

McKee, M. (2004) Winners and losers: the consequences of transition for health, in J. Figueras, M. McKee, J. Cain and S. Lessof (eds) *Health Systems in Transition: Learning from Experience*. Copenhagen: WHO Regional Office for Europe on behalf of the European Observatory on Health Systems and Policies, pp. 33–50.

Murray, C. and Lopez, A. D. (1997) Mortality for eight regions of the world: global burden of disease study, *The Lancet*, 349: 1436–42.

Nolte, E., McKee, M. and Gilmore, A. (2004) *Morbidity and Mortality in Transition Countries in the European Context: Changes in Health in Central and Eastern Europe and the Former Soviet Union: A Mixed Picture*. New York: United Nations Economic Commission for Europe.

Preker, A. and Feachem, R. (1995) *Market Mechanisms and the Health Sector in Central and Eastern Europe*. Technical Paper No. 293. Washington, DC: World Bank.

Rechel, B. and McKee, M. (2009) Health reform in central and eastern Europe and the former Soviet Union, *The Lancet*, 374: 1186–95.

Republika Srspska Health Insurance Fund (2001) *Decision on the Distribution of the Health Insurance Fund Revenues*.

Republika Srpska Ministry of Health and Social Welfare (1997) *Strategic Plan for Health Care Reform and Reconstruction in RS 1997–2000*. Banja Luka.

Roberts, E. and Mays, N. (1998) Can primary care and community-based models of emergency care substitute for the hospital accident and emergency (A&E) department? *Health Policy*, 44: 191–214.

Saltman, R. B., Figueras, J. and Sakellarides, C. (eds) (1997) *European Health Care Reform: Analysis of Current Strategies.* Copenhagen: World Health Organization Regional Office for Europe.

Shi, L. and Starfield, B. (2000) Primary care, income inequality, and self-rated health in the United States: a mixed-level analysis, *International Journal of Health Services,* 30(3): 541–55.

Shi, L., Starfield, B., Kennedy, B. and Kawachi, I. (1999) Income inequality, primary care, and health indicators, *Journal of Family Practice,* 48(4): 275–84.

Staines, V. (1999) *A Health Sector Strategy for the Europe and Central Asia Region.* Human Development Network: Health Nutrition and Population Series. Washington, DC: World Bank.

Starfield, B. (1994) Is primary care essential? *The Lancet,* 344(8930): 1129.

Starfield, B. (1998) *Primary Care: Balancing Health Needs, Services and Technology.* Oxford: Oxford University Press.

Starfield, B. and Shi, L. (2002) Policy relevant determinants of health: an international perspective, *Health Policy,* 60(3): 201–16.

Starfield, B., Shi, L. and Macinko, J. (2005) Contribution of primary care to health systems and health, *Milbank Quarterly,* 83: 457–502.

Velkova, A., Wolleswonkel-Van den Bosch, J. and Mackenbach, J. P. (1997) The east–west life expectancy gap: differences in mortality amenable to medical intervention, *International Journal of Epidemiology,* 26(1): 75–84.

Vuori, H. (1986) Health for all, primary health care and the general practitioners, keynote address: The World Organization of Family Doctors (WONCA).

WONCA Europe (2002) The European definitions of the key features of the discipline of General Practice: the role of the General Practitioner and a description of the Core Competencies of the General Practitioner/Family Physician. WONCA.

World Bank (1987) *Financing Health Services in Developing Countries: An Agenda for Reform.* Washington, DC: The World Bank.

World Bank (1993) *World Development Report: Investing in Health.* New York: Oxford University Press for the World Bank.

World Bank (1995) *Staff Appraisal Report: Estonia Health Project.* Report Number: 13297-EE, Washington, DC: The World Bank.

World Bank (1996) *Bosnia and Herzegovina The Priority Reconstruction And Recovery Program: The Challenges Ahead.* Report Number: 15564. Washington, DC: The World Bank.

World Bank (1998) *Bosnia and Herzegovina Basic Health Programme – PHC Component, Medical Equipment: Appraisal Report,* ed. P. Giribona. Washington, DC: The World Bank.

World Bank (2000) *Memorandum of the President of the International Development Association to the Executive Directors on a Country Assistance Strategy.* Sarajevo: The World Bank Group for Bosnia and Herzegovina.

World Bank (2005) *Project Appraisal Document to Bosnia and Herzegovina for a Health Sector Enhancement Project.* Human Development Sector Unit, South East Europe Country Unit, Europe & Central Asia Region, Report No. 31108-BA. Washington, DC: World Bank.

World Health Organization (WHO) (1978) *Primary Health Care. Report of the International Conference on Primary Health Care: Alma-Ata,* USSR, 6–12 September 1978; 'Health for All' Series No. 1. Geneva: WHO.

World Health Organization (WHO) (1997) *Atlas of Mortality in Europe: Sub-national Patterns 1980/1981 and 1990/1991.* Copenhagen: WHO Regional Office for Europe (European Series, No. 75).

chapter thirteen

Hospital governance: policy capacity and reform in England, France and Italy

Naomi Chambers, Maria Joachim and Russell Mannion

This chapter explores hospital-level governance. In particular, we are interested in examining the extent to which the five desirable governance attributes, of transparency, accountability, participation, integrity and capability, from the TAPIC framework outlined elsewhere in this book, are deployed in practice, and the effectiveness of the range of current arrangements for hospital governance in achieving the health policy objectives which are enduring and common to most countries. The chapter concludes by suggesting a framework for hospital governance which builds on the five attributes, augmented by an interrogation of the evidence, and which is applicable at the level of the healthcare institution.

We have chosen to focus here principally, but not exclusively, on three European countries (England, France and Italy). We have selected England as there is abundant relevant material from this country both from successive structural reforms and from high profile failures of hospital care (e.g., at the Mid Staffordshire Hospitals NHS Foundation Trust which resulted in the Francis inquiries). France is an example of a very differently organized and funded system which is also arguably high performing. Italy is different again as it is tax-funded but with significant regional devolvement of responsibilities and a track record of research and scrutiny of hospital-level governance.

To begin, we argue that there are five health policy objectives or imperatives which are to a large degree common to all advanced health care systems, and which hospital level governance has a role at the micro-level of the health care system to address. Blank and Burau and others have consistently and cogently put the case (Blank and Burau, 2006; Chambers, 2011; Smith et al. 2012) for the existence of increasing policy convergence across countries with different cultural and socio-economic backgrounds. The notion of policy convergence is also applicable at the institution level in the delivery of policies. The five common and enduring objectives can be identified as:

1 Improving patient safety
2 Improving clinical effectiveness of care
3 Delivering efficiencies
4 Improving integration of care
5 More primary and community-based care.

Improving patient safety is rightly considered a *sine qua non* in the provision of health care, ever since the Hippocratic oath adjured doctors to keep patients from harm (Edelstein 1943). It has been challenged in the modern day as an area that medicine still very much falls short on, most persuasively by Gawande in his 2014 Reith Lectures (BBC Radio 4, 2014). Patient safety includes the minimization of errors and a discipline of universally applying known best practice. Examples can range from avoiding hospital-acquired infections to ensuring there are no retained swabs after operations. A patient-safety culture requires both rigour in systems and processes, and a cultural climate in the hospital which is conducive to reflexivity and continuous learning, prioritized over blaming and shaming. It might therefore be expected that boards of hospitals would pay due attention to these matters, receiving appropriate information about organization performance in this domain, setting targets, and taking soundings about the prevailing organization culture which might inhibit or facilitate the patient-safety mission. It follows that the desirable governance attribute of integrity, with its emphasis on highly specified and predictable processes, clear allocations of responsibilities and range of mechanisms available to management, would be found in a hospital with a strong patient safety record. The WHO has developed several patient care checklists, including a surgical safety checklist, a safe childbirth checklist, a trauma care checklist and a pandemic H1N1 checklist (WHO 2015a). In addition, training and research programmes have been established in various countries to promote patient safety and patient safety research. For example, the Patient Safety Research Program (PSRP) was set up in the United Kingdom to promote patient safety research and learning from adverse events in the NHS (WHO 2015b). Over the last 10 years, significant patient safety improvements have been made in Italy. These included the creation of a national reporting system on adverse events, the implementation of several recommendations and the development of training, education and patient safety tools. Furthermore, an agreement signed in 2008 between the central government and the regions was an important step towards the governance of patient safety at the national level as well as for the clinical management at the hospital level (Ghirardini et al. 2009).

The second and allied health policy objective is about improving the quality and clinical effectiveness of care. This movement has gathered momentum since the 1990s (see Boaden 2011, for a useful summary) with growing challenges to unacceptable variation in medical practice associated with clinical autonomy, the advent of the discipline of clinical governance, and the development of clinical guidelines driven by the establishment of national bodies such as the National Institute for Health and Clinical Excellence (NICE) in England or the Institute of Quality and Efficiency in Health Care in Germany. In the last decade, recommendations for quality and effectiveness of care by the OECD have focused on cardiac care, diabetes care, primary care and prevention, mental health and patient safety (European Commission 2014). These days, the clinical effectiveness orientation of health care institutions can be assessed by the rate of adoption of best practices and by the embeddedness of service improvement tools and technologies in operational management (Boaden 2011). Boards of these organizations might therefore be expected to focus on benchmarking operational processes (e.g, lengths of stay, staffing levels) and patient outcomes (patient-reported outcome measures, complications after surgery, avoidable re-admissions, mortality rates) against similar and against 'best in their class' institutions and monitoring by management which prioritizes performance improvement over performance management. To enable clinical effectiveness of care, and the organizational capacity of the hospital to improve, boards would also need to be assured about the success of talent management and succession planning strategies so that appropriately skilled and energetic staff are in place in the organization. This board activity is related to the desirable governance attribute of capability, that is, in this case, the capacity of management and staff to implement and monitor clinical best practice guidelines with an underpinning of a culture of continuous learning.

The third policy imperative is the need to deliver efficiencies. All health care systems are experiencing fiscal stress and growing costs which are greater than increases in GDP and in generic domestic inflation. With the ever greater availability, and the allure for clinicians, of expensive and heroic technology, costs for the provision of care in the first and last weeks of life in particular are soaring. There are big variations in health care practices which threaten equity of access and outcome and which incur substantial costs – for example, in lengths of stay in hospitals for similar conditions, in rates of day case versus inpatient surgery, and in accessibility and responsiveness of services for disadvantaged groups. In addition to technology possibilities and practice variations, the workforce presents both a challenge and an opportunity when it comes to efficiencies. The workforce in health care takes up the greatest proportion of expenditure, followed by medicines. Countries appear to experience recurring cycles of shortages followed by surpluses of various health care professionals; the United Kingdom, for example, in 2015, is estimated to be short of around 20,000 nurses while there is a reported surplus of pharmacists. In order to deliver efficiencies, a focus by hospitals on patient safety and on clinical effectiveness of care, for the reasons articulated earlier, will deliver dividends. In addition, one would expect hospital boards to have a robust workforce strategy aimed not only at creative recruitment and retention in an era of human resource scarcity but also ensuring appropriate and imaginative skill mixing and skill substitution. There is evidence (Chambers et al. 2013) that a focus on talent management is an attribute of a high performing board; in relation to the themes in this book, this relates to the governance attribute of capability or policy capacity which is the potential to take good ideas and put them into action. In institution governance terms, this may also, arguably, mean the capacity for strategic competence and organizational ambidexterity – that is the mining and exploitation of known internal and external resources available to the organization, including organization memory, together with the exploration of new ideas and new solutions, combining both adaptive and generative learning (Hodgkinson and Sparrow 2002). Efficiencies can also be improved through priority setting, accountability mechanisms, performance-related pay, provider competition and stricter gate-keeping.

In the case of France, spending on health care is high but so is life expectancy. France scores as the best among the OECD countries on amenable mortality, mortality that could be avoided thanks to timely and effective health care. In addition, the French health system's efficiency in the acute care sector, as measured by disease-specific length of stays as well as the turnover rate for acute care beds, also tends to be above the OECD average (OECD 2010).

The fourth health policy drive is around the greater integration of care. The argument runs that patients using most health care resources have multiple co-morbidities, psychological as well as physical problems, and that it is counter-productive, expensive and leads to a poor patient and carer perspective to treat diseases in isolation. Improving the quality of care includes ensuring compassion, responsiveness and accessibility, all of which can be absent when there is poor integration. It appears, however, that treating the person, not the disease, is a huge challenge. In an era of clinical super and sub-specialization, a proliferation of health care providers, disputes about the funding of social as distinct from health care, and the unintended consequences of skill mixing (whose job is it these days to offer help to patients at mealtimes on the ward?), there are many fissures through which patients can fall. Coordination of care especially in the management of long-term conditions and for the frail elderly is a policy mantra. For boards of health care organizations, this relates to Pollitt's call for programme effectiveness in addition to, and indeed as superior to or trumping institution effectiveness (Pollitt 1999). A focus on good coordination of care across organization boundaries and across primary and secondary care also calls for system leadership which is gaining currency in discourses about public sector leadership (Brookes and Grint 2010). It is more difficult to locate this endeavour in one of the five desirable governance attributes outlined in this book. It relates more closely to the themes in networked governance which is increasingly embedded in the health care sector (Chambers et al. 2013). Payment mechanisms, gate-keeping and well organized referral systems as well as guidelines and protocols can encourage or weaken the practice of integrated systems of care. The WHO European Office for Integrated Health Care Services, an integral part of the WHO Regional Office for Europe, deals specifically with integrated care and aims to identify strategies and enable the coordination between levels of care through lessons from different countries to improve outcomes (Gröne and Garcia-Barbero 2001).

All the preceding health care policy objectives have somewhat fuzzy boundaries and are interconnected, which is precisely why they are common to most advanced health care systems and enduring. For example clinical effectiveness of care is dependent upon acting to improve efficiency, having a focus on patient safety, and good care coordination, all related to governance integrity, accountability and capacity. Care of older generations and frail elderly people is a prime example.

The final enduring policy objective is the provision of more health care outside the walls of hospitals, in primary care, closer to home and in the community. An argument can be made that appropriate care in the community delivers on all the above policy objectives – it is preferred by patients, is cheaper and leads to better outcomes, although the evidence for this is still in development and integration remains a huge challenge. The mantra of primary care-led health care systems has long and honourable origins going back to the declaration of Alma Ata and subsequent reinvigorations over the years (for example, the WHO's *Primary Health Care Now More Than Ever* 2008 report). The quality of primary care can be determined by several dimensions, including the accessibility of primary care, the comprehensiveness of primary care and the continuity and coordination of primary care, and those dimensions vary tremendously across different European countries (Groenewegen 2013). The policy of primary care has more recently expanded to include at times a range of quite specialized home- and community-based care including residential care (Genet et al. 2012). For hospitals to affirm this policy objective does require a measure of altruism, however, since although some of this care may be provided by them (for example, the provision of virtual wards or outreach visits to support patients on home dialysis), much of it will be provided by community-based organizations which are competing with the hospitals for a share of health care resources. The governance attribute that this relates most closely to is participation, according to which patient-centredness of care is a priority. This translates in home care to client-tailored care with consumer choice and integration.

Up until now we have assumed that the five policy objectives are interconnected and interdependent, but this last one is arguably in conflict with some of the preceding ones: patient safety and clinical effectiveness of care may be compromised by the greater risk of vulnerable patients not being constantly monitored at the hospital bedside; efficiencies may be risked by the greater complexity of care integration across institutions. This calls once again for a sophistication in framing provider governance as appropriately networked, which is particularly challenging in health care systems such as the one in England which are marketized with providers in competition with each other.

Having argued that advanced health care systems face five major challenges in delivery of care and having identified the governance attributes associated with leverage in the pursuit of this endeavour, it is useful to proceed with an account of how hospital governance at the level of the board is constructed in practice. What are boards for?

There is a common view that boards are there to set strategy and goals, to set the organization norms of behaviour, and to monitor the performance of the organization against those goals. Beyond that much of the territory is deeply contested. Boards were developed as a result of the growing commercial complexity of business and the gradual separation of ownership from control. Boards represented the interests of absent owners or shareholders (the principals), and management became the agents of the board (Pointer 1999). The earliest theory about boards was thus agency theory, based on the notion that the shareholders' and managers' interests are likely to be different and that the behaviour of both sets of actors is characterized by self-interested opportunism (Berle and Means 1932). Other theories developed later and are summarized in detail in a recent literature review (Chambers et al. 2013). These include managerial hegemony (according to which the managers rather than the owners make the key decisions), stewardship theory (in which managers and owners share a common agenda and interests), resource dependency theory (in which the main role of the board is to maximize benefits of external dependencies), and stakeholder theory, according to which board members represent the different interests of members with a stake in the organization.

Models of board behaviour can be related to the (sometimes unconscious) orientation of individual board members towards these different theories. Agency theory is connected to a challenging and defensive set of behaviours. Stewardship theory puts a premium on a high trust and collaborative style of working, with the potential disadvantage of low challenge and groupthink. In a stakeholder model, board members tend to be most engaged when articulating the interests of 'their' constituency or special interests. A resource dependency model, with members appointed for their external connections and political and social capital, can result in a 'trophy' board with inadequate grip on the business. With managerial hegemony, the board is disempowered by a chief executive and management team who control the agenda, and predetermine the outcome of meetings, with the board reduced to rubber stamping. None of these models are of themselves, in all circumstances, right or wrong, but dysfunctional boards can occur, whatever the composition and structure, when there is a conflict between members about what the fundamental *raison d'être* of the board really is or where there is a disjuncture between the prevailing context, circumstances and challenges and the characteristics, disposition and activities of that board.

Related to this are theories about the sources and use of board power, including the power of the chief executive (Herman 1981), the discretionary effort and skill exercised by non-executive board members (Pettigrew and McNulty 1995), and the increased role of the board in periods of crisis or transition (Lorsch and MacIver 1989) which can be followed by 'coasting' according to the stress/inertia theory (Jas and Skelcher 2005). These ideas suggest that board members have enormous discretion, whatever the governance arrangements, about how they deploy their power and skill for the benefit of the organization and for the benefit of patients.

The above brief summary suggests that simplistic theories of how boards *should* work are unlikely to fit all circumstances, just as (as has been argued in Chapter 1) simple models of health care system level governance are not suited to the levels of complexity found in today's advanced health care systems. In particular, a binary view is inadequate for the task – for example, proposing that either agency or stewardship is preferable for institution governance – in the same way as neither principal–agent governance nor network governance theories adequately sum up a way forward for 'good governance'.

How do boards operate in practice? An understanding of the inner working of boards is helped by considering separately the three elements of composition (board structure), focus (what the board does) and dynamics (the behavioural dimension). In addition, there are some important distinguishing characteristics of boards in the public, non-profit and health-care sectors (Chambers et al. 2013). Social performance (public value) as well as financial performance is a core purpose. Non-profit board members tend to invest more of their time and are more predisposed to 'managerial work' than their for-profit counterparts. Public boards may suffer from 'institutional isomorphism'. This is, in general, a pressure to conform to prevailing social norms and, in this case, refers to the practice of copying governance structures, rituals and procedures from the private sector without regard for their fitness for purpose for the public sector. Accountabilities on public boards may be blurred as a result of the influence of political patronage and the subversion of formal authority. Finally, as has been signalled in Chapter 1, health-care governance of individual organizations is increasingly embedded within a complex superordinate and subordinate governance network, which stretches across organizations that are interdependent in a health-care system.

Many authors argue that board practices do vary according to circumstances, in both the private and the public sectors. As well as national, geographical, cultural, market, organization size, sectoral and service differences, the following are often mentioned as key variables: organization life-cycle (start-up, mature, decline), stability compared with transformation or crisis, and degree of professionalization of the workforce. While public ownership is predominant in the European hospital sector, in the past few decades, there have been changes in hospital governance and in the level of autonomy that management and supervisory boards can exercise. Institutional boards also vary widely according to political input (Eurohealth 2013). In addition, as indicated later in this chapter, even under the same movement of New Public Management, England, France and Italy took three different approaches to implementing hospital governance changes. Choosing the appropriate mechanisms (whether it be on board composition, board focus or board behaviours) to achieve the desired outcomes appears to be important according to the particular situation. For example, for stable organizations, increased monitoring and a strengthened rein on a powerful chief executive officer (CEO) if he or she has been in position for some time may be indicated (in accordance with agency theory), in contrast to a focus on boundary spanning and on the external environment (in accordance with resource dependency theory) in circumstances of turbulence and threat. A framework for understanding how health care boards specifically may choose to operate depending on circumstances is outlined in Table 13.1.

With this framework in mind, we will now explore how far the arrangements for the management of hospitals in the three countries of England, France and Italy are focused on meeting the five key policy objectives described earlier, to what extent they are exhibiting the proposed desirable governance attributes (or others) in so doing, and how that might translate into lessons for good health care board governance. In all these countries as in most others, recent reforms demonstrate the dominance of New Public Management (NPM) philosophies at the system level and at the institution level. These philosophies draw on the alleged private sector virtues of outsourcing, delayering, decentralizing, marketizing and competition, in preference to the earlier era of classic state bureaucracy with its elaborate and deliberative planning systems of the 1960s and 1970s (Ferlie et al. 2005). Although, as we shall see below, these philosophies have been construed and operationalized differently at the level of hospital governance.

Box 13.1 Key features of health care systems in England, France and Italy with examples of key policies and reforms of hospital governance

---

England

Health system

England's National Health Service (NHS) is financed through general taxation and provides free primary and secondary healthcare at the point of service. It is based on the premise of access to health care based on clinical need, not the ability to pay. The principles, values, rights of patients and responsibilities of the NHS in England are set out in the NHS Constitution (2013). Providers of primary care, also known as General Practitioners (GPs), are the first point of contact with the health system in non-urgent cases.

Health and hospital governance reforms

The Health and Social Care Act of 2012 introduced radical changes in NHS organization and governance. First, all Primary Care Trusts (PCTs) were abolished and all GP practices are now required to be members of a clinical commissioning group (CCG), led by clinicians. CCGs enable GPs to work with other health professionals to provide health services to their local communities and to commission hospital services, which are paid for either through block contracts or through national standard or locally agreed cost per case tariffs. In addition to CCGs, provider trusts are NHS bodies that deliver health care services. The majority of NHS services, namely hospitals, are part of either an NHS Trust or an NHS Foundation Trust. Under the 2012 Act, it is expected that hospitals and other NHS trusts will all become NHS Foundation Trusts. Third, The Act aims to allow competition for NHS funding to private or charity healthcare providers that meet NHS standards on price, as well as quality and safety and as determined by the Monitor, the new regulatory body (NHS England 2013; 2014).

France

Health system

France's health care system is a social insurance model, contributions to which are made by working individuals, based on income. In addition, about 88 per cent of the French population also chooses to purchase voluntary private health insurance (Chevreul et al. 2010). The hospital sector contains public and private providers, with effective coordination between them. Hospitals which are part of the public health service (*participant au service public hospitalier*) may be either publicly owned and financed or privately owned and operated on a non-profit basis. In addition, privately owned hospitals (*cliniques*) operate on a for-profit basis. The balance of activity between public and private providers has been rather constant in the last decade with the private sector hospitals (non-profit and for-profit) accounting for about 35 per cent of general bed capacity and about 50 per cent of surgery beds (Eurohealth 2006; Steffen 2010; Galetto et al. 2014).

Health and hospital governance reforms
First, a radical reform in 2004/5 introduced a Diagnosis Related Group (DRG) payment system (also called T2A, *Tarification à l'activité*) for all acute medical and surgical procedures in public hospitals in place of the global budgets which had operated previously. The main objective of this reform was to harmonize the rules on pricing under a single fixed price model for both public and private providers (Galetto et al. 2014). Second, under the New Public Management movement, in France, as of 2010, the health care code requires public hospitals to replace the unitary system of the board of directors with the dual system comprised of the supervisory and the management boards under the reform *'Hôpital, Santé, Patients, Territoires'* or HSPT (Laouer 2010).

Italy

Health system
Italy's health care system, the *Servizio Sanitario Nazionale* (SSN), offers universal health coverage for all Italian citizens and legal foreign residents in Italy. The government finances the health system through general taxation and patients typically only pay a small co-pay to receive care at public hospitals without being enrolled in insurance coverage schemes. Hospitals had traditionally received guaranteed reimbursement for health services rendered from the central government (Lo Scalzo et al. 2009; Hall 2012).

Health and hospital governance reforms
Over the last decade, the Italian government has tried to implement various health governance reforms. First, health services have been devolved to the country's 20 regions with legal authority to adopt their own quality standards, manage accreditation of providers, set their own reimbursement rates, determine the funds allocated to hospitals, and withhold reimbursements if hospitals failed to meet the required standards of the minimum health care benefit package set centrally by the Ministry of Health. Second, the central government has been controlling the distribution of tax revenue to the regions through a weighted capitation system while regions have also been given the power to collect their own respective taxes to strengthen their regional health service delivery (Lo Scalzo et al. 2009; Hall 2012). Third, another reform has been the development of Clinical Directorates (CDs) within hospitals and across hospitals, which aimed to strengthen the role of management and streamline accountability through clinical organizational arrangements (Lega 2008).

England

Four strands of board work can be detected in health care corporate governance: the need for direction, the importance of control, the relevance of an underpinning set of values, and the requirement to demonstrate accountability

Table 13.1 An adapted realist framework for health care boards

Theory	Contextual assumptions	Mechanism	Intended outcome
Agency	Low trust and high challenge, and low appetite for risk	Control through intense internal and external and regulatory performance monitoring	Minimization of risk and good patient safety record
Stewardship	High trust and less challenge, and greater appetite for risk	Board support for management in a collective leadership endeavour	Service improvement and excellence in performance
Resource dependency	Importance of social capital of the organization; collaboration seen as more productive than competition	Institution boundary spanning and close dialogue with other health care providers	Improved external reputation and relationships
Stakeholder	Importance of representation; risk is shared by many	Collaboration and consensus-building	Sustainable organization with high levels of staff engagement and good long-term prospects

Source: Chambers et al. (2013: 24).

(Chambers 2011). The dominant discourse in England may have a strong New Public Management flavour but with more emphasis on control and accountability than on renewal and entrepreneurship. This has implications for priorities in the management of health services: one of the consequences is that lapses of control, rather than lack of attention to innovation, are more likely to be deemed governance failures. We can track this in the development of and the focus of attention paid to governance arrangements in the English NHS over the past 20 years (Chambers 2011).

Local boards in the English NHS since 1990 derive philosophically from the tenets of New Public Management and in structure from the Anglo-Saxon private sector unitary board model which predominates in United Kingdam and US business (Ferlie et al. 1996; Garrett, 1997). The unitary board typically comprises a chair, chief executive, executive directors and a majority of appointed independent (or non-executive) directors. All members of the board bear collective responsibility for the performance of the enterprise. Successful (in financial and clinical terms) hospitals can apply to be NHS Foundation Trusts (first established in 2004). These are independent public benefit corporations modelled on co-operative and mutual traditions, and now encompass more than two-thirds of acute hospitals. They have a dual board structure – a board of governors (up to about 50 people) made up of people elected from the local community membership, and a board of directors (around 11 people) made up of a chair and non-executive directors appointed by the governors, and a chief executive and executive directors, appointed by the chair and approved by the governors. This whole structure resembles the Anglo-Saxon unitary board model we have seen adopted by the English NHS but nested within a two-tier European or Senate model, commonly found in the Netherlands, Germany and France, about which more details later. The Foundation Trust board governance structure signals a desire at least to focus on the desirable governance attribute of participation in the pursuit of legitimacy, justice and effectiveness. It also relates to a hybridized stewardship (the board of directors) and stakeholder (the board of governors) model of boards.

Having adopted a unitary board and private sector business model in place of the stakeholder model for its local bodies in 1990, the English NHS (as distinct from Scotland and Wales where, with the advent of devolution, different arrangements are in place), moved quickly to embrace lessons from the private sector failures of the 1990s. A number of reports were used to strengthen corporate governance in the NHS, and health care specific guidance has also been issued (NHS Confederation 2005; The Healthy NHS Board 2010; 2013). In spite of these efforts, organizational failures in the NHS over the past 20 years have, arguably, matched or surpassed those in the commercial sector. The most high profile are the cases of neglect, unnecessary suffering and deaths at Stafford Hospital, which resulted in two inquiries (2010 and 2013), and the earlier Bristol Hospital Inquiry relating to paediatric cardiology; others have included St George's Hospital in London, where a young patient died in 2012 of thirst because ward staff mistook his medical condition for an attention-seeking mental health problem, and two cases involving murderous staff (the nurse Beverley Allitt and the GP Harold Shipman). In relation to the first policy objective of patient safety and the desirable connected governance attribute of integrity, with its emphasis on highly specified and predictable processes, clear allocations of responsibilities and range of mechanisms available to management, it would appear on the face of it, that England hospital governance is failing. The inquiry reports all pointed to a lack of focus and poor levels of challenge by the relevant board at critical junctures.

There may be some signs of recent change, however. Mannion and colleagues have found that hospital boards in England are now starting to play an important role in articulating, ritualizing and nurturing appropriate open cultures within their organization and using a variety of hard and soft intelligence in discharging their oversight duties for patient safety, albeit that many board members report that they lack adequate training in quality and safety. That research found an association between higher board scores in domains related to a strong focus on espousing organization values, and staff feeling safe to report adverse events and feeling confident that their organization would address these concerns (Mannion et al. forthcoming 2015).

France

The French health system has characteristics of a strong healthcare system, such as a satisfactory level of access to care, availability of provider choice without any significant waiting lists and a high level of life expectancy (Eurohealth 2006), however, a major problem of the French system is that the growth in health expenditure persistently exceeds the general economic growth (Steffen 2010).

Slightly later than was the case in England, in the late 1990s and early 2000s, there was a focus on strengthening the management capabilities of hospitals following the model of private corporations (McKee and Healy 2002; Kirkpatrick et al. 2013). The governance of both public and private organizations in France at the time had been predominantly characterized by the unitary board system. As the private firms seemed to benefit from the option of the dual board structure (Mallin 2007; Hirigoven and Laouer 2013; Vinot 2014), the French government was keen on adopting the dual system for the public hospital board, as well. This movement advocated for the modernization of public management under the name of 'New Public Management' or NPM, or 'new clinical governance' (Vinot 2014). Even though NPM was attempted in France earlier, the movement only saw a sustained push in 2005. The two main components of the NPM involved a new governance structure for hospitals through the establishment of management boards. In addition, hospitals were encouraged to rearrange clinical units into larger activity centres or medical 'poles' (Dent 2003; Or and de Pouvourville 2006; Kirkpatrick et al. 2013). In France, the health care code has been effective since 2010 and requires public hospitals to substitute the unitary system (the board of directors) with the dual one system comprised of the supervisory and the management boards under the reform '*Hôpital, Santé, Patients, Territoires*' or HSPT.

This change in the structure of governance has been labelled as one of the most important reforms in the history of the management of French hospitals. According to the health care authorities, by changing the governance system, the public hospitals would be able to achieve the desired performance objectives (Hirgoven and Laouer 2013). HSPT has redefined roles of both managers and physicians as part of the supervisory and management boards. The two boards are mutually exclusive, thus dividing physicians into two categories: those who are responsible of formulating and executing hospital strategy and those who participate in monitoring and advising hospital managers (Laouer 2010). Compared with the United Kingdom, the French support and motivation for NPM was not driven by a belief in market forces, but by the need to rationalize public sector decisions by involving key actors in management and to decrease the growing debts of regions (Simonet 2013). Even though there was support for NPM and the possibility of advocating greater accountability, it has been challenging to implement as expected, with one of the reasons being that stakeholders seem to have had different definitions and interpretations of quality indicators and their measurement (Simonet 2013).

Italy

In Italy, guaranteed reimbursements have resulted in reduced incentives for hospitals to improve the quality of their services or lower their costs. Over the last decade, the Italian government has tried to minimize some of those inefficiencies through several reforms. First, health services have been devolved to the country's 20 regions with legal authority to adopt their own quality standards, manage accreditation of providers, set their own reimbursement rates, determine the funds allocated to hospitals, and withhold reimbursements if hospitals fail to meet the required standards of the minimum health care benefit package set centrally by the Ministry of Health.

In Italy, the main New Public Management reform has been the development of Clinical Directorates (CDs) within hospitals and across hospitals. CDs aimed to strengthen the role of management and streamline accountability through clinical organizational arrangements. An in-depth analysis of accounts concerning the establishment of CDs from 1999 to 2006 revealed that CDs struggled to be successful due to unspecified goals and expectations, lack of incentives and administrative support, and resistance from clinicians. This resistance came about because the position of the CD Chair was not considered by physicians as a career track but instead a career that could change every 3–4 years with the change in tenure of the hospital's CEO. Clinicians also expressed concerns about losing their practical clinical expertise during that time because of administrative workload in their CD responsibilities as well as competitive colleagues who only focused on hands-on medicine. As a result, this resistance by clinicians led to only the oldest physicians being willing to take on roles in CDs. The development of CDs has been and remained a major issue for large and teaching hospitals, both for governance and cost optimization reasons (Lega 2008).

In addition, recommendations for quality improvement in different Italian hospitals have been numerous. The demand for outpatient services, referrals and diagnostic procedures has been rising in Italy, making access increasingly difficult and increasing waiting times in hospitals. As a result, a number of local health units have implemented Homogeneous Waiting Groups (HWGs) as an approach to the redistribution of out-patient referrals on the basis on clinical priority. To ascertain the acceptability and transparency of the HWG approach, three surveys on citizens' perceptions on HWGs were conducted in 2006, 2007 and 2009 in a HWG study in the province of Trento. Mariotti et al. (2014) report that the percentage of respondents who agreed about adopting HWGs rather than the traditional 'first-come, first-served' approach was 85 per cent, 87 per cent and 95 per cent for the three respective years. Moreover, in 2009, 81 per cent of respondents agreed that the implementation of HWGs was effective in reducing waiting times for more severe pathologies and urgent conditions, thus encouraging the uptake and implementation of HWGs (Mariotti et al. 2014). The study also reports that although most local health units have been implementing the HWG approach, its uptake and implementation have not been homogeneous on a national level.

In relation to the policy objective of efficiency, administrative data has shown that the number of hospital days in acute wards has been significantly high in some hospitals in Italy, contributing to a waste of resources and an increased risk of hospital-acquired infections and iatrogenic risk, while also preventing care of patients who need it. In a study at the University Hospital of Parma, researchers have shown that simple strategies involving physician direct accountability can reduce unnecessary hospital days. The researchers recommend that relatively simple interventions such as using a validated hospital delay tool and audits by autonomous physicians can be implemented in hospitals to reduce excessive lengths of stay (Caminiti et al. 2013).

The evaluation of quality is central for the enactment of public transparency and accountability in health care, argued in this book as two desirable governance attributes. To evaluate whether reporting of hospital performance was associated with a change in quality indicators in Italian hospitals, researchers launched the most comprehensive comparative evaluation programme for health care outcomes in the Italian region of Lazio and made the performance data available to the public. The investigators evaluated 54 outcome indicators and the results were published online. Public disclosure of the indicators' results caused initial mixed reactions but finally promoted discussion and refinement of some indicators. Based on the Lazio evaluation experience, the Italian National Agency for Regional Health Services has launched a National Outcome Programme aimed at systematically comparing outcomes in hospitals and local health units in Italy (Fusco et al. 2012; Renzi et al. 2012). This initiative is in line with the governance attribute of transparency, allowing the public and a range of external actors to scrutinize information about clinical quality. There are parallels with the NHS in England, where publication of hospital performance across a range of indicators from waiting times to deaths after surgery is now in place.

Conclusion

Kirkpatrick and colleagues describe how editing rules apply in the translation of management models from one country and one context to another (Kirkpatrick et al. 2013). In all three countries that we have examined in this chapter, the dominant influence of New Public Management can be seen in the structures and processes that have been mandated by their governments for hospital level governance over the past 20 years. In each country, NPM tenets have been broadly followed but the story that has unfolded is different. England has been attracted by a market model which has pitted hospitals in competition with each other, has fallen prey to the allure of incessant structural reform, and has been bruised by successive waves of hospital scandals; and is therefore very focused at the hospital level on costs and on patient safety. France is primarily concerned with strengthening public sector accountability, reining in costs and producing efficiencies. Italy has focused on improving patient flow and on stimulating improvements in clinical quality through publication of comparative performance.

In relation to the pursuit of the five policy objectives of improving patient safety, improving clinical effectiveness of care, delivering efficiencies, improving integration of care and providing more care closer to home, evidence from the published literature shows concern and focus *at the hospital governance level* with the first three of these five, prioritized slightly differently in each country. The last two, on care integration and on community based care, relate to a focus on network governance which is relatively absent in the discourse of hospital-level governance. The evidence, however, is, particularly with the advent of the range of ehealth technologies, that these two are likely to continue to be policy priorities into the future: to ignore them therefore may be short-sighted and unstrategic but predictable. Corporate governance research from the private sector signals that high-performing boards pay close attention to strategy; health care governance research suggests that in this sector boards generally pay less attention to strategy and more to performance monitoring (Chambers et al. 2013).

How far can we discern the governance attributes of accountability, transparency, participation, integrity and capability in the practices of hospital level governance in these countries? Attention to patient safety, improving clinical quality of care and delivering efficiencies indicate at least the architecture of accountability, transparency and integrity. The lack of attention to care integration and to community care indicates some weakness in the governance attribute of capability (if that can be translated to mean strategic understanding and implementation of different future models of care) and in participation (if that is taken to mean patient-centredness of care).

Hospitals provide health care on a day-to-day basis as well as delivering policy objectives. They face crises and experience serendipity. They may either operate in a context of intense competition or bask in a monopoly. We have argued earlier that there is no one simple model of how boards *should* operate but there are clues about what works in different circumstances and there are consequences in terms of outcomes in their choice of *modus operandi*. Table 13.2 suggests which governance attributes may be most closely associated with which theories, contexts, mechanisms and outcomes. The governance attributes elsewhere in this book also have relevance at the hospital level. They are more or less foregrounded in different countries and are more or less associated with some common health policy objectives. The embeddedness of health care governance across networks and the coming of community-based models of care does suggest that a stakeholder model of governance, with an effort to build long-term collaborations and consensus and to improve patient experience and staff engagement, may gain ground. This does not negate the need for performance monitoring, accounting to the public and to regulatory agencies or the need, through a stewardship board mentality, to build trust, and encourage and drive innovation and renewal. The evidence, however, is growing that there are consequences, some of which are unforeseen, in espousing a particular governance approach and that a combination of mechanisms and governance attributes may be called for.

Hospital governance in England is broadly characterized by a strong agency approach with corresponding governance attributes of accountability and integrity. The evidence from England suggests, however, that, despite all the essential management and infrastructure building blocks in place – and however hard you 'turn up' the control knobs of performance monitoring and regulation, using as an analogy the Harvard–WHO Model (Hsiao and Sparkes 2011) – the impact continues to be unacceptable variation in practice and failings in care. The Francis Inquiries have highlighted a problem in England with a lack of care and compassion which contributed to this state of affairs – governance attributes of ensuring participation, transparency and workforce capability alongside an emphasis on accountability and integrity may therefore be required to change the organizational climate. This would help to create a situation where patients and staff can 'call in' unacceptable behaviours and standards of care.

Table 13.2 Governance attributes for health care boards

Theory	Context	Mechanisms	Outcomes	Governance attributes
Agency	Low trust and high challenge, and low appetite for risk	Control through intense internal and external and regulatory performance monitoring	Minimization of risk and good patient safety record	Accountability and integrity
Stewardship	High trust and less challenge, and greater appetite for risk	Board support for management in a collective leadership endeavour	Service improvement and excellence in performance	Capability
Resource dependency	Importance of social capital of the organization; collaboration seen as more productive than competition	Institution boundary spanning and close dialogue with other health care providers	Improved external reputation and relationships	Transparency
Stakeholder	Importance of representation; risk is shared by many	Collaboration and consensus building	Sustainable organization with high levels of staff engagement and good long-term prospects	Participation

In France, we have seen that reforms in hospital governance have attempted to inculcate a more business-like approach to drive efficiencies and to involve doctors either in management or in monitoring the activities of management. The introduction of the dual hospital board structure is similar to the governance structure of the Foundation Trusts in the NHS in England. Early reports in France indicate some confusion about definitions and interpretations of relevant quality indicators. The building blocks, however, for the desirable governance attributes of accountability and transparency are there, although, as we have seen in the case of hospitals in England, the structure and the building blocks may not be sufficient in themselves without the appropriate governance mechanisms being deployed. In relation to the involvement of clinicians in management, on boards and in the direction of 'medical poles', evidence from the US is now strong that having doctors involved in the top management team is associated with better clinical performance and lower rates of mortality (Chambers et al. 2013). France would therefore appear to be well placed to hold on to its high ranking in the delivery of clinically effective care. The French health care system continues to be relatively weak in the area of primary and community health care and in the absence of a gate-keeping function to the more expensive hospital services. The governance reforms so far do not address this, which suggests that in the area of efficiency, the health care system may still lag behind those such as England where this is a prominent feature. This indicates the need for a networked, inter-organizational, collaborative governance attribute that is not entirely encapsulated by the five desirable attributes that this book focuses on.

The Italian health care reforms have focused on improving efficiencies through the development of hospital clinical directorates, through the publication of comparative performance information and proactively managing waiting lists. Although there has been a reported lack of enthusiasm on the part of some of the doctors to engage in the clinical directorate initiative, it appears from the evidence (see, for example, the case of France above) that this is the 'right' thing to do from a governance perspective. There is a recurring and international theme around the benefits of involving clinicians in management. This move, in the context of a professionally led bureaucracy such as the case in health care, can be related to the stakeholder model of corporate governance, according to which all those with a vested interest, are involved in setting the direction for the organization. It is also closely associated with the desirable governance attribute of participation but with the focus more on workforce than patient or public engagement in this case. In connection with the other Italian health care reforms described, it is interesting that the focus for driving up performance has been to publish comparative information and to engage clinicians and the public in this process, rather than, as in England, a focus on a target culture and the naming and shaming of hospitals with poor performance against targets. This suggests again a stakeholder or stewardship approach rather than an agency one and with a focus on the governance attribute of transparency.

The learning from the experiences of these three countries in relation to the management of hospitals is that there are definitely trade-offs in the deployment and prioritization of a particular set of governance arrangements. At the same time, there are also uncertainties, in some contexts, in relation to the impact of certain mechanisms, used on their own, on intended outcomes. A judicious combination or requisite variety of governance approaches used in tandem may be most fruitful to mirror the complexity of the policy and management challenges in health care. In general, the missing governance attribute is the one related to capacity; the variability of practice, the relative lack of strategic focus of health care boards, the lack of attention to talent management, are all indicators of underdevelopment of capacity, as that term is explicated elsewhere in this book. This also indicates that hospitals may be under-prepared for the organizational virtuosity required to embrace the future of health care which will increasingly lie outside their walls.

References

BBC Radio 4 (2014) The Reith Lectures. Available at: http://downloads.bbc.co.uk/radio4/transcripts/2014_reith_lecture1_boston.pdf (accessed 15 December 2014). Also http://downloads.bbc.co.uk/radio4/open-book/2014_reith_lecture2_wellcome.pdf

Berle, A. A. and Means, G. C. (1932) *The Modern Corporation and Private Property*. New York: Macmillan.

Blank, R. and Burau, V. (2006) Setting health priorities across nations: more convergence than divergence? *Journal of Public Health Policy*, 27: 265–81.

Boaden, R. (2011) Quality management. In K. Walshe and J. Smith (eds) *Healthcare Management* (2nd edition), Maidenhead: Open University Press.

Brookes, S. and Grint, K. (2010) *The New Public Leadership Challenge*. Basingstoke: Palgrave Macmillan.

Caminiti, C., Meschi, T., Braglia, L., Diodati, F., Iezzi, E., Marcomini, B. and Borghi, L. (2013) Reducing unnecessary hospital days to improve quality of care through physician accountability: a cluster randomized trial, *BMC Health Services Research*, 13: 14.

Chambers, N. (2011) Leadership and governance. In K. Walshe and J. Smith (eds) *Healthcare Management*, (2nd edition). Maidenhead: Open University Press, pp. 377–400.

Chambers, N. (2012) Health systems. In C. De Vincenti (ed.) *Fair, Robust and Sustainable: A Recipe for Europe's Growth*. Rome: Foundation for European Progressive Studies and Fondazione Italiani europei, pp. 148–58.

Chambers, N., Harvey, G., Mannion, R., Bond, J. and Marshall, J. (2013) Towards a framework for enhancing the performance of NHS boards: a synthesis of the evidence about board governance, board effectiveness and board development, *Health Services and Delivery Research*, 1(6).

Chevreul, K., Durand-Zaleski, I., Bahrami, S. B., Hernández-Quevedo, C., and Mladovsky, P. (2010) France: Health system review, *Health Systems in Transition*, 12 (6): 1–291.

Cortez, N. (2009) International health care convergence: the benefits and burdens of market-driven standardization, *Wisconsin International Law Journal*, 26 (3): 646–704.

Dent, M. (2003) *Remodelling Hospitals and Health Professionals in Europe: Medicine, Nursing and the State*. London: Palgrave.

Edelstein, L. (1943) *Hippocratic Oath trans from Greek*. Baltimore, MD: Johns Hopkins Press. Available at: http://www.medicinenet.com/script/main/art.asp?articlekey= 20909 (accessed 15 December 2014).

Eurohealth (2006) French health system reform: implementation and future challenges, *Eurohealth*, 12(3).

Eurohealth (2013) Governing public hospitals, *Eurohealth*, 19(1).

European Commission (2014) *Public Health: Healthcare Quality Indicators*. Available at: http://ec.europa.eu/health/indicators/other_indicators/quality/index_en.htm (accessed December 31, 2014).

Ferlie, E., Lynn, L. and Pollitt, C. (eds) (2005) *The Oxford Handbook of Public Management*. Oxford: Oxford University Press.

Ferlie, E., Pettigrew, A., Ashburner and Fitzgerald, L. (1996) *The New Public Management in Action*. Oxford: Oxford University Press.

Fusco, D., Barone, A. P., Sorge, C., D'Ovidio, M., Stafoggia, M., Lallo, A., Davoli, M. A. and Perucci, C. A. (2012) P.Re.Val.E.: outcome research program for the evaluation of health care quality in Lazio, Italy, *BMC Health Services Research*, 12: 25.

Galetto, M., Marginson, P. and Spieser, C. (2014) Collective bargaining and reforms to hospital healthcare provision: a comparison of the UK, Italy and France, *European Journal of Industrial Relations*, 20: 131–47.

Garrett, G. A. (1997) *World Class Contracting*. Arlington, VA: ESI International.

Genet, N., Boerma, W., Kroneman, M., Hutchinson, A. and Saltman, R. (eds) (2012) *Home Care across Europe: Current Structure and Future Challenges*. Copenhagen: WHO Regional Office for Europe on behalf of the European Observatory on Health Systems and Policies.

Gerlinger, T. anf Urban, H. J. (2007) From heterogeneity to harmonization? Recent trends in European health policy, *Cad. Saúde Pública*, 23(2): S133-S142.

Ghirardini, A., Murolo, G. and Palumbo, F. (2009) The Italian strategy for patient safety, *Clinica Chimica Acta*, 404(1): 12–15.

Groenewegen, P. (2013) The strength of primary care in Europe: an international comparative study, *The British Journal of General Practice*, 63(616), e742–e750.

Gröne, O. and Garcia-Barbero, M. (2001) Integrated care: a position paper of the WHO European office for integrated health care services, *International Journal of Integrated Care*, e21.

Hall, A. (2012) Italy's Health care system: reducing regional disparities for at-risk populations, *Annals of the Health Law*, 21: 126–38.

The Healthy NHS Board (2010) A review of guidance and research evidence, *National Leadership Council*. Available at: http://www.leadershipacademy.nhs.uk/wp-content/uploads/2013/06/NHSLeadership-HealthyNHSBoard-2010-LiteratureReview.pdf

The Healthy NHS Board (2013) *Principles for Good Governance*. NHS Leadership Academy. Available at: http://www.leadershipacademy.nhs.uk/wp-content/uploads/2013/06/NHSLeadership-HealthyNHSBoard-2013.pdf

Herman, E. S. (1981) *Corporate Control: Corporate Power*. Cambridge: Cambridge University Press.

Hirigoyen, G. and Laouer, R. (2013) *Convergence of Corporate and Public Governance*. SAGE Open, 1–8.

Hodgkinson, G. and Sparrow, P. (2002) *The Competent Organisation*. Buckingham: Open University Press.

Jacobs, R., Mannion, R., Davies, H. T. O., Harrison, S., Konteh, F. and Walshe, K. (2013) The relationship between organizational culture and performance in acute hospitals, *Social Science & Medicine*, 76: 115–25.

Jas, P. and Skelcher, C. (2005) Performance decline and turnaround in public organizations: a theoretical and empirical analysis, *British Journal of Management*, 16: 195–210.

Kirkpatrick, I., Bullinger, B., Lega, F. and Dent, M. (2013) The translation of hospital management models in European health systems: a framework for comparison, *British Journal of Management*, 24: S48–S61.

Laouer, R. (2010) The equivocality between control and management by physicians: an overview from hospital boardroom, *International Journal of Arts and Sciences*, 3(12): 432–42.

Lega, F. (2008) The rise and fall (acy) of clinical directorates in Italy, *Health Policy*, 85(2), 252–62.

Lo Scalzo, A., Donatini, A., Orzella, L., Cicchetti, A., Profili, S. and Maresso, A. (2009) Italy: health system review, *Health Systems in Transition*, 11:6.

Lorsch, J. W. and MacIver, E. (1989) *Pawns or Potentates: The Reality of America's Corporate Boards*. Boston: Harvard Business School.

Mallin, A. (2007) *Corporate Governance* (2nd edition). Oxford: Oxford University Press.

Mannion, R., Freeman, T., Millar, R. and Davies H (2015 in press) *Effective Board Governance of Safe Care* (NIHR report under review).

Mariotti, G., Siciliani, L., Rebba, V., Fellini, R., Gentilini, M., Benea, G. and Liva, C. (2014) Waiting time prioritization for specialist services in Italy: the homogeneous waiting time groups approach, *Health Policy*, 117(1): 54–63.

McKee, M. and Healy, J. (2002) *Hospitals in a Changing Europe*, Maidenhead: Open University Press.

NHS Confederation (2005) *Effective Boards in the NHS?* London: NHS Confederation.

NHS England (2013) *Guide to the Healthcare System in England*. London: The NHS Constitution.

NHS England (2014) *Understanding the New NHS: A Guide for Everyone Working and Training Within the NHS*. London: Charlesworth Press.

Organization for Economic Co-operation and Development (OECD) (2010) Health care systems: getting more value for money, *OECD Economics Department Policy Notes*, No. 2.

Or, Z. and de Pouvourville, G. (2006) French hospital reforms: a new era of public-private competition? *Eurohealth*, 12: 21–4.

Pettigrew, A. and McNulty, T. (1995) Power and influence in and around the boardroom, *Human Relations*, 48(5): 845–73.

Pointer, D. (1999) *Board Work: Governing Health Care Organizations*. San Francisco: Jossey-Bass Inc.

Pollitt, C., Girre, X., Lonsdale, J., Mul, R., Summa, H. and Waerness, M. (1999) *Performance or Compliance? Performance Audit and Public Management in Five Countries*. Oxford: Oxford University Press.

Renzi, C., Sorge, C., Fusco, D., Agabiti, N., Davoli, M., and Perucci, C. A. (2012) Reporting of quality indicators and improvement in hospital performance: the P.Re.Val.E. Regional Outcome Evaluation Program, *Health Services Research*, 47(5): 1880–901.

Simonet, D. (2013) New public management and the reform of French public hospitals, *Journal of Public Affairs*, 13(3): 260–71.

Smith, P. C., Anell, A., Busse, R., Crivelli, L., Healy, J., Lindahl, A. K., Westert, G., and Kene, T. (2012) Leadership and governance in seven developed health systems, *Health Policy*, 106(1): 37–49.

Steffen, M. (2010) The French health care system: liberal universalism, *Journal of Health Politics, Policy and Law*, 35(3): 353–87.

Vinot, D. (2014) Transforming hospital management à la francaise, *International Journal of Public Sector Management*, 27(5): 406–16.

World Health Organization (WHO) (2015a) *Programmes: Patient Safety Checklists*. Geneva: WHO. Available at: http://www.who.int/patientsafety/implementation/checklists/en/ (accessed December 31, 2014).

World Health Organization (WHO) (2014b). *Programmes: Patient Safety*. Geneva: WHO. Available at: http://www.who.int/patientsafety/links/en/ (accessed December 31, 2014).

Index